Welcome to the All About Space Annual

Mankind has gone to great lengths to explore space. It is a natural curiosity that has led us to build incredible machines and push the boundaries of what we thought was possible. We're constantly trying to gather more information, hoping that we can uncover the mystery of what life was like prior to the big bang or what is in store for our future. In this, the All About Space Annual 2014, we bring you some of the best nuggets from the magazine over the last year and explore space in a way that NASA would be proud. In this book, we explore the impact that neighbouring galaxies could have on our Milky Way and what parts of science fiction could eventually become science fact – from tractor beams and underwater space cannons to next-gen spacesuits and supersonic parachutes. We'll look at the wonders of the Solar System, how we've explored space, and what lies beyond the Oort Cloud. This annual gives you the very best of the magazine in one place and is an absolute must for anyone interested in learning more about space. Hopefully it will inspire you to discover the next dwarf planet or uncover the big secrets that make up our solar system...

All About Space Annual

Imagine Publishing Ltd
Richmond House
33 Richmond Hill
Bournemouth
Dorset BH2 6EZ
☎ +44 (0) 1202 586200
Website: www.imagine-publishing.co.uk
Twitter: @Books_Imagine
Facebook: www.facebook.com/ImagineBookazines

Head of Publishing
Aaron Asadi

Head of Design
Ross Andrews

Edited by
Jen Neal & Jon White

Senior Art Editor
Greg Whitaker

Design
Moe Hezwani

Photographer
James Sheppard

Cover images courtesy of
NASA, ESO, ESA, JPL

Printed by
William Gibbons, 26 Planetary Road, Willenhall, West Midlands, WV13 3XT

Distributed in the UK & Eire by
Imagine Publishing Ltd, www.imagineshop.co.uk. Tel 01202 586200

Distributed in Australia by
Gordon & Gotch, Equinox Centre, 18 Rodborough Road, Frenchs Forest, NSW 2086. Tel + 61 2 9972 8800

Distributed in the Rest of the World by
Marketforce, Blue Fin Building, 110 Southwark Street, London, SE1 0SU

ISBN 978 1909 758 094

Part of the All About Space bookazine series

IMAGINE PUBLISHING

Contents

Page 8
A-Z
of the universe

"For one priceless moment in the whole history of man, all the people on this Earth are truly one"

РОСКОСМОС

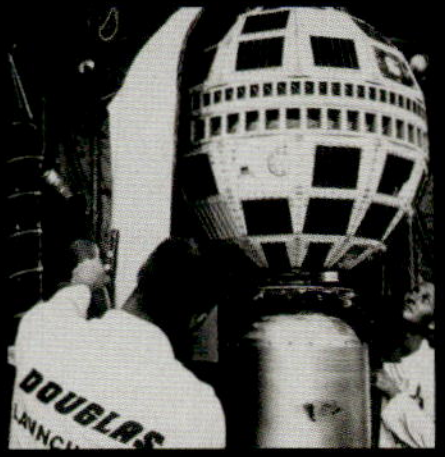

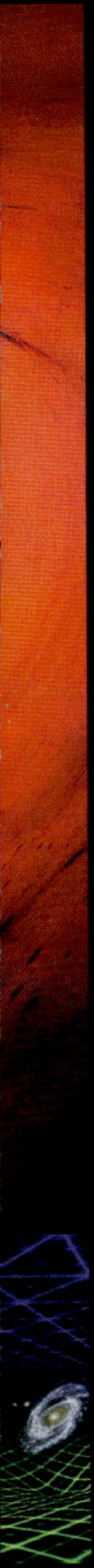

A-Z of the UNIVERSE

From Alpha Centauri to Zeti Reticuli, we take you on an amazing journey through the alphabet of space

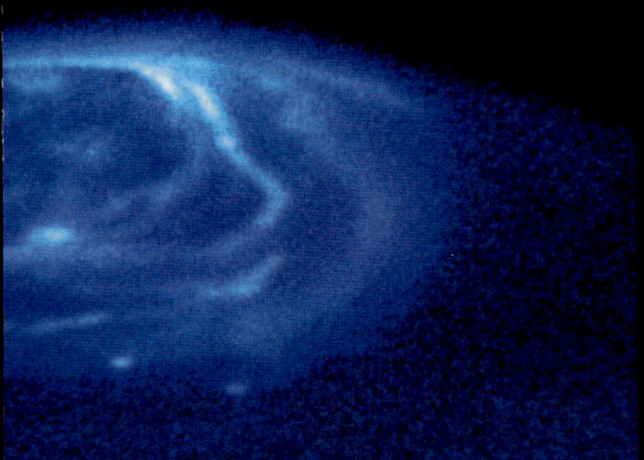

Space is fascinating, but there is so much to cover that sometimes it can be difficult to comprehend it all. What is a binary star system? What does a black hole really do? Why is the search for water so important? What types of astronomy are most useful to scientists?

And that's just the start of it. What about some of the pioneering moments in space exploration, or the seemingly unexplainable phenomena that exist throughout space?

Thankfully, we're here to help. In this feature we'll take you on a journey through the alphabet of the cosmos and introduce you to some of the most important things in space. If you've wanted to know what the most abundant element in the universe is, why Mars has been the focus of so many space agencies, what the biggest observatory in the world is or how fast light travels, you'll find out the answers to all your questions and much more here in our A-Z of the universe.

Alpha Centauri

Alpha Centauri is particularly interesting for a number of reasons. Not only is it the nearest star system to our Solar System, but it is also a prime example of a binary system around which there may be one or several planets.

The Alpha Centauri system is about 4.37 light years from the Sun. It consists of two stars, Alpha Centauri A and B, and a possible third star known as Proxima Centauri or Alpha Centauri C. The distance between A and B varies from the distance between the Sun and Pluto to the distance between the Sun and Saturn. Alpha Centauri C, meanwhile, orbits at a distance equivalent to 400 times the size of Neptune's orbit.

In October 2012, it was discovered that there is at least one planet in orbit around this binary system. The planet discovered, named Alpha Centauri Bb, is slightly more massive than Earth but has a close orbit lasting just over three days, meaning it is likely to be extremely hot and inhospitable to life.

Black Holes

A black hole is what happens when you compress a star ten times more massive than the Sun into an area the size of New York City from which nothing, not even light itself, can escape. They are regions of space-time that have the most intense gravity we know of, pulling everything within their vicinity into their centre and, in some cases, driving the rotation of massive objects like galaxies. They predominantly come in two shapes and sizes: stellar mass black holes form when a star collapses at the end of its life, while supermassive black holes millions of times more massive than the Sun result from the merging of other smaller black holes.

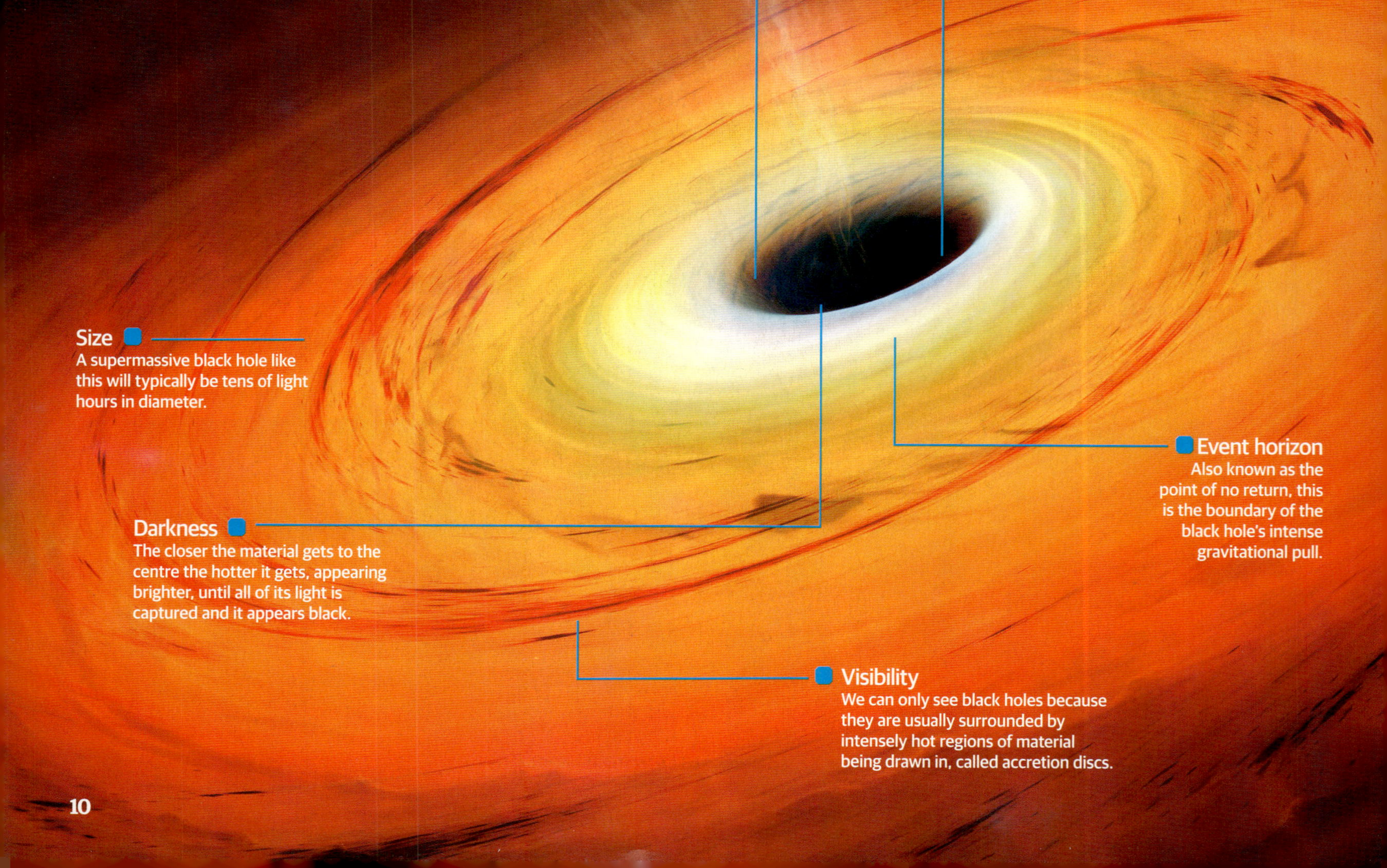

Constellations

In the night sky there are a whole host of constellations that have been categorised and named over many centuries for observational purposes. Constellations are useful when looking for a particular star, or even when navigating on Earth. However, it is often the case that a particular constellation is made up of stars that are in actuality nowhere near each other, but from Earth they appear very close. Here, we've taken a look at the Cancer constellation to show you what's actually going on.

Pattern
From Earth, the Cancer constellation appears to be made up of various stars in proximity to each other.

Magnitude
Together, the magnitudes of the different stars make them seem at the same distance but at different brightness.

Shape
Because of the huge distances involved, constellations generally appear to retain the same shape as observed from Earth.

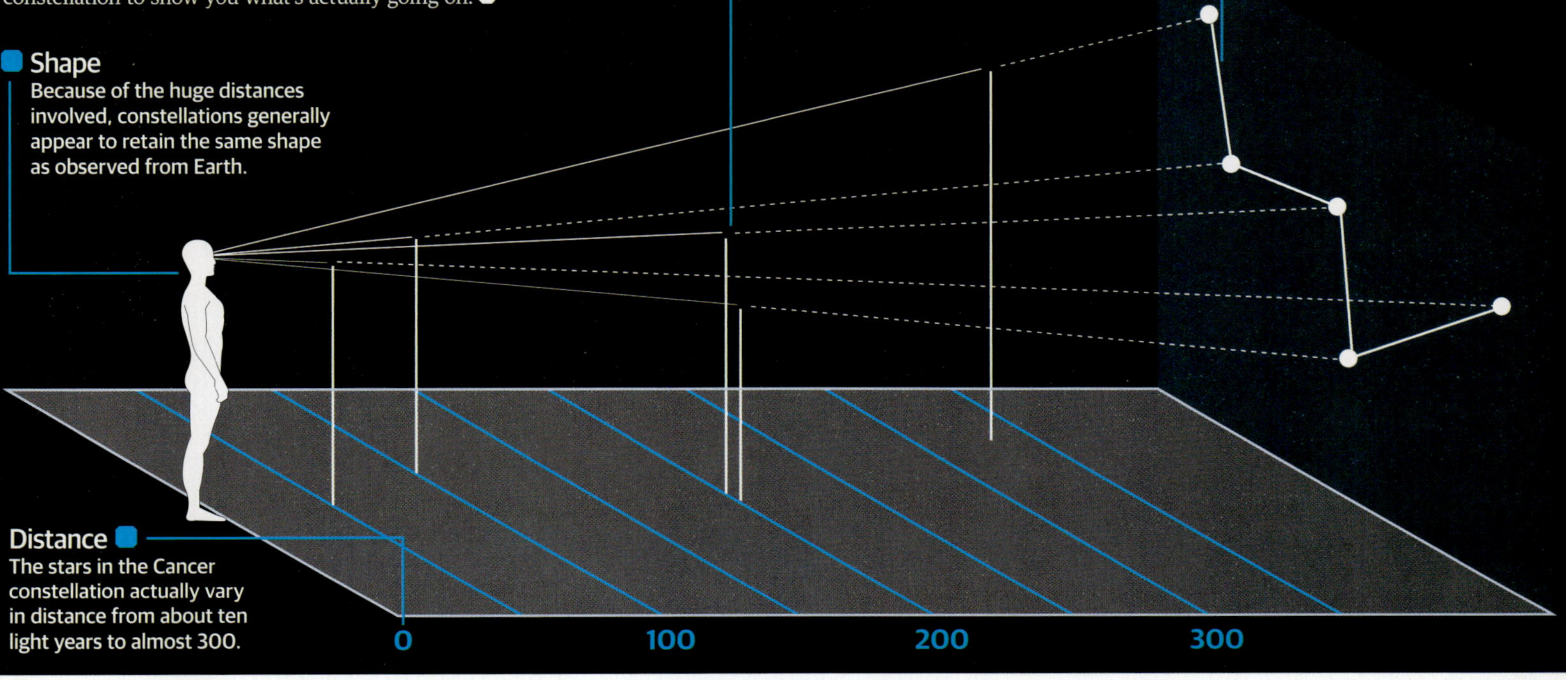

Distance
The stars in the Cancer constellation actually vary in distance from about ten light years to almost 300.

Dragon

SpaceX's Dragon spacecraft has been heralded as ushering in a new age of private spaceflight. Where previously space travel was the sole pursuit of national space agencies, this company based in California, USA has proven that, with the right application, a start-up company can also conquer the challenges of space exploration

The Dragon spacecraft is a cargo vehicle that is under contract with NASA to resupply the International Space Station. In May 2012 it docked with the ISS for the first time, the first privately built spacecraft to do so. SpaceX, however, has bigger plans for the Dragon. The company is planning a manned version, tentatively known as DragonRider, which will be able to take astronauts to the ISS by the end of the decade. Further into the future, it has stated its ambition to land humans on Mars.

Exoplanets

Planet hunting is a very new area of astronomy. The first planet outside our Solar System was not discovered until 1992, but since then many hundreds more have been found, most by NASA's Kepler space telescope. The discovery of exoplanets has led scientists to believe that we are just one of many, many planetary systems in the universe. It is thought that every star plays host to an average of 1.6 planets, with a potential 17 billion Earth-sized planets resident in the Milky Way alone, itself just one of over 100 billion galaxies.

To date most of the planets that have been found are gas giants, planets resembling ones like Jupiter or Neptune. This is because our current method of finding planets relies on measuring the dip in their host star they cause as they pass in front of it, known as the 'transit' method. In future, however, we will have bigger and more powerful telescopes (like NASA's James Webb Space Telescope) that will be able to find more planets at a range of sizes.

The holy grail of planet hunting is to find an Earth-sized planet orbiting in the habitable zone of a star, the area in which the planet's temperature and orbit would be suitable for water, and possibly life, to form. To date no such planet has been found, but the hunt continues and it will likely only be a matter of time until we find such a 'second Earth', and possibly many more similar planets, in our Milky Way.

Galaxies by numbers

Stats and facts about these massive structures

600

Not all stars are found inside galaxies; Hubble has found over 600 stars in intergalactic space

100 billion

The universe is thought to contain over 100 billion galaxies

2

Occasionally galaxies collide, affecting the orbits of many stars and planets and, on rare occasions, merging their central black holes

100 trillion

Galaxies range in size from dwarf galaxies, containing tens of millions of stars, to giants with 100 trillion stars

380 million

The most distant galaxy from us formed just 380 million years after the Big Bang

3

Galaxies come in three main shapes: spirals, ellipses and irregular

1

Most galaxies, such as our own Milky Way, have a supermassive black hole at their core

Force of gravity

Gravity is one of the most important forces in the universe that holds everything together

Without gravity, the universe would be a chaotic place. Pretty much everything we know of in the universe is influenced by gravity in one way or another. Our Solar System, for example, is in a finely tuned balance of gravity around the Sun. Planets and moons orbit on fixed paths, as do some asteroids, while comets are occasionally plucked from the Oort cloud at the edge of the Solar System and flung inwards towards the Sun by the force of gravity.

While the exact cause of gravity on a subatomic scale is still largely unknown, we can see its effects all over the universe. An object's mass will determine its gravitational pull, but all objects exert a gravitational influence on another. Right now, while the Earth is pulling you downwards, you in turn are pulling the Earth upwards, albeit by a tiny amount. The formation of new stars and planets in the universe, meanwhile, is only possible because of gravity; when a star explodes as a supernova, the resultant material is gradually drawn together by gravity and eventually might form new celestial bodies. ●

Hydrogen

Hydrogen is the most abundant element in the universe and, as it turns out, it is also one of the most useful. When the universe formed in the Big Bang, the resultant matter was about three quarters hydrogen, one quarter helium and a tiny fraction of lithium. Some of this matter formed stars, which in turn burned hydrogen and helium to produce the heavier elements that make up many other celestial bodies such as planets and asteroids. Hydrogen and helium remain the main sources of fuel for stars. In fact, 99.9 per cent of the atoms in the Sun are either hydrogen or helium (but mostly the former). Hydrogen is also vital for space exploration, being a major source of fuel for rockets, in the form of liquid hydrogen. ●

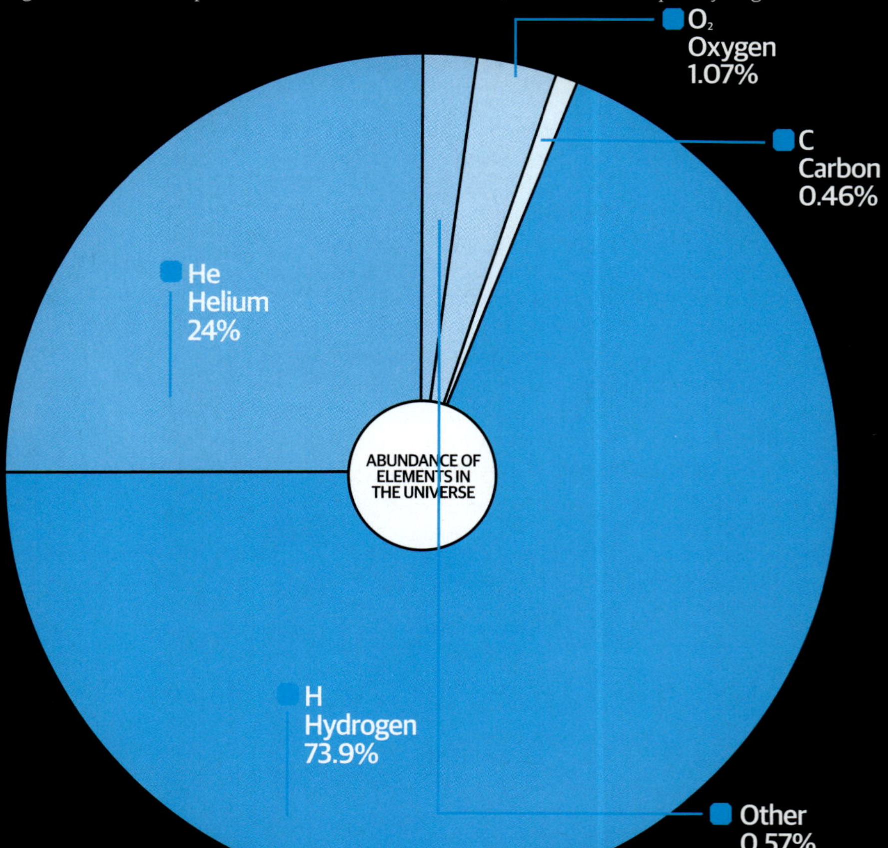

Io

Including Earth, Io is the most volcanically active body in the Solar System and, therefore, it is one of the most interesting worlds we know of. The surface of this moon of Jupiter is strewn with over 400 active volcanoes, which produce plumes of sulphur that travel several hundred kilometres high. The plumes have left Io's silicate rock surface covered in sulphur, which gives it its yellowish appearance. Aside from volcanoes, lava flows and craters are scattered across Io's surface. The cause of the moon's volcanism is thought to be its orbit around Jupiter, which is highly elliptical and therefore causes stretching and compression of the moon's molten core, heating it up and causing more volcanic eruptions.

A volcanic plume 138km (86 miles) high is seen here erupting from Jupiter's moon Io

Jet Propulsion Laboratory

The Jet Propulsion Laboratory (JPL) is NASA's main centre of cutting-edge research and development for space exploration. Formed in 1936, JPL was transferred to NASA in December 1958 and has become its main centre of unmanned planetary exploration. It is located near Pasadena, California, and has about 5,000 full-time employees.

Over the decades JPL has amassed a huge number of missions under its belt, and in the process it has sent spacecraft to every planet in the Solar System. These include Voyager 1 and 2, Cassini-Huygens, the Spitzer Space Telescope, the Mars rovers Spirit and Opportunity, and recently the Curiosity rover.

"Over the decades JPL has sent spacecraft to every planet in the Solar System"

NASA's Jet Propulsion Laboratory was responsible for successfully landing the Curiosity rover on Mars in August 2012

The coldest naturally occurring place we've found in the universe is the Boomerang Nebula

Kelvin

When discussing the temperature of things in the universe, such as stars or the universe itself, scientists often use the Kelvin range. 0 Kelvin (-273.15°C or -459.67°F) is defined as absolute zero, the coldest temperature possible where molecules stop moving altogether. The hottest temperature of all, meanwhile, would have occurred during the Big Bang as, with all matter squeezed into a point, there would have been a theoretical infinite temperature limit. Since then the universe has cooled and now everywhere in space is generally the same temperature: 2.7 Kelvin (-270.45°c or -454.81°F).

Light year

The speed of anything in the universe is limited by the speed of light, about 300,000 kilometres per second (186,000 miles per second) in a vacuum. Nothing can travel faster than this, and even approaching this speed would require an almost infinite amount of energy. But just how far and fast does light travel in a set amount of time?

How fast does light travel?

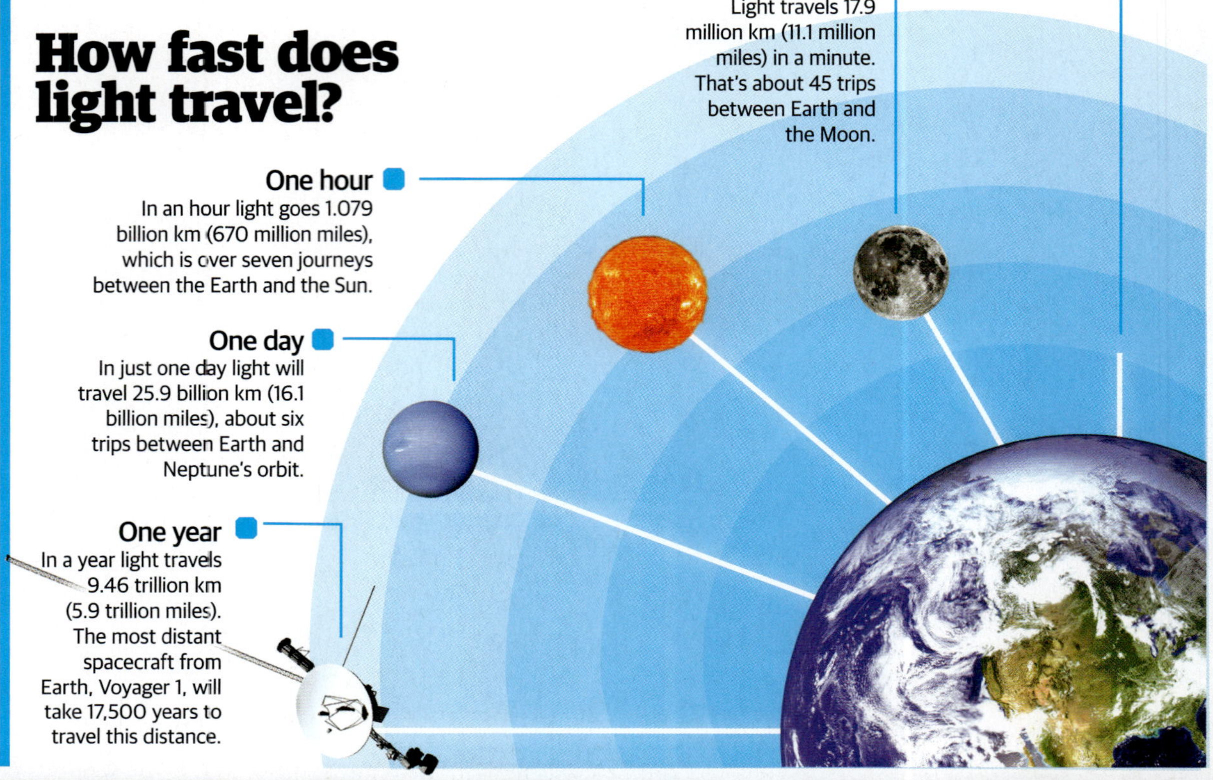

One second
In a second light travels 299,792km (186,282 miles), which is equivalent to seven-and-a-half trips around the world.

One minute
Light travels 17.9 million km (11.1 million miles) in a minute. That's about 45 trips between Earth and the Moon.

One hour
In an hour light goes 1.079 billion km (670 million miles), which is over seven journeys between the Earth and the Sun.

One day
In just one day light will travel 25.9 billion km (16.1 billion miles), about six trips between Earth and Neptune's orbit.

One year
In a year light travels 9.46 trillion km (5.9 trillion miles). The most distant spacecraft from Earth, Voyager 1, will take 17,500 years to travel this distance.

Mars

Aside from Earth, Mars is the most studied world in the Solar System, and for good reason. This planet, often called the Red Planet, bears tantalising hints that it once played host to water, and possibly even life. This has been evidenced by imagery data from the numerous rovers we have sent to the surface, and the spacecraft that we have sent to orbit the planet. Recently, NASA's Curiosity rover discovered an ancient riverbed on the Martian surface, a clear indication that water once flowed there.

Since the dawn of the space age in the Sixties we have sent 50 different spacecraft to Mars but, such is the difficulty of travelling to the Red Planet that only 21 have succeeded. NASA and other space agencies continue to place Mars as a high priority in their planetary exploration missions, not only because of its interesting past but also because, in the present, it might still play host to some form of life. Indeed, by understanding what became of Mars and how it might have lost a once habitable environment, we may uncover clues as to the future of our own planet.

Length
This mammoth canyon is over 4,000km (2,500 miles) long, 200km (120 miles) wide and 7km (4.35 miles)

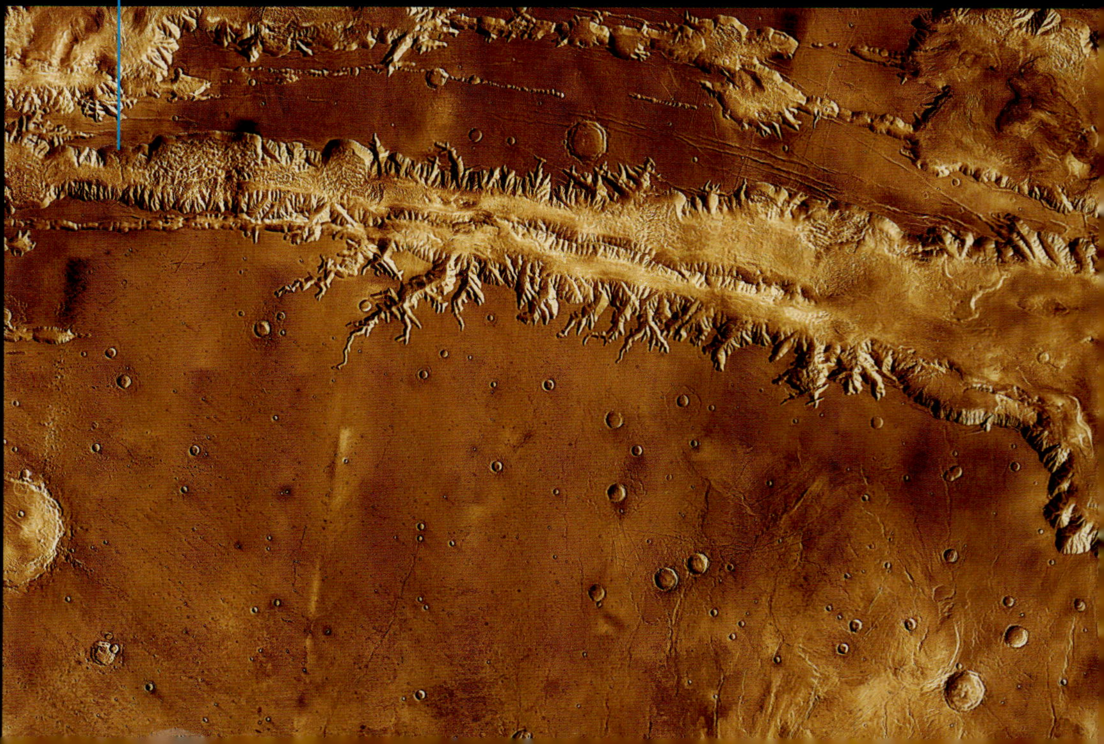

The Crab Nebula is one of the most famous and most studied supernova remnants

Nebulae

When a star comes to the end of its life it will often collapse and may eject material into the surrounding interstellar space via a supernova. As this dust and gas spreads out, different areas of the resultant 'cloud' will have different compositions and therefore, when we observe it from Earth in different wavelengths it will appear to have shape and form, often resulting in fantastic images. We call this a nebula.

Nebulae are important in the universe as they are responsible for recycling the elements that make up stars, and ultimately spark the formation of new celestial bodies such as planets. It is believed that our own Solar System formed from a previous nebula, with the dust and gas coalescing into the planets, asteroids and comets, and of course the star, that now reside here. Nebulae are also important in the study of supernovas, as by observing the speed the nebula is growing and diffusing we can discern what type of star may have caused the original explosion. ●

Observatories

Observing the universe has been a pastime of humanity for millennia. From primitive early contraptions to modern marvels, astronomers have used observatories to increase their understanding of the cosmos. Whether it's calculating the distance to a star, mapping a portion of the night sky or getting close-up imagery of a cosmic phenomenon, they have forever been a cornerstone of our attempts to understand the universe. With some upcoming constructions, they will only increase in power and scope and therefore allow us to discover even more about the universe around us.

Observatories work by gathering light, or another form of radiation, and composing the resultant data into an image. The largest optical observatory is the 10.4-metre (34-foot) wide Gran Telescopio Canarias in Spain but this will be dwarfed by the European Extremely Large Telescope upon its completion in the 2020s, which will have an aperture 39.3 metres (129 feet) wide. ●

"The European Extremely Large Telescope will dwarf its rivals"

The WM Keck Observatory at the summit of Mauna Kea in Hawaii is the largest observable telescope in the world

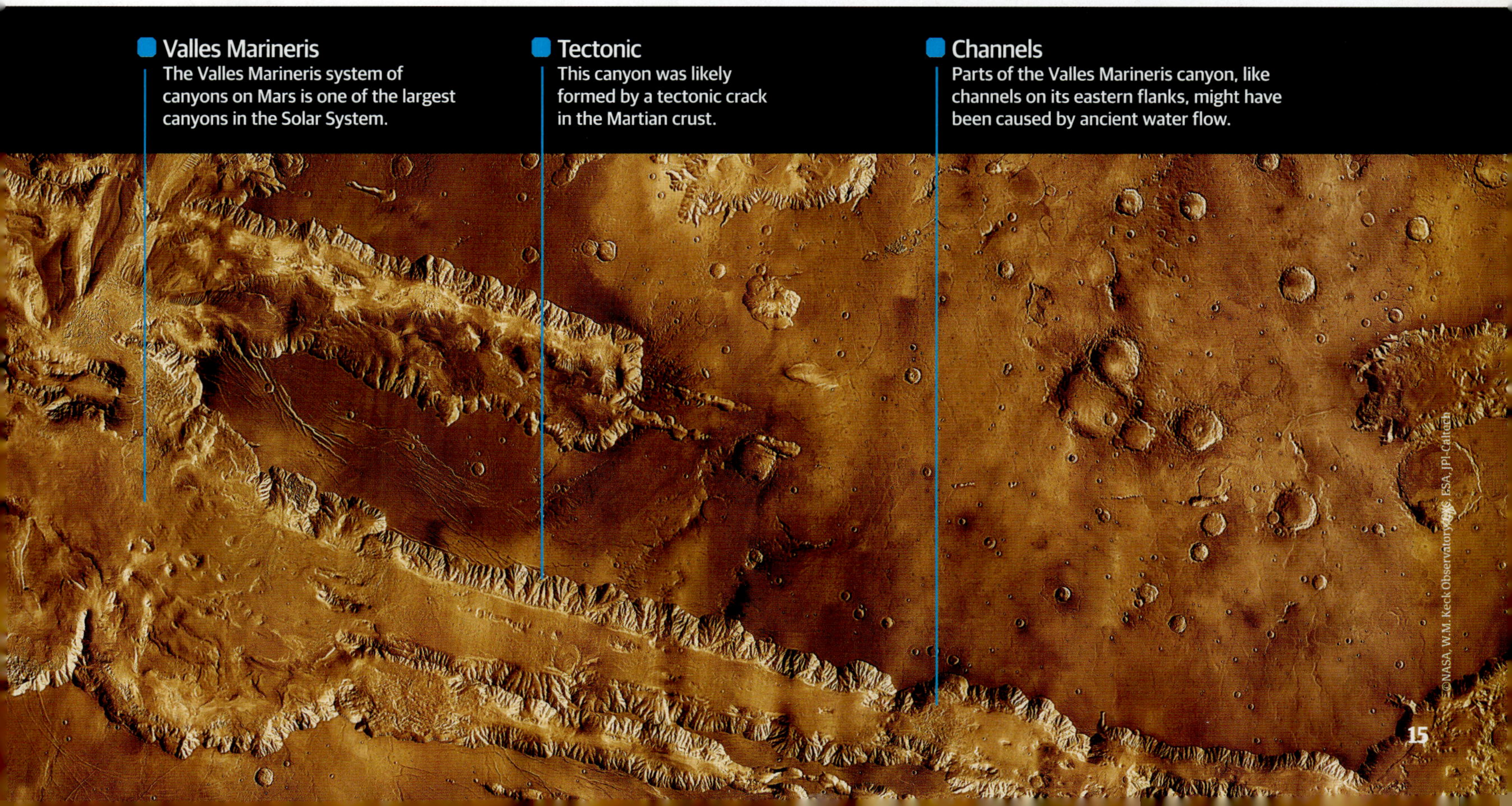

Pulsars

When a star explodes as a supernova it will sometimes leave behind its small but massive core. This object, generally with a mass several times that of our Sun but a diameter of only a few tens of kilometres, is known as a neutron star. It is super dense, equivalent in scale to the mass of a jumbo jet rammed into a grain of sand, and is made almost entirely of neutrons.

On some occasions, the resulting neutron star will retain much of its original angular momentum and, owing to its new smaller size, it forms with a rapid rotational speed. The rapid rotation, coupled with the high density, forms a strong magnetic field that fires beams of radiation away from the star's poles in opposite directions, spinning with the rotation of the star. This object is known as a pulsar, and it is one of the most rapidly rotating things in the universe that we know of. Some pulsars are known to rotate at speeds up to a quarter of the speed of light and, as they spin, their beams of radiation sweep around. Despite their apparently hostile characteristics, some pulsars are thought to play host to exoplanets. Indeed, the first exoplanets ever discovered in 1992 were found around a pulsar.

Quaoar

Quaoar is one of five dwarf planets in the Solar System, worlds big enough to be spherical but not large enough to be classified as true planets. But just what does it take to become a planet? A body is classed as a planet when it has a diameter greater than 2,000 kilometres (1,240 miles), has a stable orbit around the Sun, has a spherical shape as a result of its own gravity and is the dominant object in its immediate neighbourhood. Most dwarf planets fill all of these classifications barring the last one; this is the reason Pluto was demoted from a planet to a dwarf planet in 2006.

CMBR was found by accident at the Holmdel Horn Antenna in New Jersey, USA in 1964

Radiation

Radiation is the movement of particles across a medium, usually a vacuum. It is the predominant method through which energy is transferred around the universe and, through our understanding of radiation, we are able to understand the nature and characteristics of stars, planets and more.

All types of electromagnetic radiation are covered by the electromagnetic spectrum, which ranges from radiation such as radio waves and TV to X-rays and gamma rays. Visible radiation constitutes a small part of the spectrum but, when observing the universe, we often use telescopes that are susceptible to different types of radiation to gather different data from objects in the universe. For example, observing in ultraviolet light allows us to discern the composition and temperature of stars.

The most widespread radiation in the universe is the Cosmic Microwave Background Radiation (CMBR), a glow of thermal radiation left behind after the Big Bang. This glow of microwaves is one of the strongest indications for a uniform explosion leading to the birth of the universe, and by understanding it we are able to discern how our universe has expanded and cooled.

Spacewalks

When an astronaut leaves a vehicle to go out into space alone it is called a spacewalk, which is also known as an extra-vehicular activity (EVA). The first spacewalk was performed by Russian Alexey Leonov on 18 March 1965. Spacewalks have been used since then to perform external actions on a spacecraft such as carrying out repairs, deploying satellites and much more. While early spacewalks lasted just tens of minutes, modern spacewalks on the ISS can last for hours. Here, we've taken a look at some spacewalks that have been performed over the ages.

1. First US spacewalk
Ed White performs America's first ever spacewalk during the intrepid Gemini 4 mission on 3 June 1965.

2. Vital repairs
Scott Parazynski moves towards a tear in one of the ISS's solar arrays in 2007.

3. Hanging out on the ISS
Chris Hadfield dangles upside down in the shadow of the ISS in 2003.

4. Hubble EVA
US astronaut Andrew Feustel manoeuvres the piano-sized Wide Field Camera 3 on to NASA's Hubble Space Telescope in 2009.

5. Expedition 22
Russian astronaut Oleg Kotov performs a spacewalk lasting five hours and 44 minutes during Expedition 22 on the ISS in 2010.

In 1962, Telstar 1 became the first satellite to transmit TV pictures around the world

Telstar 1

The world's first communications satellite, Telstar 1 ushered in the modern age of satellite TV, GPS and much more. It was the first satellite to ever transmit television pictures around the world, something we take for granted today.

An international collaboration between AT&T, Bell Telephone Laboratories, NASA, the British General Post Office and several other institutions, Telstar 1 launched on a Delta rocket on 10 July 1962. It was tiny, about three times the size of a basketball, and used just 14 watts of power from its 3,600 solar panels on its hull. It could carry just 600 phone calls and one black-and-white television channel but, by doing this, it was able to transmit the first ever TV show across the Atlantic, albeit only for about 18 minutes during every orbit. That first transmission was a live feed transmitted to France of an American flag waving outside the receiving station in Andover, Maine - not exactly thrilling programming, but a pioneering moment in our ability to communicate around the world.

This ultraviolet image shows an aurora at Jupiter's north pole

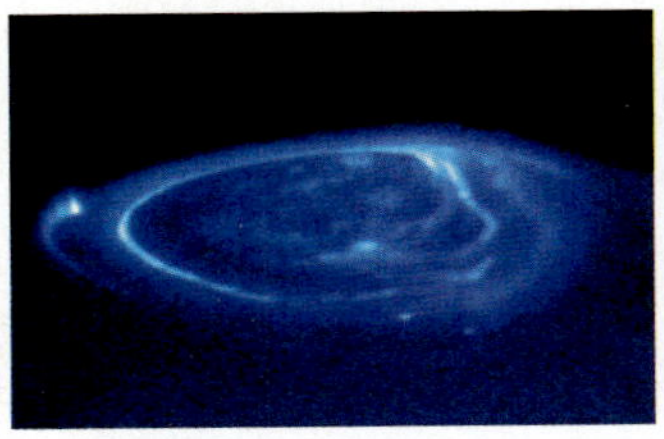

Ultraviolet

Ultraviolet astronomy is useful for discerning the composition, temperature and density of stars, and also for studying the evolution of galaxies. It allows us to see particular features that would otherwise be invisible in other portions of the electromagnetic spectrum. Ultraviolet radiation is generally associated with hot objects, with cool objects emitting very little ultraviolet radiation, and therefore it is useful to see objects evolving at the start or end of their lives such as stars. Ultraviolet light is mostly absorbed by the Earth's atmosphere, so to observe anything in ultraviolet a space observatory located outside the Earth's atmosphere must be used. Examples of such telescopes include the Hubble Space Telescope and the Galaxy Evolutionary Explorer (GALEX).

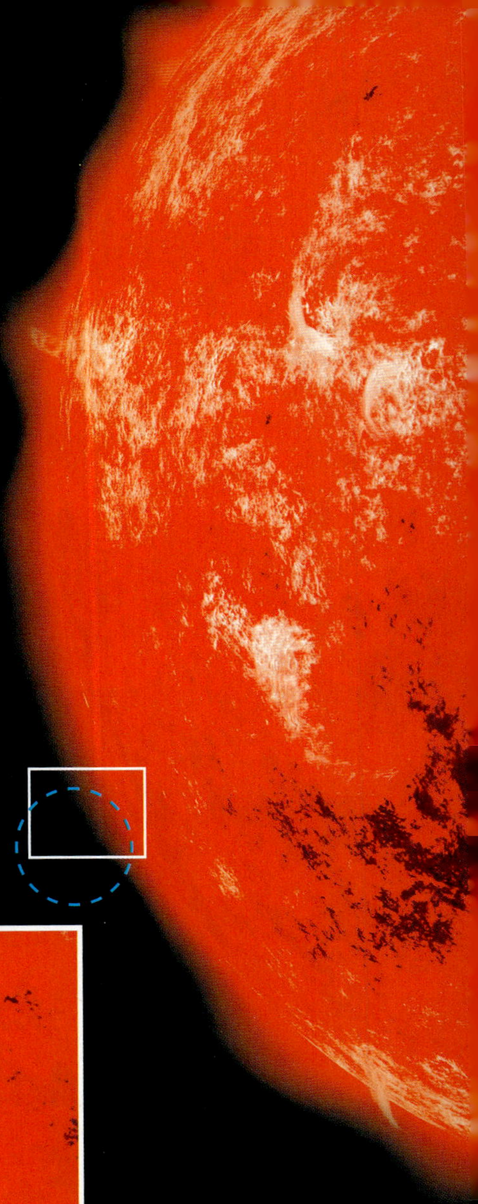

VY Canis Majoris

Compared to Earth the Sun is massive, dwarfing it by about 110 times, but in the grand scheme of the universe the Sun is a relatively small star. One of the largest stars we know of is VY Canis Majoris, a red supergiant 1,400 times bigger than the Sun. If it were placed at the centre of the Solar System, its surface would extend out to the orbit of Saturn. Humongous stars such as this have very short life spans in astronomical terms, typically only a few million years compared to the estimated 10 billion-year lifetime of our Sun, owing to the huge rate of fuel consumption they undergo. At the end of their lives, massive stars such as these will often explode as a supernova, resulting in the formation of a nebula and possibly new stars and planets.

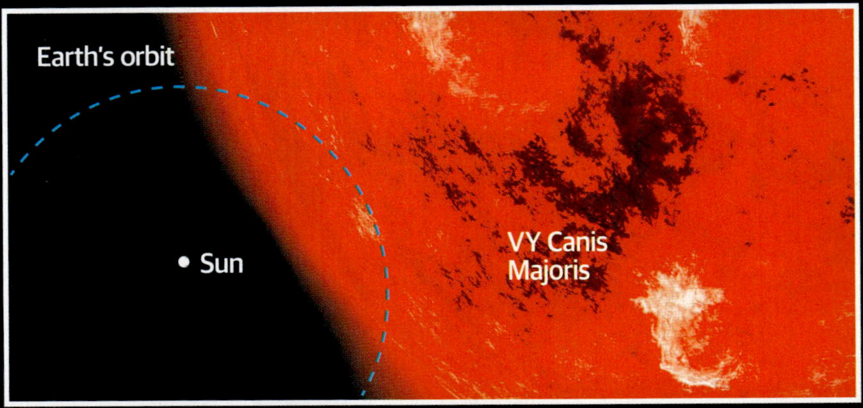

Water

For life to form on a world in the universe there are many conditions that must be met, but one of the main ingredients that must be present is water, and therefore the search for it in our Solar System has become of huge importance. Without it, life as we know it simply cannot survive. This is one of the reasons Mars is of such interest to scientists, as it bears tantalising hints of having an ancient wet environment. Studies of other worlds in our Solar System, such as Europa, suggest that they may be harbouring subsurface oceans hidden from the radiation of the Sun. These are of increasing importance in our understanding of how life can form in the universe. In terms of planet hunting, finding an exoplanet residing in the habitable zone of a star is often the goal, as within this zone (not too hot and not too cold) water, and therefore life, might be able to form on a planet. Some theories suggest that water may be transported between bodies by water-bearing comets; our own water on Earth may have originated in such a fashion.

Planet Earth is the only world we know to have liquid water - so far...

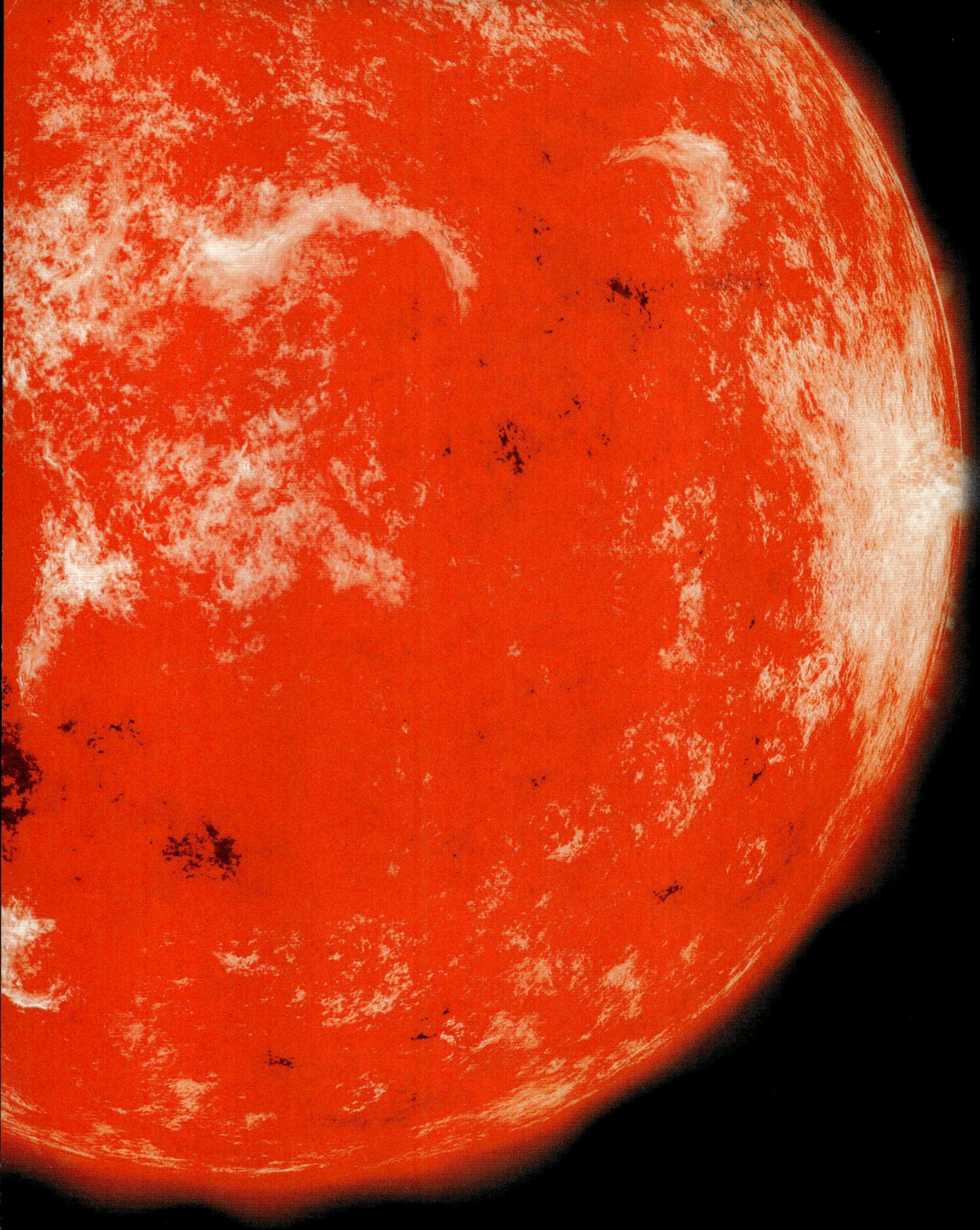

You

The late astronomer Carl Sagan once said that we are all made of "star stuff," and he wasn't just being poetic. When stars explode they release their elements into nebulae, as mentioned earlier. Over time the resultant material coalesces into other stars and planets, but that isn't the only thing that is created. All of the heavier elements in the universe like oxygen and carbon were created deep in the hydrogen-burning furnaces of stars, and therefore the elements that make everything around us, including ourselves, originated within stars. ●

Nearly every celestial body was formed from the dust and gas of an exploded star

X-rays

While ultraviolet astronomy is useful for studying relatively hot objects or regions of space, those that are extremely hot are more easily observed in the X-ray band of the electromagnetic spectrum. Neutron stars and black holes, for example, are prime sources of X-rays and therefore our best way to observe them is with X-ray telescopes like the Chandra X-ray Observatory. ●

Chandra took this X-ray image of the fantastic Pac-Man Nebula

Zeta Reticuli

Zeta Reticuli is interesting because it is one of the only examples of a binary star system composed of two Sun-like stars that we know of. The system is located about 39 light years from Earth, and recent evidence suggests that one of the two stars is orbited by a debris disc similar to our own Kuiper belt, therefore suggesting there may be a planetary system also residing there. ●

A real image of the Zeta Reticuli system

"Zeta Reticuli is composed of two Sun-like stars"

Exploration

Over 50 years of space travel celebrated

34
Mission to Mars
22
Amazing spacecraft
50
Hayabusa
©masamic
©NASA

10 Spacecraft that changed the World

We take an in-depth look at the past, present and future of the world's greatest spacecraft, from the early pioneers to the modern marvels that have explored the Solar System

1 Apollo 11 Lunar Module

The first manned spacecraft to land on the Moon

To perform the first Moon landing the Apollo 11 mission used two very different spacecraft. The first was the pressurised, conical-shaped Command Module that served as the main living quarters. It was attached to an unpressurised Service Module containing the main rocket engine and propellant.

At launch, the Apollo 11's Command and Service Module (CSM) was mounted above the Lunar Module (LM) on top of the Saturn V rocket. When they moved out of Earth orbit, the CSM separated itself and turned around to attach to the docking port on the LM.

On 20 July 1969 at 21:17 (BST), Neil A Armstrong and Edwin 'Buzz' Aldrin touched down on the Sea of Tranquility, and deployed exploration equipment from a bay on the side of the Descent module.

On leaving the Moon, the Ascent stage's own rocket motor blasted off the Descent stage that remained on the moon. After docking with the CSM, the Ascent stage was jettisoned and left to crash back on the Moon. Prior to re-entry, the Service Module was jettisoned, and after re-entry, the Command Module parachuted down to a splashdown in the sea.

2 Saturn V

The most powerful rocket of all time

The mighty three-stage Saturn V rocket towered to a height of 110.6 metres (363 feet) and weighed 3 million kilograms (6.7 million pounds) fully fuelled. It was constructed under the direction of Dr Wernher von Braun, the German rocket pioneer, at the Marshall Space Flight Center, Huntsville, Alabama.

A workforce of 5,000 people took four months to fit the Saturn V's rocket stages together in the Vehicle Assembly Building at the Kennedy Space Center, Florida.

Altogether, 15 Saturn V rockets were built, and even today, they remain the biggest rockets ever put into service. The closest to it was the Soviet Union's N1 Moon rocket that measured 105 metres (344 feet) tall, but it exploded on all four attempts to launch it.

In comparison, the Space Shuttle was only 56 metres (184 feet) tall. Only the Ares I, at 94 metres (308 feet) tall, has come close to the size of the Saturn V, but it was cancelled due to NASA budget cuts.

© NASA

3 Vostok 1

The original manned spacecraft

Vostok 1 was the spacecraft that took the first ever human to space, Yuri Gagarin, on 12 April 1961.

Although troubled by performance issues, Vostok 1 was a technical marvel. Never before had a vehicle been able to take a human to orbit and return them intact, and therefore Vostok 1 was almost entirely autonomous to prevent any human error. Gagarin could only take control in an emergency, unlike Alan Shepard a few weeks later in the Freedom 7 spacecraft who had almost full control of his flight.

Although Yuri Gagarin spent just 1 hour 46 minutes in orbit he, along with Vostok 1, will forever be remembered for kick-starting the age of human space exploration.

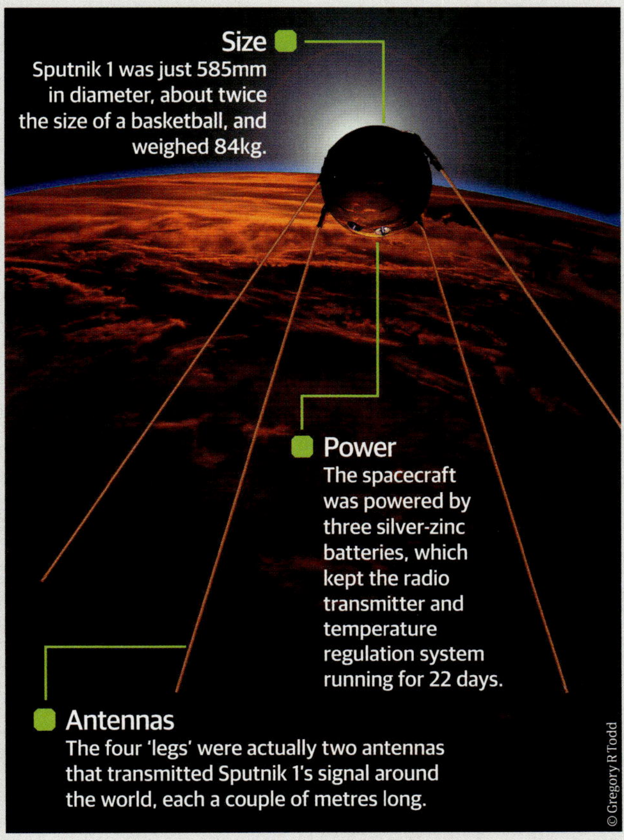

© Gregory R Todd

4 Sputnik 1

This pioneering man-made object was the first to go into orbit around Earth

On 4 October 1957, the Soviet Union successfully sent the first ever artificial object into Earth orbit, using an R-7 rocket to get it there. The small, spherical satellite with four pronged legs was named Sputnik 1.

It was a major milestone not only for the Soviets but also for humanity as a whole, signifying that Earth orbit was both possible and feasible. Sputnik 1 led directly to the Space Race between the USA and USSR. However, it also gleaned some scientific data, such as measuring the electron density in the ionosphere.

Upon reaching orbit it entered an elliptical orbit, reaching over 900km (560 miles) from the surface of Earth. It transmitted radio signals for 22 days that were monitored around the world and eventually fell back into the atmosphere and burned up on 4 January 1958.

5 Voyager 1 & 2

Reaching the edge of the Solar System and beyond

The two unmanned Voyager spacecraft are on a long journey to escape our Solar System and enter the realms of interstellar space.

After achieving the primary mission to explore Jupiter and Saturn, they progressed to explore the outer planets, and are now studying the outer limits of the Sun's solar wind and magnetic field as part of the Voyager Interstellar Mission (VIM).

They are now passing through the heliosheath, where the compressed solar wind turbulently interacts with the interstellar medium. The goal is for them to reach and cross the heliopause, which is thought to be the edge of the Solar System.

They have enough power and fuel to operate until 2020, and it is hoped they will reach the heliopause by then. Indeed, Voyager 1 might be close already. After that they'll drift through space, with Voyager 1, in about 40,000 years' time, passing within 15 trillion kilometres (9.3 trillion miles) of the star AC+79 3888. In 296,000 years, Voyager 2 will pass Sirius by 42.1 trillion kilometres (25 trillion miles).

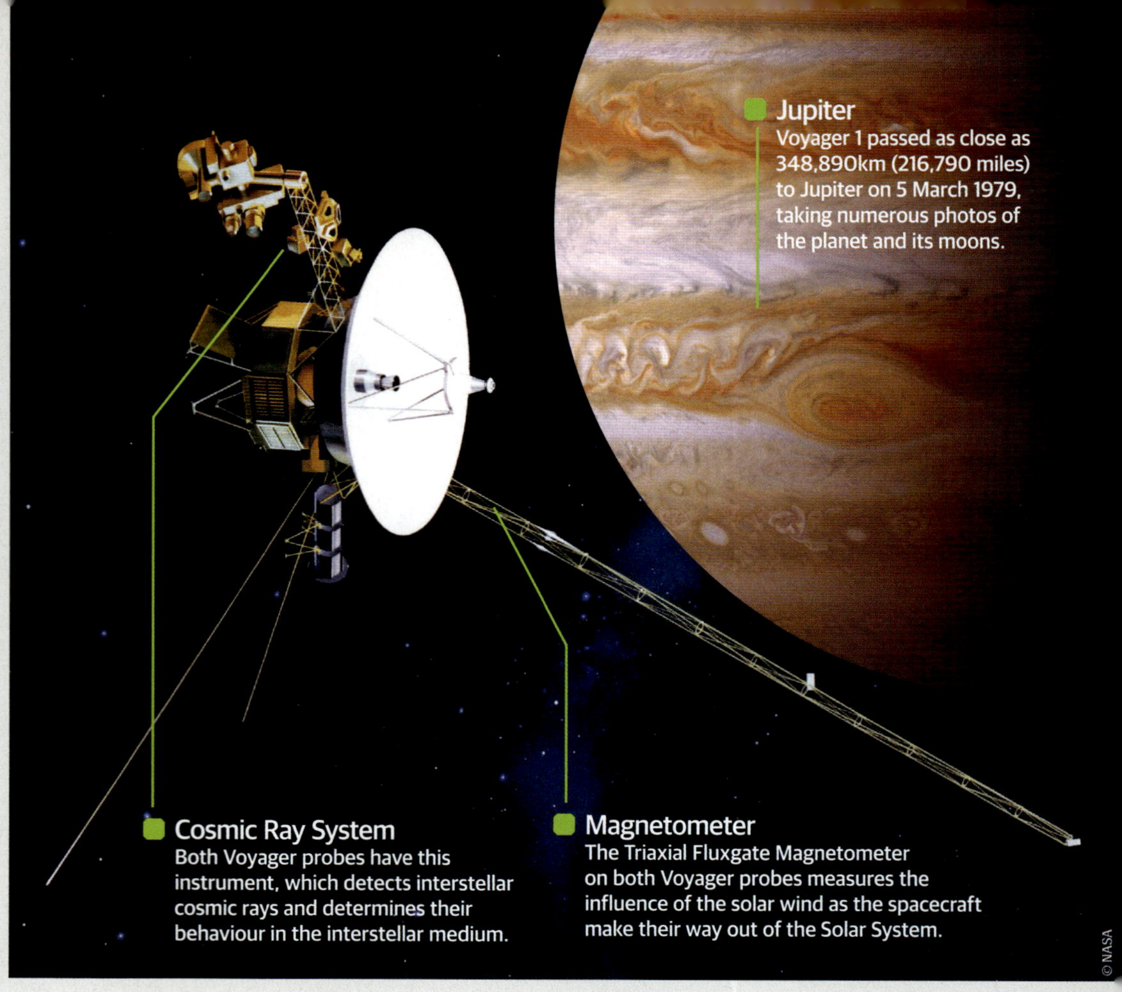

6 Galileo

The first craft to enter Jupiter's atmosphere

Galileo was taken into space inside the payload bay of Space Shuttle (STS-34) Atlantis on 18 October 1989. The unmanned craft consisted of a main orbiting vehicle and a Jupiter atmosphere probe.

During its journey, it discovered extensive volcanism on the Moon and a huge impact basin on the Moon's far side. It passed within 1,600 kilometres (990 miles) of the Gaspra asteroid and when passing the Ida asteroid at a distance of 2,400 kilometres (1,500 miles) Galileo's instruments discovered a small moon (Dactyl) orbiting it.

Galileo released the Jupiter probe on 13 July 1995, and on 8 December 1995, it fired its main engine to become the first man-made object to orbit Jupiter.

During the mission, Galileo made numerous surprising discoveries about the nature of Jupiter's atmosphere. These included finding a radiation belt 50,000 kilometres (31,000 miles) above its cloud layer, strong winds blowing at 600 kilometres per hour (400 miles per hour) and ten per cent less lightning activity than on Earth, though it can be up to a thousand times more powerful.

After making 34 orbits of Jupiter, Galileo was nearly empty of fuel, so it was decided to crash the craft into Jupiter. After travelling a total of 4.6 billion kilometres (2.8 billion miles) Galileo disintegrated in Jupiter's dense atmosphere on 21 September 2003.

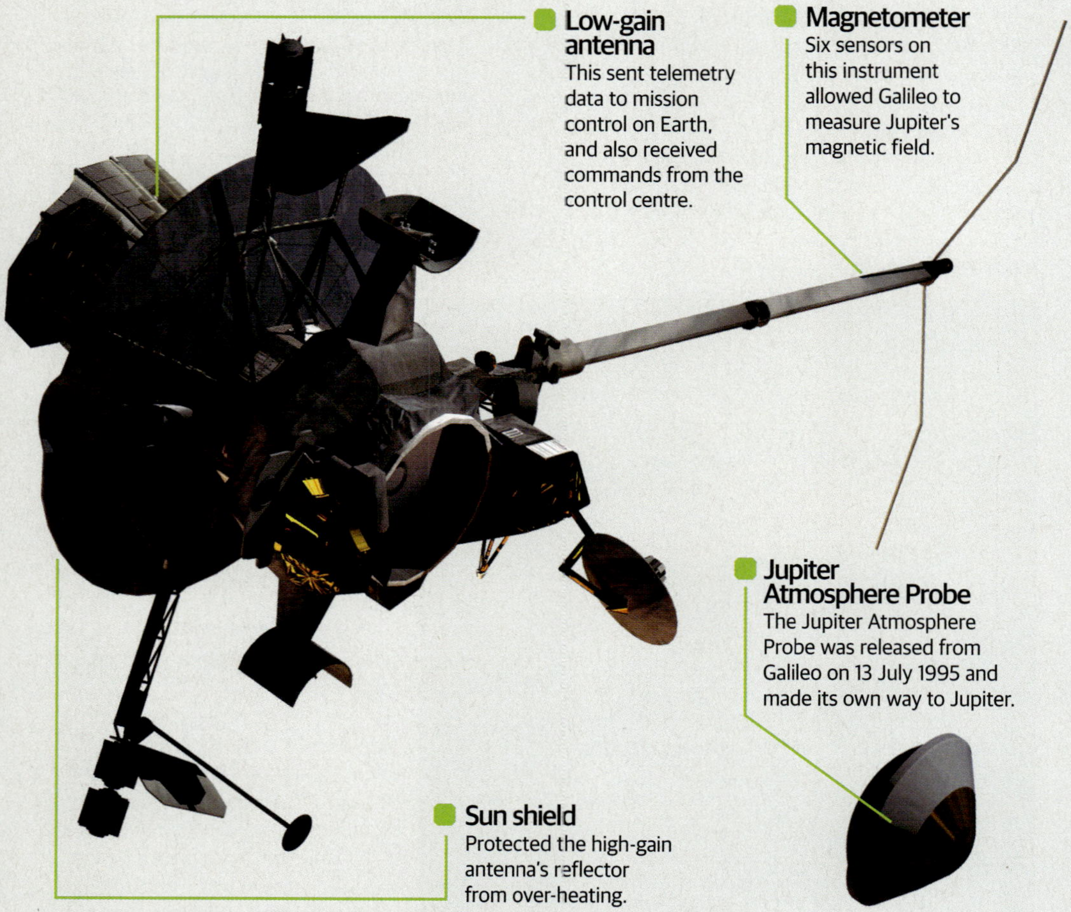

Spacecraft missions

And how they changed the world

Vostok · Sputnik · Apollo · Saturn V · Voyager · Galileo · Cassini-Huygens · Space Shuttle · Soyuz · Orion

- 4 October 1957 — **Sputnik 1**: First man-made object reaches orbit
- 12 Apr 1961 — **Vostok 1**: First human spaceflight
- 14 Jun 1963 — **Vostok 5**: Longest ever solo Earth orbit flight
- 16 Jun 1963 — **Vostok 6**: First woman in space
- 23 Apr 1967 — **Soyuz 1**: First manned Soyuz flight, crashes on re-entry
- 9 Nov 1967 — **Apollo 4**: First unmanned Saturn V flight
- 21 Dec 1968 — **Apollo 8**: First manned Saturn V flight

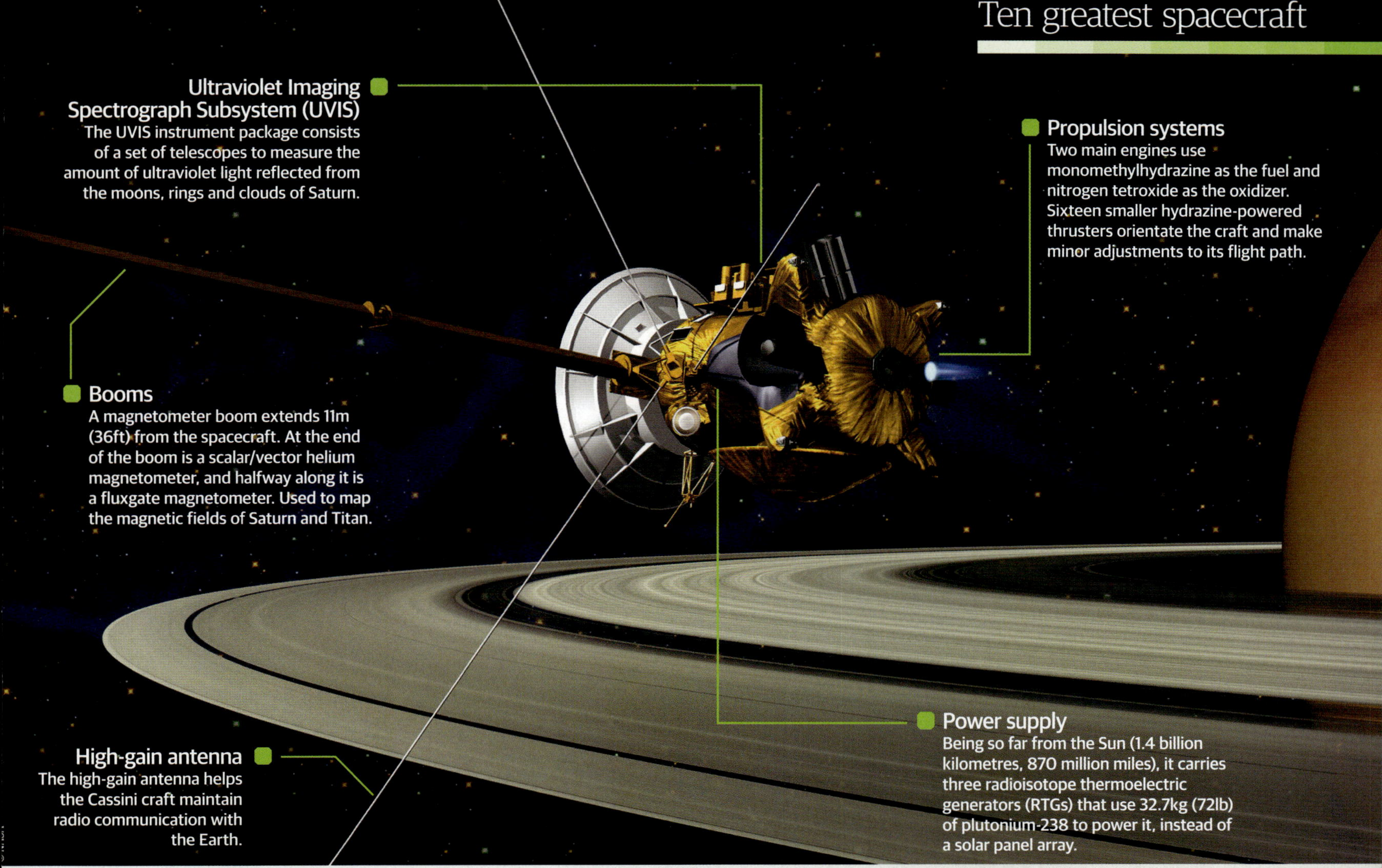

7 Cassini-Huygens

The most complex interplanetary probe ever launched

At 6.7 metres (22 feet) tall and four metres (13 feet) wide, and with a weight of 5,712 kilograms (12,593 pounds), Cassini is the largest and most complex unmanned interplanetary spacecraft ever launched.

Its main objective was to use 12 on-board scientific instruments to conduct a four-year long study of Saturn's atmosphere, surface details, the behaviour of its rings, magnetic environment and the composition of its moons, as well as to carry the Huygens lander spacecraft to Saturn's moon, Titan.

It began orbiting Saturn in 1 July 2004 and completed its prime objectives on 30 June 2008. Under the 'Cassini Solstice Mission', it still remains in operation. Early in 2012, it studied the moons of Jarnsaxa and Mundilfari, and passed Enceladus. In the summer of 2012, it is set to pass Titan, Saturn's largest moon.

Cassini has detected several new moons and revealed that Enceladus sprays out jets of ice crystals that feed into the rings of Saturn. On Saturn, lightning storms and hurricanes have been discovered, and on Titan they have found under its smoggy atmosphere, mountains, clouds, snow, and liquid methane rivers and lakes, much like the conditions on Earth before life evolved here.

To end the mission, it is planned to crash Cassini into Saturn in 2017. ●

"On Titan, they have found mountains, clouds, snow, and liquid methane rivers and lakes, much like the conditions on Earth before life evolved here"

On the surface of Titan

The Huygens lander was the first spacecraft to land on a body in the outer Solar System. Its mission was to carry six instruments to sample the chemical composition of Titan's atmosphere and to take photographs of its surface.

During its flight, the Huygens lander was checked every six months, and before being separated from Cassini its systems were checked and programmed to reactivate itself four hours before it entered Titan's atmosphere.

It landed at 10.2°S, 192.4°W and transmitted data for over three hours during its descent and from the surface before its batteries ran out.

Its photographs showed an orange surface littered with rocks and a ground mist composed of ethane or methane. The temperature of the surface was measured at -144°C (-291°F) and the wind speed was recorded at 241kph (150mph).

20 Jul 1969	14 Apr 1970	30 Jul 1971	11 Dec 1972	14 May 1973	27 Sep 1973	12 Aug 1977	20 Aug 1977	5 Sep 1977	12 Nov 1980
Apollo 11 First lunar landing	**Apollo 13** Mission aborted after oxygen tank exploded	**Apollo 15** First use of lunar rover	**Apollo 17** Last manned landing on the Moon	**Skylab** First American space station launched	**Soyuz 12** First flight of two-person Soyuz	**Enterprise** First manned Shuttle test flight	**Voyager 2** Voyager 2 launches	**Voyager 1** Voyager 1 launches	**Saturn** Voyager 1 flies by Saturn

> "The flight of Columbia proved that the 2.5 million parts of the Space Shuttle were fully functional"

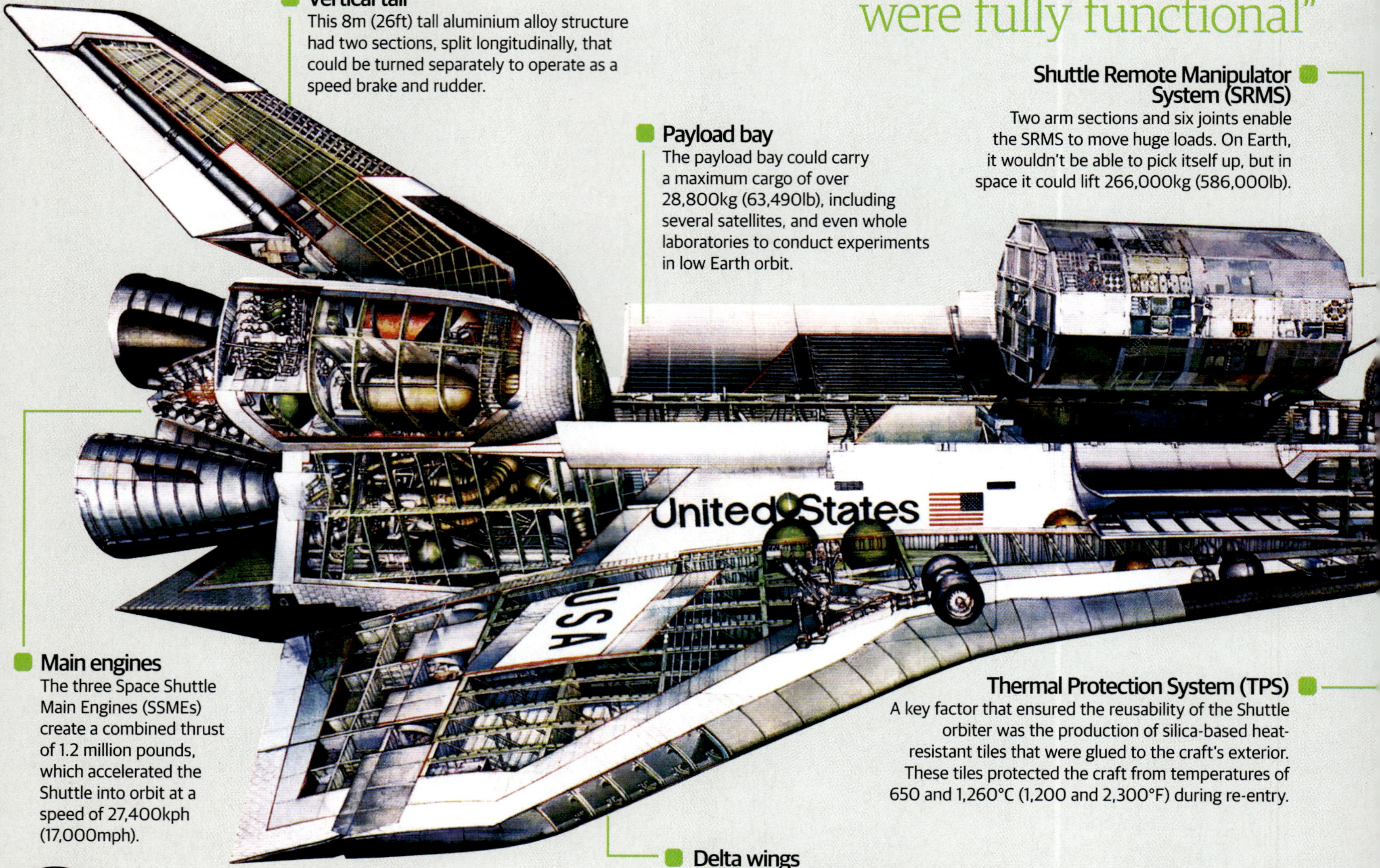

Vertical tail
This 8m (26ft) tall aluminium alloy structure had two sections, split longitudinally, that could be turned separately to operate as a speed brake and rudder.

Payload bay
The payload bay could carry a maximum cargo of over 28,800kg (63,490lb), including several satellites, and even whole laboratories to conduct experiments in low Earth orbit.

Shuttle Remote Manipulator System (SRMS)
Two arm sections and six joints enable the SRMS to move huge loads. On Earth, it wouldn't be able to pick itself up, but in space it could lift 266,000kg (586,000lb).

Main engines
The three Space Shuttle Main Engines (SSMEs) create a combined thrust of 1.2 million pounds, which accelerated the Shuttle into orbit at a speed of 27,400kph (17,000mph).

Thermal Protection System (TPS)
A key factor that ensured the reusability of the Shuttle orbiter was the production of silica-based heat-resistant tiles that were glued to the craft's exterior. These tiles protected the craft from temperatures of 650 and 1,260°C (1,200 and 2,300°F) during re-entry.

Delta wings
The delta wings were constructed of a conventional aluminium alloy, and had a 'cranked delta' bend near the midpoint. This gave the Shuttle better aerodynamic lift than any other type of wing.

8 Space Shuttle

The world's first reusable manned spacecraft

Columbia was the very first Space Shuttle to blast off from the Kennedy Space Center on 12 April 1981. It was mounted on a huge 47-metre (154-foot) long and eight-metre (27-foot) diameter external tank, and two solid fuel booster rockets to take it into orbit. The boosters were jettisoned into the Atlantic Ocean where they were recovered and reused, and nine minutes after launch the external tank fell away into the atmosphere and burnt up over the Pacific Ocean. After its mission, the Shuttle 'orbiter' landed on a runway like a conventional aircraft. It could then be refurbished to be launched once more into space.

The flight of Columbia proved that the 2.5 million parts of the Space Transportation System (STS), as it was officially called, were fully functional. The Shuttle fleet consisted of Columbia, Challenger, Discovery, Endeavour and Atlantis. Atlantis flew the very last mission in July 2011. During this 30-year period, the combined fleet conducted 133 successful missions, made over 21,000 Earth orbits, travelled almost 873 million kilometres (543 million miles) and carried more than 850 astronauts.

Two major disasters struck the Shuttle programme. Challenger broke-up and exploded during lift-off on 28 January 1986, while Columbia disintegrated during re-entry on 1 February 2003.

Nonetheless, the Shuttle craft made many notable achievements, including 37 missions to the ISS. On 25 April 1990, Discovery deployed the Hubble Space Telescope, the world's first space-based optical telescope. In May 1992, Endeavour, built to replace Challenger, sent three astronauts to recover, repair and re-launch the INTELSAT VI communications satellite. From 1993 to 2009, the Shuttle programme made five trips to repair and service the Hubble Space Telescope, with Endeavour getting it functioning properly in December 1993.

NASA's concept of the reusable Shuttle as a cost-effective vehicle that could make space travel safe and routine was never fulfilled. In the light of this it was decided to cancel the programme after it had assembled the International Space Station, and focus on new space exploration projects. ●

Should the Space Shuttle programme have been cancelled? @spaceanswers #SpaceShuttle

Spacecraft missions

- 27 Nov 1980 — **Soyuz T-3**: First flight of redesigned three-person Soyuz
- 12 Apr 1981 — **Columbia**: First manned Shuttle orbital flight
- 26 Aug 1981 — **Saturn**: Voyager 2 flies by Saturn
- 24 Jan 1986 — **Uranus**: Voyager 2 has first-ever Uranus encounter
- 25 Aug 1989 — **Neptune**: Voyager 2 becomes first spacecraft to observe Neptune
- 18 Oct 1989 — **Launch**: Galileo spacecraft launches
- 24 Apr 1990 — **Discovery**: Shuttle deploys Hubble Space Telescope
- 7 Dec 1995 — **Probe**: Galileo space probe enters Jupiter's atmosphere
- 8 Dec 1995 — **Orbit**: Galileo orbiter enters orbit around Jupiter

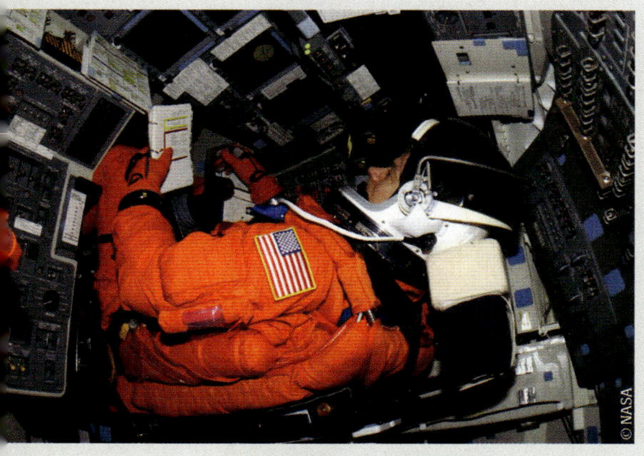
© NASA

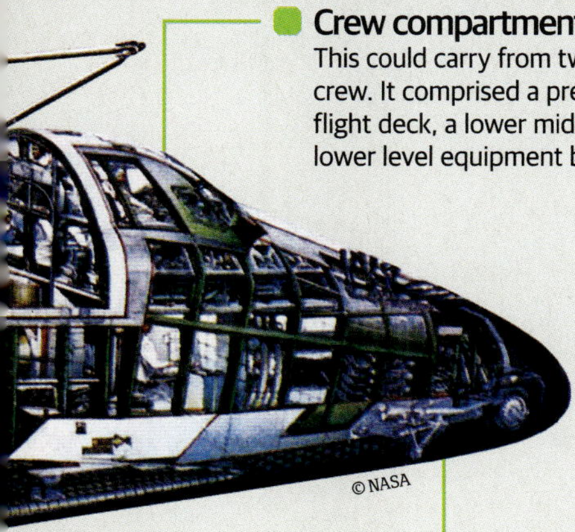
© NASA

Crew compartment
This could carry from two to eight crew. It comprised a pressurised flight deck, a lower mid-deck and a lower level equipment bay.

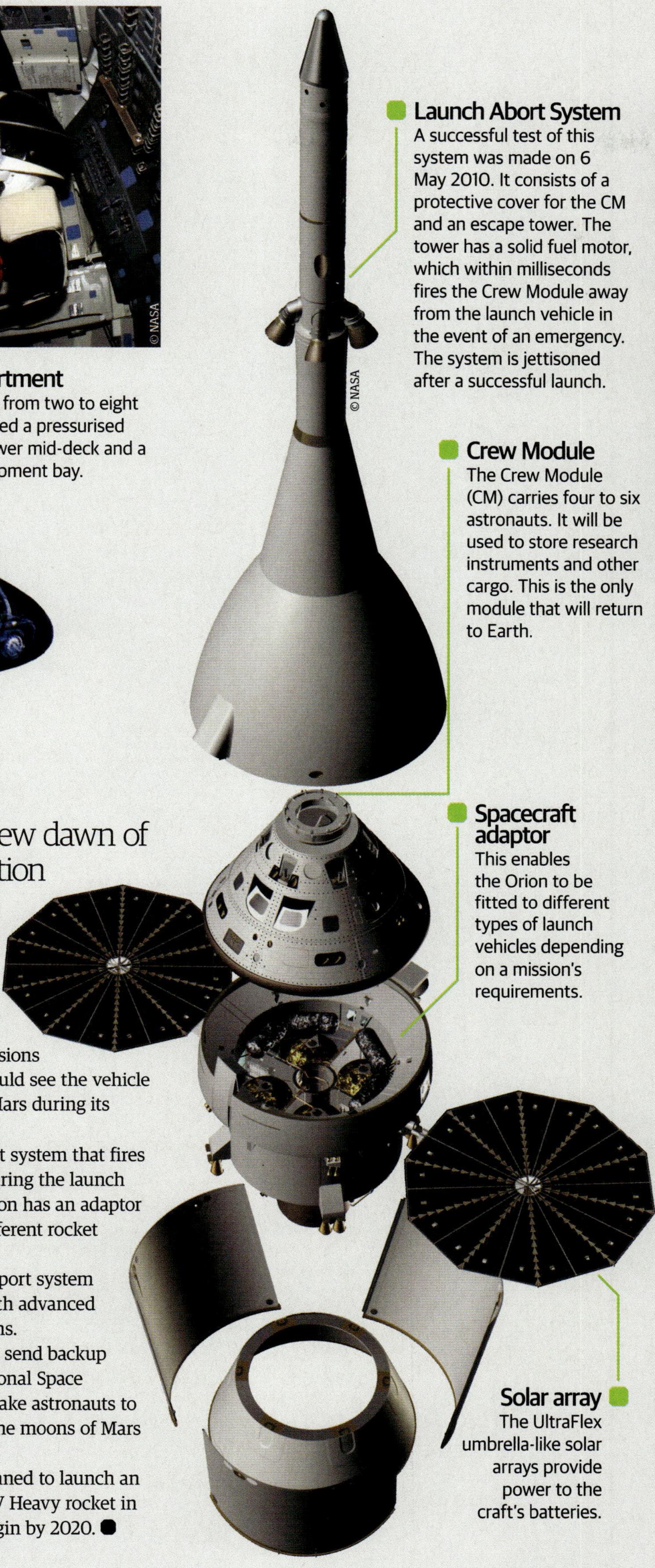
© NASA

Launch Abort System
A successful test of this system was made on 6 May 2010. It consists of a protective cover for the CM and an escape tower. The tower has a solid fuel motor, which within milliseconds fires the Crew Module away from the launch vehicle in the event of an emergency. The system is jettisoned after a successful launch.

Crew Module
The Crew Module (CM) carries four to six astronauts. It will be used to store research instruments and other cargo. This is the only module that will return to Earth.

Spacecraft adaptor
This enables the Orion to be fitted to different types of launch vehicles depending on a mission's requirements.

Solar array
The UltraFlex umbrella-like solar arrays provide power to the craft's batteries.

9 Orion

Heralding a new dawn of space exploration

Although still in development, the Orion spacecraft is already world-changing in terms of its advanced design and scale of ambition. Unlike other craft of its kind the Orion is being designed for long-term space missions lasting over six months which could see the vehicle being used for manned trips to Mars during its service lifetime.

It will use a revolutionary abort system that fires the capsule away from danger during the launch and lift-off stages. At its base, Orion has an adaptor unit so that it can be fitted to different rocket launch vehicles.

The craft has a unique life-support system and thermal protection, along with advanced propulsion and navigation systems.

When necessary the Orion can send backup crews and cargos to the International Space Station, and can also be used to take astronauts to the Moon, near-Earth asteroids, the moons of Mars and Mars itself.

To test all its systems, it is planned to launch an unmanned Orion using a Delta IV Heavy rocket in 2014. Manned missions could begin by 2020. ●

A Soyuz spacecraft orbiting the Earth with its solar array deployed
© NASA

10 Soyuz

The longest-serving manned spacecraft

The Soyuz spacecraft was originally designed as an essential part of the mission to land Soviet astronauts on the Moon.

A modified (L1) two-man version of it was planned to be the equivalent of the Apollo Command Module, which would release a manned lander to the Moon.

On 23 April 1967, Soyuz 1 was launched to rendezvous and dock with another Soyuz craft in Earth orbit but it ended in failure. After this inauspicious start and the cancellation of the Moon programme, the Soyuz became a manned ferry to the Salyut space station in the Seventies.

Soyuz 19 docked with an Apollo spacecraft on 17 July 1975, marking the end of the Space Race between the USA and the Soviet Union.

The Soyuz T, with its improved electronics and navigation equipment, was introduced in June 1980 as the successor to the Soyuz 40, while the Soyuz TM replaced the Soyuz T in 1986 and serviced the Mir space station until its de-orbit in 2001. The latest version is the upgraded TMA that is used to service the International Space Station.

The basic craft carries three crew in a spherical orbital module, who are returned to Earth in a re-entry module that is positioned behind it. It can automatically dock to a spacecraft, though a manual override can be used when needed.

The Soyuz spacecraft has remained successful due to its modular design and ability to be modernised and modified to adapt to changing mission requirements. ●

- 15 Oct 1997 — **Launch** — Cassini-Huygens launches
- 17 Feb 1998 — **Voyager 1** — Voyager 1 becomes the most distant man-made object
- 31 Oct 2000 — **Soyuz TM-31** — First visit of Soyuz to ISS
- 21 Sep 2003 — **De-orbit** — Galileo orbiter intentionally crashes into Jupiter
- 1 Jul 2004 — **Orbit** — Cassini enters orbit around Saturn
- 14 Jan 2005 — **Huygens** — The Huygens probe lands on Titan
- 8 Jul 2011 — **Atlantis** — Final flight of Space Shuttle programme
- 15 May 2012 — **Soyuz TMA-04M** — Soyuz takes recent crew to ISS
- 2014 — **Launch** — First unmanned test flight of Orion spacecraft
- 2020 — **Manned** — First manned flight of Orion

NASA's Moon buggy

This small, four-wheel-drive, electric-powered buggy may look flimsy, but this intrepid vehicle is also the most expensive car in the history of humankind

Officially known as the Lunar Roving Vehicle (LRV), NASA's state-of-the-art, $38-million-dollar Moon buggy was more spacecraft than regular vehicle. Its designers were tasked with producing a buggy that could carry two astronauts in heavy spacesuits along with their scientific equipment over the rugged Moon terrain where temperatures can range from plus or minus 120 degrees Celsius (250 degrees Fahrenheit) and the gravity is one-sixth weaker than on Earth.

To fit the buggy inside the 1.8 x 1.2 metre (6 x 4 foot) Quadrant 1 bay of the Descent Stage of the Lunar Module, the wheels folded inwards and the whole body was folded in half. A set of ropes, cloth tapes, pulleys and springs enabled it to be swung out from the craft, and the wheels and body semi-automatically snapped into place. It took the Apollo 15 astronauts 26 minutes to deploy it in this fashion – ten minutes longer than originally planned.

The buggy was the size of a small car at 3.1 metres (10.1 feet) long, 1.83 metres (six feet) wide, 1.14 metres (3.7 feet) high. It didn't have a roof and the seats were like webbed patio furniture with Velcro strips on the surface. The astronauts had special spacesuits that could bend at the waist to enable them to sit in the vehicle, and the main steering and speed control was a T-shaped handle that could be easily operated with bulky spacesuit gloves.

Electric drive
The front and rear wheels each had an electric motor to control the steering mechanism. Each wheel was driven by its own 0.25hp electric motor that was powered by two 36-volt silver-zinc potassium hydroxide batteries.

Tool carrier
The buggy had a mass of 210kg (460lb) and could carry 490kg (1,080lb). This included the two astronauts, equipment and Moon rock samples.

Wheels
The 818mm (32in) diameter, 230mm (9in) wide tyres were made out of zinc-coated steel strands that covered the aluminium hub. To provide traction, titanium chevrons covered the outside of the tyre.

Each wheel had its own electric motor, so that if one or more failed the buggy was still driveable. The front and rear wheels each had their own steering motor, with the option to steer with four wheels or with just the front or rear wheels. The buggy had a turning circle of 3.1 metres (10.1 feet) and had an average speed of nine kilometres per hour (5.6 miles per hour). During the Apollo 17 mission, Eugene Cernan set the speed record for the buggy at 18 kilometres per hour (11.2 miles per hour).

Only three buggies ever flew to the Moon, on the Apollo 15, 16 and 17 missions. On each mission, they made three separate journeys beyond the Lunar Module, to a maximum distance of 7.6 kilometres (4.7 miles). It was a very stable vehicle, although under the low gravity the wheels had a tendency to float off the ground and return to the Lunar surface much slower than expected.

It only took 17 months to design, test and build the buggy at a cost of $38 million USD (£24 million), making it the most costly car in history. Nonetheless, it was a great success as it enabled the Apollo 15 astronauts to explore four times more territory than the previous Apollo 11, 12 and 14 missions put together. As Apollo 15 astronaut Dave Scott put it: "I think the vehicle is about as optimum as you can build."

"The astronauts had special spacesuits that could bend at the waist to enable them to sit down in the vehicle"

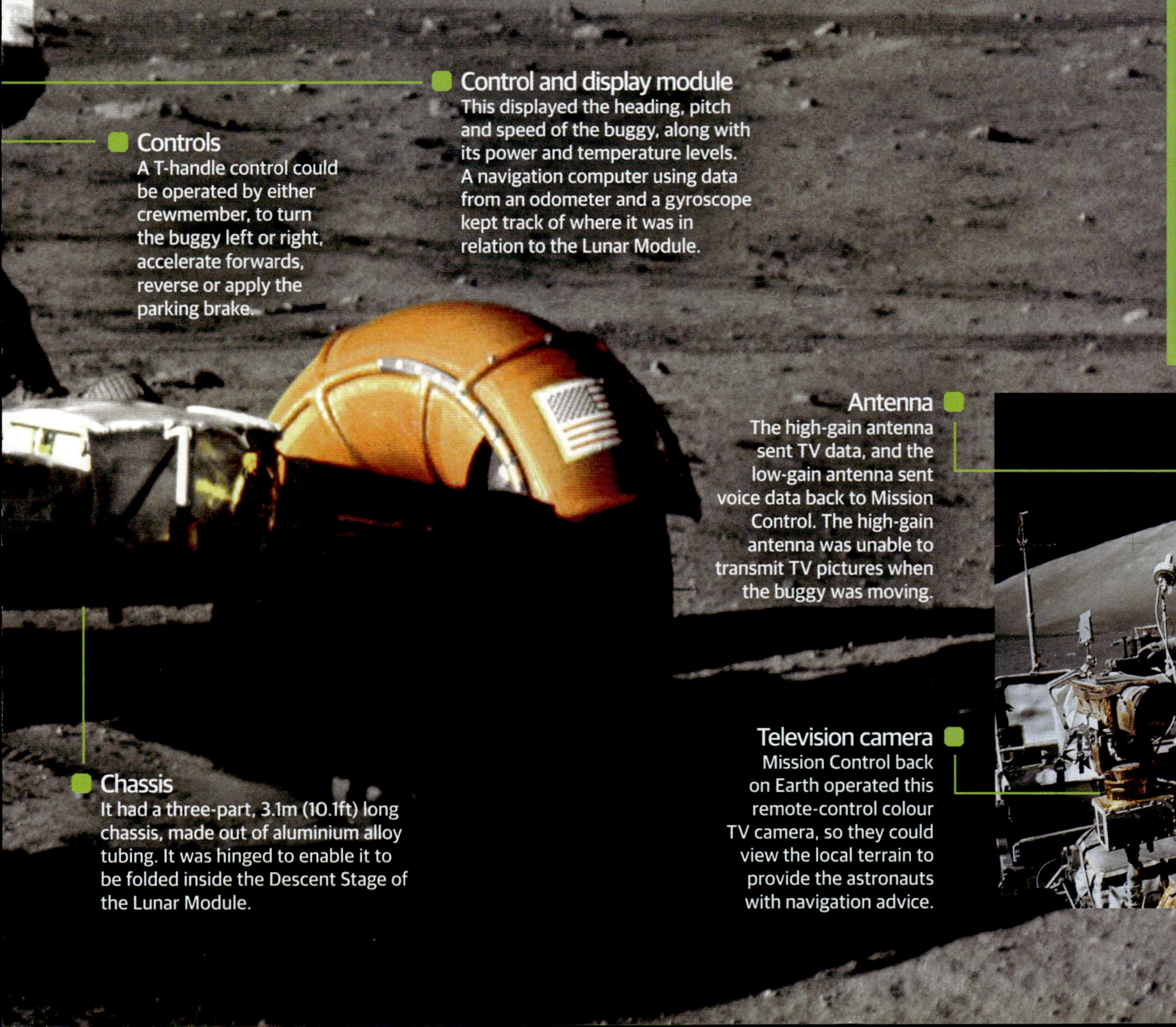

Moon buggy missions

Apollo 15

Landing date:
30 July 1971
The first astronauts to use the Moon buggy were David Scott and James Irwin during the Apollo 15 mission, travelling a total of 27km (17 miles).

Apollo 16

Landing date:
21 April 1972
John Young and Charles Duke Jr used the moon buggy in their Apollo 16 mission to travel 4.5km (2.8 miles) from the Lunar Module.

Apollo 17

Landing date:
11 December 1972
The last astronauts to use the buggy were Eugene Cernan and Harrison Schmitt, with the former setting the unofficial lunar land-speed record of 18km/h (11.2mph).

Neil Armstrong descends the Lunar Module's ladder on his way to the Moon's surface

Neil Armstrong and the first moonwalk

The late Neil Armstrong will forever be remembered as the first human being to set foot on the Moon. We look back at that historic Apollo 11 moonwalk

On 21 July 1969 (UTC), 530 million television viewers sat transfixed by the first grainy, black-and-white transmission from the surface of the Moon. At 109 hours, 24 minutes and 15 seconds into the Apollo 11 mission, Neil Armstrong, the soft-spoken mission commander, climbed down the ladder of the Lunar Module and became the first human being to place his foot on celestial soil. Armstrong, who died in 2012 at the age of 82, was ready with his now famous pronouncement, "That's one small step for man; one giant leap for mankind."

The logistics of the journey were staggering. It required a three-stage Saturn V rocket, a slingshot around the Moon and a final descent in a tiny capsule, barely avoiding a rock-strewn field to land safely on the edge of the Sea of Tranquillity. Inside the landing module, nicknamed the 'Eagle', were Armstrong and his co-pilot Edwin E 'Buzz' Aldrin, Jr. Their third comrade, Michael Collins, was 100 kilometres (62 miles) overhead, orbiting in the Command/Service Module.

The men had rehearsed every step of their eight-day journey, including the experiments they would conduct during the moonwalk, known in NASA circles as extra-vehicular activity (EVA). But even with their extensive training, the Moon was very much terra incognita. Would the dust on the lunar surface be so fine and deep that they would sink into it like quicksand? Would their spacesuits, designed to keep the astronauts cool in the Moon's 100 degree Celsius (212 degree Fahrenheit) temperatures, work? To ensure the astronauts' safety, this first moonwalk would be quick - just two and a half hours of scientific exploration, photo documentation and a chat with the President.

The two astronauts knew that the mission could be aborted at any time. That's why Armstrong's first act, before planting the flag or posing for a photo, was to grab the closest hunk of Moon rock as a contingency sample. If nothing else worked, at least they would have something to show the eager NASA geologists back home.

15 minutes after Armstrong made his fateful 'leap', Aldrin stepped from the landing module hatch and descended to the surface. The two men snapped photos of the landing site and described the feel of the lunar surface and the effect of the module's descent engines on the lunar dust.

Next, Armstrong read from a plaque mounted on the Lunar Module ladder. The ladder, and the plaque, would remain on the Moon when the rest of the craft eventually brought the astronauts back to rendezvous with Collins. Armstrong read the plaque to the rapt millions back home: "Here men from planet Earth first set foot upon the Moon. July 1969 AD. We came in peace for all mankind."

Photo documentation was a critical focus of the Apollo 11 mission. Armstrong and Aldrin were armed with high-end Hasselblad 70mm still cameras, a 16mm movie camera, plus super-wide focus lenses and a 35mm stereoscopic close-up camera. The men were on orders to photograph or film nearly every aspect of the moonwalk: from panoramic vistas to extreme closeups of the lunar surface.

The television camera was equally, if not more, important than the still cameras. Not only was the live TV footage 'proof' of NASA's momentous achievement, but every frame would be recorded and analysed back home for clues to the physical and environmental properties of the Moon. Look how the dust settles. See how the soil colour changes after it is compressed by a boot. Check out Aldrin's stiff gait as he tries to bunny hop in his bulky suit. After reading the plaque, Armstrong carried the TV camera about 25 metres (80 feet) from the landing module so it would have a clear, wide shot of everything the astronauts did.

One focus of the TV footage was the moonwalkers' mobility. Aldrin was the chief subject of these tests, which show the former Air Force pilot running, skipping, hopping and cutting sharply from left to right as he describes the ease or difficulty of each manoeuvre. Aldrin was also assigned the tasks of kicking lunar soil to evaluate its trajectory.

The planting of the American flag has been a flashpoint for conspiracy theorists who shout that a flag cannot 'wave' in a vacuum. That's true, which is why the one metre by 1.5 metre (three foot by five foot) flag was held open by a telescopic horizontal rod. The astronauts struggled to open the rod completely, which gave the flag a slightly ruffled appearance. The men also received a brief congratulatory phone call from President Richard Nixon, who described the feelings of those watching below. "For one priceless moment in the whole history of man," said Nixon, "all the people on this Earth are truly one."

But most of the work of that first moonwalk was dedicated to scientific experimentation. Armstrong collected 22 kilograms (48.5 pounds) of samples containing rocks, pebbles and fine lunar dust. Aldrin set up a solar wind collector made of aluminium foil. The foil was exposed for 77 minutes and it captured the first measurement of the solar particle stream outside of the Earth's magnetic field.

The men installed a seismometer that would beam back information about 'moonquakes' and give clues to the internal structure of the rocky orb. They also set up a special mirror called a lunar ranging retroreflector that would be used by Earth telescopes to bounce back long-range laser beams. The lasers would give the first hyper-accurate measurements of the Moon's distance from the Earth and how fast it is drifting away from us (38 millimetres or 1.5 inches annually).

Once the experiments were deployed, the famously by-the-books Armstrong momentarily veered from the game plan. Moving quickly across the lunar surface, he bounded to the nearby Little West Crater to snap a last-minute panoramic shot of its sloping interior. At a distance of 60 metres (196 feet) from the Lunar Module, this is the farthest either man strayed during the entire moonwalk.

At over 111 hours and 35 minutes into their mission, and only two hours and 32 minutes after Armstrong popped the hatch on the Lunar Module, the commander sealed it shut again. After some rest, the men would begin their journey home, ending with a splashdown in the Pacific. ●

"For one priceless moment in the whole history of man," said Nixon, "all the people on this Earth are truly one"

The first moonwalk explained

Distance covered

In their two and a half hours on the lunar surface, Armstrong and Aldrin never strayed more than 60 metres (196 feet) from the lunar module - less than the length of a football pitch. The fear was that the astronauts' water-cooled spacesuits would run out of H_2O, leaving them exposed to 100°C (212°F) lunar temperatures.

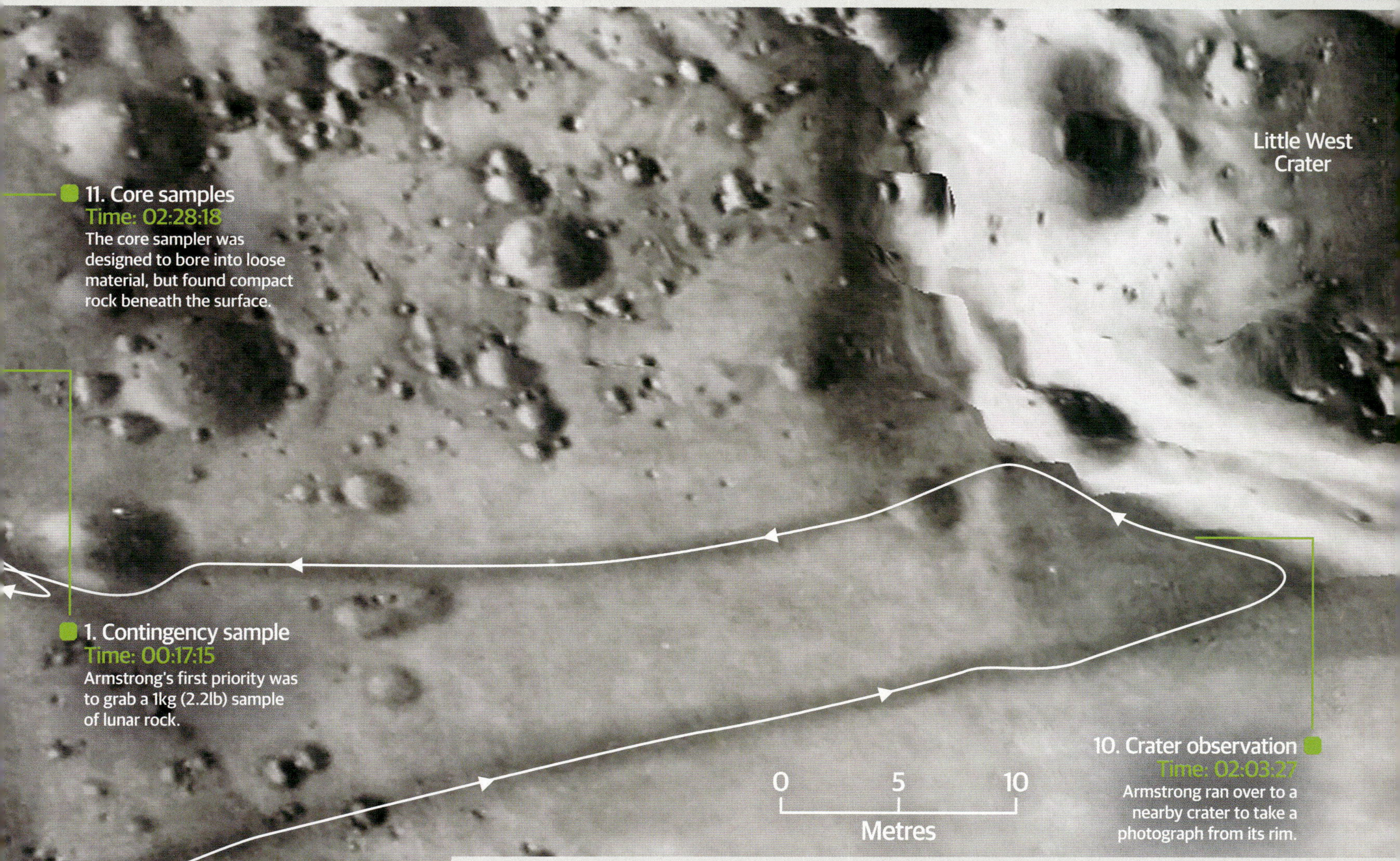

11. Core samples
Time: 02:28:18
The core sampler was designed to bore into loose material, but found compact rock beneath the surface.

1. Contingency sample
Time: 00:17:15
Armstrong's first priority was to grab a 1kg (2.2lb) sample of lunar rock.

10. Crater observation
Time: 02:03:27
Armstrong ran over to a nearby crater to take a photograph from its rim.

Exploring Mars

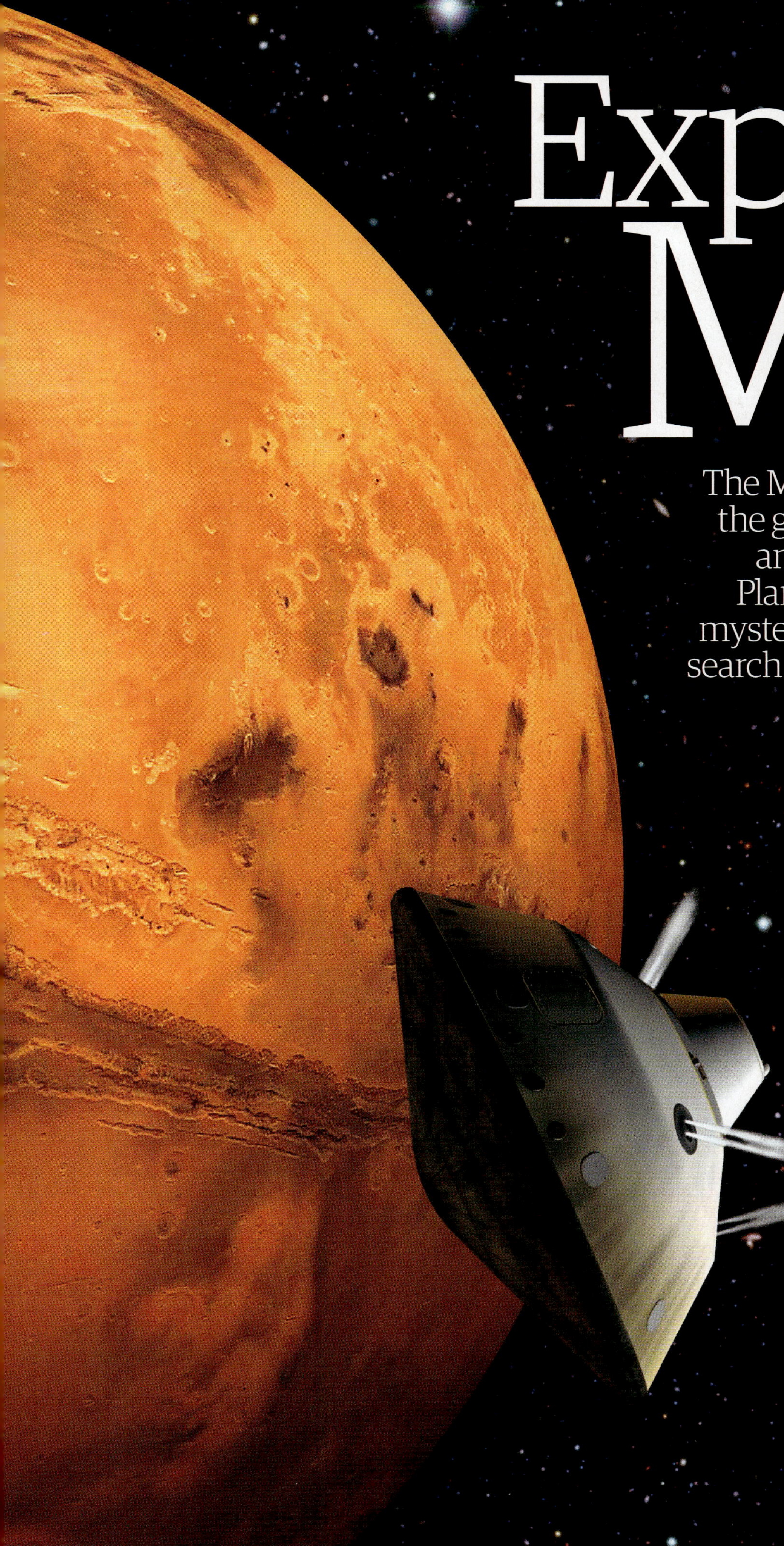

The Mars Science Laboratory will be the greatest mission to ever explore another world. It'll probe the Red Planet's ferocious past, uncover its mysterious present and, through the search for life, it may be a precursor to future manned missions

The Mars Science Laboratory (MSL), also known as the Curiosity rover, is NASA's most ambitious robotic mission to date. It is the largest and most sophisticated machine to ever land on another world, and its ultimate objective is driven by the fact that life is thought to have once existed, or perhaps still does, on the Red Planet. Mars has been the subject of numerous missions over the past four decades but Curiosity is set to rove its surface like never before.

The rover is huge and complex, with ten different instruments on board that will probe the surface of Mars in unprecedented detail. "It's our most ambitious robotic mission," says Michael Meyer, program scientist for the MSL mission and lead scientist for the Mars Exploration Program, when we spoke to him. "This is the most complicated mission we've done and it's designed to last for [at least] a Mars year, so we're going to take it slow and make sure we don't break anything in our rush to get data."

Curiosity is the largest landing vehicle ever to operate outside the confines of Earth, a behemoth of a machine almost 1,000 kilograms (2,200 pounds) in weight and the size of a car that is revolutionising our understanding of Mars since it landed on 6 August 2012. With a multitude of sample analysis instruments, cameras and even a hi-tech laser it is absolutely unmatched in its design.

The mission is designed to last 686 Earth days, approximately one Martian year. During this time Curiosity will carry out some groundbreaking science on the surface in addition to testing out new technologies and methodologies. The rover is somewhat autonomous, possessing the ability to move between two points while avoiding obstacles. However, to do so requires extensive daily input from the ground. "The challenge of [MSL] is that you can't just program it and collect your data in two weeks to see how it's going. You actually have to tell it what to do every day. That's what's going to pose a real challenge.

"One of the things that really makes this mission pretty exciting is that the amount of information that we have about the landing site from our orbital assets is phenomenal," says Meyer. "We've already plotted out likely pathways of where to go, and it's great to approach it with that sort of prior knowledge because when we find something that's different it's a real 'aha!' moment."

Curiosity will be the fourth rover to land on Mars, succeeding Sojourner, Spirit and Opportunity, and NASA has made sure to learn from the previous missions to optimise the data returned from this one. "Certainly we have greatly improved operations, and we have a much better sense of the kind of realistic timing for what we can do and what we can ask the rover to do." Indeed, as previously mentioned, one of Curiosity's greatest advancements on its predecessors is a greater degree of autonomous navigation. "On any of the runs where the rover goes more than 30 metres [100 feet], it can be done autonomously because we'll have enough data to plot out a good path," explains Meyer. "If we don't have enough information [about the topography] the rover can decide if it has an obstacle in the way and avoid it. The big science driver for this mission is not within the landing area, it's actually going up Mount Sharp, so because of that there'll be a fair amount of driving to get to the minerals we're most interested in early on in the mission." The rover, however, won't be speeding along the Martian landscape. It will take its time, going very slowly indeed. "To go 100 metres [330 feet] is doable in a day," says Meyer. "In theory you could maybe go 150 to 200 metres [490 to 650 feet]. Part of that is the wheels don't roll that fast, and the other part is that after a certain distance it has to stop and reassess its environment."

The Mars Science Laboratory landed in an area known as the Gale Crater, a 3.8-billion-year-old crater 154 kilometres (96 miles) in diameter. At its centre is the aforementioned Mount Sharp, towering 5,500 metres (18,000 feet) high. It was one of four candidates for a landing site and ultimately received the nod, but why was it picked? "All four [proposed] landing sites were pretty compelling," explains Meyer. "All four sites give you evidence of a place that has had water in the past, so they all met our criteria of a place that we think could have been habitable at one point. Any one of them would have been fantastic, but Gale has evidence of water in its past and it has two major minerals that we think are indicative of different periods of time on Mars: clays and sulphates. There's also layering there, which we think will give a somewhat ordered history of Mars. Gale has sedimentary deposits that we think traverse a period of time when Mars went from being relatively warm and wet to what it is now: cold and dry."

Curiosity dwarfs the other Mars rovers by quite a margin

The most interesting thing about Gale, though, is that it has the possibility of organics or, in other words, past or present signs of alien life. This ties in directly with one of the key goals of Curiosity's mission, namely discerning whether Mars was or is habitable, a question that no other mission has yet been able to definitively answer. "With any sedimentary deposit you have the potential for preservation of organic material," says Meyer. "One of the surprises of the Viking probe was actually that they didn't find organics. You would expect to find some because you get them from meteorites and the like. So the big science revelation [from Viking] was that something's happening on Mars that destroyed the organics, at least on the surface. So we're hoping that by going to a place where you have these deposits laid out, that something buried may be preserved."

To find these hidden clues to the Martian past, Curiosity has a variety of hi-tech instruments on board. These include ChemCam, a laser that will vaporise areas of rock for Curiosity to analyse, and SAM (Sample Analysis at Mars), an instrument suite that will discern the molecular and elemental chemistry of soil samples collected by a drill on Curiosity's extendable arm. Meyer is fairly confident that Curiosity would be the mission that would find signs of habitability. "We expect to find organics from meteorite impacts, brought in from outer space. We also expect to find organics that were made on the planet, so this is a great lead into that. And then of course the million dollar question is: are there organics made by Martian life?"

So, will MSL be able to answer that question? "Definitively, no," says Meyer, "but there is a possibility, there is always a possibility. Carl Sagan [the American astronomer] said that even a camera is a life-detection instrument. If something hops in front of the camera then you know it's alive. But the camera was not designed to specifically look for things to hop in front of it. MSL is designed to understand the environment in which it lands."

One of the most fascinating features of this Mars mission, and one that scientists hope might be used in future Mars missions, is the

Mars mission history

Dozens of robotic spacecraft have made the hazardous journey to the Red Planet since the Sixties, with mixed results...

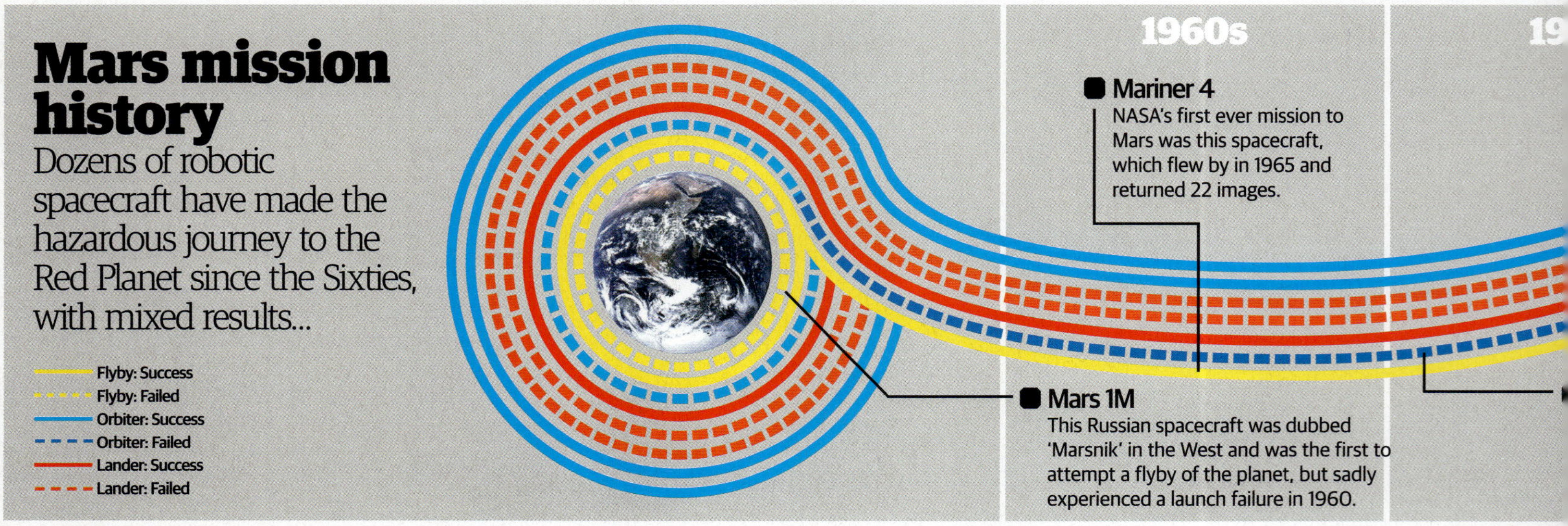

4 goals of going to Mars

The Mars Science Laboratory has four primary scientific goals that it will be looking to fulfil in its time on the surface of Mars. While it will perform other research as well, it is these goals that pose the greatest unanswered questions about the Red Planet

Curiosity will be able to return high-resolution images and video from the surface of Mars thanks to its on-board cameras

Is, or was, Mars habitable?

One of the strangest things about Mars, surprisingly, is that life has not yet been found. The planet has been pummelled by meteorite impacts, thanks largely to its thin atmosphere, and therefore we would expect to find organics of some kind. Curiosity will tackle this problem head-on, studying the mineralogical composition of the surface to discover what mysterious past this planet is hiding.

What is Mars's climate like?

It is thought that in the past Mars may have been warmer and therefore had a thicker and wetter atmosphere compared to the thin, cold atmosphere it has now. The determination of whether water exists underground or once gouged the surface is imperative as life as we know it cannot exist without water. By measuring elements such as carbon, Curiosity will look for abrupt changes in the abundance of certain elements that could be associated to life forms.

Does Mars have a volatile history?

It is generally accepted that Mars is a much different world to what it was a few hundred million years ago, but what caused this change is still unknown. Of great interest to Curiosity will be Mount Sharp, in the Gale Crater. This mountain could have layers of sedimentary deposits of Martian history, similar to the layers of deposits we see on Earth. By studying various rocks and soils on Mars, Curiosity will be able to understand some of the geological processes that sculpted Mars.

Could we launch a human mission to Mars?

The Sky Crane is the only current landing method that can land 1,000kg (2,200lb) on the surface of another world, a necessity for a manned mission. By demonstrating that the Sky Crane works, Curiosity will pave the way for human explorers to use the same design to land on Mars. In addition, Curiosity will also study the levels of radiation to unearth any potential hazards that might face future explorers.

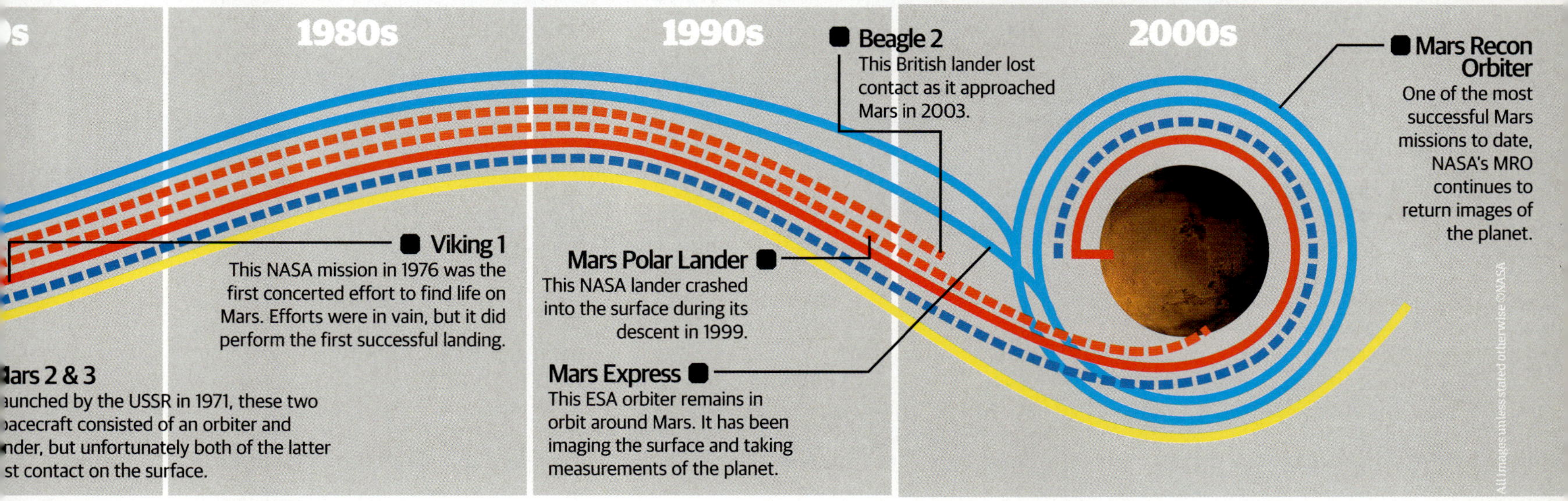

revolutionary Sky Crane concept that will land Curiosity in the Gale Crater. We were keen to find out why this design had been picked. "It wasn't just the desire to have something that looked like a Rube Goldberg device," explains Meyer. "When it came to Curiosity we wanted to build a system that we could use not only for this mission but also for future missions. We needed to find out how we could get a metric ton to the surface. With Sky Crane, we can do that."

However, as incredible as the Sky Crane concept looks there's still a significant chance of failure, especially as the whole routine is handled autonomously. "If you just look at statistics, like the percentage success rate of going to Mars, the odds aren't very good. We've been lucky in our US landed missions, we've been very successful. We are confident in that we're well over a probability of 90 per cent for landing but it's a tough one where one rock can do you in. You can do everything right and be unlucky. That's kind of why I would prefer to go somewhere else [during the landing] and find out a couple of days later if we actually made it, so I don't have to go through all that anxiety!"

While Curiosity will probe the Red Planet in an unprecedented manner, it's not too soon to consider what missions might come next. Of course, human exploration is one of the ultimate goals, but Meyer has some other thoughts on what would be best for the future. While orbiters like NASA's Mars Reconnaissance Orbiter will continue to play a role, he asserts that landing on Mars is the real driver for future missions. "I really think the science is on the surface. I think what will happen is that we'll have small rovers with different and more sophisticated instruments, and they might not be quite so ambitious in terms of the number of instruments [like MSL]. The expectation is that we'll have these things that are smaller and work just as well. And I think we ultimately need to work towards sample return, because there's so much we can do with a sample when we bring it back to Earth."

But does Meyer think sample return would be best done by humans or robots? "I think the first time we go and get samples on Mars, we want to do it robotically," he says. "Part of the reason is you can make a robot a lot cleaner than an astronaut! And there's also an issue with astronaut safety and that sort of thing. How you actually bring it back can be done robotically or you can have astronauts orbit Mars and pick it up."

There's little doubt, then, that the Mars Science Laboratory will be set to change Mars exploration completely, increasing our understanding of the past and present and leading the way to future missions.

At the time of going to print there's still the chance the landing will be unsuccessful, but NASA is confident and we'll certainly be sitting with fingers crossed as it descends to the surface. Through this incredible mission we will be able to answer some mysterious questions about Mars and maybe, finally, discover if it was or is a truly habitable world. ●

Is this the most ambitious space exploration mission of all time? @spaceanswers #GreatestMission

"You can't just program it and collect your data in two weeks and see how it's going. You actually have to tell it what to do every day. That's what's going to pose a real challenge"

Michael Meyer, lead scientist for NASA's Mars Exploration Program

Building the Mars Science Laboratory

The key steps in the development of this incredible rover

1. Mars heat shield constructed
2. Parts assembled
3: Wheels tested
4: Core of Curiosity assembled
5: Arm tested
6: Obstacle avoidance
7: Further testing
8: Instruments adjusted
9: Vacuum test
10: Sky Crane attached
11: MSL enters capsule
12: MSL readied for final assembly
13: Heat shield and capsule aligned
14: Mars spacecraft sealed
15: Inside the Atlas V payload fairing
16: MSL prepared for enclosure
17: Protective payload fairing sealed
18: MSL prepped for Atlas V
19: Atlas V launches on 26 Nov 2011
20: MSL begins surface operations

How Curiosity measures up

The Mars rovers that led the way for Curiosity

Sojourner

Size: 0.63 x 0.48 x 0.28m
Weight: 10.5kg
The first rover to operate on another planet was this tiny NASA vehicle, the size of just one wheel of Curiosity, which landed on 4 July 1997 near the Martian equator and lasted until 27 September 1997.

Spirit

Size: 1.6 x 2.3 x 1.5m
Weight: 174kg
Spirit, the first of the two Mars Exploration Rovers, landed at the Gusev Crater on 4 January 2004. It operated until May 2009 when it got stuck in soft soil and succumbed to the Martian weather.

Opportunity

Size: 1.6 x 2.3 x 1.5m
Weight: 174kg
Opportunity landed on 24 January 2004 at Meridiani Planum, three weeks after its sister rover. Until the arrival of Curiosity it is the only vehicle currently operational on the surface of Mars.

Curiosity

Size: 3.0 x 2.8 x 2.1m
Weight: 900kg
More than twice the weight of all the other Mars rovers combined, the MSL is a monster. Eight years in the making, its hi-tech instruments will probe the fourth planet from the Sun like never before.

01

02

03

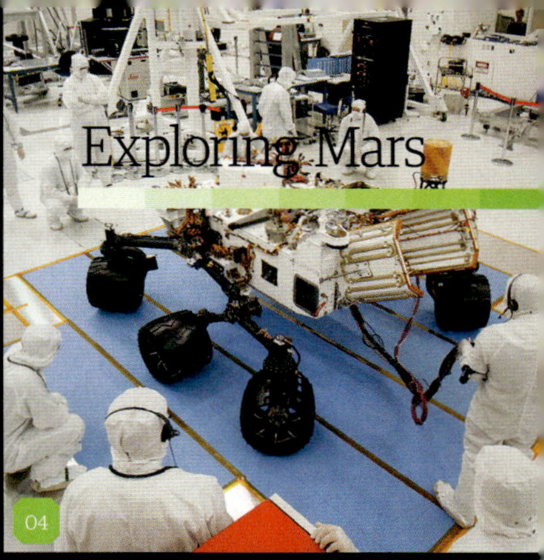
04

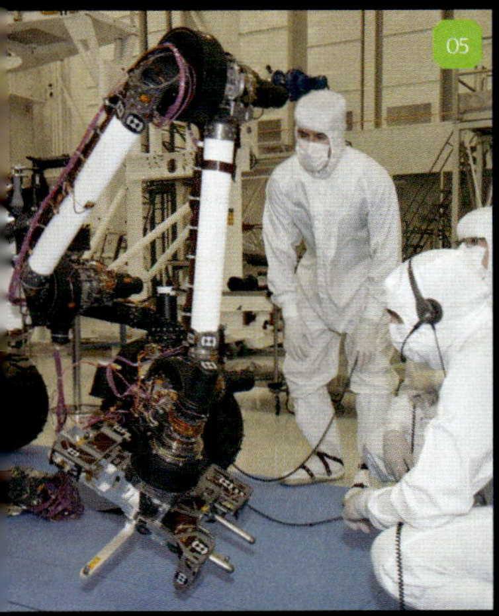
05

06

07

08

09

10

11

12

13

14

15

16

17

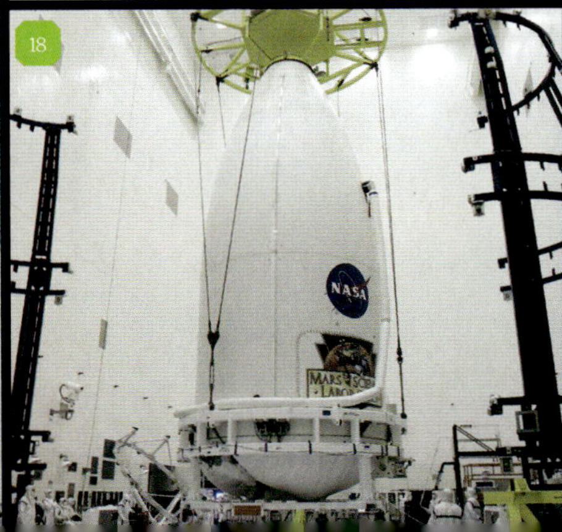
18

19

20

"Seven minutes of terror"

How do you slow a spacecraft down from 13,000mph to zero in just over 400 seconds?

Having landed on 6 August 2012, MSL's groundbreaking Sky Crane enabled the craft to traverse Mars's atmosphere before its make-or-break touchdown on the planet's surface in a descent which NASA described as "seven minutes of terror".

A landing mechanism that was as thrilling as it is terrifying, the Sky Crane could revolutionise how we land on other worlds. Previously, it was thought that air bags would be the only option to land on a planet such as Mars, but now it's widely believed that future off-Earth landings will use a Sky Crane design.

Curiosity had a much greater degree of control as it plummetted through the Martian atmosphere than any mission before it. As it descended it jettisoned some weights, putting the centre of mass of the descent capsule off balance and allowing the craft to manoeuvre through the atmosphere. Such is the accuracy of the descent that NASA was able to pinpoint a fairly precise area in which it expected Curiosity to land. The landing culminated with a rocket-powered descent after the parachute phase.

One of the benefits of this landing design is that Curiosity is placed straight down onto the surface rather than rolling off a ramped platform like Sojourner, Spirit and Opportunity. While alleviating some hazards, such as the ramp getting stuck, Curiosity might still have encounter problems. If it landed on top of a rock, engineers will have needed to carefully manoeuvre it to a safer position. Mission controllers had to make sure there were no hazards immediately around the vehicle, such as rocks or an uneven surface, before it began scientific operations.

01

02

03

1st minute: Dead or alive
Curiosity encounters the Martian atmosphere travelling at 21,000kph (13,000mph), more than 17 times faster than the speed of sound on Earth. The whole landing lasts seven minutes but it takes 14 minutes for Curiosity to communicate with Earth, so when ground control receives word that the rover has hit the atmosphere, it will have been alive or dead on the surface for seven minutes.

2nd minute: Into the frying pan
The atmosphere of Mars is 100 times thinner than Earth's. However, while it is not too thin to slow a spacecraft down completely, it is thick enough to tear an unprotected spacecraft apart. Therefore, as the capsule slams into the atmosphere, its heat shield bears the brunt of a 1,600°C (2,900°F) heat from atmospheric drag, glowing like the surface of the Sun.

3rd minute: Steering through the fire
As MSL makes its way through the atmosphere it is constantly steering itself with reaction thrusters, guiding itself like an aeroplane so that it can land in a precise area. In fact, it can manoeuvre so much that it could even perform an 'S' turn in the air.

4th minute: Chute for glory
After exiting the atmosphere the capsule will still be travelling at 1,600kph (1,000mph). To continue the deceleration, the largest and strongest supersonic parachute that has ever been built is deployed, snapping open at an incredible 5gs. Weighing just 100 pounds, it must withstand a force of 29,500kg (65,000 pounds) as it slows down the rover.

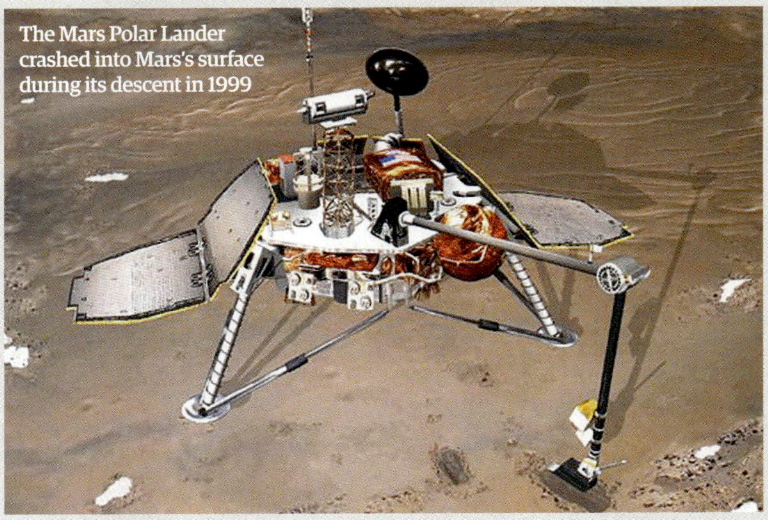
The Mars Polar Lander crashed into Mars's surface during its descent in 1999

What could go wrong?

At the time of going to print, Curiosity is roaming across Mars's surface. As you read this, it shall be taking readings and sending them back to NASA. But what could go wrong? As this is such a precise mission there is so much that could fail. During the intricately choreographed process every single aspect had to work perfectly for the rover's seven-minute landing procedure to be a success. For example, if the parachute deployed too early it will be ripped to shreds. If the Sky Crane failed to disconnect it would pull the rover back into the sky before coming back to collide with Mars. Or, the mission could work flawlessly, but MSL could have accidentally land on a large rock or loose sand, leaving it stuck on the surface.

However, NASA was optimistic. Not only was every eventuality accounted for, but it has successfully completed a rocket landing before. Its Phoenix lander, in 2008, used rocket propulsion to lower itself to the surface of Mars's North Pole, although it didn't employ the same Sky Crane winch concept as Curiosity. As Curiosity landed, it remains one of the greatest achievements to date and its findings will be some of the most important.

6th minute: Sky Crane

Eight rockets on the Sky Crane suddenly spring into action, taking the rover off to the side to avoid the parachute overhead. This mechanism must then kill the horizontal and vertical velocity of the spacecraft and head for the planned landing site at the bottom of Gale Crater, right beside the 5.5km (3.4-mile) high Mount Sharp.

7th minute: Touchdown

The last minute of the mission is the riskiest. At this point the Sky Crane lowers the rover down from a height of 20 metres (65 feet) on four cables that are each 6.4 metres (21 feet) long. Slowly, the rover is touched down on the surface, the cables are released from the rover and the Sky Crane flies off to crash in the distance so that it does not land on the rover. Seven minutes later, ground control will receive a signal from the rover confirming it has made it to the surface, and the crux of the mission can begin.

5th minute: Cut off point

The parachute slows the craft down to 320kph (200mph), but this is not slow enough to land. The lower heat shield is no longer needed, so this is jettisoned, and then the upper portion of the parachute flies off, leaving the rover and its Sky Crane in freefall.

Landing Zone at Gale Crater

A year on Mars

What will Curiosity do once it has landed?

After landing, Curiosity entered the first drive phase, when engineers conducted tests on the rover for five days to ensure it was in a "safe state" before moving it for the first time.

During the first five days several instruments were deployed and tested, including the High Gain Antenna for communications with Earth and the sampling system. Once this had been completed, the rover then ran through some further checks before it was ready to move into uncharted Martian terrain for the first time.

Curiosity has a primary mission time of one Martian year, about 686 Earth days. It will travel up to 20km (12 miles) from its landing site and is expected to analyse about 70 samples of soil and rock throughout its primary mission. It is likely that Curiosity's operations on Mars will be extended if the primary mission is successful.

The ChemCam laser will allow Curiosity to examine the composition of rocks and soil on Mars

Curiosity's technologies

What's on board the rover?

Sample Analysis at Mars

This instrument uses a sophisticated chemical lab to analyse samples from the Martian surface. A robotic arm will pick up samples and place them in the chamber to be investigated.

Autonomous

It can take up to 40 minutes for a signal to be sent to Curiosity and a response received, so planning what the rover will do is of utmost importance. While Curiosity is somewhat autonomous, allowing itself to dodge rocks and other obstacles, it largely relies on input from the ground to carry out a task. This can be a very long process, from several days to weeks.

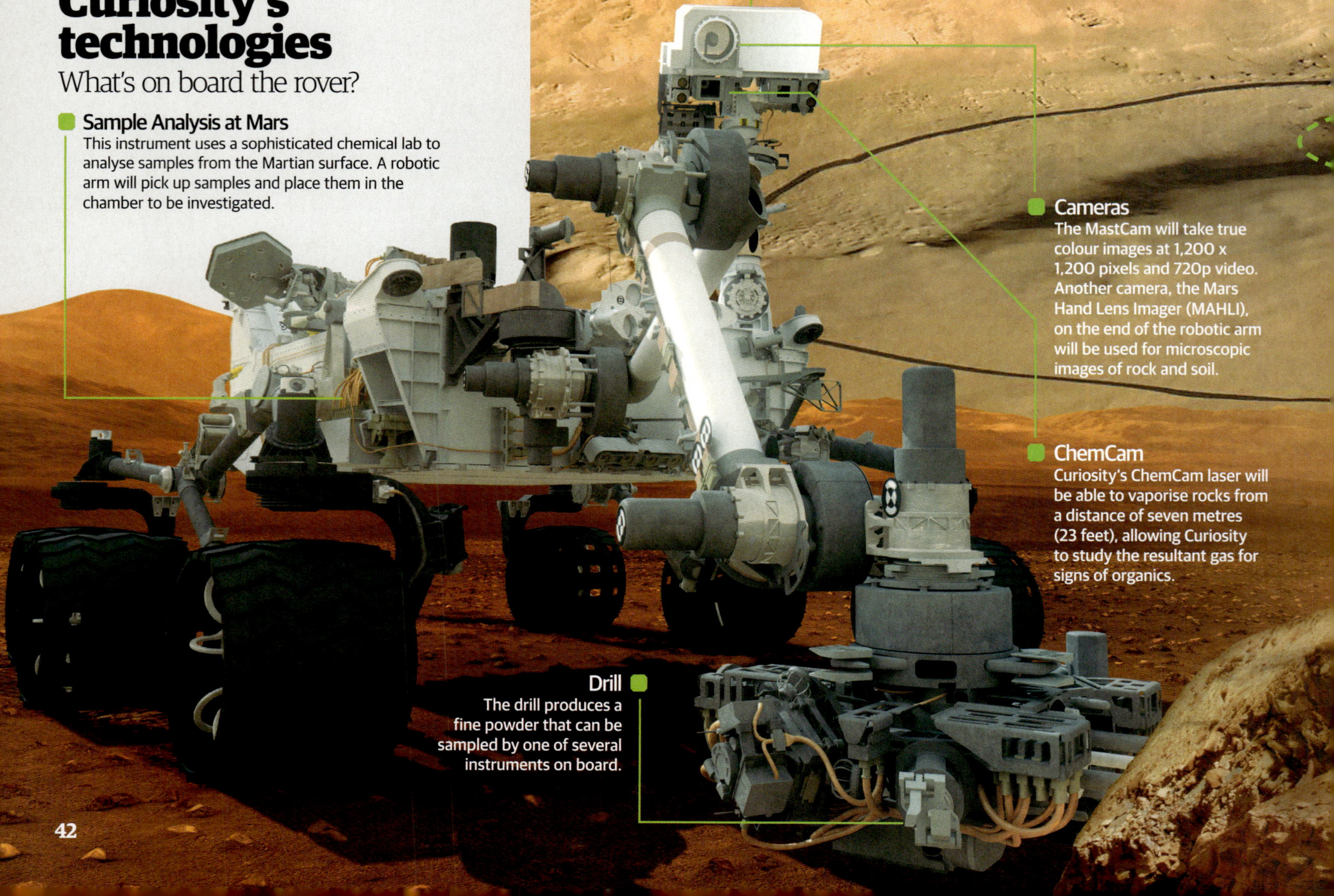

Cameras

The MastCam will take true colour images at 1,200 x 1,200 pixels and 720p video. Another camera, the Mars Hand Lens Imager (MAHLI), on the end of the robotic arm will be used for microscopic images of rock and soil.

ChemCam

Curiosity's ChemCam laser will be able to vaporise rocks from a distance of seven metres (23 feet), allowing Curiosity to study the resultant gas for signs of organics.

Drill

The drill produces a fine powder that can be sampled by one of several instruments on board.

Mission destination
Curiosity is scheduled to last for 668 Martian sols, which is equivalent to 686 Earth days. At this point it will have reached a significant distance up Mount Sharp, but the rover is actually expected to last for many years after this just as Opportunity has done.

Mars is strewn with interesting rocks that could provide clues to its possibly wet past

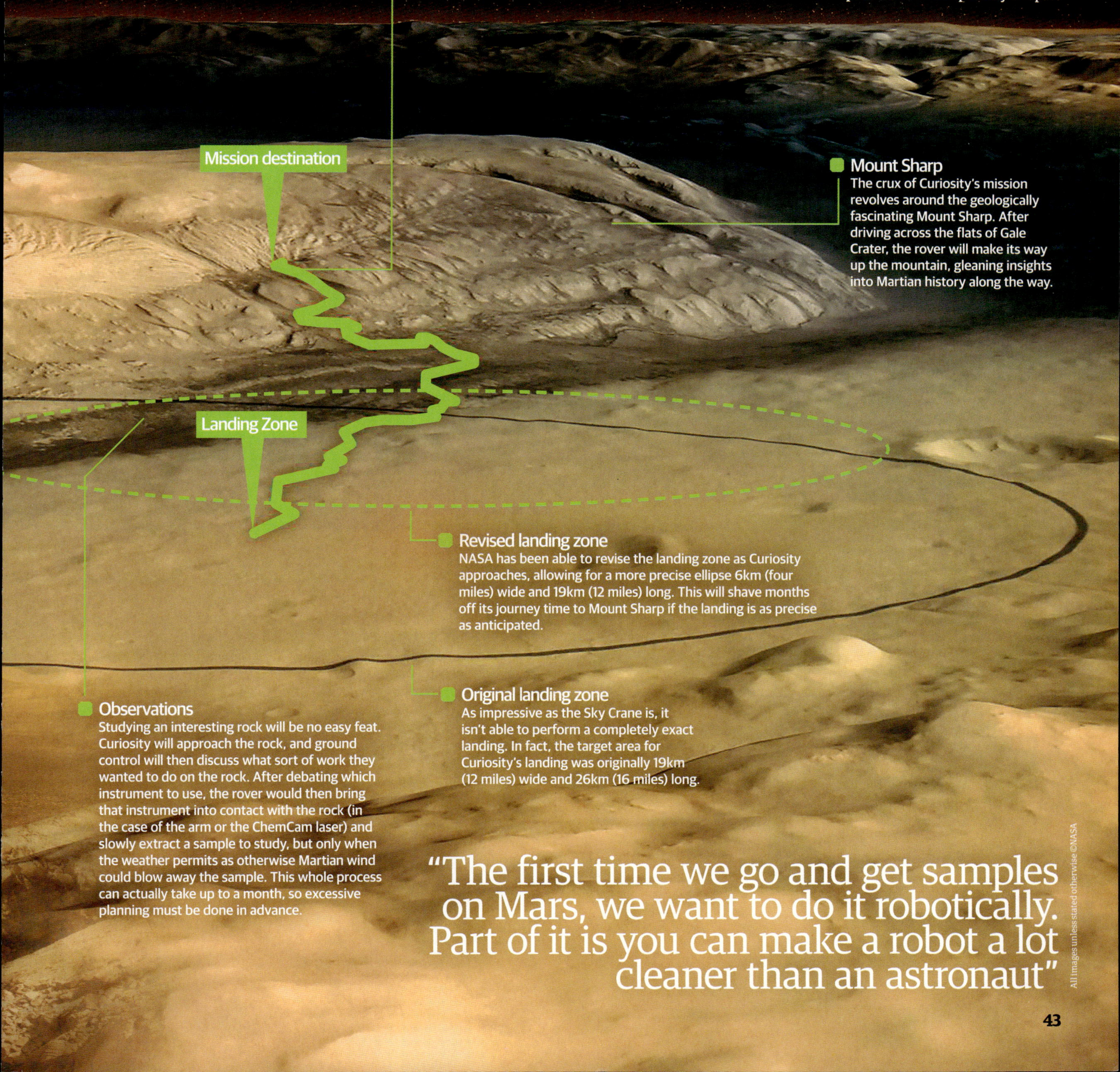

Mount Sharp
The crux of Curiosity's mission revolves around the geologically fascinating Mount Sharp. After driving across the flats of Gale Crater, the rover will make its way up the mountain, gleaning insights into Martian history along the way.

Revised landing zone
NASA has been able to revise the landing zone as Curiosity approaches, allowing for a more precise ellipse 6km (four miles) wide and 19km (12 miles) long. This will shave months off its journey time to Mount Sharp if the landing is as precise as anticipated.

Original landing zone
As impressive as the Sky Crane is, it isn't able to perform a completely exact landing. In fact, the target area for Curiosity's landing was originally 19km (12 miles) wide and 26km (16 miles) long.

Observations
Studying an interesting rock will be no easy feat. Curiosity will approach the rock, and ground control will then discuss what sort of work they wanted to do on the rock. After debating which instrument to use, the rover would then bring that instrument into contact with the rock (in the case of the arm or the ChemCam laser) and slowly extract a sample to study, but only when the weather permits as otherwise Martian wind could blow away the sample. This whole process can actually take up to a month, so excessive planning must be done in advance.

> "The first time we go and get samples on Mars, we want to do it robotically. Part of it is you can make a robot a lot cleaner than an astronaut"

JUNO
The journey to Jupiter

Does this unique probe hold the key to demystifying the gas giant's composition and unlocking secrets of our Solar System's origins in the process?

Stargazers have pondered Jupiter for millennia – as the third brightest object in the sky, it demands attention. When Galileo pointed his telescope that way 400 years ago, he was greeted by colourful clouds and orbiting moons, intensifying the fascination. But even after all these years scrutinising with increasingly powerful telescopes and spacecraft, we still haven't unlocked all its mysteries, because the outer cloud cover has hidden its interior workings from view. Now Juno is on its way, armed with an array of instruments to peek behind the curtain.

The investigation could also tell us a lot about our own origins. According to the prevailing theory of our beginnings, a nearby stellar explosion 5 billion years ago caused a cloud of gas and debris to collapse into a disc. Most of this cloud came together to form the Sun. The lion's share of the leftovers collapsed to form Jupiter 4.5 billion years ago, followed by the formation of the other planets. Because its intense gravitational pull kept the original material from escaping, Jupiter is like a time capsule that captured the nature of that cloud.

Like the Sun, Jupiter's atmosphere is 99 per cent hydrogen and helium. The other elements are more perplexing. When the Galileo spacecraft dropped a probe through the clouds in 1995, it found that heavy elements like nitrogen and carbon were two to four times more abundant on Jupiter than the Sun, indicating Jupiter picked up the gases from icy bodies we would expect to find in more distant, colder regions of the Solar System. One possibility is comets carried the debris to Jupiter. But it's also possible that Jupiter formed further away from the Sun than it is today.

The various theories predict different volumes of water in Jupiter's atmosphere. By detecting the volume of oxygen and other elements, Juno could tell us which theory is more likely correct or point us to a new theory. Understanding how oxygen, carbon, and other life essentials arrived on Jupiter will also help us understand how they arrived on Earth.

Juno's Microwave Radiometer (MWR) should help us unravel this mystery. It will measure microwave radiation emanating from the interior cloud levels. At each depth, only microwave radiation in a certain wavelength range has sufficient energy to make it past Jupiter's outer cloud level. With six radiometers each measuring distinct wavelengths of radiation, MWR will be able to detect six separate cloud layers in the atmosphere. This will give us a 3D model of the atmosphere extending from the cloud tops, where the pressure is similar to Earth, to hundreds of kilometres deep, where the pressure is much greater. MWR will also help us understand whether distinct structures on the cloud top surface, such as the Great Red Spot, float on the atmosphere or extend down to the lower layers.

Juno's Jovian Infrared Auroral Mapper (JIRAM) will also peer into Jupiter's atmosphere, using a combination of an infrared camera and a spectrometer, which splits light into its component wavelengths. Probing 50 to 70 kilometres (31 to 43 miles) below the cloud tops, JIRAM's camera will detect heat to gauge the make-up of water and other compounds in deeper clouds. Different gases, such as ammonia and methane, absorb different wavelengths of infrared light. By analysing the missing wavelengths of light with a spectrometer, JIRAM will be able to determine the chemical composition of the clouds.

JIRAM will also examine Jupiter's magnetic field. Astronomers believe that a third to half of the way down to the centre of the planet, the pressure gets so intense that the hydrogen and helium takes liquid form. This churning liquid conducts electricity, creating a powerful dynamo that generates a huge magnetic field.

Juno's Magnetometer (MAG) will create a 3D map of the magnetic field by detecting its Birkeland currents, electrical currents that align with the field. To avoid contamination from Juno's other instruments, which have small magnetic fields of their own, the two flux gate magnetometer sensors sit on a 3.6-metre (11-foot) boom on the end of one of the solar arrays. Jupiter offers an excellent opportunity to investigate magnetic field properties because it doesn't have an outer crust to get in the way of measuring the dynamo. Juno is likely to capture the most detailed view of a dynamo yet.

Several Juno instruments will examine the magnetic field's most striking manifestation, the auroras over Jupiter's poles. As electrons and ions stream over the northern and southern hemispheres, they interact with the magnetic field and emit light photons. The result is a spectacular light show 1,000 times bigger than Earth's northern lights. Juno's Jupiter Energetic Particle Detector Instrument

Technicians conduct an illumination test on the solar array panels

Jovian Auroral Distributions Experiment (JADE)

JADE will examine the processes behind Jupiter's aurorae by detecting the individual electrons and ions that interact with the atmosphere to create the light show.

Waves

The Waves rabbit-ear antenna will measure radio and plasma waves to examine Jupiter's magnetosphere, a bubble of plasma captured by Jupiter's magnetic field.

Gravity Science Experiment

By measuring the effect of minute changes in Jupiter's gravitational field on Juno's orbit, the Gravity Science Experiment will paint a picture of the planet's internal makeup.

Microwave Radiometer (MWR)

MWR's six radiometers will measure the microwave radiation emitted from six cloud levels, revealing details of Jupiter's composition going hundreds of kilometres deep.

JunoCam

Juno's wide-angle visible light camera will take photos of Jupiter's cloud tops during the probe's closest approaches.

Jupiter Energetic Particle Detector Instrument (JEDI)

Working closely with JADE, JEDI will measure how high-energy electrons and ions interact with Jupiter's magnetic field.

Solar Arrays

The three 8.5-metre-long arrays include 18,000 solar cells that will convert the Sun's energy into electricity, generating 420 watts to power all of Juno's equipment.

Mission Profile

Juno

Mission dates: Aug 2011-Oct 2017
Launch: Lifted off from Cape Canaveral on 5 August 2011
Objectives: Reach Jupiter in July 2016; study multiple levels of Jupiter's distinctive clouds; analyse water content in the atmosphere; measure the gravitational field to analyse Jupiter's centre; examine Jupiter's magnetic field and northern and southern auroras; test theories of Jupiter's development and evolution; search for evidence of how the Solar System began; investigate the source of oxygen on Solar System planets; complete 33 orbits over the course of a year; end mission and de-orbit to burn up in Jupiter's atmosphere in October 2017.

Exploring Jupiter - where Juno fits

1970

Pioneer 10
Date: 3 December 1973
Type: Flyby
The probe examined Jupiter's magnetosphere and radiation belts determining that the planet is mostly liquid.

Pioneer 11
Date: 2 December 1974
Type: Flyby
The probe made the first observations of Jupiter's polar regions.

1980

1990

Ulysses
Date: 8 February 1992
Type: Flyby
The solar observation probe used Jupiter to slingshot itself into a trajectory over the Sun's poles for its solar observations.

The orbit explained

One of the most remarkable things about Juno is its unconventional polar orbit. If it took a simpler orbit around the equator, Juno would only get a look at the middle region of the planet. By taking a carefully co-ordinated, highly elliptical path over the north and south poles, Juno will be able to see every bit of Jupiter over the course of its 33 laps. The orbit will also allow Juno to stay very low on each pass - just a few thousand kilometres above the clouds - ducking safely below Jupiter's radiation belt, which would otherwise damage on-board electronics.

(JEDI) and Jovian Auroral Distributions Experiment (JADE) will examine the particles to determine the amount of energy each carries, exactly how the auroras form, and how the interaction with the magnetic field adds energy to Jupiter's atmosphere. Additionally, Juno's Ultraviolet Imaging Spectrograph (UVIS) will capture ultraviolet light images of the auroras.

Juno's Waves instrument will examine Jupiter's magnetosphere, a giant bubble created by the magnetic field that traps plasma (electrically charged gas). Waves measures the electrical and magnetic components of the magnetosphere's radio and plasma waves, using four-metre (13-foot) rabbit ear-style antennas and a compact antenna made of coiled wire. Electricity moves through the entire magnetosphere, making it something like a giant electrical circuit. By tuning in to the activity at any one point, Waves can monitor what's happening throughout the magnetosphere.

Juno will also look at Jupiter's deepest mystery: what's at its centre. The prevailing theory is Jupiter has a dense, solid core of heavy elements formed in the early days of the Solar System. According to this hypothesis, Jupiter began to form when debris, asteroids and comets clumped together to form a rocky, icy planetoid. When the planetoid gained enough mass, its gravitational pull captured hydrogen and helium gas left over from the Sun's formation, steadily growing into a gas giant. The leading alternative theory is there is no rocky core. Instead, Jupiter formed directly from a cloud of gas and dust, making the planet a hydrogen and helium mix all the way down.

Juno will examine Jupiter's internal structure for evidence supporting or refuting these theories. It's not feasible to descend to the centre of the planet, but Juno can learn a lot from orbit. Jupiter's inner composition will result in characteristic variations in the gravitational field at different points around the planet. Those gravitational field changes, in turn, will shift Juno's path very slightly as it orbits. The Gravity Science Experiment (GSE) instrument will measure these changes by tracking shifts in radio signals. An on-board radio transponder and the massive radio antennas of Earth's Deep Space Network will send continual signals back and forth. The Doppler shift of the signals will indicate changes in Juno's position moment-to-moment, allowing GSE to map Jupiter's gravitational field.

> "It's also possible that Jupiter formed further away from the Sun than it is today"

On top of unlocking Jupiter's secrets, the Juno team also faced the challenge of completing the spacecraft's five-year, 2.8 billion-kilometre (1.7 billion-mile) journey. On 5 August 2011, Juno left Earth on an Atlas V rocket. In space, it used an on-board rocket engine to manoeuvre into a trajectory that will take it within 500 kilometres (310 miles) of Earth in October 2013. On this pass, Earth's gravitational pull will boost Juno's velocity, flinging it towards Jupiter.

Juno continually spins as it travels, which offers two key benefits. First, the gyroscopic effect of the spin stabilises its flight. Second, it allows Juno to continually scan Jupiter's surface in orbit. The 2rpm spin gives each of the various instruments, positioned around the spacecraft, a turn to observe the planet.

Juno is the first outer Solar System spacecraft to run wholly on solar power. It will capture the energy it needs in Jupiter orbit, using 18,000 solar cells on three massive arrays.

One of the journey's main challenges is intense cold and radiation. Shiny thermal blankets protect Juno's surface from extreme temperatures, while an armoured titanium vault houses its sensitive electronics. Outside the vault, Juno will receive the equivalent of 100 million dental X-rays. Inside the vault, the exposure will be a more manageable 120,000 dental X-rays.

The Juno crew will keep in contact with the spacecraft's on-board brain - the Command and Data Handling System (CDH) - via radio signals. It takes radio signals 45 minutes to travel between here and Jupiter, making instantaneous control impossible. Instead, Juno will make many adjustments itself. When it encounters a problem, it enters a standby mode, alerting Earth and staying in safe orbit until it receives new orders.

When Juno reaches Jupiter in 2016, the control crew will be in constant contact. And the people who designed the spacecraft and instruments will be eagerly awaiting its new discoveries. ●

Juno blasts off for Jupiter aboard an Atlas V

2000 | 2010 | 2020

Galileo
Date: 7 December 1995
Type: Orbiter
In a 58-minute trip below Jupiter's clouds, Galileo's descent probe measured 720km/h (450mph) winds.

Cassini-Huygens
Date: 30 December 2000
Type: Flyby
On its way to Saturn the probe observed Jupiter, yielding new details about the planet's atmospheric circulation.

New Horizons
Date: 28 February 2007
Type: Flyby
New Horizons used Jupiter's gravitational pull to boost its speed by 4km/s (2.5 miles/s), shortening its journey to investigate Pluto.

Juno
Date: 5 August 2011
Type: Orbit
The only outer Solar System 'craft to be powered wholly by solar power, Juno's thorough orbit will shed new light on the gas giant.

Engineers use a rotation stand to gauge Juno's weight, balance, and centre of gravity

Technicians install guidance and navigation systems

NASA asked Lego for some special passengers to accompany their hi-tech instruments: custom aluminium minifigures of the Roman god Jupiter, goddess Juno, and Galileo

Juno's journey

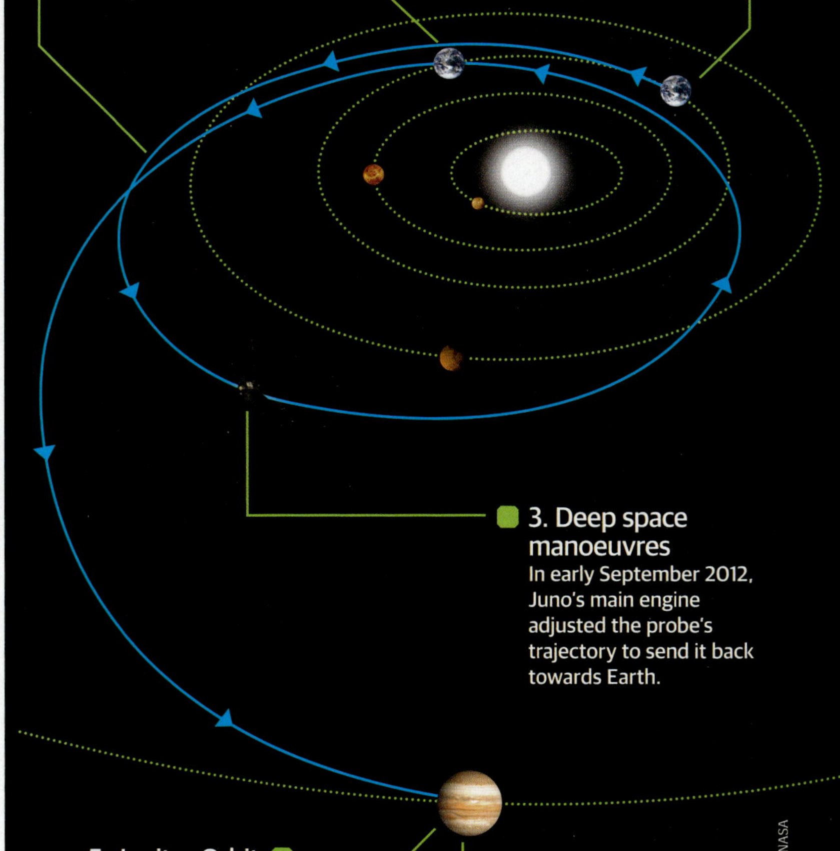

1. Launch
On 5 August 2011, when the planets were properly aligned for the journey, an Atlas V rocket launched Juno on its way to Jupiter.

2. Near orbit
The Atlas rocket doesn't provide enough power to pull Juno away from the Sun's gravitational pull. The probe will stay in our neighbourhood for two years.

3. Deep space manoeuvres
In early September 2012, Juno's main engine adjusted the probe's trajectory to send it back towards Earth.

4. Gravitational slingshot
When Juno comes within 500km (310 miles) of the Earth in October 2013, the planet's gravitational pull will boost the probe's velocity enough to sling it towards Jupiter.

5. Jupiter Orbit Insertion (JOI)
As Juno approaches Jupiter at top speed in July 2016, the probe will have to fire rockets exactly right to slow down and fall into Jupiter orbit.

6. De-orbit
In October 2017, after 33 observation passes, Juno will end its mission by descending into Jupiter's atmosphere.

Exploring asteroids with The Dawn spacecraft

Asteroids are like time machines. So as the Dawn spacecraft visits Vesta and Ceres, scientists are reeling back the years to our Solar System's beginnings

Technicians at Astrotech do spin-balance testing of the Dawn spacecraft before launch

Launched in 2007, Dawn's goal is to bring back photographs and information from two of the asteroid belt's largest residents: Ceres and Vesta.

Dawn used a 'gravity assist' from Mars to get to its first science stop, Vesta, whipping past the Red Planet in February 2009 to pick up speed and soar to its destination.

The spacecraft has an engine on board to kick up additional speed, if needed. Powered by solar panels, it alters the molecules of the xenon fuel to create an electrical charge. The ionised fuel is then passed through an electric field to make it go faster.

This engine – called an ion engine – can accelerate Dawn to a speed ten times faster than conventional rockets. The downside is it takes much longer to fire the ion engine to produce the high speed needed. In 12 days, according to NASA, Dawn can increase its velocity by more than 290 kilometres per hour (180 miles per hour). Wait a year, and the speed will increase by 8,850 kilometres per hour (5,500 miles per hour).

Since flying to space is expensive, fuel efficiency is a priority for spacecraft designers. Ion engines, for these engineers, are a fuel-saving dream. In a year of firing the engines, Dawn will only use 15 gallons of fuel. In car equivalents, that's how much fuel it takes to power a mid-sized car – on just one tank of gas.

Dawn plunked itself into an orbit at Vesta, a 525-kilometre (326-mile) wide asteroid, in July 2011. Vesta is the third-largest asteroid in the belt. It was found in 1807 by Heinrich Olbers.

After adjusting the orbit and calibrating instruments, Dawn got to work. Below on Vesta was a dry, basaltic surface covered in craters. The spacecraft began in a high orbit before spiralling down to get a closer look.

"We had the hypothesis that a set of meteorites that are on the Earth... were from Vesta. It was the parent body," says Christopher Russell, the University of California's principal investigator for the Dawn mission.

"If you believe that, then analyse geochemically the composition of the meteorites, it implies Vesta has an iron core with a basaltic surface, and in particular, minerals such as pyroxene."

The scientists were initially surprised to find a large mountain on Vesta's surface, but some research in the Fifties and Sixties had predicted it.

Three times larger than Everest, the 24-kilometre (15-mile) high mountain in Vesta's southern atmosphere is among the tallest in the Solar System.

Another interesting finding: Vesta appeared to have a very young surface in its southern atmosphere. From counting craters, the scientists estimated that features there are as young as 1 billion to 2 billion years old. That's less than half the age of our 4.5-billion-year-old universe.

Long-term observations yielded a temperature map of the entire surface, which led scientists to speculate that ice water could survive in the areas around the north and south pole.

This is an important finding, as some scientists believe life on Earth was 'seeded' by comets and other small bodies – similar to Vesta – in the Solar System.

Scientists have seen ice on Mercury and the Moon, so such a hypothesis is not wholly unexpected – although on those worlds, the ice exists in craters that are permanently shielded from sunlight. Vesta's craters are too shallow to protect ice from the Sun, but the little world is a lot further away from the Sun. Less heat warms its surface, giving it an average temperature of less than -138 degrees Celsius (-200 degrees Fahrenheit) at the poles.

Science results are still pouring in from Vesta, but in September 2012, Dawn began its journey to its final planned destination: Ceres.

This rocky body is so big – 933 kilometres (580 miles) – that it is now known as a 'dwarf planet'. Ceres officially received that designation in 2006, at the same time that Pluto was taken off planetary status.

Scientists suspect there could be water ice below Ceres's surface because its density is much less than that of Earth. Also, the dwarf planet's surface has evidence of 'water-bearing minerals', or minerals that tend to form in the presence of water.

Ceres probably has a 'differentiated' interior. It would have a more dense core, with the lighter materials moving towards the surface. Earth and our rocky neighbours also have differentiation, suggesting Ceres has planetary characteristics.

We've known about Ceres since Father Giuseppe Piazzi spotted it in 1801. Ceres turned out to be the first in a long series of asteroid discoveries that is ongoing today.

The Dawn team is even offering 'citizen scientists' a chance to get involved. Asteroid Mappers recently launched, inviting the public to scour unprocessed Vesta images for craters, boulders and other interesting features.

"I'm happy with not just the fact that these people are doing work that we're going to find useful, but also that it satisfies their curiosity," Russell said.

"Perhaps it will inspire some of the younger ones to go into planetary science and contribute to the ongoing exploration of the Solar System."

Despite some setbacks, Dawn is in good shape to keep exploring the Solar System for the next few years, at least. "The spacecraft is beginning to age," Russell admits, but he expects Dawn will have no trouble completing its mission at Ceres. ●

The destinations

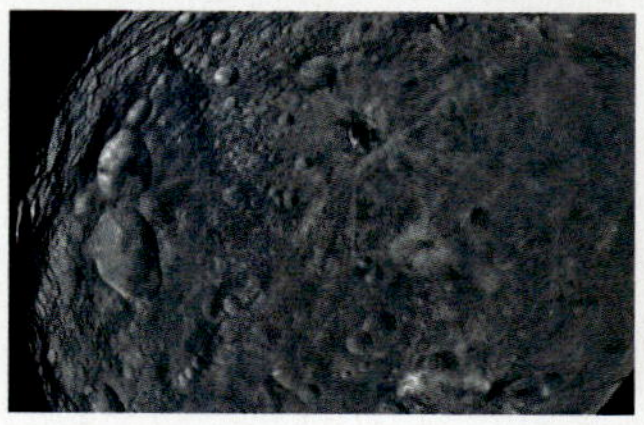

Vesta

Vesta revealed a few surprises when Dawn visited in 2011 and 2012. It has a mountain three times taller than Everest, and possibly has ice sprinkled on its surface. The possible ice is important, as it gives clues to how water formed in the Solar System – and possibly, how it came to be on Earth.

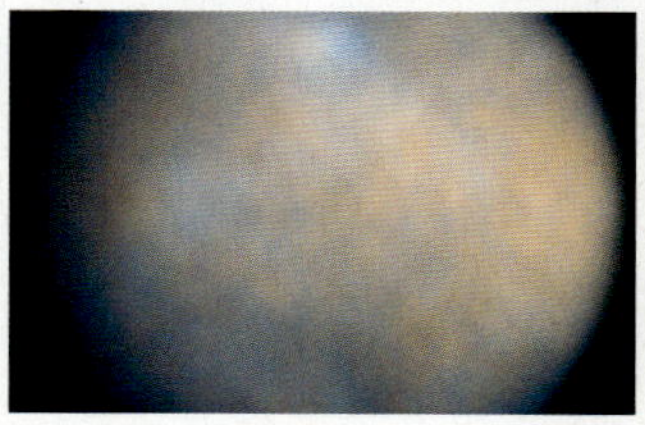

Ceres

Dawn will arrive at Ceres in 2015. Scientists expect to find evidence of water ice based on past Hubble Space Telescope observations. So far, they know that Ceres has a small density (which suggests water) and that the surface possibly has 'water-bearing minerals'.

Dawn's flight trajectory

1. Liftoff

Dawn left Florida's Cape Canaveral in a quest to understand more about the early Solar System. To do so, NASA planned to visit the asteroid Vesta and dwarf planet Ceres.

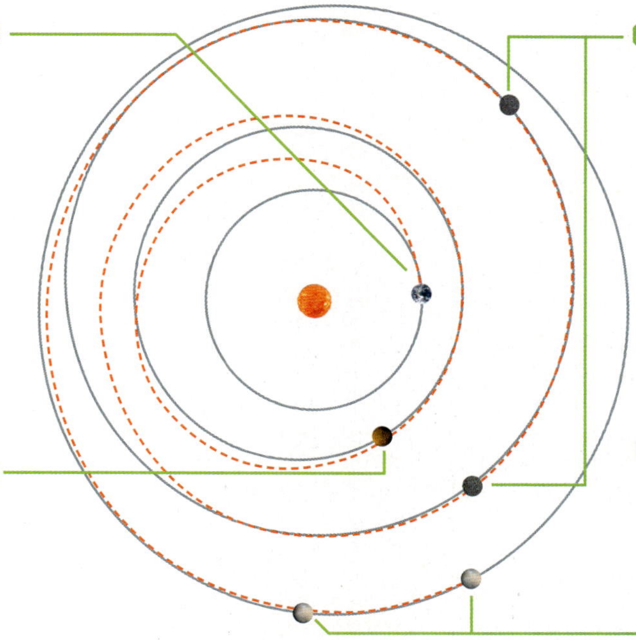

2. Gravity boost

To pick up speed at low cost, NASA swung Dawn by the planet Mars. The procedure, known as a gravity assist, cuts down on the amount of fuel necessary for the mission.

3. Vesta

Dawn spent about a year orbiting Vesta, discovering features such as a large mountain and possible ice below the surface regolith, or soil.

4. Ceres

Dawn is currently en route to Ceres, a dwarf planet. The spacecraft will search for water ice when it arrives there in 2015.

The story of Hayabusa

How this spacecraft overcame all the odds to return the first asteroid samples to Earth and inspire a nation to invest in space

In the early-2000s, Japan was one of the largest economies in the world not to have a dedicated space agency, lagging behind even its fierce rival China. Despite a variety of missions in the 20th Century, the space industry in Japan was something that was yet to receive much public interest.

Unlike Russia and the United States, Japan's space programme had until 2003 been limited to a variety of demonstrations and experiments in space that did little to enthuse any real interest in the country's under-funded cosmic exploits.

But when Japan announced in 2002 that it would attempt to become the first nation to return a sample from the surface of an asteroid, the public was instantly hooked. Here was something they could be genuinely excited about, something that would put Japan firmly on the radar in the space industry.

The revolutionary spacecraft for this mission would be called Hayabusa (originally MUSES-C), and aside from landing on an asteroid it would perform key tests on ion drives that would be a necessity for any nation hoping to launch a future deep space mission using ion engines. In fact, this was the primary objective of Hayabusa; the sample return from an asteroid was merely a useful way to test out the technology, but it became much more than that throughout the course of the mission.

From the initial target launch date to the return home seven years later, however, this would be a mission dogged by problems. But where other nations might see failure, the Japanese instead saw Hayabusa as the inspiring team effort the nation's space programme needed to ensnare the public in a cosmic grip like never before. Just as Apollo 13 sparked national pride in the USA, so too would Hayabusa prove to be Japan's pivotal moment in its long overlooked space industry.

Hayabusa (which translates as 'peregrine falcon') was scheduled to launch in July 2002 to either of the asteroids 4660 Nereus or (10302) 1989 ML, but the failure of a Japanese rocket pushed the launch back to May 2003 and the target was changed to the asteroid 25143 Itokawa. Five months after the launch in October 2003, Japan's three separate space agencies merged into a single one: the Japanese Aerospace Exploration Agency (JAXA). The country now had a dedicated space agency. All it needed next was a successful mission.

On 9 May 2003, Hayabusa lifted off from what is now known as the Uchinoura Space Center in Japan. Four xenon ion engines would take the spacecraft on a two-and-a-half year journey to the vicinity of Itokawa in June 2005. Hayabusa would remain in a heliocentric orbit (one around the Sun), similar to Itokawa's, in order to approach the asteroid relatively slowly. But just several months after launching, disaster struck.

The Sun, with unfortunate timing, unleashed a huge solar flare that bathed Hayabusa in solar radiation, crippling the cells on its solar panels. Engineers at JAXA frantically sought a solution to the early setback, and they eventually found a way to operate the ion engines on limited power. Hayabusa's rendezvous with Itokawa would have to be delayed from June to September in 2005 as the spacecraft could only limp towards its target.

By the time Hayabusa was settled in position near Itokawa in late 2005, maintaining a distance of 20 kilometres (12.4 miles) from the asteroid, it was looking worse for wear. Not only were its ion engines subdued, but it had also lost functionality in two of its three reaction wheels that allowed the spacecraft to rotate in the X and Y-axis. Through a clever workaround, engineers were able to use the one remaining reaction wheel and two chemical thrusters to maintain attitude control (orientation).

Now, thankfully, the true science of the mission could begin. Hayabusa began surveying Itokawa, mapping the surface and analysing the characteristics of the asteroid. Itokawa is an S-type ellipsoid asteroid that is roughly 630 metres (2,070 feet) long and 250 metres (820 feet) wide. It has a fragmented appearance that suggests it may have formed when two smaller asteroids stuck together, but a lack of impact craters on its surface, which itself is rough and covered in boulders, suggests that several smaller asteroids rather than just two may have coalesced into a 'rubble pile'. Itokawa's elliptical 556-day orbit around the Sun takes it from outside the orbital plane of Mars to within Earth's.

On 4 November 2005, Hayabusa moved closer to Itokawa and attempted a rehearsal touchdown, but an anomalous signal at an altitude of 700 metres (2,300 feet) sent it scampering back to safety. A second practice landing was attempted on 12 November, but this would prove even more disastrous. Hayabusa carried with it a small lander called Minerva,

The story of Hayabusa

1. Capsule
The sample capsule was successfully retrieved from the Woomera Prohibited Area in south Australia in June 2010.

2. Shadow
Hayabusa's shadow can be seen here on the asteroid Itokawa in an image taken by the spacecraft.

3. Assembly
Hayabusa was assembled in a clean room before it launched on its way to Itokawa.

4. Dust
Hayabusa specialists get ready to open the sample container and examine its contents.

5. Sample
The capsule had to be carefully retrieved so that the sample inside was not contaminated.

6. Study
Two scientists at the German Aerospace Center study asteroid dust collected by Hayabusa, one of several samples sent out for study.

weighing just over half a kilogram and measuring ten centimetres (3.9 inches) in height and 12 centimetres (4.7 inches) in width. The tiny solar-powered vehicle was designed to take advantage of Itokawa's low gravity and 'hop' across the surface, relaying images to Hayabusa.

However, Hayabusa's distance from Earth meant that it could take upwards of 40 minutes to communicate with the spacecraft, meaning that a lot of its tasks were carried out autonomously. It was creeping towards the asteroid at just three centimetres (1.18 inches) per second, and an order was given to release Minerva when Hayabusa was just 55 metres (180 feet) above the surface of Itokawa, close enough for the asteroid to grab hold of the tiny space hopper. When the signal was sent, however, Hayabusa had already reached the 55-metre mark and had begun its ascent from the asteroid back to its 'parking' distance. When the signal arrived, Hayabusa released Minerva at much too high an altitude. Unable to move itself closer to the asteroid and therefore be grabbed by its gravity, Minerva drifted off into space, never to be heard from again.

It was yet another setback for the now seemingly ill-fated Hayabusa, which had encountered problem after problem, but JAXA pushed ahead. A week later they attempted to land for real. On 19 November, Hayabusa began its descent towards Itokawa at 12 centimetres (4.7 inches) per second, releasing a target marker (containing 880,000 autographs) at an altitude of 40 metres (130 feet) to track its descent to the surface. Hayabusa inched towards the surface until, 17 metres (56 feet) up, the unthinkable happened: contact was lost.

It's not clear what happened next. It's thought that it 'bounced' twice off the surface before actually landing on the asteroid. This was something it wasn't quite supposed to do; instead, it should have fired two bullets into the ground while hovering above Itokawa, which would have kicked dust up into its sample collector, but these failed to deploy. After half an hour Hayabusa left the surface, and in doing so inadvertently carried out the only controlled landing and ascent from any other Solar System body, except the Moon, to date.

On 25 November, it reached the surface again, but it's not clear if the bullets worked here either. However, just by hovering and touching the surface engineers were convinced that dust from the asteroid would have been kicked up into the sample collector, and they made the decision to return home. They would not know until the sample capsule was retrieved on Earth whether Hayabusa had been successful or not in collecting a sample, but it was a risk they would have to take.

Things went from bad to worse on 9 December. A thruster leak altered the direction that Hayabusa's antenna was pointing, and JAXA lost all communications with the spacecraft. After a month having to face the possibility that their pioneering spacecraft might be lost in space, contact was made again in late January 2006. It would be a year until the journey home began.

That fuel leak had caused another problem, though. The chemical thrusters, which had been used to orientate the spacecraft, were now no longer useable. Hayabusa needed to be able to move in three axes to make it home. The one remaining reaction wheel controlled the yaw, while the ion engines could be slightly tilted to alter the pitch, but the spacecraft was unable to roll. Ingeniously, JAXA engineers discovered they could utilise the Sun's photon pressure on the solar panels. It was a tiny force, but it was enough to roll the spacecraft.

With just two of its four ion engines operational, Hayabusa soldiered home on a journey that lasted over three years, starting in February 2007. With the engines' functionality continually fluctuating, Hayabusa finally made it back to Earth in June 2010 and, on 13 June, it re-entered our atmosphere. The main spacecraft burned up as planned, while the sample capsule separated and parachuted safely to Earth in south Australia.

The sample it carried weighed less than a gram, with barely 100 particles each smaller than 0.001 millimetres present, but it wasn't known if they originated from Itokawa or not. Then, on 16 November 2010, the news JAXA had been hoping to hear for almost a decade arrived: the particles were from the surface of Itokawa. Japan had become the first nation to return a sample from the surface of an asteroid, thanks to a little spacecraft and a dedicated team. Now, work is underway on a successor, tentatively named Hayabusa 2, which will have advanced capabilities and return more samples from an asteroid that is yet to be chosen. Despite the ultimate success of Hayabusa, JAXA could be forgiven for hoping that Hayabusa 2 goes a little more smoothly. ●

Yoshiyuki Hasegawa, associate executive director of JAXA, briefs media ahead of the re-entry of Hayabusa in 2010

"Hayabusa 'bounced' twice off the surface before coming to rest on the asteroid"

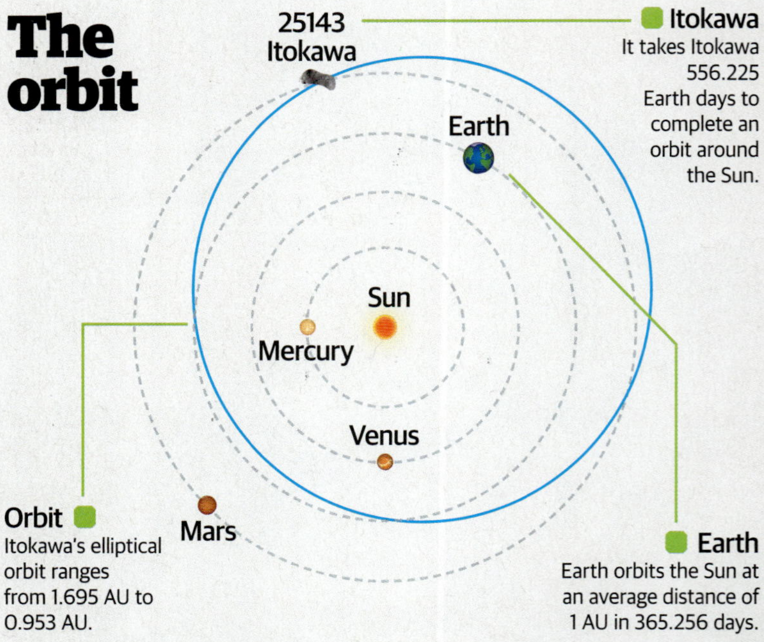

Mission timeline

Hayabusa's shadow seen on Itokawa

1. Launch
Hayabusa launched on its mission towards Itokawa on 9 May 2003.

2. Approach
The spacecraft arrived at Itokawa in September 2005, but lost the use of two of its three reaction wheels.

Second landing attempt

3. Landing
In mid-November 2005, Hayabusa lost the Minerva mini-lander and failed a landing attempt.

4. On the surface
In late-November Hayabusa successfully touched down on the asteroid and collected a sample.

5. Re-entry
After limping home, Hayabusa re-entered the Earth's atmosphere on 13 June 2010.

Mission Profile

Hayabusa

Launch: 9 May 2003
Agency: JAXA
Mass: 510kg
Cost: $100m
Mission duration: 7 years, 1 month, 4 days
Re-entry: 13 June 2010

Second landing attempt

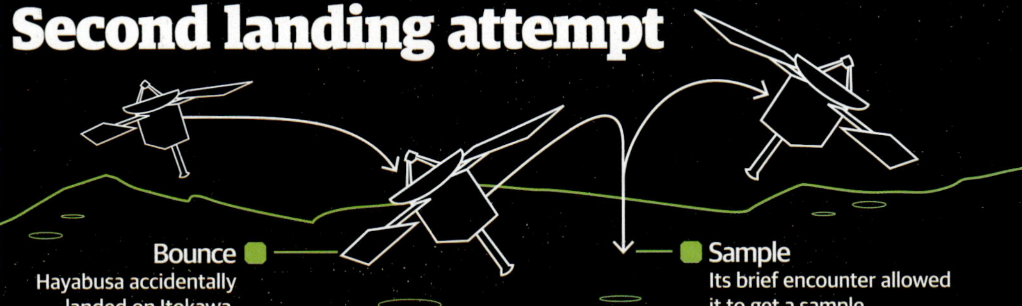

Bounce
Hayabusa accidentally landed on Itokawa.

Sample
Its brief encounter allowed it to get a sample.

NASA's Deep Impact

Discover the secrets behind NASA's Deep Impact spacecraft's unique mission to fire an impactor into the surface of a speeding comet in 2005

Deep Impact's primary goal was to fire an impactor into a speeding comet to help scientists better understand these fascinating denizens of the Solar System. So where did the idea for Deep Impact come from and why is there so much interest in comets?

Comets are relics of the early Solar System, left over from when it first formed. By studying them, scientists can learn more about the history of our Solar System, how it came to be and our place in it.

Deep Impact was first conceived by Alan Delamere, an engineer at Ball Aerospace & Technologies Corp, and Mike Belton, from the National Optical Observatory. "In 1996 we decided to submit a proposal to explore the exterior of a dead comet, Phaethon, using an impactor," says Delamere. "At this point Mike A'Hearn, now principal investigator for Deep Impact, joined our team. We proposed to the NASA Discovery Program using a large mass hitting the comet at about 38km/sec (24 miles/sec). We found a way to hit the comet and observe the crater development. However, the proposal wasn't funded because they did not believe we could hit it. But the idea evolved and in 1998 Mike A'Hearn took over the team and proposed to hit an active comet, Tempel 1. We added a fine guidance system to the impactor. This convinced reviewers we could hit the comet."

Deep Impact was launched on 5 January 2005. It travelled for about six months to reach Tempel 1, 431 million kilometres (268 million miles) away from Earth at the time. On 4 July 2005, the impactor separated from the main craft, hitting the comet 24 hours later. A huge bright cloud of dusty material was seen emanating from the impact site.

The debris plume was found to be rich in organics, the building blocks of life. This supports the possibility that comets delivered these materials to the early Earth. Other key results included the discovery of both water ice and craters on the surface. The ice was anticipated, while the craters were a surprise. Tempel 1's interior was found to be very porous, indicating that it is shielded from solar heating. While the surface can heat up and cool down almost instantly, the inside is perpetually cold.

After Deep Impact's rendezvous with Tempel 1, it was decided that it would be too risky for the spacecraft to return to the comet. Deep Impact may encounter another comet in the future, but it has already provided enough data to keep scientists busy for years to come.

"A huge bright cloud of dusty material was seen emanating from the impact site"

Deep Impact travelled for six months after launch before impacting with Tempel 1

Solar System

Exploring the wonders of our solar system

82
Observing asteroids

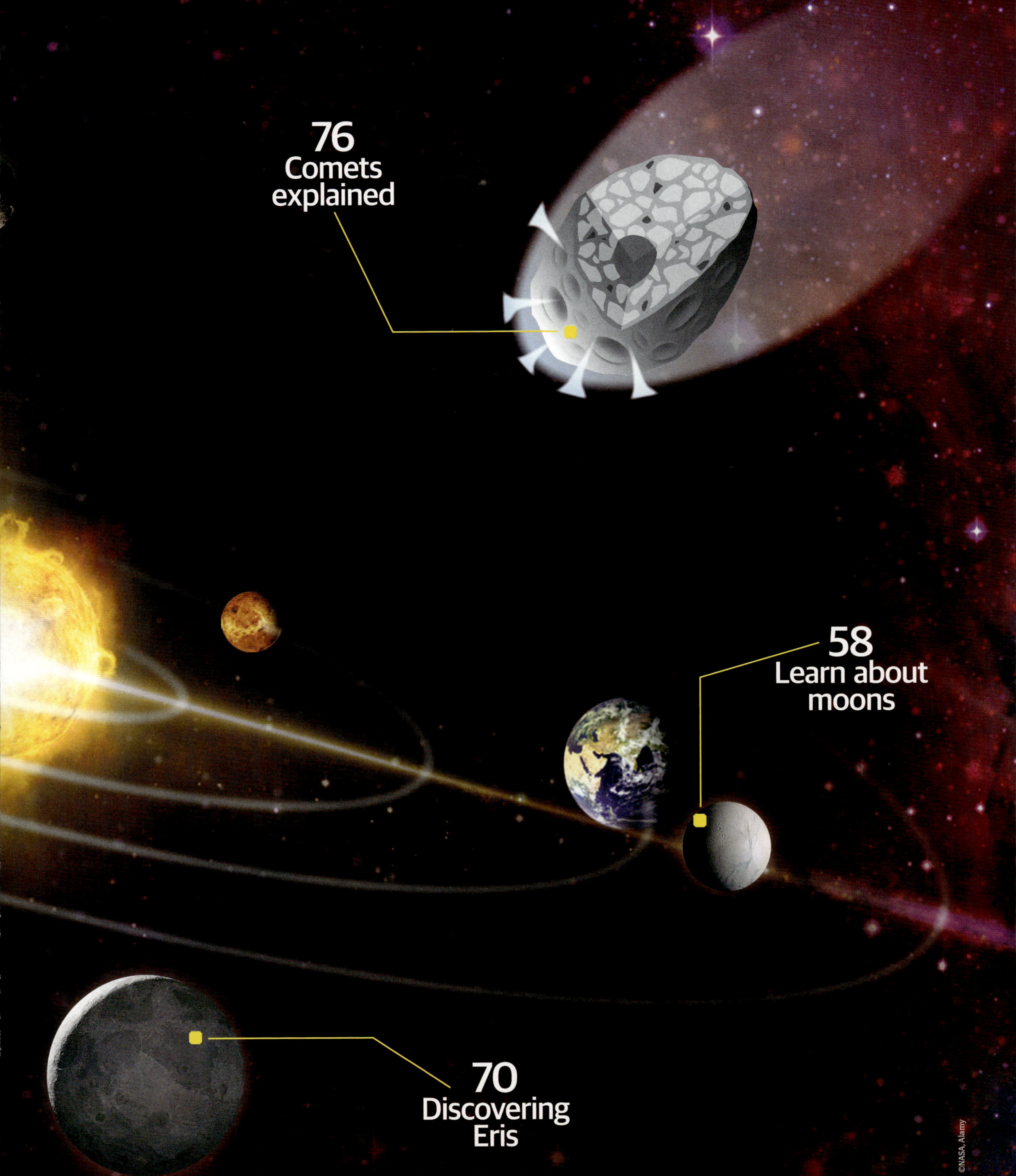
76
Comets explained
58
Learn about moons
70
Discovering Eris
©NASA, Alamy

Mo
the
Sy

There are
System. I
the mo

Until the 16th Century most of the moons in the Solar System were regarded as planets. Early astronomers were so baffled by these large spherical objects that they had no explanation other than they must be additional worlds. Now, though, we know that these moons are objects within their own right. They do not have the same level of influence on their surroundings as planets, and nor do they dominate their orbital planes. However, many possess a host of astounding features and characteristics that rivals the activity seen on some of the planets.

The very existence of moons is remarkable. The Sun exerts an overriding gravitational pull on every planet in the Solar System but, somehow, six of the eight major planets have been able to create their own mini-planetary systems within which natural satellites are in orbit. From dozens of moons to just one, each of these planets has been able to grab on to and hold these space rocks, clinging on to them as the Sun does its best to drag them away. Many moons, however, are in turmoil, torn between the gravitational influence of their host planet and nearby objects, giving rise to bizarre features. Worlds such as Jupiter's moon Io are twisted and heated by their neighbours, while others like Saturn's moon Dione share their orbit with other moons. The difference between the moons is staggering. They range in size from a mere 0.5 kilometres (0.3 miles) in radius to over 2,600 kilometres (1,600 miles), bigger even than planet Mercury.

An artist's impression of the surface of Triton (centre), the largest moon of Neptune (right)

The inner two planets of our Solar System, Mercury and Venus, do not have moons. As mentioned earlier, this is most likely due to the influence of the Sun. Mercury would not have been able to hold onto a natural satellite early in its formation, and therefore anything caught in its orbit would have gradually been pulled into the Sun and out of Mercury's orbit. As it is also the smallest planet in the Solar System it simply doesn't have the muscle to keep a moon in its orbit. Venus has a similar problem, but it also rotates in the opposite direction to the other planets. This means that a moon in orbit around the planet would have been slowed considerably by the Sun and eventually crashed into Venus, although there is no evidence that this has ever happened. The simple fact is that these two planets are just too close to the Sun to be able to hold on to moons.

This does, however, pose something of a conundrum for Earth. We are the third planet from the Sun and, relative to the other five planets with moons in the Solar System, we're pretty close and experience a significant gravitational force from the Sun. How, then, have we been able to keep hold of a moon when Venus and Mercury could not? The answer most likely lies in the formation of our Moon. It is thought that early in the Earth's life, perhaps a couple of billion years ago, a Mars-sized object impacted the Earth, which would be the largest known impact in the Solar System. The debris thrown out in this collision would have gradually coalesced into an object, which we now know as the Moon. However, the gravitational force between the Moon and the Sun was, and still is, greater than that between the Moon and the Earth. The only way we could have held on to the Moon was through what's known as the 'tidal force'. The pull between the Earth and the Moon has tidally locked the latter to the former, and therefore we've been able to keep hold of our only natural satellite.

The next planet from the Sun also has a rather bizarre planetary system. Discovered in 1877, Mars's moons Phobos and Deimos both bear more of a resemblance to asteroids than spherical moons, and therefore it is thought that they were captured

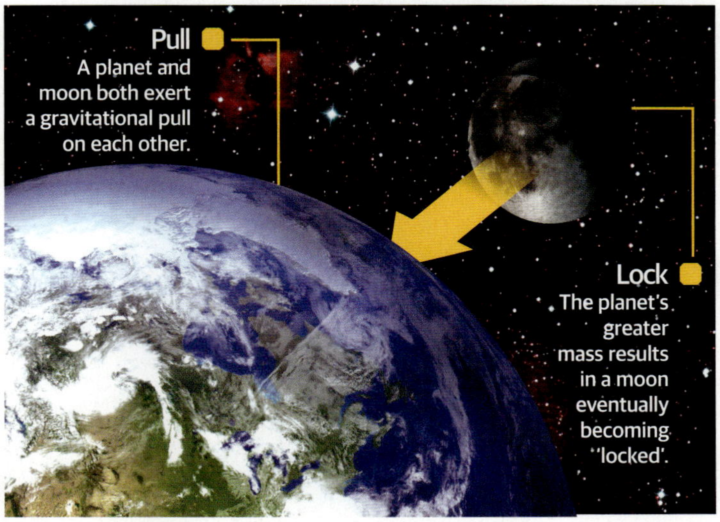

Tidal locking

Why do some moons have the same face always pointing towards their host planet?

Tidal locking is the effect of a planet continually exerting a gravitational influence on a rotating moon and gradually slowing its orbit. Imagine a record spinning on a hypothetical record player, with the arm and stylus pressing down on the record. The record is the moon, and the arm is the planet. Over time the force of the arm pressing down on the record would slow its rotation until, eventually, it would come to a halt.

This is in essence what happens in a moon and planet system. A rotating moon in orbit is pulled by its host planet, causing the moon's rotation to slow down. Eventually the moon stops spinning, but continues in its orbit, and so the same face also looks towards the planet. The same effect occurs with planets in orbit around the Sun, with those nearer the Sun spinning slower than those further away. Our Moon is tidally locked to Earth, while 32 other moons in the Solar System are tidally locked to their host planet, with others approaching tidal locking.

Total number of moons

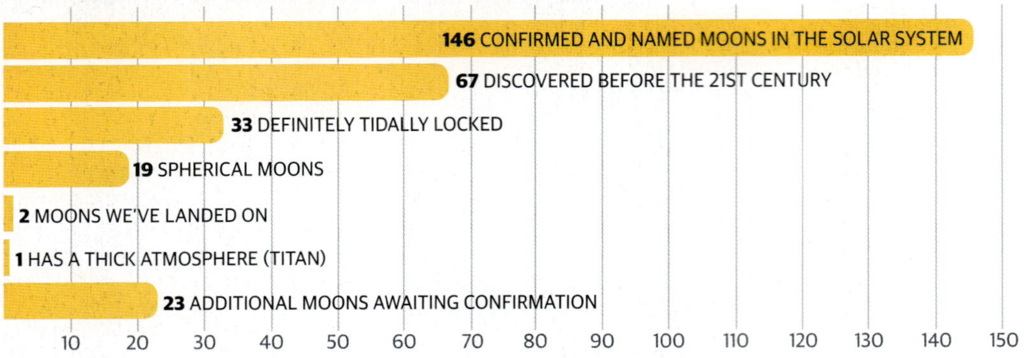

"The simple fact is that these two planets are just too close to the Sun to hold on to moons"

from the asteroid belt by the orbit of the Red Planet. However, the moons may also have formed from a collision event on Mars, like our Earth-Moon system, and so may hold material from the Martian surface. This has made them a desirable place to visit, highlighted by a Russian mission in late-2011 that aimed to return soil from Phobos. Unfortunately, it experienced a failure immediately after launching.

The moons are tiny, with Phobos having a diameter of just 22.2 kilometres (13.8 miles) and Deimos 12.6 kilometres (7.8 miles), but they are also unusual in that they orbit very close to Mars, closer than any other moons in the Solar System. Phobos is just over 9,000 kilometres (5,600 miles) away from the centre of Mars and Deimos just over 23,000 kilometres (14,300 miles), completing orbits of the Red Planet in 7.65 and 30.4 hours respectively. Both the moons are tidally locked to the planet, always showing the same face towards it like our own Moon and many others in the Solar System. Phobos is so close, and orbits so rapidly, that its orbital radius is slowly decreasing. In just a few million years – a minuscule amount of time in astronomical terms – it is expected to either crash into the Martian surface or break up in the atmosphere. Indeed, craters on Mars suggest that a similar fate may have befallen other moons of Mars if it once had them. Deimos, on the other hand, is slowly drifting away from Mars.

Past the four inner planets of the Solar System and beyond the asteroid belt, the Sun's influence lessens and therefore the four outer giant planets are able to more easily control their surrounding planetary systems. Such is the extent of Jupiter's planetary system that it is often regarded as its own mini-Solar System. Indeed, Jupiter appears to possess most of the characteristics to become a star and, had it been 75 times more massive, it would likely have ignited like a star. Jupiter's moons are diverse, varied and numerous. It currently has 50 known and named moons and at least 14 more awaiting confirmation. Its four largest moons (Io, Europa, Ganymede and Callisto) are the Galilean satellites, named after Galileo Galilei, who discovered them in 1610. Io is the most volcanically active body in the Solar System, owing to the push-and-pull effect it experiences from Jupiter and nearby moons. Europa is the smoothest body in the Solar System, with a surface covered almost entirely in ice and a vast ocean of water (containing more water than is on Earth) likely residing underneath. Ganymede is the largest moon we know of, bigger even than planet Mercury, and is the only moon known to have its own magnetic field. And finally Callisto, an ancient world devoid of almost any activity, might hold answers to what the early Solar System was like.

Aside from these major moons, Jupiter has a multitude of other celestial bodies in orbit around the planet. Most of these are small asteroid-like rocks just a few kilometres across, which were likely snared from the nearby asteroid belt, and they are so minute that they make up just 0.01 per cent of Jupiter's orbital mass, with the other 99.99 per cent coming from the Galilean satellites. Such is the scale and variety of the moons that their characteristics vary wildly. The orbits of some minor moons are nearly perfectly circular, while others are highly elliptical. Some rotate in the direction of Jupiter's spin and others against it, while the time taken to complete an orbit of Jupiter ranges from several hours to several years. A number of Jupiter's small inner satellites are also known as shepherd moons. They orbit within Jupiter's rings and 'sweep up' superfluous debris, clearing the vicinity of the rings and giving them more crisply defined boundaries.

Of the confirmed and named moons, Saturn has the most with 53 (although with unconfirmed moons, Jupiter has 64 and Saturn 62). This gas giant, with a more visibly obvious ring system than Jupiter, also plays host to one of the most interesting worlds in the Solar System, Titan, which is also the second

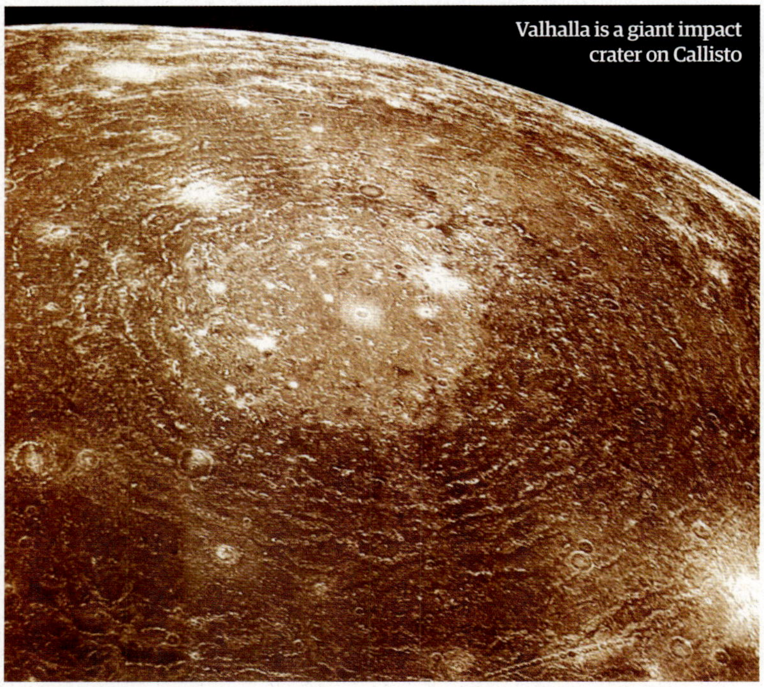
Valhalla is a giant impact crater on Callisto

Apollo 17 astronauts snapped this shot of Earth from the Moon in 1972

largest moon. Titan is the only moon known to have a thick atmosphere, and one of the only places other than Earth where liquid has been definitively imaged on its surface, making it a possible residence for alien life in the Solar System. Elsewhere, Saturn's moon Enceladus emits jets of dust and gas in the form of geysers from its surface, while underground there may also be liquid water. Four of Saturn's moons are in Trojan orbits with larger moons, which is an orbit within which there is more than one body. All of Saturn's major moons orbit in or around the rings of the planet, in addition to several minor shepherd moons. Outside the ring system are a number of irregular satellites with wildly inclined orbits, with the largest of these being Phoebe. Saturn's planetary system has been extensively studied by the Cassini spacecraft, which continues to return stunning imagery of the moons and rings to further our understanding of these worlds.

The next planet out from the Sun is Uranus, which has the unusual accolade of being the only planetary system with moons named after characters from the works of William Shakespeare and Alexander Pope, rather than the Roman and Greek mythological names given to every other moon. Found in 1787 by William Herschel, its first two moons were Titania and Oberon. Five of Uranus's moons are large enough to be spherical, while the other 22 moons are irregular satellites. However, despite having more moons than Neptune, Uranus's planetary system is the least massive in the Solar System. The combined mass of all of its satellites is just half that of Neptune's biggest moon (and the seventh largest in the Solar System), Triton. All 13 of Uranus's inner moons are connected to its ring system and contribute to some shepherding, but their orbits are erratic. They consistently cross over each others' orbital planes and two of the moons, Desdemona and Cressida, are expected to collide within the next 100 million years. Owing to Uranus's distance from the Sun, most of the moons are very dark. Many are composed of equal parts rock and ice, leading to some speculation that there could be liquid water beneath the surface of some of them.

Finally, we reach the last planet in the Solar System, Neptune. This blue ice giant has 13 known moons, but they are all fairly insignificant in size when compared to its largest moon, Triton, which is several hundred times more massive than the rest of the moons combined. Neptune's six inner moons orbit around the equator and some may be responsible for shepherding Neptune's faint ring system. Triton, along with six others, is an irregular moon, meaning it rotates in the opposite direction to the spin of Neptune. All except Triton have elliptical orbits. It is thought that Triton was captured by Neptune after its other satellites had entered orbit, possibly accounting for the erratic and varied motion of the moons apart from Triton.

There's little doubt that the moons of the Solar System are a diverse bunch. From the tiny rocks to the giant, seemingly Earth-like worlds, there's plenty of objects of interest in the Solar System. 146 named moons and counting, we'll continue to find out more about some of these wonderful worlds in the coming years as more spacecraft traverse and study the Solar System at large. ●

How do moons form?

Moons in the Solar System come in all sorts of shapes and sizes, and in some instances this can be due to how they were formed in the first place. Our understanding of how exactly moons were created is growing every year, and as we continue to study this varied bunch of worlds we'll undoubtedly glean more information about how they are all able to have such different appearances. Those moons that are large and spherical were likely formed at the birth of the Solar System around the same time as the major planets, while the more irregular moons could have once been asteroids that were then captured by their host planets. Each moon has its own story to tell, but they generally fall into these three main categories.

1 Early formation

Some moons, particularly those that are spherical and in circular orbits around their host planet, are thought to have formed at the birth of the Solar System around 4.7 billion years ago.

2 Collisions

Some moons have evidence that they were formed from a nearby collision. As Mercury, Venus and Earth are all close to the Sun, they may have been unable to acquire natural satellites in the early Solar System. Instead, a Mars-sized object may have struck Earth, sending off a huge amount of debris that, over time, formed into the spherical Moon.

3 Captured

There are many more small, irregular moons than there are large spherical ones. The reasoning for this is that they could be asteroids that were captured by their host planet. The Earth has several asteroids that are influenced by its gravitational pull, but a larger planet such as Jupiter would be able to exert a strong enough influence to pull small objects into its vicinity in highly elliptical orbits and, over time, squash their orbits into more circular ones. This is evidenced by a wide variety of asteroid-like moons having different orbits, from highly eccentric ones to more circular ones. Indeed, with the asteroid belt between Mars and Jupiter, it is likely that some asteroids could have strayed from the belt into the orbital vicinity of the two mentioned planets, and possibly Saturn, Neptune and Uranus as well.

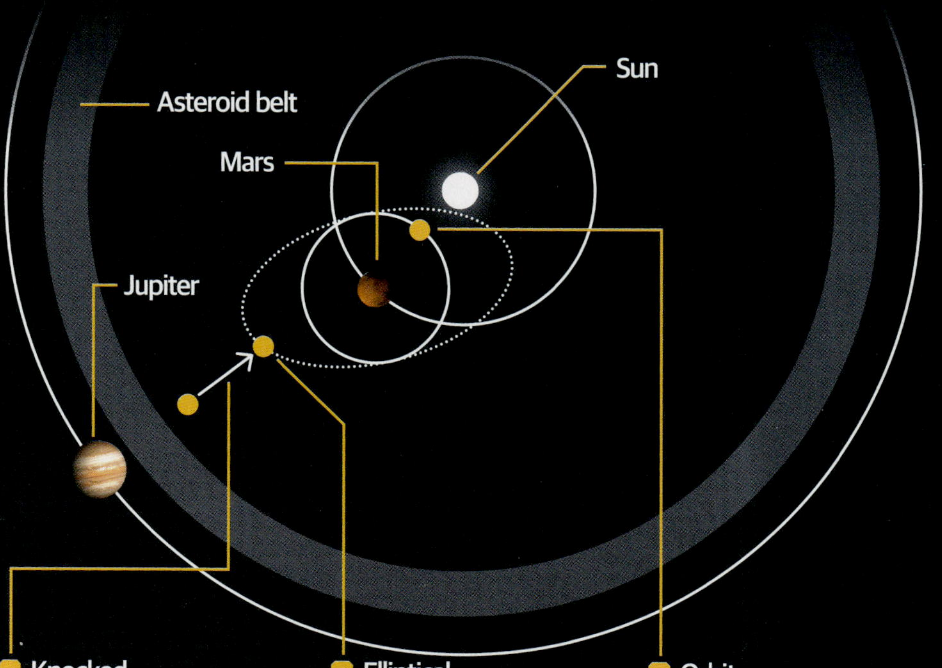

Knocked
An asteroid could be knocked out of the asteroid belt, or elsewhere, by a collision with another body or simply the vicinity of a planet.

Elliptical
The asteroid would fall into an elliptical orbit with the planet, moving out to great distances before coming back for a close approach.

Orbit
Over time the orbit would be squashed as the planet continually pulls the asteroid, eventually bringing it into a more stable circular orbit.

Neptune's dominant satellite

Mass: 0.00359 Earths

Triton

Planet: Neptune

Like Saturn's Enceladus this moon of Neptune, which is far bigger than any other natural satellite of the furthest planet from the Sun and also the seventh biggest moon in the Solar System, has several cryovolcanoes in its southern polar region. Triton's icy surface is most likely liquid underground and, as the pressure builds, the liquids are forced up from the moon's surface and out as vapour and gas.

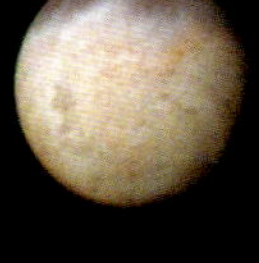

Triton is the least studied of the most active moons

The 'Death Star' moon

Mass: 0.0000063 Earths

Mimas

Planet: Saturn

Mimas has been nicknamed the 'Death Star' moon owing to its obvious physical similarities to the famous space station in the *Star Wars* movies. The 'dish' of the 'Death Star' moon is a 130km (80 mile) wide impact crater named Herschel after Sir William Herschel who discovered the moon in 1787. Mimas is also the smallest known celestial body to be spherical due to its own self-gravitation.

The surface of Mimas is strewn with impact craters

The moon that's nearing its end

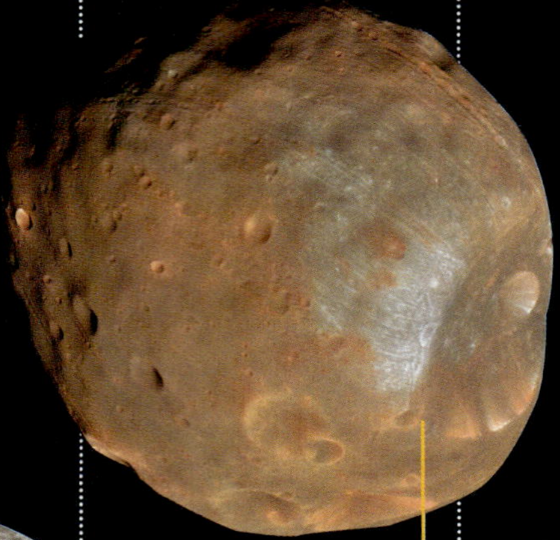

Mass: 0.0000000018 Earths

Phobos

Planet: Mars

The larger of Mars's two natural satellites, the other being Deimos, Phobos orbits just 6,000km (3,700 miles) from the Martian surface, closer than any other known moon. It orbits Mars faster than the planet rotates, meaning it rises and sets about twice per day in the Martian horizon. In several million years it will impact the Red Planet or break apart and become a planetary ring.

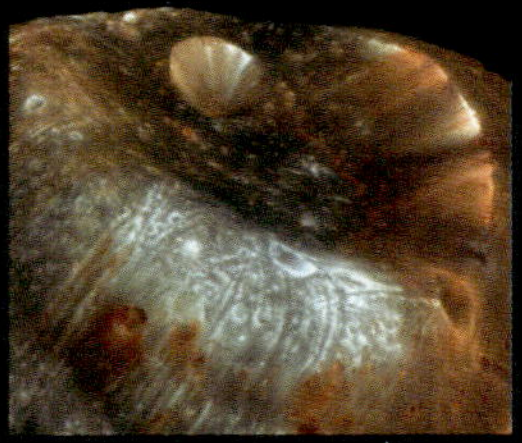

Stickney is the largest crater on Phobos

The best bet for life?

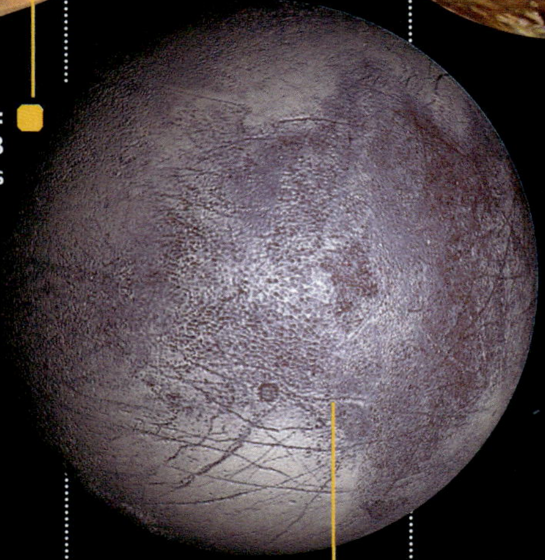

Mass: 0.008 Earths

Europa

Planet: Jupiter

Europa is the smoothest body in the Solar System, thanks to its vast and icy surface. Cracks on its surface suggest that underground there is a huge ocean of liquid water pressing against the bottom of the ice. This continued motion of the liquid and the icy surface heats up the bottom of the ice and, as cracks and vents appear, the liquid can escape out of the planet as jets of vapour and gas.

Cracks on Europa's surface hint at subsurface activity

The most violent moon

Mass: 0.015 Earths

Io

Planet: Jupiter

Io is the most volcanically active body in the Solar System (including Earth). This poor moon is being pushed and pulled by both Jupiter and Europa, and therefore its interior is constantly being heated. In fact, the surface of Io moves up and down by tens of metres. Under the surface vast lakes of lava build up and, once the pressure has built up enough, they are launched upwards out of volcanoes.

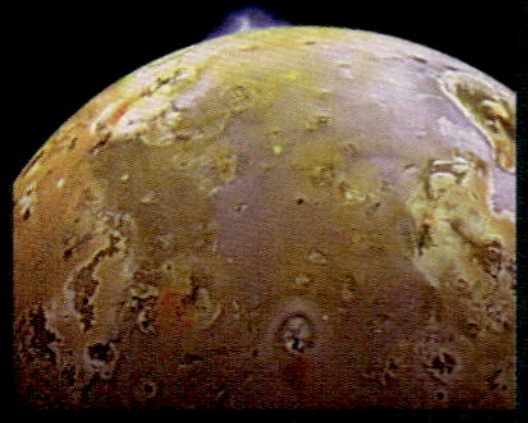

Io's massive volcanoes dwarf those on Earth

The only ringed moon?

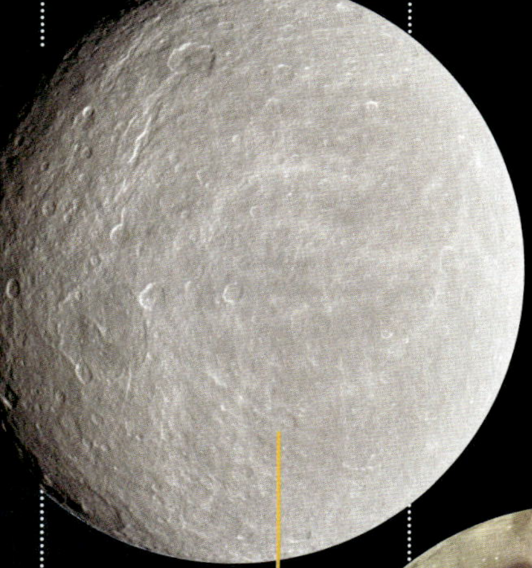

Rhea

Planet: Saturn

Rhea, the second-largest moon of Saturn, is an icy world with two mysteries that we are yet to solve. The first is the presence of a very tenuous atmosphere made of oxygen and carbon dioxide detected around the moon, which could be the result of organics. Second, Rhea is thought to have a very faint ring system, the only moon to have one, although images from the Cassini spacecraft were inconclusive.

Rhea could be the only moon with rings

The biggest moon of them all

Ganymede

Planet: Jupiter

The largest moon in the Solar System, Ganymede is composed of almost equal parts silicate rock and water ice. It has a liquid core, like a planet, giving it the only known magnetic field of a satellite. Beneath its surface it is thought to house a salt-water ocean, and it also has a thin atmosphere that has traces of oxygen within it. Its features have made it one of the subjects of the ESA's JUICE spacecraft, to be launched in 2022.

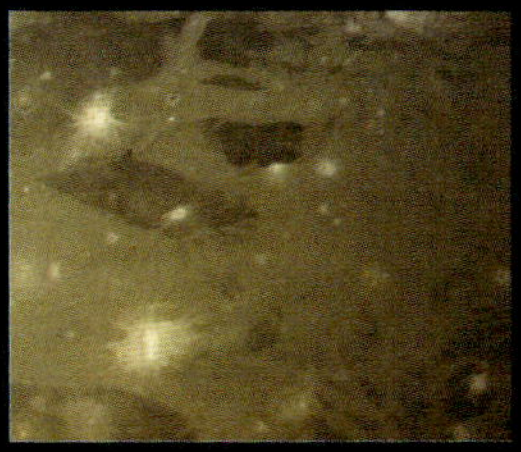

Ganymede might be hiding a subsurface ocean

A bizarre world with astounding features

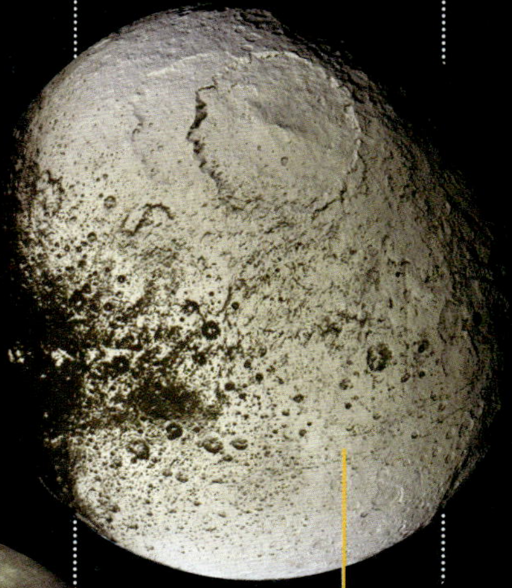

Iapetus

Planet: Saturn

Probably one of the most striking moons in the Solar System, Iapetus is immediately noticeable for its two-tone colouration. Its leading side is incredibly bright while its trailing side is mysteriously dark, possibly due to the influence of the Sun and nearby moons. Around its equator on the dark side it also has a 1,300km (800 mile)-long ridge that rises up to 13km (eight miles), but its origins are unknown.

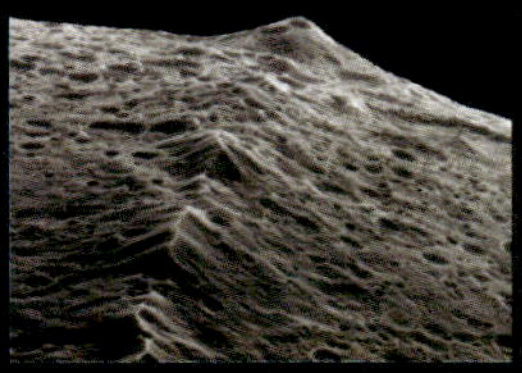

An equatorial ridge runs across this strange moon

The young moon that was recently altered

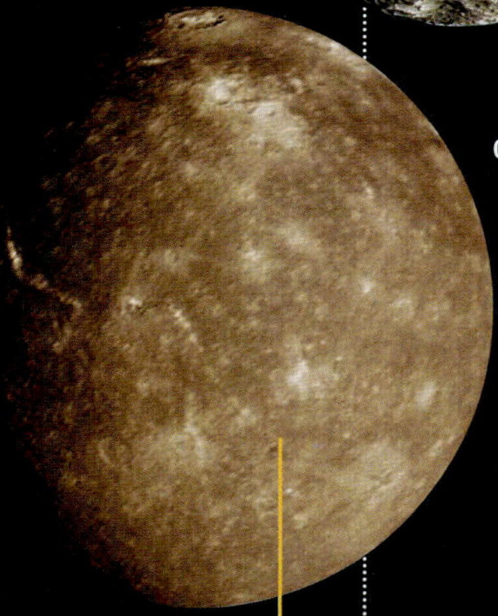

Titania

Planet: Uranus

Titania, discovered in 1787 by William Herschel, is interesting for its seemingly young surface. The walls of many of its craters are partially submerged, suggesting this moon, the largest of Uranus, underwent a resurfacing event at some point in its past, possibly as a result of geological activity. A valley 1,600km (1,000 miles) in length is further evidence for this sort of activity.

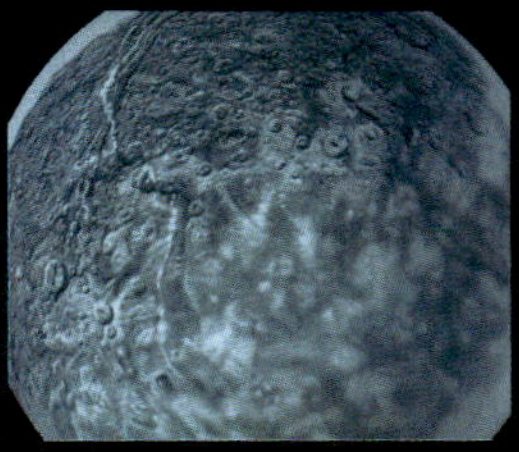

This false colour image of Titania shows its features

Saturn's sponge-like satellite

Hyperion

Planet: Saturn

Hyperion is one of the largest irregular objects in the Solar System, but its most noticeable feature is its strange, sponge-like appearance. Dark-floored craters and pock-marks are scattered across its surface, suggesting it was once involved in a collision that blew part of the Moon away, further evidenced by its erratic orbit and chaotic rotation. It was also the first non-spherical moon to be discovered.

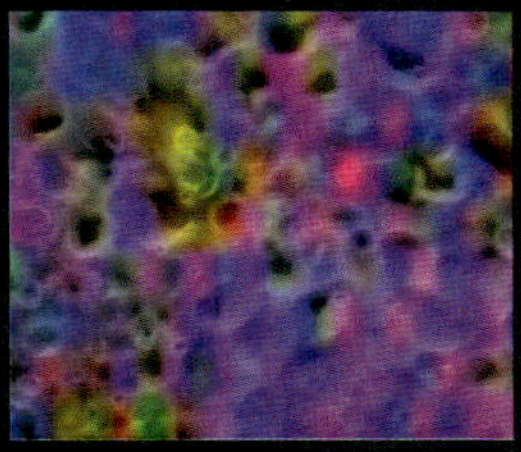

Hyperion's porous surface is unique

146 Moons
A Complete Guide

How do all of the moons in the Solar System compare to one another? Find out in this guide to every single confirmed natural satellite

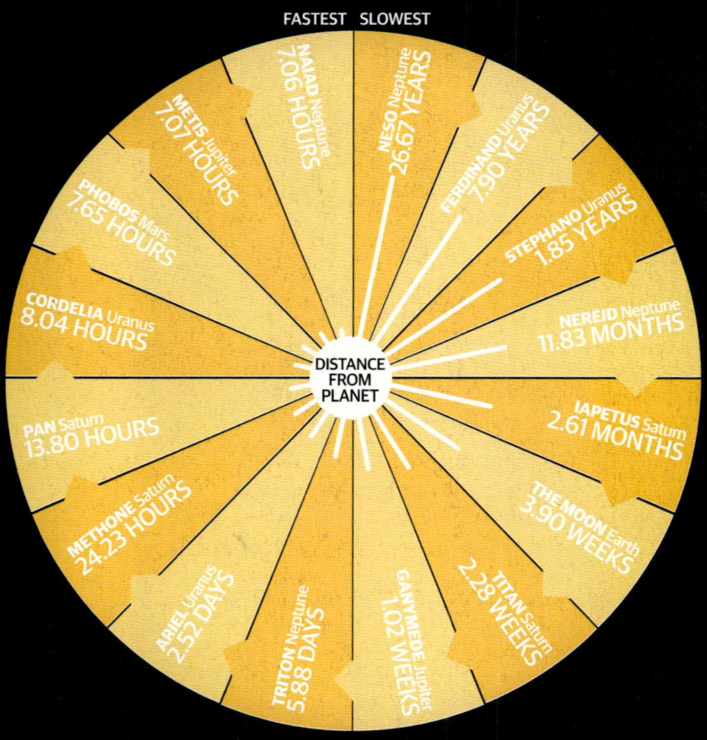

Orbital periods

A year is defined as the time taken to orbit a host body, while a day is the time taken for the orbiting body to complete a rotation. Generally, the further a moon is from a planet the longer it will take to orbit it. However, it also depends on the mass of the planet. Here we compare the time taken for various moons to orbit their host planet and their distance from that planet. All times are given in Earth measurements.

Moons of the Solar System

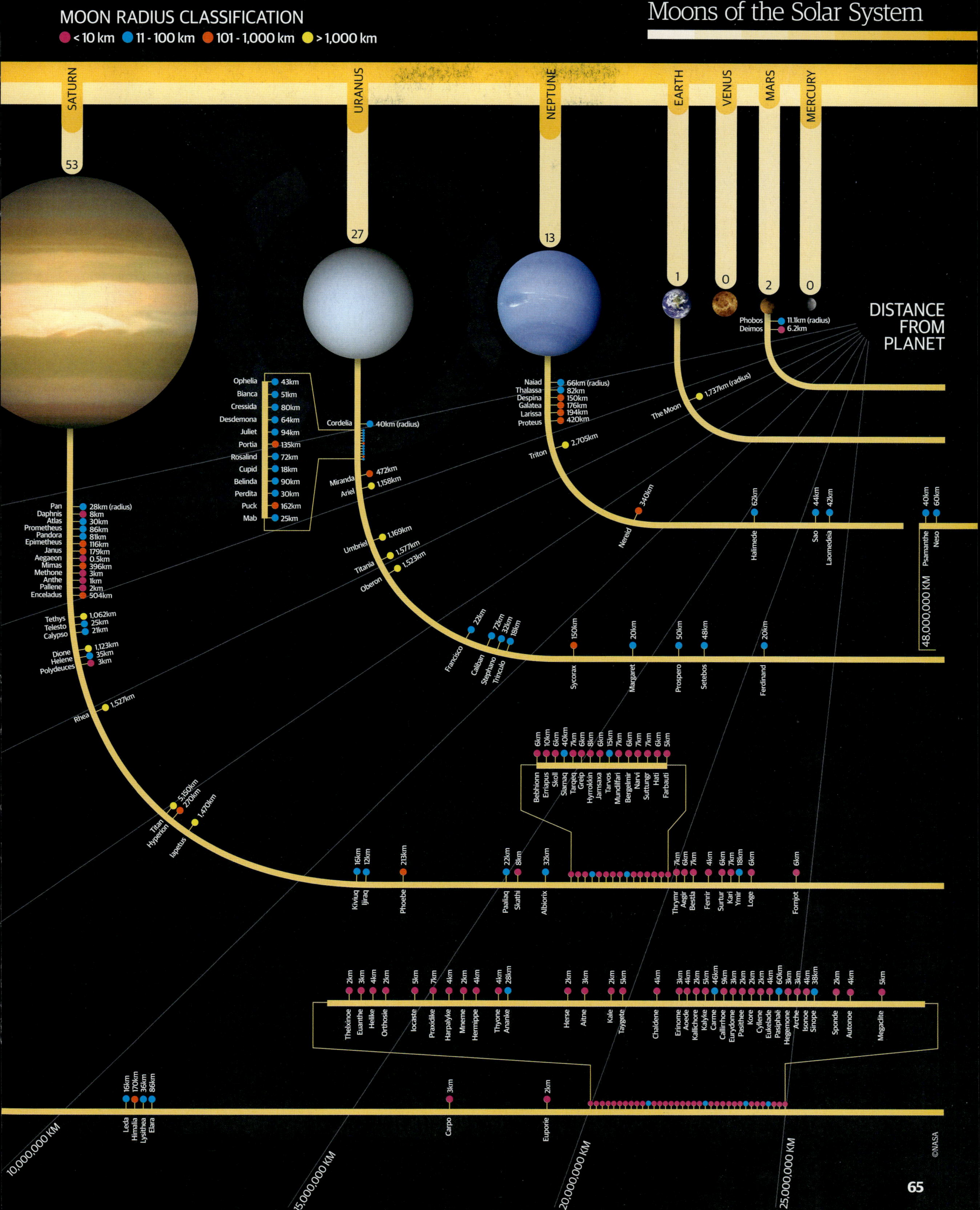

The mysteries of Saturn's rings

Despite their simple appearance Saturn's rings are incredibly complex structures

Saturn's rings are arguably the most awe-inspiring element of the planet's system. Made up from billions of ice, rock and dust particles, they grant the planet one of the most distinctive appearances in our Solar System. However, despite their simple appearance from Earth, upon closer inspection Saturn's rings are a fervent system of constantly evolving formations permanently in flux.

The probing of Saturn's ring system's secrets began with the Pioneer and Voyager probes of the Seventies, which revealed that far from them being made up from a mere handful of large rings, they were in fact composed of thousands of ringlets, incredibly narrow, varying composition circular and elliptical rings. However, it was not until the Cassini probe arrived in 2004 that the ringlets' true nature was uncovered.

Cassini revealed that gravitational interactions between the ringlets' particles orbiting within the larger rings along with some of the planet's larger moons, were driving huge levels of dynamism within them. These processes involved Saturn's moons stabilising and destabilising the planet's rings, generating incredibly bright radial spokes across many rings' horizontal planes and instigating vast tsunami-like vertical waves running outwards towards ring edges, distorting them massively.

Further, in 2006 Cassini discovered that hundreds of moonlets (small moons) were embedded within the ring discs. The probe identified them through their generation of propeller-like structures within the ring planes, which left a characteristic trail of particle disturbance in their wake. As such, since 2006 Cassini has helped identify more than 150 moonlets.

However, the exact nature of Saturn's rings' particulate material is still unknown. Analysis has revealed that they are made up of 99.9 per cent pure water ice, however, what impurities make up the remaining 0.1 per cent, the impurities that grant the rings their appearance and unique characteristics, remain a mystery. Unfortunately, any mission to analyse one would entail a perilous journey that would likely be a one-way ticket for the spacecraft in question.

"Instigating vast tsunami-like vertical waves running outwards towards ring edges, distorting them massively"

Plugging the gap

There are over ten major gaps within Saturn's rings, ranging in width from 3km (1.8 miles) to more than 285km (177 miles). These gaps are also partnered by two major divisions, the Cassini Division and Roche Division, which are far grander in scale and filled with heavily destabilised loose ring-like material.

The destabilisation, the same destabilisation that created and maintains the Cassini Division between A Ring and B Ring, is generated by Saturn's moon Mimas being embedded within it. The position of Mimas causes particle density to drop sharply through a destabilising orbital resonance, a process that involves any ice particles in the Cassini Division being drawn towards the moon every two orbits, thereby maintaining the division between rings. Interestingly, the orbital resonances of Saturn's moons not only destabilise particles but stabilise them also, thereby maintaining certain ring formations around the planet.

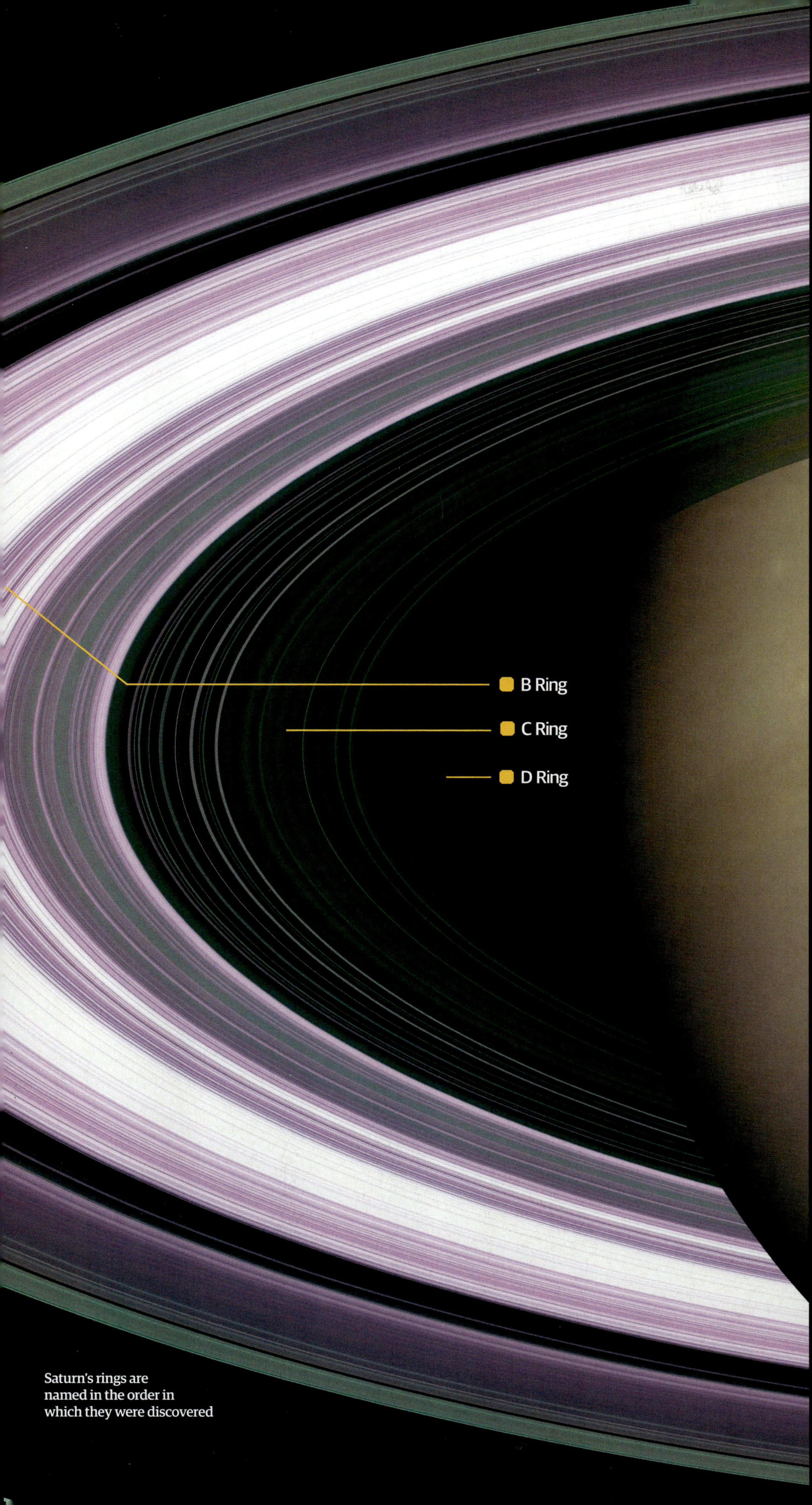

Saturn's rings are named in the order in which they were discovered

Saturn's rings analysed

The most fascinating properties and features of Saturn's rings

A Ring
A Ring was the first of Saturn's rings to be discovered and is the outermost of the large, bright rings. The ring's width is estimated to be roughly 20m (66 feet) while the entire ring is thought to have the approximate mass of Hyperion.

B Ring
B Ring is the largest and brightest of Saturn's rings and is famed for its uneven and disturbed structure. Indeed, the outer edge of the ring appears vaulted out from its plane and is interspersed with propeller-like ridges and vertical structures.

C Ring
C Ring is a wide but faint ring that appears almost transparent from above and is only noticeable on an angle. Within C Ring lies the Colombo Gap, and within that the Titan Ringlet, a bright but narrow ring of material that is elliptical rather than circular.

D Ring
One of the faintest of Saturn's rings, D Ring was only discovered by Voyager 1 in 1980. Within it is a structure of numerous waves about 30km (19 miles) apart that are postulated by NASA to have been generated by an impact event from a disrupted comet.

E Ring
E Ring is Saturn's outermost ring and is extremely wide. It begins at the orbit of Saturn's moon Mimas and ends around the orbit of Rhea. Unlike other rings, E Ring has a large concentration of carbon dioxide and ammonia, which help give it a very diffuse appearance.

F Ring
F Ring is the outermost of Saturn's discrete rings and is arguably the most active ring in the Solar System. F Ring is very thin and its structure is maintained by Saturn's moons Prometheus and Pandora, which orbit inside it and outside it respectively.

G Ring
G Ring is very faint and roughly halfway between F Ring and the start of E Ring. At its inner edge lies a bright arc, which is stabilised by the orbital resonance of Mimas. It constantly loses mass by its interaction with Saturn's magnetic field.

Opportunity's view of Mars

This extraordinary image, taken by NASA's Opportunity rover, provides an awesome landscape of the Red Planet

Dust buildup
Martian dust accumulates on Opporunity's solar panels over time, so during the winter the rover must maximise the amount of sunlight it receives.

Tracks
Here you can see the path Opportunity took to reach its resting spot at Greeley Haven.

Opportunity's continued fight for survival sees it undertake some clever manoeuvres in order to survive the harsh conditions on Mars. This particular image shows the steps taken to ensure it outlasts the treacherous Martian winter as it camps out at Greeley Haven.

Throughout the rover's activities it slowly accumulates dust on its solar panels, although the Martian wind gradually cleans them. In the winter when the Sun spends the least amount of time in the sky, the rover needs to maximise its time in sunlight to generate as much power as possible in order to stay alive. The winter period lasts for four months until days begin to lengthen during the southern winter solstice.

In this particular instance, the rover headed to the flats of Greeley Haven where it could get a decent amount of exposure to the Sun. During its stationary time at Greeley Haven, Opportunity gathered data about perturbations in the rotation of Mars, which will help scientists understand more about the planet's core.

With its winter rest over, Opportunity is now heading north to continue to study the interior of Endeavour Crater, which has a variety of light-coloured soil patches that might be indicative of subsurface liquid and also plays host to some of the oldest features on Mars yet seen by the rover.

Opportunity has been active on Mars since it landed on 25 January 2004, far exceeding its expected lifetime. Its sister rover, Spirit, landed about three weeks earlier on 4 January 2004 but succumbed to the Martian weather and ceased operating in March 2010.

Opportunity is still going strong despite landing on the Martian surface over eight years ago

Endeavour wall
A 20km (12 mile) wall is visible here, an interior feature of the Endeavour Crater that Opportunity is now inside.

800 images
During its winter stopover at Greeley Haven, Opportunity snapped over 800 images of its surroundings, many of which were combined into this 360-degree digital panorama.

Eris The missing planet

To us, Eris is just a small point of light in the sky. But within months of its discovery, this tiny world changed our definition of a planet

Mike Brown, an astronomer at the California Institute of Technology, was the lead discoverer of Eris. He knew that this world was about the same size or larger than Pluto and he realised that he would be hailed as the discoverer of the tenth planet. However, he didn't agree that Eris, or even Pluto, were big enough objects to actually qualify as planets.

Before Eris's official announcement in 2005, his wife joked Brown's discovery meant that some day their daughter could afford college. But Brown maintained his hypothesis: Eris was the biggest known member of the Kuiper belt - a region of icy objects orbiting beyond Neptune.

Today, Brown says that it was tempting to keep the title as the founder of the tenth planet, but as a scientist he couldn't let that stand. "It's hard to pretend that was not in my head," he tells **All About Space**. "But I felt like there was no way to leave this argument. It made no scientific sense."

Prior to Eris's discovery, Brown was a new faculty member at Caltech trying to secure tenure. He chose planet-hunting to make his mark. In 1997, his team began using an ageing 120-centimetre (48-inch) Schmidt telescope at the university's Palomar Observatory. The telescope was so old that it could only use photographic plates. Each photo would then be scanned into a computer for analysis.

After two years of hunting, Brown determined this method was not working. They resumed the search in 2001 using up-and-coming digital technology. Within months, the team discovered small worlds in the Kuiper belt. The largest ones, Quaoar and Sedna, were announced to some fanfare. Brown's tenure was secured. Then came a tiny point of light on 5 January 2005 that would change astronomy forever. It was close: 90 Earth-Sun distances away, the equivalent of the Solar System's backyard. And it was bright: 18.8 magnitude, easily visible in a professional telescope.

The object was officially labelled 2003 UB313, but Brown nicknamed it Xena in a subtle nod to the mythical Planet X on the outside of our Solar System. He planned to take his time to confirm the discovery, which is standard practice among astronomers. Among other tools, his team used a telescope in Chile. Brown was tracking a number of small worlds with this telescope, including one later named Haumea. Unfortunately for Brown, a public University of Ohio website had records of which objects the telescope was looking at (this was later rectified).

News of Haumea leaked out. According to Brown, a Spanish astronomer falsely claimed its discovery based on the Ohio data. However, the International Astronomical Union (IAU) never made a ruling. Brown nevertheless knew the positions of Xena and another object he was confirming were also in danger of discovery. Hastily, he made an announcement on 29 July 2005. When the IAU realised that Xena was about the same size as Pluto, it decided to call a meeting to vote on the definition of a planet.

Its decision to demote Pluto in 2006 to dwarf planet was controversial among astronomers. As such, Brown suggested the official name of Eris, after the Greek goddess of strife and discord. The IAU accepted it. That dispute has faded in the years since, Brown says, although the public still feels it's controversial.

According to Brown, Eris is the furthest dwarf planet we have ever spotted orbiting the Sun. It is almost 15 billion kilometres (9 billion miles) away - about three times further than Pluto. Eris takes 560 years to make one trip around the Sun and its orbit is eccentric. Its distance from the Sun varies from 38 Sun-Earth distances to 97 Sun-Earth distances. The dwarf planet is around 2,326 kilometres (1,450 miles) in diameter. Eris also has a moon, Dysnomia. From watching Dysnomia orbit Eris, Brown estimates Eris is 27 per cent more massive than Pluto and has a density of around 2.6 grams per cubic centimetre (1.5 ounces per cubic inch). The high density implies Eris is mostly made of rock.

It is also surprisingly bright, reflecting almost 97 per cent of the light that comes to it. Brown's team believes it's because Eris's atmosphere is frozen, due to its estimated minimum temperature of -240 degrees Celsius (-405 degrees Fahrenheit). The dwarf planet is at its furthest distance from the Sun right now, and will warm up to -215 degrees Celsius (-360 degrees Fahrenheit) as it gets closer. Eris's atmosphere is likely made

up of methane and nitrogen, and astronomers believe that it's currently just a thin layer of substance lying over the surface.

Brown says there's still much to learn about Eris. His team is trying to find its pole. This is important because the direction of Eris's spin determines how much heating the dwarf planet receives as it goes around the Sun. Brown also keeps up on the latest news on the dwarf planets he found.

"There's a paper that just came out... on the first precise measurement of Makemake," Brown says, referring to another of his discoveries. "I didn't have anything to do with [the paper], and it's hard. I always assumed it was like having your kid grow up and start dating and get married. You don't always want it to happen, except you know it should happen."

But Brown is focusing on other things. One of his near-term goals is to restart the search for dwarf planets with more advanced digital technology. "It's hard to justify doing the entire survey again, except each one of the big bright [objects] is just so interesting that it's worth going and finding out if they're there." ●

"Each of the objects is so interesting that it's worth finding out if they're there"

Mike Brown, **California Institute of Technology**

A trans-Neptunian orbit

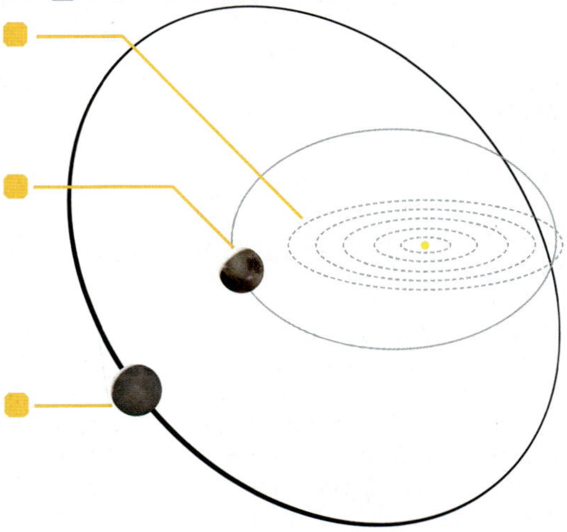

A moon called Dysnomia

Eris's moon, Dysnomia, was discovered on 10 September 2005. Brown and his team were working at the Keck Observatory in Hawaii when they found the moon.

They nicknamed it Gabrielle (after the character in *Xena: Warrior Princess*), which stuck until the IAU approved the official name of Dysnomia. In mythology, Dysnomia is the daughter of Eris. The name also closely honours the first two letters in Brown's wife's name, Diane.

Keck and Hubble were used several times to figure out Dysnomia's orbit. It takes about 16 days for the moon to go around Eris. More importantly, Dysnomia's movements around the dwarf planet allowed astronomers to figure out how massive Eris is: about 27% more than Pluto.

It's difficult to tell just how big the moon is because of its size and distance, but the astronomers figured Dysnomia is about 200 times fainter than Eris. Brown estimates Dysnomia is about 100km (62 miles) in diameter, but that could range as high as 250km (155 miles). There is no direct evidence showing what Dysnomia might be made of. However, Brown suspects it is mostly made up of frozen water, based on similar objects he has studied.

Dysnomia's discovery is important because it appears that most of the largest Kuiper belt objects have moons. This implies they all had similar origins, which would give us a window into the early years of our Solar System.

Eris and its moon, Dysnomia, in a WM Keck Observatory image from 2007. Its high density implies Eris must be partly made of rock

Planetary Auroras

These vast light shows, predominantly found near the poles of a planet, are simply astounding in appearance

The Sun is constantly giving out energy in the form of charged particles that make their way throughout the Solar System unheeded by the vacuum of space. However, around most of its eight major planets is a magnetosphere caused by activity in that planet's core, namely the induction of currents. When these charged particles from the Sun come into contact with the magnetosphere of a planet, the results are nothing short of remarkable.

A planet's magnetosphere extends in a circle from pole to pole, with the pressure of the solar wind also extending its tail far beyond the planet. When the particles from the Sun come into contact with a magnetosphere they run along the magnetic field lines as it is the point of least resistance. They move along these lines until they are destroyed by coming into contact with other particles. This usually happens around the poles of a planet where the magnetic field lines are concentrated and the atmosphere becomes thicker. The solar wind hits particles in the atmosphere at the poles, ionising them during the collision and releasing photons (packets of light) in the process. The colour of the resultant light emitted depends on the atmospheric particle: oxygen atoms give off a green light while nitrogen atoms emit blue or red light.

It is for these reasons that on Earth, and indeed on other planets in the Solar System, fantastic auroras appear at the poles. They don't usually appear near the equator of a planet as the magnetic field lines of the magnetosphere are concentrated at the poles, although occasionally the intensity of the incoming solar wind can force the aurora quite far from the poles. As the solar wind continues to interact with a planet's atmosphere more and more light is produced, often in sweeping waves or huge bands of light. For this reason, as Venus and Mars have insignificant magnetic fields, their auroras (if there are any at all) are virtually nonexistent and certainly very difficult to detect, while Mercury barely has an atmosphere and therefore does not have noticeable auroras.

In this feature we have taken a look at the fantastic auroras produced on Earth, Jupiter, Saturn, Uranus and Neptune.

On Earth the Northern Lights are known as the aurora borealis, while the Southern Lights are the aurora australis

Green light is given off when the solar wind hits oxygen particles in the atmosphere

Auroras in the Solar System

Jupiter

Jupiter's magnetic field is more than 14 times as strong as our own, and therefore the biggest planet in our Solar System produces some startlingly huge auroras even though it is much further from the Sun (and therefore receives less solar wind). One of the reasons for the large auroras is that, as well as interaction with the solar wind, Jupiter's atmosphere is also ionised by its moons, mostly the volcanically active Io which releases a huge number of particles into Jupiter's magnetosphere. Interestingly, three of Jupiter's four Galilean moons, Io, Europa and Ganymede, have all been observed to have auroras, indicating they have noticeable atmospheres.

If Jupiter's magnetosphere was visible to the naked eye it would be as big as the Sun in the night sky on Earth

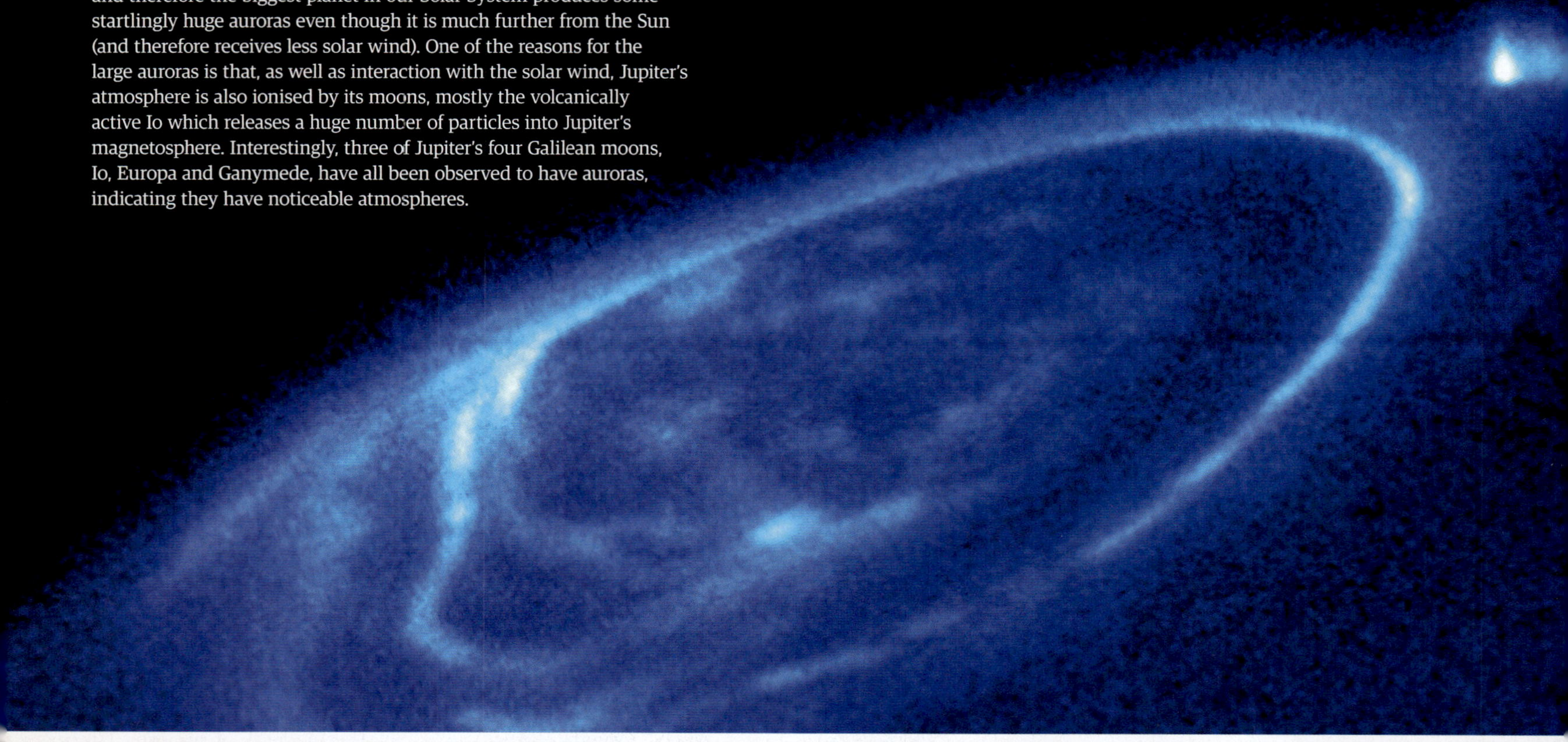

Uranus

Auroras on Uranus were not seen until 2011 when the Hubble Space Telescope snapped a picture of the small light shows in action. These auroras are driven by the solar wind like on Earth. However, Uranus is unique in that it rotates on its side relative to its motion around the Sun and its poles are offset by about 60 degrees relative to the rotation axis. Therefore, its auroras can appear to form at the equator of the planet but in actuality they are the planet's poles.

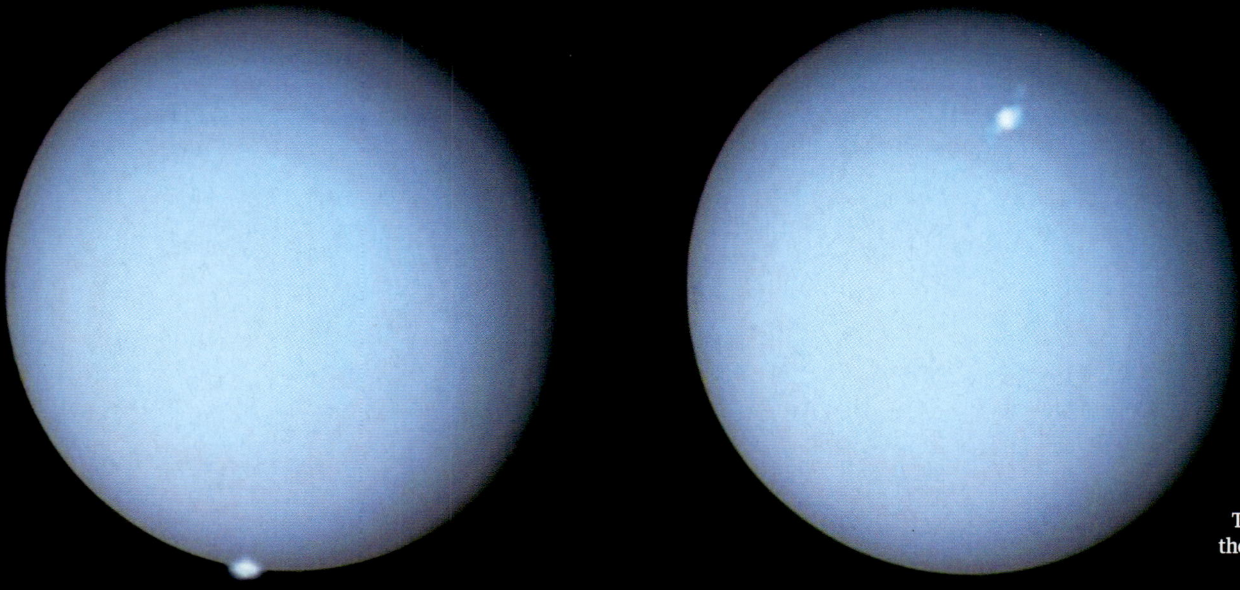

The Hubble Space Telescope snapped these images of the unusual auroras on Uranus in November 2011

Saturn

Saturn's magnetosphere is the second largest only to Jupiter in the Solar System, and contains plasma both from the giant ringed planet itself and its nearby moons. Auroras on Saturn form large ovals at the poles, with the northern aurora appearing closer to the pole than the southern aurora. The auroras on Saturn are more similar to those on Earth than they are to those on Jupiter in that they are driven largely by the solar wind, despite being further from the Sun than Jupiter.

Auroras on Saturn and Earth share more similarities than those on Jupiter

Neptune

The Voyager 2 spacecraft provided the first evidence for auroras on Neptune in 1989. However, the auroral power on Neptune is very weak, with its magnetosphere estimated to have a power of just 50 million watts compared to 100 billion watts on Earth. Therefore the auroras, which are driven by the solar wind, do not appear near the poles but rather in widespread regions across the planet at very low intensity. Like Uranus, Neptune's magnetic field is highly tilted to its rotational axis, which also contributes to the varied location of the auroras.

Auroras on Neptune are very low in intensity and so are difficult to detect

Comets explained

Are these cosmic snowballs the building blocks of life on Earth?

NASA's Deep Impact spacecraft fired an impactor into Comet Tempel 1 in 2005 in an attempt to study the resultant debris

Almost 5 billion years ago our Solar System was born from a hot and dense cloud of dust and gas. In this cloud could be found a whole manner of elements, both light and heavy, and various other material including water and ice. At the heart of the system a protostar took shape, eventually evolving into what we now know as the Sun, taking with it many of the heavy elements and igniting a nuclear fusion process that would become its hot core. The remaining rock, metal and gas formed into the various planets and asteroids in the Solar System.

All that was left at this point were small lumps of frozen gas and ice in the outer regions of the Solar System, where the temperature was low enough for them to remain. They formed into bodies ranging from just a few metres to dozens of kilometres wide and entered into highly elliptical orbits around the Sun due to its gravitational pull. Tearing through the Solar System at great speeds, we call these objects comets.

The formation of comets and their unique characteristics make them a fantastic window into the conditions in the early Solar System. Speaking to **All About Space**, NASA's comet expert Dr Joseph Nuth said: "From a scientific perspective comets preserve invaluable evidence for the conditions in the primitive solar nebula that we can attain from no other source. Comets very likely formed on a much shorter timescale than the 5 to 10 million years that the solar nebula persisted. This means that the solids and volatiles preserved in comets represent grab-bag samples of the materials found in the nebula at the time of their formation. The materials are preserved because comets were never hot enough to lose significant quantities of water and it is unlikely that much (if any) of this water was ever liquid."

This has made comets one of the most intriguing subjects of study among astronomers. They have been observed by humanity for thousands of years, with many comets returning to Earth periodically for repeated study. For example, Halley's Comet, one of the most widely known of these fascinating objects, was included in the Bayeux Tapestry of the 1070s. Its eccentric orbit was calculated by English astronomer Edmond Halley, who correctly predicted its return in 1758 and therefore had the honour of the comet being named after him.

> "Comets may have been responsible for transporting the building blocks of life, like water and organic compounds, to Earth"

The name 'comet' derives from the Latinisation of the Greek word komētēs, translating as 'long-haired'. This was in reference to the their appearance as stars with long strands of hair trailing behind them. We now know that these trails are the tails of comets, extending far back beyond the comet's nucleus (centre). The tails of comets are interesting as they contain various elements and material from the comet, allowing them to be studied without visiting the surface. In 2004, NASA successfully flew its Stardust spacecraft within the tail of the comet Wild 2, collecting samples and returning them to Earth for study.

Comets originate in two distinctive regions - the Kuiper belt, which is a disc-like belt found beyond the orbit of Neptune, and the Oort cloud, which is 100,000 times further from the Sun than the Earth is. Short-period comets, found in or near the Kuiper belt, are occasionally nudged by gravity into an orbit that brings them closer to the Sun, allowing us to observe them as they make their way past, usually within a period of under 200 years. Less predictable are the long-period comets, which originate in the Oort cloud. These comets have highly irregular orbits and can take as long as 30 million years to complete one trip around the Sun or, in some cases they may simply be thrown out of the Solar System by the Sun and never return.

Comets are interesting for many reasons, but in particular for providing us with a window into how the Earth became habitable. Comets may have been responsible for transporting the building blocks of life, like water and organic compounds, to Earth in the early Solar System. They may contain some of the rarer ingredients for life compared to other objects like asteroids, which are generally just hunks of rock left over from the formation of the planets. "Establishing the relationship between comets and asteroids and charting the course of their evolution over the last several billion years can inform our understanding of the processes that formed the planets," explained Dr Nuth. "This includes the evolution of the atmosphere and oceans and the origin of the unique chemistry that might have led to life on Earth (and possibly elsewhere in the Solar System). This would naturally lead to predictions of the probability of life elsewhere in the universe."

The perceived importance of comets has led to several missions being launched to try to better understand these drifting balls of ice. The Stardust mission of 2004, as mentioned earlier, was important in helping to understand the structure of comets. Later, in 2005, NASA's Deep Impact spacecraft launched an impactor into Comet Tempel 1, ejecting huge amounts of powdery material from the comet and allowing the resultant debris to be studied. The Stardust spacecraft, after delivering its comet sample back to Earth, went back to re-study Tempel 1 in 2011 to see how the comet had reacted to the impact. One of the next comet-visiting spacecraft will be the ESA's Rosetta, launched in 2004 and now on its way to comet 67P/Churyumov-Gerasimenko, which will place a lander on the comet's surface to perform various experiments.

Our understanding of comets has greatly increased in the past several decades, but there is still much to learn. Future missions and observations of both short and long-period comets will help us understand them even further, and perhaps unlock more of their secrets that may offer clues as to our beginnings. ●

Tell us about your comet sightings @spaceanswers #comets

Orbital paths

What happens as a comet orbits the Sun?

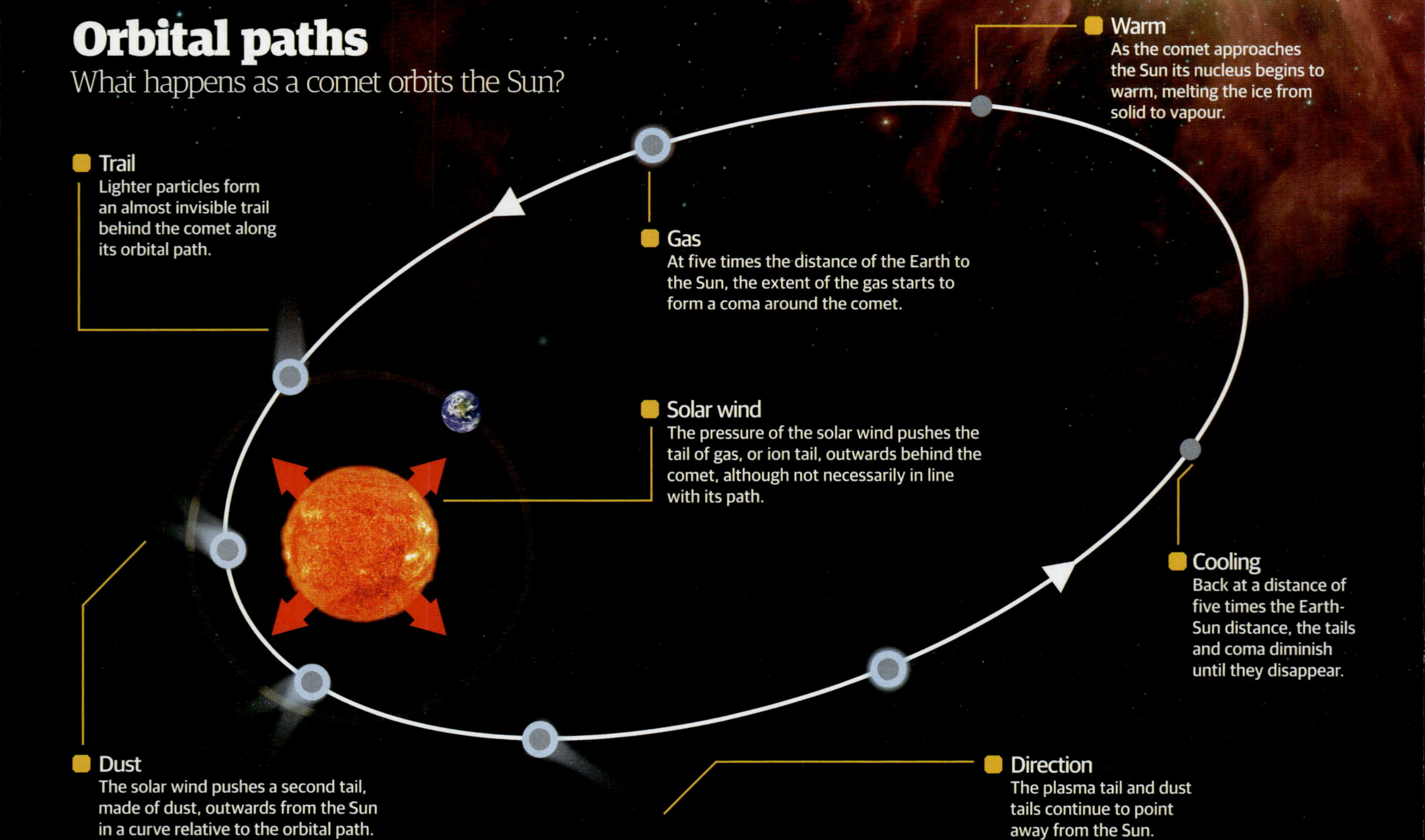

Inside a comet

What's going on inside these balls of ice?

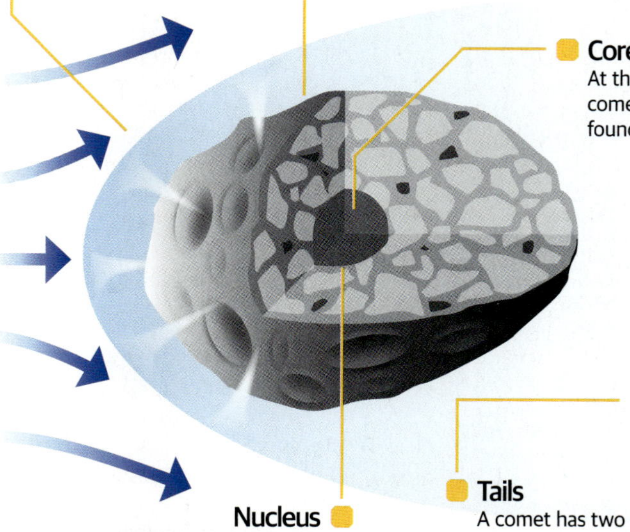

Coma
When a comet approaches the Sun its surrounding gas, known as a coma, is heated and becomes visible.

Fragments
Most comets are only loosely held together and can be pulled apart by the gravity of the Sun and the planets.

Core
At the core of some comets can be found solid rock.

Nucleus
The hard nucleus of a comet, made of ice, water and rock, ranges from a few hundred metres to dozens of kilometres in diameter.

Tails
A comet has two primary tails, one made of gas and the other made of dust. The former can extend over 500 million km (310 million miles) in length.

This crater chain on Jupiter's moon Ganymede was the result of a comet breaking apart and impacting the surface

NASA's Ulysses spacecraft inadvertently crossed the paths of several comets

Why studying comets could save life on Earth

Other than being a history lesson, NASA's comet expert Dr Joseph Nuth tells us why understanding comets is so important

"From a purely practical perspective a comet dropping into the inner Solar System for the very first time has the potential to destroy all life on Earth with very little advanced warning, though the probability of such an occurrence is minuscule. A more likely scenario would be for the orbit of the comet to gradually evolve to the point where it collides with the Earth, thus yielding us some time to formulate a plan to divert or destroy the agent of our destruction.

"A comet's destructive potential is related to its composition, mass and relative velocity. While the properties of its orbit will determine its relative velocity with the Earth, the mass and composition of a comet could vary over a very wide range: from a highly porous, fluffy ice ball, to a dense, water-bearing chunk of space rock. Ironically, the fluffy, porous ice ball will look like a huge threat as it enters the inner Solar System whereas the water-bearing space rock may be barely detectable until it is quite close and might therefore appear to be less of a problem. The collisional consequences, however, are opposite in severity.

"Understanding the range in potential properties of comets will help us to more accurately estimate the threat from any particular body and will guide our response in dealing with any potential threat. Without knowledge of a comet's likely internal structure, formulating plans to break it up or to push it aside will suffer from being forced to anticipate a very wide range in the characteristics of such an object: pushing too hard on a small spot could break it off or bury a probe in the body of a fluffy ice-ball, while trying to blow a space rock into pieces could merely dent the surface."

History of comet observations

1070s — Bayeux Tapestry
The comet ezlater known as Halley's Comet is pictured in the Bayeux Tapestry.

1450 — First tracking
For the first time, astronomers record the paths of comets in the night sky.

1705 — Halley's Comet
Edmond Halley predicts the return of the comet in 1758, later named Halley's Comet.

1986 — Fleet
An international effort saw five different spacecraft approach and study Halley's Comet.

1994 — Collision
Scientists watch in amazement as comet Shoemaker-Levy 9 smashes into Jupiter.

2005 — Deep Impact
Comet Tempel 1 is impacted by NASA's Deep Impact collider, revealing its nucleus.

2006 — Stardust
NASA's Stardust spacecraft successfully returns particles from comet Wild 2 to Earth.

2014 — Rosetta
The ESA's Rosetta spacecraft will arrive at and study comet 67P/Churyumov-Gerasimenko.

The Great Comets

Here we take a look at some of the most notable Great Comets from recent history

Arend-Roland

Last visit: 1957

Next visit: Never

In 1957, comet Arend-Roland flew into the Solar System and reached a distance of just 0.316 AU from the Sun. However, upon orbiting the Sun it was thrust into a hyperbolic orbit, meaning its speed is fast enough for it to escape from the Solar System, never to return.

Ikeya-Seki

Last visit: 1965

Next visit: 3000

This long-period comet (one with an orbital period of more than 200 years) drifted into view in 1965 and passed as near as 0.008 AU to the Sun. Its close encounter with the Sun caused it to break into three pieces, but all remained in a near-identical orbit. It will return to the inner Solar System just before 3000 AD.

Halley's Comet

Last visit: 1986

Next visit: 2061

This comet is one of the most well-known short-period comets (an orbital period of less than 200 years). It's orbit brings it in to the Sun at a distance about half that of the Earth-Sun distance (one Astronomical Unit (AU), 150 million km or 93 million miles). It travels out beyond the orbit of Neptune before returning on its approximate 75-year-long journey.

West

Last visit: 1976

Next visit: 256,000 AD

In 1976 this spectacular comet tore through the inner Solar System, reaching just 0.197 AU from the Sun. Its highly chaotic orbit will take it up to 70,000 AU (1.1 light years) from the Sun, but it is expected to eventually return any time in the next 254,000 to 6.5 million years.

Hyakutake

Last visit: 1996

Next visit: 72,000 AD

Dubbed 'The Great Comet of 1996', Hyakutake was one of the closest cometary approaches to Earth in 200 years. It came as close as 0.23 AU to the Sun and, on its journey, NASA and ESA's Ulysses spacecraft unwittingly crossed its 500 million km (310 million miles) long tail.

Hale-Bopp

Last visit: 1997

Next visit: 4385

One of the most widely observed comets of the 20th Century, Hale-Bopp was visible to the naked eye for 18 months, although it only came to 0.914 AU of the Sun. Now on its way out of the Solar System, it will remain observable by telescopes until 2020 on its way to its distance of 370 AU from the Sun.

McNaught

Last visit: 2007

Next visit: 95,000 AD

This long-period comet was easily visible to the naked eye when it approached in 2007. It reached 0.17 AU from the Sun, during which its motion was observed by NASA's Sun-orbiting telescope the Solar and Heliospheric Observatory (SOHO). Amusingly, the Ulysses spacecraft again accidentally passed through the tail of this comet, just as it did Comet Hyakutake in 1996.

Lovejoy

Last visit: 2011

Next visit: 2633

The last 'Great Comet' to visit Earth to date, Lovejoy passed within just 0.00555 AU of the Sun. It travelled through the solar corona but emerged unscathed. It's 622-year orbital period will see it return to Earth some time around 2633.

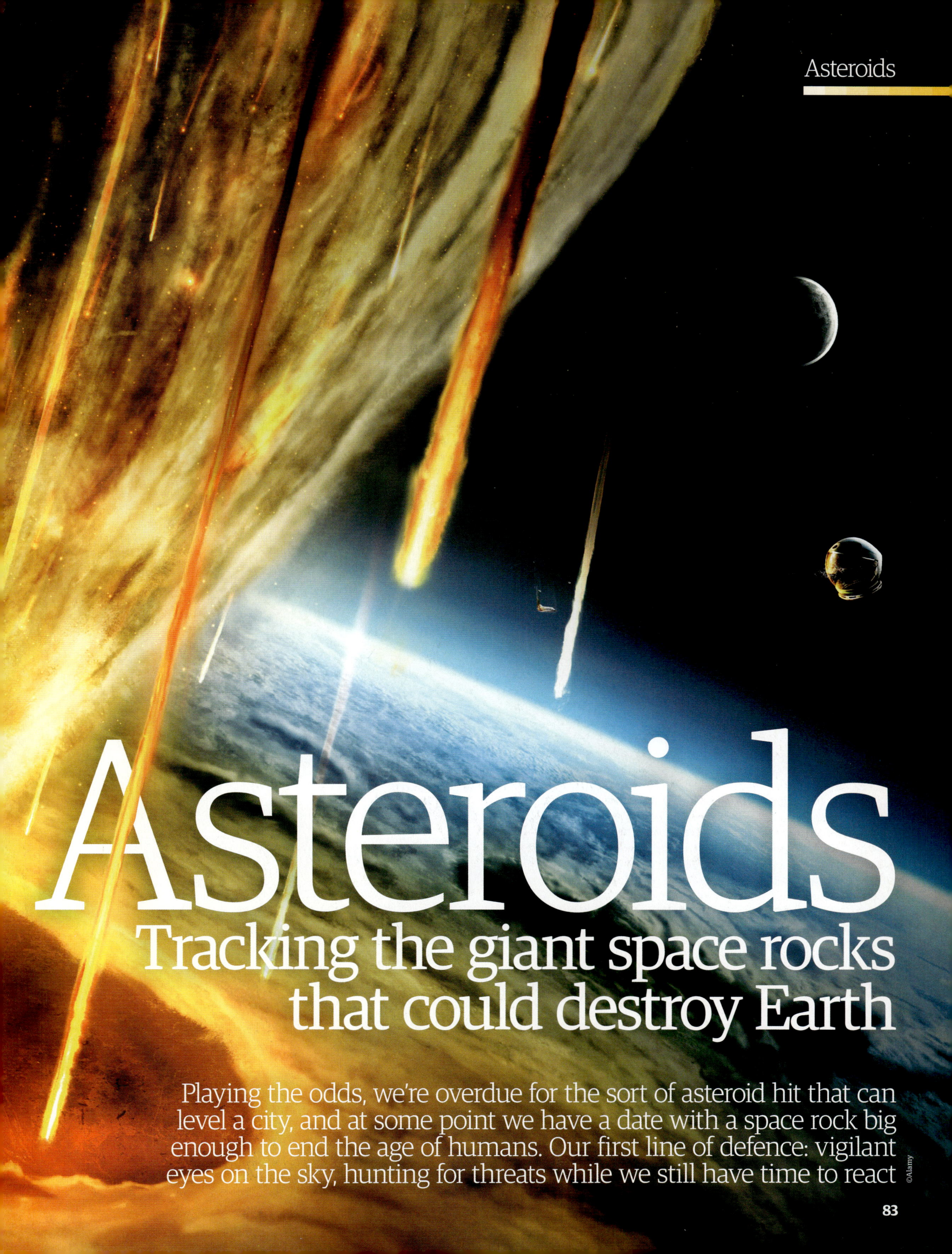

©Alamy

Asteroids

Tracking the giant space rocks that could destroy Earth

Playing the odds, we're overdue for the sort of asteroid hit that can level a city, and at some point we have a date with a space rock big enough to end the age of humans. Our first line of defence: vigilant eyes on the sky, hunting for threats while we still have time to react

Dr Don Yeomans and his Near-Earth Object (NEO) Program are responsible for tracking the asteroids that could potentially threaten the Earth

The unsung heroes are a small team of astronomers who scour the night sky for near-Earth objects (NEOs), asteroids and comets that are headed for our neighbourhood. "There are probably a couple dozen folks who are doing this more or less on a full-time basis," explains the manager of NASA's Near-Earth Object Program Office, Dr Don Yeomans. "The vast majority of discoveries are made in the US Southwest and Hawaii, by NASA-supported telescope facilities."

The searchers have been enormously successful, cataloguing more than 9,000 NEOs - objects projected to travel within 1.3 astronomical units of the Sun (195 million kilometres, or 121 million miles). Smaller ones do still sneak up on us, though.

"That happens all the time," Yeomans says. "We had an object about the size of a small or fairly good-sized automobile that actually hit in October 2008. It was discovered about 24 hours in advance. We predicted it would impact over northern Sudan, and it did. It was observed by a KLM airline pilot and somebody with a cell phone camera on the ground. Astronomers actually went over there and looked for fragments of the asteroid and they found several."

Far from a catastrophe, the impact turned out to be an exceptional stroke of luck. "That was a scientific bonanza," Yeomans says. "They can examine these fragments in Earth-based laboratories to find out exactly what the chemical composition is, and they also had observations of this object in space, so they know its spectral characteristics. They could say, all right, this particular type of asteroid is made up of this chemical composition."

On top of identifying planetary threats ahead of time, this is a key benefit of tracking NEOs. "That's sort of the holy grail of asteroid science: to try and take the meteorites that we have in museums and have been studied to death in terms of the composition - chemical and elemental composition - and say, 'All right, this meteorite is an example of that type of asteroid in the sky.'"

There's no shortage of errant debris in the Solar System, left over from its earliest days as a massive cloud of gas and dust. Beginning about 4.6 billion years ago, much of this dust clumped together, forming larger chunks of matter. Many of these chunks, in turn, steadily formed planets and moons. But a lot never joined the big leagues. In fact, about 100 tons of the stuff shows up at Earth's door every day. Fortunately, almost all of it is sand-sized particles that burn up on contact with our atmosphere. There are plenty of bigger pieces out there, though. Most are found in a belt between Mars and Jupiter. It's home to millions of asteroids - chunks of rocky, metallic or carbon-based material. There are even more of their smaller counterparts, meteoroids. Some think Jupiter's gravitational pull has kept the debris in place, preventing it from coalescing into a planet.

For the most part, these asteroids stay within the belt, revolving around the Sun in an orderly fashion. But now and then, a collision or a gravitational tug knocks an asteroid out of its orbit, into a path that takes it closer to the centre of the Solar System. A fraction of those end up heading our way.

Most of the asteroids that reach Earth come from the inner part of the belt, which is primarily made up of S-type asteroids, composed of silicate rock. We also encounter a good number of C-type asteroids, composed of carbon-rich material. The third variety, metallic M-type asteroids, are rare.

It's a similar story with comets, mixtures of dusty ice and rock that typically travel in the outer regions of the Solar System. The distinction between comets and asteroids is blurry, as some asteroids may contain ice, and comets may be fairly rocky. One of the chief distinctions is where you find them. Comets are concentrated in a region beyond Neptune and in a more distant comet concentration, called the Oort Cloud, about a light year from the Sun.

All told, there are potentially trillions of comets in the Solar System, though nearly all will never get anywhere near us. They stick to their wide orbits, the most distant potentially taking 30 million years for a single trip around the Sun. But, just as with asteroids, chance collisions and gravitational tugs occasionally set a comet into an orbit that takes it through the centre of the Solar System. Fortunately, comets' tails - streams of icy gaseous material vaporised by the Sun's heat - make them easier to spot. For instance, when the Hale-Bopp comet gets close to the Sun, it grows a tail spanning millions of kilometres. Comets and asteroids have played a critical role in our history

"If we detect a larger threat - the sort that could devastate a wide area or wipe out humanity - we'll need to alter its path"

"You don't have to go and stop each one. You just have to know that it's coming"

as a species. In fact, we most likely owe our very existence to them, a few times over.

First, of course, our planet formed from asteroids colliding and clumping together. But beyond that, many scientists believe that comets delivered much of the water and carbon-based molecules that set the stage for the beginning of terrestrial life, 3.8 billion years ago. Flash forward to 65 million years ago, and a foreign object intervened again. A massive asteroid or comet collision brought about a rapid shift in our atmosphere that caused the extinction of about 75 per cent of life on Earth, including the dinosaurs. While it was surely no picnic for our mammalian ancestors either, the elimination of so many predators ultimately gave them a chance to thrive and evolve.

Asteroids and comets may play a critical role in our future, too, but the next hit isn't likely to be so beneficial to us. Scientists estimate the sort of impact that took out the dinosaurs – a collision with a comet or asteroid measuring ten kilometres (6.2 miles) or greater – comes along on average every 50-100 million years, but any day could be the day.

Objects measuring 30-100 metres (165-328 feet), big enough to cause substantial local damage or kick up tidal waves, hit every few hundred years or so. The last one was the Tunguska event, a massive explosion caused by an estimated 40-metre (132-foot), 80,000-ton asteroid fragment bursting over Siberia in 1908. It claimed no human casualties, but only because it happened to strike an uninhabited region. With an explosive energy about 500 times more powerful than the Hiroshima bomb, it cleared millions of trees across a 40-kilometre (25-mile) area and generated a shockwave powerful enough to shatter windows and knock people down many miles away. If it had hit a major city, the impact would have been the most devastating disaster in human history.

Fortunately, the odds are against such a hit. About 71 per cent of the Earth's surface is ocean, making the sea the most likely destination for an impact. On top of that, huge, uninhabited areas of land, such as Antarctica, increase our odds. Because of this, we've been blissfully unaware of most hits throughout human history. In this sense, the Tunguska event was a stroke of luck. It woke us up to the risks, spurring us to search the sky for potential dangers.

We've had other reminders since, including the first observation of a spectacular impact with a fellow planet. In 1994, the comet Shoemaker-Levy 9 collided with Jupiter, breaking up in its atmosphere into 21 fragments, some as large as two kilometres (1.25 miles) in diameter. On Earth, an impact of this calibre would have brought about global destruction.

NASA's main objective is identifying and tracking potentially hazardous asteroids (PHAs), defined as objects measuring at least 100 metres (328 feet) that have the potential to get within 0.05 astronomical units (about 4.7 million miles) of Earth.

The key equipment is a powerful telescope that captures detailed images of the night sky with a charge-coupled device (CCD), the same array of light-sensitive cells at the heart of a digital camera. But, Yeomans explains, successful asteroid and comet-hunting ultimately depends on something a little more low-tech: "Persistence."

He describes a simple but painstaking process: "Basically, what they do is point their telescopes

Our eyes on the sky

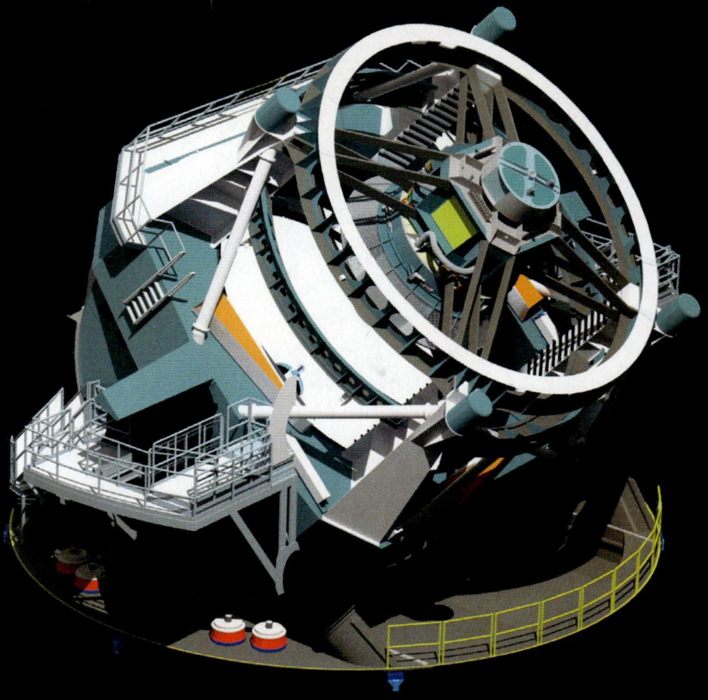

The Large Synoptic Survey Telescope (LSST)

When it comes online, the 8.4-metre (27.5-foot) LSST in Chile will mark a substantial leap forward. It will combine a large aperture, a wide field of view, a 3-billion-pixel camera, and advanced data processing to monitor the night sky. It will be able to capture 800 panoramic images every night, covering the visible sky twice in a week.

Maui Space Surveillance Site (MSSS)

The MSSS is part of a US Air Force satellite-tracking and research facility on Maui, Hawaii. It sits on the crest of Haleakala, an extinct volcano. The combination of minimal light pollution and a stable climate of dry, clean air gives the location exceptional year-round visibility.

In 2000, the Jet Propulsion Laboratory began using one of the two 1.2-metre (3.9-foot) telescopes to hunt for NEOs. To optimise the telescope for this, the US Air Force and JPL configured it for a larger field of view and installed a specialised camera.

In June, the MSSS team completed a modernisation of a range of equipment.

The Palomar Observatory

As a key observatory in the NASA Jet Propulsion Laboratory's NEO search programme going back to 1973, Palomar has been the site for thousands of discoveries, including hundreds of NEOs. The observatory is located in north San Diego county, California, and is owned and operated by the California Institute of Technology, which partners with JPL, Cornell, and many other institutions on a wide range of projects.

The observatory is home to five telescopes, including the 508-centimetre (200-inch) Hale, which was the world's largest telescope when it went into operation in 1947. The telescopes have seen regular upgrades, including a camera for NEO observations, the Near-Earth Asteroid Tracker, installed in 2001.

NASA BOUNDARY FOR POTENTIAL HAZARDOUS ASTEROID DESIGNATION
7,500,000km

Approaching threats, closer than the Moon

390,000km
NAME: 1999 AN10
DATE: AUGUST 2027
Soon after asteroid AN10's discovery in 1999, observations suggested it could get as close as 30,577km (18,999 miles) to Earth. Additional data puts it farther out.

800m

MOON ORBIT
385,000km

381,774km
NAME: 99942 APOPHIS
DATE: APRIL 2171
In 2004, initial observations suggested a 2.7 per cent probability that Apophis would hit in 2029. It was briefly a 4 on the Torino Scale, the high rating record, before additional observations ruled out an impact.

270m

332,000km
NAME: 2005 WY55
DATE: MAY 2065
Astronomers discovered Asteroid WY55 in November of 2005, using the Spacewatch telescope at the University of Arizona's Lunar and Planetary Laboratory.

200m

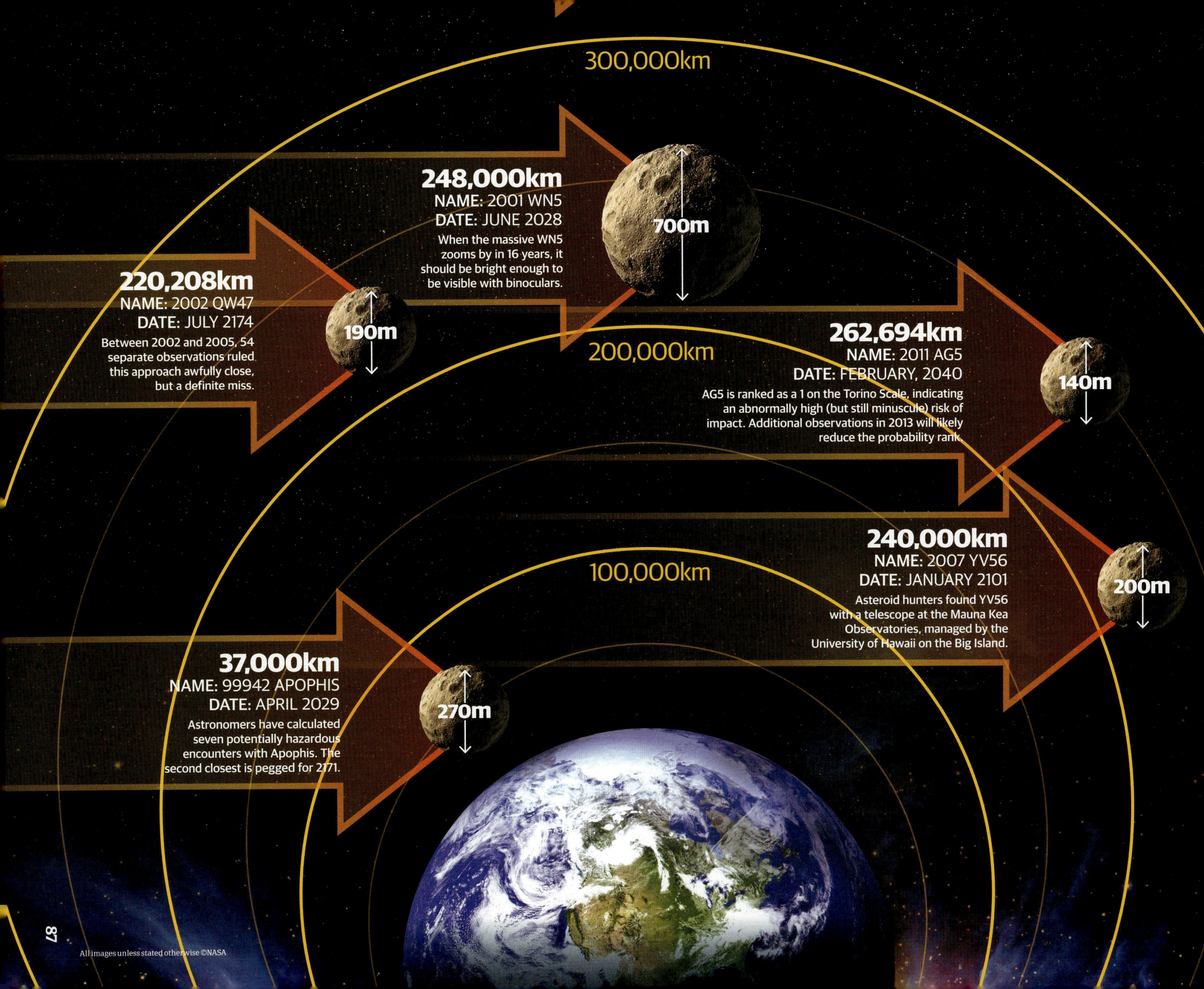
300,000km
200,000km
100,000km
248,000km
NAME: 2001 WN5
DATE: JUNE 2028
When the massive WN5 zooms by in 16 years, it should be bright enough to be visible with binoculars.
700m
220,208km
NAME: 2002 QW47
DATE: JULY 2174
Between 2002 and 2005, 54 separate observations ruled this approach awfully close, but a definite miss.
190m
262,694km
NAME: 2011 AG5
DATE: FEBRUARY, 2040
AG5 is ranked as a 1 on the Torino Scale, indicating an abnormally high (but still minuscule) risk of impact. Additional observations in 2013 will likely reduce the probability rank.
140m
240,000km
NAME: 2007 YV56
DATE: JANUARY 2101
Asteroid hunters found YV56 with a telescope at the Mauna Kea Observatories, managed by the University of Hawaii on the Big Island.
200m
37,000km
NAME: 99942 APOPHIS
DATE: APRIL 2029
Astronomers have calculated seven potentially hazardous encounters with Apophis. The second closest is pegged for 2171.
270m

at a region of the dark sky and take a CCD image, come back to that same region 15 minutes later and take another image, come back to that same region 15 minutes later and take a third, or a fourth image. Then you can compare those three or four images to see if anything in the field has moved during the times that you took those images. The stars, of course, will remain stationary and will not have appeared to have moved, but any near-Earth asteroids will have appeared to move from one image to another, and the computers are good at picking up motions like that."

While it can be monotonous, computer technology has expedited the process immensely. Astronomers used to do it the hard way, examining two photographic plates under a microscope. "You would compare the images taken a few minutes apart one after the other, back and forth," Yeomans says. "The stars hadn't moved between when the two images were taken but the asteroid would have, so its image would appear to be hopping back and forth."

Today, computers make some of the discoveries themselves. Yeomans says the most successful search observatory today, the Catalina Sky Survey near Tuscon, Arizona, depends on close human-computer collaboration. "They routinely have the computer find candidates, and then a human observer looks at them to confirm that, in fact, the object that the computer picked was a near-Earth asteroid. So these computer programs, at least in this one case with the Catalina Sky Survey, don't actually completely replace humans. They simply make it easier for the humans to consider only the likely suspects."

Yeomans says the key is getting high-fidelity images of large sections of the night sky: "Ideally, you would like to have a telescope with a large aperture, so you could collect a lot of light, and you'd have a wide field of view that covers a lot of sky. I think the perfect telescope would be one that went very deep to find faint objects and then at the same time covered a lot of sky so that you could cover a fair bit of the accessible sky every night."

Asteroid hunters have had to make do with less than perfect equipment, Yeomans says. "In fact, most of the telescopes that are currently being used were not built for the express purpose of finding near-Earth objects. So, they're one-metre class aperture - that is, their mirrors are usually one metre. There are a couple that are one and a half metres, 1.8 metres. But they weren't built with near-Earth object discovery in mind, so they're not all that wide field."

The NEO watch is getting a major upgrade with the Panoramic Survey Telescope & Rapid Response System (Pan-STARRS), a new telescope facility on top of the volcano Haleakala on the island of Maui. Designed with near-Earth object observation in mind, the system will boast 3-16 times the collecting power of other telescopes. A larger field of view will allow the system to scan the sky much more quickly, while massive CCD arrays will be able to pick up far fainter objects than other NEO survey telescopes. With 1.4 billion pixels apiece, the system's four cameras will be the largest in existence. Its prototype telescope, PS1, began regular survey operations in 2010. The finished four-telescope array will follow.

In the future, Yeomans is looking forward to the Large Synoptic Survey Telescope (LSST), a facility

Massive Earth impacts

1. Wolfe Creek Crater

Location: Australia
Size: 1.2km (0.7 miles)
Age: 300,000 years
While the crater was long-known to the Aboriginal people, Europeans didn't discover it until 1947, while conducting an aerial survey.

6. Aorounga Crater

Location: Chad
Size: 13km (8 miles)
Age: 350 million years
Additional circular features near the larger crater indicate a multiple impact event.

2. Pingualuit Crater
Location: Canada
Size: 3.4km (2.1 miles)
Age: 1.4 million years
As a lake with no connection to other bodies of water, Pingualuit Crater has preserved sediments from before the Pleistocene ice age, capturing a wealth of geological history.

3. Chicxulub
Location: Mexico
Size: 200km (124 miles)
Age: 65 million years
Scientists believe this massive crater in the Yucatan Peninsula is probably from the comet or asteroid impact that killed the dinosaurs.

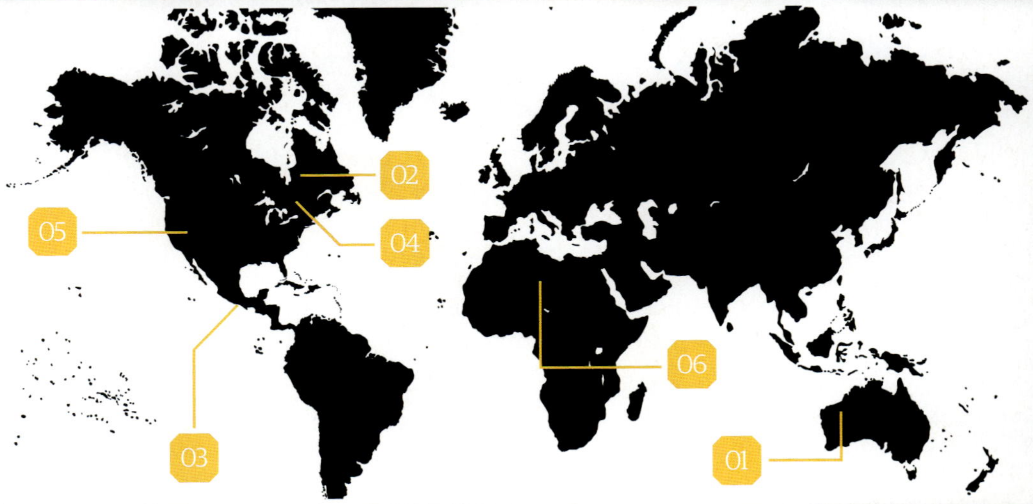

5. Barringer Crater
Location: USA
Size: 1.2km (0.7 miles)
Age: 49,000 years
Geological research suggests the crater came from a 45m (148ft) nickel-iron asteroid, which mostly vaporised on impact.

4. Manicouagan Crater
Location: Canada
Size: 70km (43.5 miles)
Age: 206-214 million years
Today, the huge crater – two semicircular lakes with a protruding land in the middle – is one of the more striking natural formations visible from space.

in Chile that will deliver unprecedented detail when it comes online around 2020. "It's an 8.4-metre (27.5-foot) aperture, and it's extremely wide-field. So although it's not being built expressly for near-Earth objects, they simply can't avoid them."

In the effort to catalogue potential hazards, discovering a new comet or asteroid is only the beginning. To assess the possibility of Earth impact, astronomers need to figure out where each is going, which means pinpointing its position and trajectory.

Yeomans says stars provide the starting point: "Say you've got four stars in the background and you've got an asteroid in the foreground. You can measure the distance between asteroid and star 1, the distance between asteroid and star 2, the distance between asteroid and star 3 and so on. Since you know the positions of the stars you can determine the position of the asteroid when you took that image. If you have a bunch of these observations, then you know where the asteroid was - its angular position in the sky."

The key to improving accuracy, he explains, is multiple observations: "As the asteroid is observed more and more, day after day, we get more of these observations, and so the orbit gets better and better. What we do is we start with a preliminary orbit and then we project that orbit forward in time through all of the observations we have in hand, and we ask the question, 'Well, how well did that preliminary orbit match where that asteroid was observed to have been?' Then we say, 'Oh well, it wasn't a perfect fit, but we can use the differences between the observed and the predicted position of the asteroid to refine the orbit and the next time we observe it we'll know better where it is.' We can predict its motion much better in the future as we get more and more observations on which to base the orbit."

The necessary follow-up observations have a surprising source. "The majority I would say are done by amateurs, actually," Yeomans says. "They're really amateurs in name only because they're extremely sophisticated observers, most of them."

Yeomans says the hub is the Minor Planet Center in Cambridge, Massachusetts, which acts as clearing house for all data on the Solar System: "The amateurs, or the professionals for that matter, will take their data, report the time at which they

"We had an object about the size of a small or fairly good-sized automobile that actually hit in October 2008. It was discovered about 24 hours in advance"

observed, and the so-called right ascension and declination, which are two measurements of where that asteroid was at that given time. They will send those observations to the Minor Planet Center, and the Minor Planet Center will do a preliminary orbit and ask the observer community to follow up. Then amateurs take a look at the Minor Planet Center's follow-up list and say, 'All right, if this object has been just discovered, it needs additional observations so that the orbits can be computed more accurately.'"

With sufficient observations in hand, it's time to crunch the numbers. Yeomans says the Minor Planet Center sends preliminary orbit data to the Jet Propulsion Laboratory in Pasadena, California, as well as a team in Pisa, Italy: "As more and more data comes in, we in our office here and our colleagues in Pisa also, run the orbits for these objects forward 100 years and see if there's any interesting close-Earth approaches. And if there are, we also do impact probability calculations."

To understand the risk of impact, astronomers consider the uncertainty ellipsoid - the possible positions and orbits of the object - and then perform a Monte Carlo analysis to assess the chance of a hit.

"The Monte Carlo analysis takes every orbit in that uncertainty ellipsoid, even the ones at the edges, runs them forward 100 years, and asks will that orbit run into the Earth," Yeomans says. "Then you take another one inside the uncertainty ellipsoid at the current time and run it forward 100 years and ask will that orbit hit the Earth at any time. If a hundred out of a thousand hit, you have a ten per cent impact probability."

To date, Yeomans says, the analysis hasn't shown any objects with a high likelihood of hitting us: "Dozens of them have non-zero impact probability, but most of them are extremely small. They're 10^{-5}, 10^{-6}. There are none that reach one per cent. There are some that reach 1 in 500 or 1 in 300. That's about as high as we get at the moment."

The NEO Program hopes to locate at least 90 per cent of the asteroids and comets that approach Earth

Inside an asteroid

Yeomans says NASA's first priority has been to find the asteroids that are big enough to cause worldwide problems if they struck Earth: "Their initial goal was to find at least 90 per cent of the near-Earth asteroids that were larger than a kilometre (0.6 miles). There's about a thousand of those, and we've discovered already about 94 per cent, about 940 of them. And none of them represent a threat in the next century."

While the search for the missing six per cent goes on, the hunters have broadened their scope. "Now NASA's goal is to find 90 per cent of the objects 140 metres (459 feet) and larger, because those are the objects that cause regional damage or tsunamis should they hit," Yeomans says. "About 40 per cent of those have been found, and none of those represent a significant threat in the next hundred years."

For smaller asteroids, Yeomans reports more modest progress: "When you get down to around 30 metres [98 feet], we've found less than one per cent of the total population, because there's so many of them. For those guys, it might make sense to have a telescopic survey engineered to find them on their last approach, because you're not going to discover them until they get very close or they're about to hit."

Yeomans says, in these cases, an early warning system makes more sense than deflecting the threat. "If it's only a 30-metre [98-foot] object, it would be sufficient to find it a few days in advance of an impact because you know the line along which it will strike, and if that line went through any populated areas you could evacuate. More than likely it would hit over the ocean and not be a problem. We could do the calculation and say, 'All right, if it's going to hit the Earth, it's going to hit along this line, which could run from South America out to the Pacific Ocean to China, say.' And if any of that line goes near a population centre, we could say, 'All right, you folks would be wise to move a couple of hundred kilometres from that line.' You don't have to go and stop each one; you just have to know it's coming."

If we detect a larger threat – the sort that could devastate a wide area or wipe out humanity – we'll need to alter its path. Contrary to Hollywood predictions, blowing it up wouldn't be a good option, as it would only create more chunks to contend with.

Yeomans describes the more practical reality: "The easiest technique would simply be to run into it with a spacecraft and slow it down or speed it up so that in 20-30 years, when it was predicted to hit the Earth, it wouldn't. We would alter its trajectory just a bit, a millimetre or two a second."

NASA took this plan through a successful dry run in 2005 with its Deep Impact probe. "We purposely ran into a comet, Tempel 1," Yeomans says. "But the technology that was employed would be the same that would be used to hit an asteroid. So, we've demonstrated that it can be done. All you have to do is find it early enough that will give you enough time to get your spacecraft up there and run into it several years in advance of the projected impact because you need time for the change in velocity to build into a change in the position at the time."

Another possibility is to attach solar sails that would use the Sun's energy to nudge the object into a different orbit. Some have even proposed detonating a nuclear bomb far enough away that it doesn't break the asteroid apart, but irradiates the surface, making the asteroid recoil enough to shift its trajectory.

The elaborate schemes are conjecture at this point. "For my money, the simplest and easiest technique is the best," Yeomans says. "And simply running into it, if you have the time, is the way to go." ●

The Torino Scale

The Torino Scale is to near-Earth objects what the Richter Scale is to earthquakes. Astronomers assign each potentially hazardous asteroid and comet a hazard score of 1-10, based on a combination of its impact probability and estimated kinetic energy. The number score indicates the specific threat and recommended course of action, while the colour bands show the general danger level at a glance. The scale is named for Torino, Italy, the site of a 1999 international conference on near-Earth objects that adopted the currently used revised version of the scoring system.

No hazard	0	At this level the likelihood of an asteroid or comet striking Earth is effectively zero.
Normal	1	A near pass is predicted, but it poses no unusual level of danger and a hit is extremely unlikely.
Meriting attention by astronomers	2	Makes a near pass and may merit attention, but inspection will likely reduce threat.
	3	A collision has a 1 per cent or greater chance, capable of localised destruction.
	4	The threat of a collision remains one per cent, but observations will probably deem it no threat.
Threatening	5	A close encounter that could cause regional devastation. Critical attention needed.
	6	Poses a serious but uncertain threat of global catastrophe, requiring contingency planning.
	7	A close encounter that would require immediate planning if it is within a century.
Certain collisions	8	A collision with Earth is certain. Localised destruction or a tsunami will result.
	9	Unprecedented devastation, including major tsunami. Occurs every 100,000 years.
	10	May threaten the future of civilisation. Occur less than once per 100,000 years.

Secrets of the Oort cloud

At the fringes of the Solar System lies a vast cloud of icy bodies. Like a museum, this region holds the pieces of the Solar System as it first formed

This icy swarm was first proposed by Dutch astronomer Jan Hendrik Oort, who said that some comets might come from a cloud of millions of small objects at the edge of the Solar System.

Some comets are frequent visitors to our Solar System, such as Halley's Comet. These are believed to come from an area just beyond Neptune, known as the Kuiper belt. The Oort cloud comets, however, are from a different realm altogether. The cloud probably has anywhere from 0.1 to 2 trillion icy comets lurking between 5,000 and 100,000 AU from the Sun.

We haven't been able to spot objects in the cloud yet, because it is so far from Earth and the objects would be tiny. This leaves them out of reach of many of today's telescopes. But using numerical models, astronomers have come up with a typical life cycle of a comet originating from this cloud.

Every so often, a stray bit of gravity kicks an icy body out of the cloud and towards the inner Solar System. They then get sucked in to the Sun's gravitational well and fly past Earth.

As a comet gets closer to the Sun, heat and solar particles hit it and begin to melt the frozen ice. Gas and debris stretches behind the comet, producing spectacular tails that are sometimes visible from our planet.

Since these comets come from so far away, it can take thousands of years for them to make one trip around the Sun. Jan Oort observed that these so-called 'long-period comets' had a similar inclination, which implied that they must come from a similar origin.

The Oort cloud is so vast that it has at least two separate regions: an outer cloud and a more populated Hills cloud in the inner region. The inner region, first detailed by astronomer JG Hills, would occur as the gravity of passing stars and Jupiter pulled on the icy bodies after their formation.

Since the Oort cloud is too far away for us to study right now, our best bet in understanding its composition is to observe the comets that swing by our Solar System. It's hard to send a spacecraft out to comets because they are so unpredictable. Funding a mission takes years, and then there's the work that needs to go into plotting trajectories to make sure the spacecraft is in the right place at the right time.

For that reason, the spacecraft that have visited comets, such as NASA's Stardust, stick to those that have predictable, regular trips through the Solar System. For the Oort comets, astronomers rely on observations from the ground or space telescopes.

We can still see quite a bit from a distance. In 1997, scientists used two NASA observatories - the Hubble Space Telescope and the International Ultraviolet Explorer - to check out what was happening as Comet Hale-Bopp swung near the Earth.

Astronomers were surprised to see that water ice in the nucleus of the comet changed directly from a frozen state to a gas (called sublimation) at a different rate than other types of ices on the comet. This essentially rewrote our understanding of comet nuclei.

Before, we thought that the comet's water ice acted as a container for all the other ices. If that had been the case, we would have seen the sublimation happen at similar rates.

Astronomers are now awaiting another Oort cloud visitor: Comet ISON. It is on its way to the inner Solar System and, if predictions are right, will put on a bright show around November and December 2013. ●

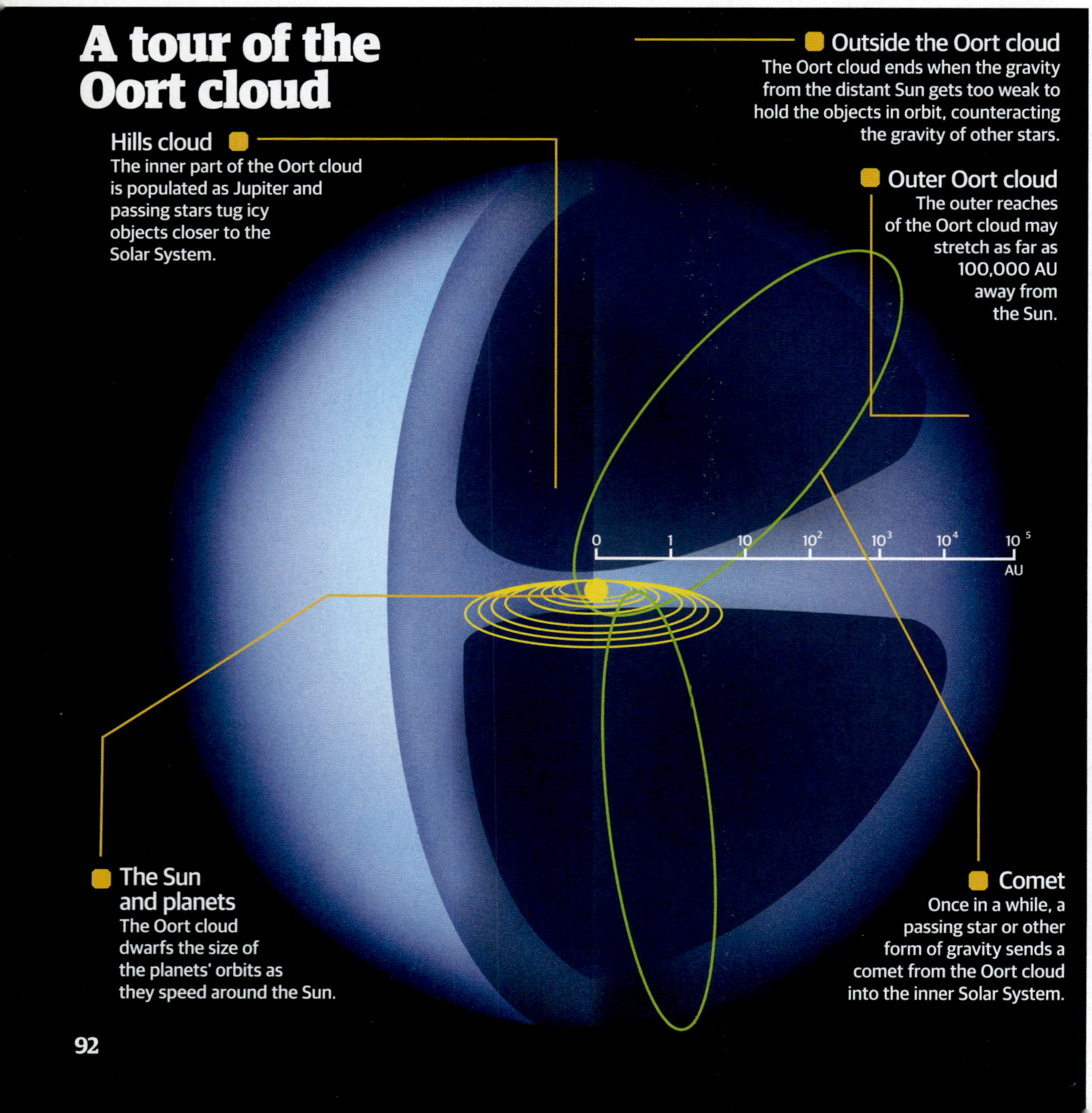

The existence of the Oort cloud was theorised by astronomer Jan Oort

Where is the Oort cloud?

Deep Space

Take a look at what lies past our own galaxy

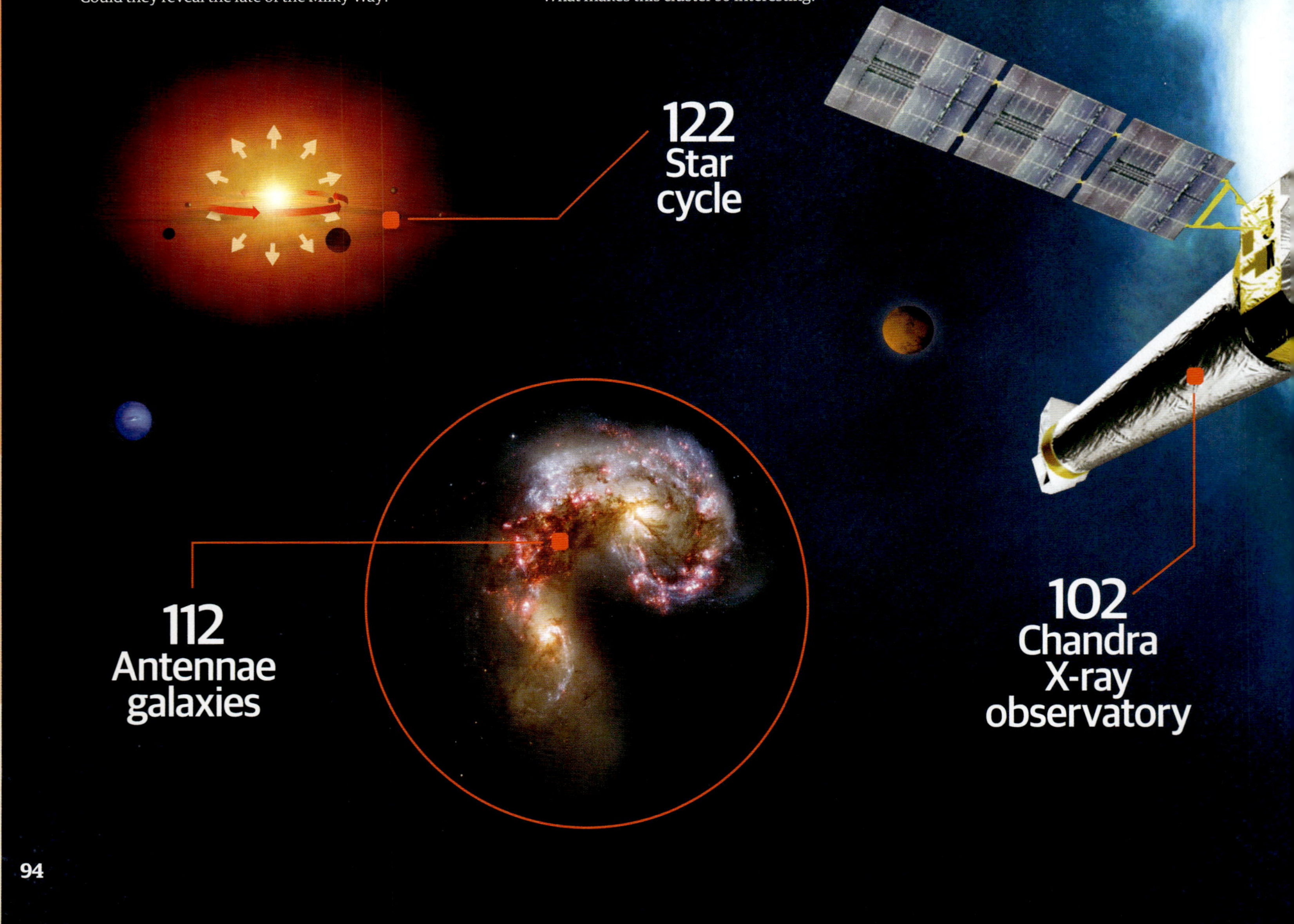

©NASA, Alamy

Exploring deep space

Join us on a journey beyond the frozen orbit of Pluto and into a universe dominated by supermassive black holes, colossal galaxy clusters and mysterious 'dark' matter

Imagine the brilliance and clarity of a night sky on the Greek island of Samos in 300 BCE. No city lights to drown out the view of the thick streak of the Milky Way and the countless bright stars in every direction. This is the sky the Greek philosopher Epicurus was gazing at when he wrote, "There are infinite worlds both like and unlike this world of ours. We must believe that in all worlds there are living creatures and planets and other things we see in this world."

Nearly 2,300 years later, the Hubble Space Telescope trained its powerful eye for ten straight days on a single patch of the night sky. The picture it took, known as the Hubble Deep Field, would have floored Epicurus. The image shows more than 3,000 galaxies, some that are millions of times larger than our own Milky Way, and each containing billions of stars orbited by incalculable scores of planets. Incredibly, this cosmic panorama represents only the smallest fraction of the visible night sky. Extrapolate this image to the entire observable universe - 93 billion light years across - and the results are staggering. With a nearly infinite number of solar systems, Epicurus would ask again, what are the chances that we are really alone?

Modern astronomers are closer than ever to answering some of the most ancient of questions: Where did life on Earth come from? How are stars and planets formed? How big is the universe? How old is it? And when, if ever, will it come to an end? The answers, we believe, are out there, if only we can see deep enough into space. The Hubble Deep Field image hints at the nearly infinite potential for discovery. Now it's time to get out there and explore.

At the edge of our Solar System are two frozen regions: the Kuiper belt and the Oort cloud. Pluto is a citizen of the Kuiper belt, as are more than 70,000 other icy rocks. The Kuiper belt covers a region that is 30 to 55 astronomical units (AU) from the Sun. One astronomical unit is equal to the Earth's distance from the Sun (150 million kilometres or 93 million miles). To compare, Jupiter is less than 5 AU from the Sun.

The Kuiper belt was discovered in 1992 during a search for slow moving objects (SMOs) in the far reaches of the Solar System. It is widely believed that the Kuiper belt is the source for most short-period comets, those that orbit the Sun every 200 years or less. Halley's Comet is the most famous of the bunch. Astronomical study of the Kuiper belt is critical to understanding planet formation in all solar systems, not just ours. Astronomers currently believe that Kuiper belt objects are the oldest remnants of a tremendous disc of matter that surrounded our young Sun roughly 4.6 billion years ago. The Sun's gravity helped to condense most of the matter into our planets, but the material in the Kuiper belt was too far away for gravity to have its full effect, leaving a trail of scattered debris.

The Oort cloud is even more distant than the Kuiper belt, occupying the huge swath of space between 5,000 and 100,000 AU from the Sun. Astronomers estimate that as many as 2 trillion icy objects float through this no man's land of interstellar space. In fact, the movements of some of these Oort cloud objects are influenced less by the Sun's gravity than other stars. In 2003, astronomers discovered a distant dwarf planet occupying the inner reaches of the Oort cloud. Named Sedna after a famously frosty Inuit goddess, the dwarf planet orbits the Sun every 10,500 years, is less than a third of the diameter of the Moon and has an estimated surface temperature of -261°C (-438°F).

NASA's New Horizons spacecraft will be the first to explore the Kuiper belt up close. The probe, launched in 2006, is scheduled to reach Pluto in 2015 and tour the Kuiper belt from 2016 to 2020. Objects in the Kuiper belt are believed to be rich with organic (carbon-bearing) molecules and covered with water ice. New Horizons will closely analyse Pluto, its large moon Charon and other Kuiper belt objects for clues to our own planet's evolution.

"Hubble has surveyed 30 nearby galaxies and found supermassive black holes at each of their cores"

One of the most amazing things about deep space exploration is that it doubles as time travel. The deeper you gaze into space with a telescope, the further you see back in time. If you view a star that is 400 light years away, you are seeing the star as it looked 400 years ago. If you use a really powerful telescope, like the twin giants at the Keck Observatory in Hawaii, you might see a galaxy that is hundreds of millions of light years away, or hundreds of millions of years in the past. Astronomers use their powerful new instruments as 'time machines' to explore the evolution of the universe as a way of understanding how we got here and where we might be going.

As we continue our journey into deep space, some of the closest objects - on a cosmic scale - to our Solar System are nebulae, those brilliantly colourful cosmic displays of swirling dust, gas and newborn stars. Two of the most famous nearby nebulae are the Orion and Horsehead nebulae, 1,300 and 1,500 light years from Earth respectively. A light year, which is the distance travelled at the speed of light for an entire year, is much longer than an AU, roughly 10 trillion kilometres or 6 trillion miles.

First discovered in the 1800s, the Horsehead Nebula is a thick cloud of cool dust swirling along a large magnetic field. Until recently, nebulae were thought to be nothing more than diffuse blobs of interstellar gas and dust. But more powerful telescopes, especially those scanning for infrared light waves, have recast nebulae as cradles of star formation. Inside those thick clouds are protostars, relatively cool balls of condensing gas. If a protostar never gets big enough and hot enough to trigger a thermonuclear reaction, it's labelled a brown dwarf. But if its gravity continues to draw in hydrogen, the heat will convert that hydrogen to helium and a star is born.

In 2011, the European Space Agency's infrared Herschel Space Observatory uncovered a string of fledgling stars hidden in the haze of the Orion Nebula. The stars were observed to fluctuate in intensity by as much as 20 per cent over the course of a few weeks. Astronomers theorise that the variable intensity could result from clumps of gas moving from the outer edge of the forming star into the centre, stoking the flames of the thermonuclear reaction. Discoveries like this show how much we have yet to learn about star formation.

Another mystery lies at the very centre of our galaxy, roughly 25,000 light years from the Sun. In 1997, the Hubble Space Telescope gave us the first clear images of the stars closest to the theoretical centre of the Milky Way. Some of the stars

An artist's view of star formation in the early universe

The observable universe

Space is almost entirely empty. One of the hardest things to wrap our heads around is the totality of the nothingness that surrounds us. When considering the distances on this chart, remember that a light year is the distance travelled over an entire year of travelling at the speed of light.

1. GRB 090429B

NASA's Swift satellite is a burst-spotter. Gamma ray bursts, or GRBs, are the most energetic events in the universe, formed during the dramatic death of a supermassive star. On 29 April 2009, a five-second burst of gamma rays triggered the Swift satellite's Burst Alert Telescope. The GRB faded after only ten seconds, but the data collected during that short span proved that GRB 090429B was the new record-holder for the furthest observable object in the universe.

2. The edge of the observable universe

Our view of the universe - 93 billion light years in diameter - is limited by its age. Here's why. Roughly 13.75 billion years ago, during the super-hot expansion of matter after the Big Bang, radiation was blocked by hordes of free electrons. When the universe began to cool, those free electrons joined with elemental particles to form the first atoms, and radiation was free to shine forth. This 'first light', known as Cosmic Microwave Background radiation, switched on 379,000 years after the Big Bang. Thanks to the Wilkinson Microwave Anisotropy Probe, we have a full picture of the observable universe from that first light until today.

3. Hubble Ultra Deep Field

Between 24 September 2003 and 16 January 2004, the Hubble Space Telescope trained its eyes on a tiny patch of sky one-tenth the diameter of the Moon. This ultra-long exposure, taken by two separate cameras, produced our deepest image of the universe dating back over 13 billion years. The Hubble Ultra Deep Field image is like a cosmic core sample. Of the more than 10,000 galaxies in the image, the brightest are younger star formations while the faint red specs represent some of the oldest galaxies in the universe.

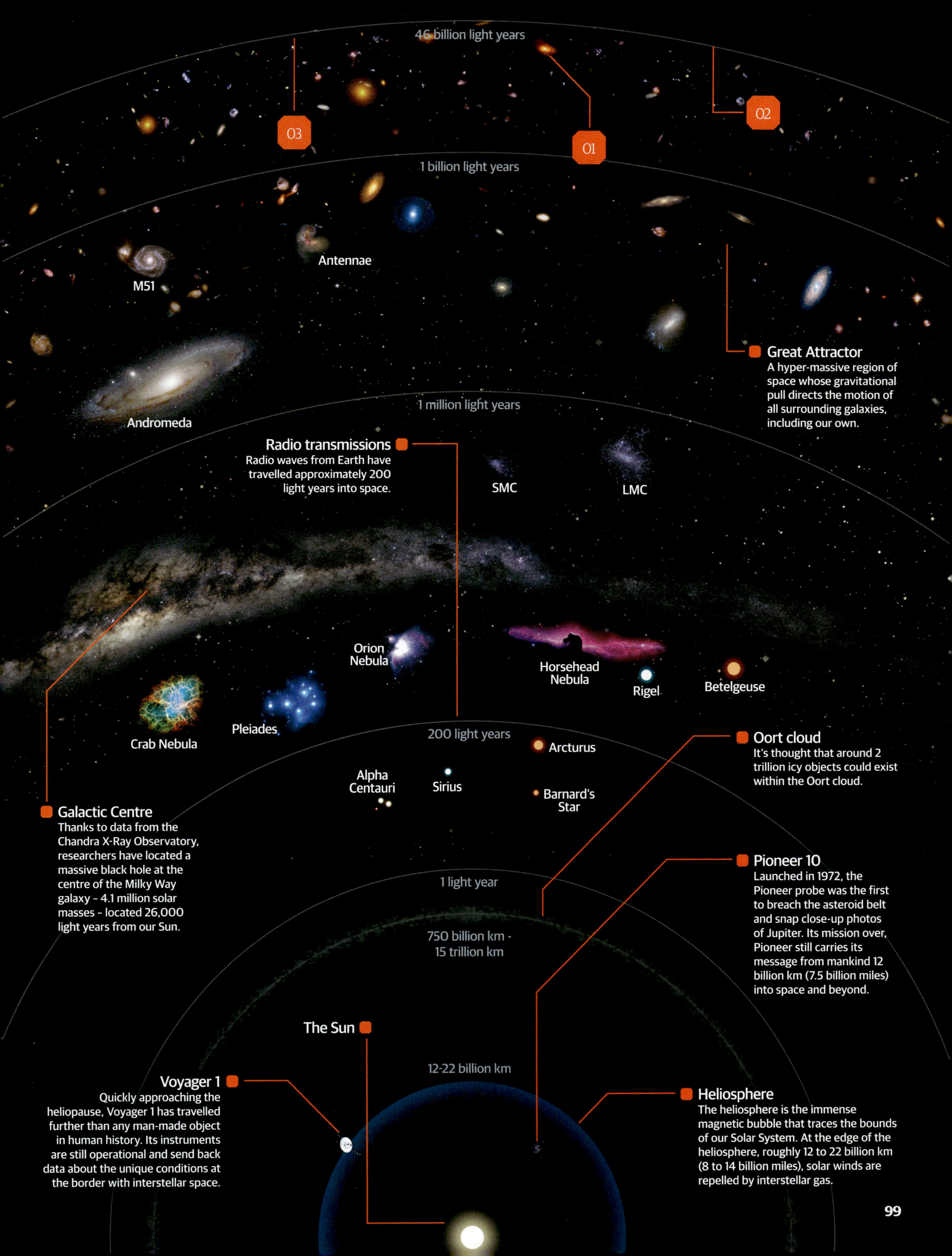

46 billion light years
03
01
02
1 billion light years
Antennae
M51
Great Attractor
A hyper-massive region of space whose gravitational pull directs the motion of all surrounding galaxies, including our own.
Andromeda
1 million light years
Radio transmissions
Radio waves from Earth have travelled approximately 200 light years into space.
SMC
LMC
Orion Nebula
Horsehead Nebula
Rigel
Betelgeuse
Crab Nebula
Pleiades
200 light years
Arcturus
Oort cloud
It's thought that around 2 trillion icy objects could exist within the Oort cloud.
Alpha Centauri
Sirius
Barnard's Star
Galactic Centre
Thanks to data from the Chandra X-Ray Observatory, researchers have located a massive black hole at the centre of the Milky Way galaxy - 4.1 million solar masses - located 26,000 light years from our Sun.
Pioneer 10
Launched in 1972, the Pioneer probe was the first to breach the asteroid belt and snap close-up photos of Jupiter. Its mission over, Pioneer still carries its message from mankind 12 billion km (7.5 billion miles) into space and beyond.
1 light year
750 billion km - 15 trillion km
The Sun
12-22 billion km
Voyager 1
Quickly approaching the heliopause, Voyager 1 has travelled further than any man-made object in human history. Its instruments are still operational and send back data about the unique conditions at the border with interstellar space.
Heliosphere
The heliosphere is the immense magnetic bubble that traces the bounds of our Solar System. At the edge of the heliosphere, roughly 12 to 22 billion km (8 to 14 billion miles), solar winds are repelled by interstellar gas.

were rocketing around a central point at a rate of 5,000 km/s (3,000 miles/s). To compare, our Sun cruises through space at a leisurely 220 km/s (137 miles/s). The only thing that could cause such a high-velocity orbit is a central object of colossal mass. Since no such object was visible, astronomers theorised the existence of a supermassive black hole. More recently, the Chandra X-ray Observatory detected large jets of X-rays pouring from the galactic centre, confirmation that a black hole is swallowing up tremendous amounts of matter.

The supermassive black hole at the centre of the Milky Way - named Sagittarius A* - has a diameter less than half the distance between Earth and Sun, but is 4 million times more massive than the Sun. Hubble has surveyed 30 nearby galaxies and found supermassive black holes at each of their cores. Some astronomers theorise that black holes play a necessary role in galaxy formation, providing the seed gravity to pull in free-floating star clusters. As the young stars shed interstellar gas, the black hole feeds on this material to grow larger and stronger, pulling even more objects into its orbit.

Moving still deeper into space, we exit our galaxy entirely. From a distance of 500,000 light years, we see that our spiral Milky Way exudes a gravitational pull on a series of orbiting dwarf galaxies. The two largest dwarf galaxies are called the Large and Small Magellanic Clouds. Bright and clear, they are the most distant cosmic objects visible by the naked eye at 160,000 light years and 200,000 light years respectively. The Small Magellanic Cloud holds 3 billion stars and the Large contains 33 billion.

In 2006, the Hubble Space Telescope helped to measure the movement of these galaxies. Hubble scientists were surprised to learn that the Milky Way's largest orbiting galaxies weren't orbiting us at all. Instead, they are cosmic visitors on a much larger and erratic journey that has only brought them into our vicinity once before. This explains why the clouds contain so much interstellar gas - which is usually robbed by the larger central galaxy - and why they are such productive star factories.

Travelling beyond our neighbouring galaxies, we arrive at the closest large spiral galaxy, Andromeda. At 2.5 million light years from the Sun, Andromeda has a similar structure to the Milky Way, a many-armed spiral

What we've seen

Stunning images from the furthest reaches of the universe

GRB 090429B
Created by the death of a massive star 30 times larger than our Sun, GRB 090429B is currently the furthest known object in the universe, as well as the oldest.

Milky Way
This image taken by the ESO's Very Large Telescope offers the most detailed view yet of the heart of the Milky Way Galaxy.

Large Magellanic Cloud
This image shows the star-forming region 30 Doradus in the Large Magellanic Cloud dwarf galaxy, which, at around 160,000 light years away, can still be viewed by the naked eye.

HUDF-JD2
Massive galaxy HUDF-JD2 was the most distant galaxy discovered in the Hubble Ultra Deep Field image in 2005. It is most likely being viewed when the universe was around 800 million years old.

M31
This X-ray and infrared image of the Andromeda Galaxy was taken by the Chandra and Spitzer telescopes. Andromeda is around 2.5 million light years from Earth.

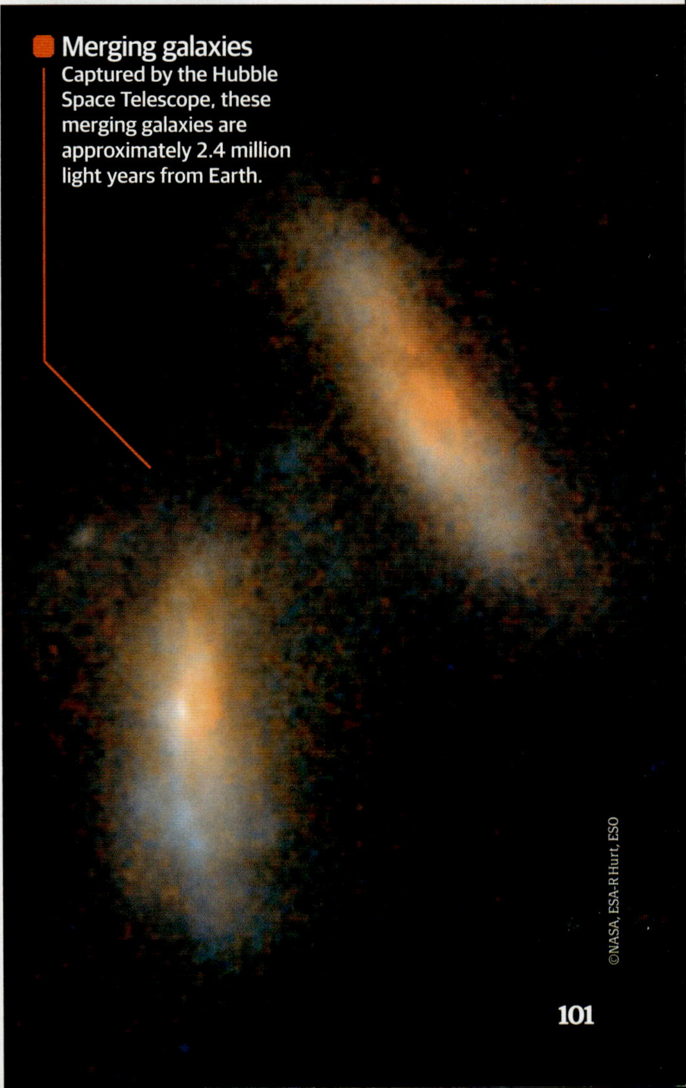

Merging galaxies
Captured by the Hubble Space Telescope, these merging galaxies are approximately 2.4 million light years from Earth.

How we see into deep space

The telescopes that let us look into the universe's past

Chandra X-ray Observatory

Location: Between 16,000 and 133,000km from Earth

X-rays are high-energy photons produced by some of the hottest regions in the universe, including exploding stars and matter being eaten up by black holes. Since X-rays are deflected by particles in and near the Earth's atmosphere, astronomers set their sites on a space telescope. Since its launch in 1999, Chandra has explored the black hole at the centre of the Milky Way and discovered countless others across the universe.

It discovered a supermassive cluster of galaxies 5.7 billion light years away with a central galaxy that churns out more than 740 new stars a year. The previous record holder spawned 150 new stars a year.

Hubble Space Telescope

Location: 560km above Earth

Launched in 1990, the Hubble Space Telescope is the oldest and most famous of NASA's space telescope fleet. The heart of the Hubble is its 2.4m (94.5in) primary mirror, which deflects light onto a secondary mirror before being captured by any of five different on-board cameras. Some of the most striking early Hubble images are from the visible light portion of the spectrum. Hubble transmits 18 DVDs worth of data every day. By analysing this data, researchers have measured the age of the universe, discovered the role of dark energy and revolutionised our understanding of the origins of the universe.

The colossal mass of the universe should be slowing its expansion, but Hubble helped confirm that a 'weak force' called dark energy had overtaken gravity and was accelerating the universe's expansion.

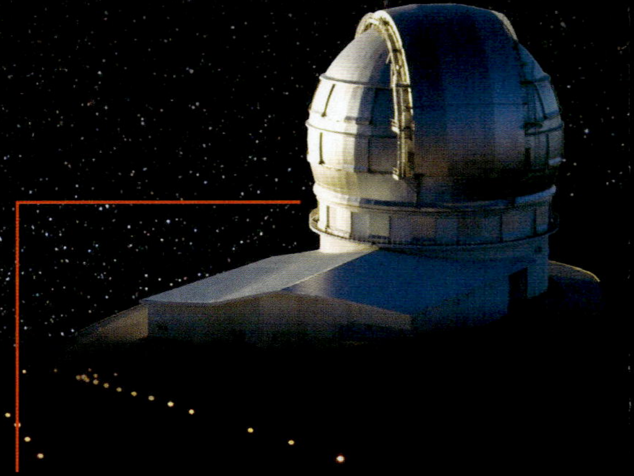

Large Binocular Telescope

Location: Arizona, USA

The Large Binocular Telescope employs the largest mirror surface in the world to detect the furthest objects in the universe. Each of its concave mirrors is 894mm (35in) thick at the edges and weighs 16,000kg (35,000lb). Using adaptive optics, the LBT cancels out atmospheric distortion to produce image resolution ten times greater than its rivals.

The LBT captured the first glimpse of the innermost planet in a galaxy 128 light years away, using adaptive optics to smooth the distortion of the nearby star.

South African Large Telescope

Location: Sutherland, South Africa

The South African Large Telescope can detect light from objects a billion times too faint to be seen by the naked eye. SALT's 11m (36ft) mirror is split into 91 hexagonal components. SALT scans the night skies over South Africa's Karoo Desert searching for hints to the origin of the planets, stars, galaxies and universe.

Researchers at SALT spotted a solar system with two small stars so closely aligned that they orbit each other every couple of hours. Orbiting the twin stars are two colossal planets with masses six to eight times greater than Jupiter.

Gran Telescopio Canarias

Location: Canary Islands

The Gran Telescopio Canarias is one of the most technologically advanced stargazers in the world. The CanariCam 'sees' the full electromagnetic spectrum, plus it uses coronagraphy to mask the glare of distant stars to spot unseen exoplanets. Its other advanced piece of imaging equipment is called OSIRIS and is mounted with tunable filters for zeroing in on a portion of the spectrum.

Researchers from the University of Florida peered over 9 billion years into the past to refute the idea that galaxies in the young universe were more dense than today.

Spitzer Space Telescope
Location: 159 million km from Earth
The Spitzer Space Telescope is the largest infrared telescope ever launched into space. Any object in the universe that has a temperature emits radiation in the infrared spectrum. Spitzer is especially useful for detecting cosmic objects that are shrouded in thick clouds of cosmic dust.

Using Spitzer, researchers spotted two tiny planets orbiting the Sun from an extreme distance near the Kuiper belt. One of the planets, Eris, was larger than Pluto, convincing the International Astronomical Union to re-categorise Pluto and its two new friends as dwarf planets.

Keck Observatory
Location: Hawaii, USA
The twin Keck observatories sit atop Mauna Kea, a dormant Hawaiian volcano. Since volcanic disturbances aren't a concern, the designers of the Keck focused on distortions caused by temperature and gravity. Steel and mirrors expand and contract with temperature changes, so both observatories are kept at 0°C (32°F).

Looking back 10.7 billion years, the Keck Observatory focused on a rare spiral-shaped galaxy. Researchers credit the galaxy's spin to the pull of a nearby galaxy, and theorise that all spinning galaxies need such a dancing partner.

"By studying protoplanets of nearby solar systems, astronomers hope to track the sequence of evolutionary events"

of stars and gas swirling around a supermassive black hole. Andromeda's diameter is 260,000 light years.

Andromeda played a critical role in the early discoveries that shaped modern astronomy. In the Twenties, Edwin Hubble took the first rough measurements of the distance of Andromeda - which he believed was a nebula - using a technique pioneered by Henrietta Swan Leavitt in 1908. Swan Leavitt discovered that a certain type of bright star, called a Cepheid star, fluctuated with a calculable frequency. The longer the period of the star's vibration, the greater its intrinsic brightness. By knowing how bright a star should be, she compared that number with the observed brightness to determine its distance.

By calculating the period of Cepheid stars embedded in Andromeda, Hubble came up with a distance of 900,000 light years. Sure, he was off by a million or so light years, but his 2.5m (98in) telescope was feeble compared with 10m (33ft) mirrors and space 'scopes used today.

Hubble's more important discovery built on the work of another astronomer, Vesto Slipher. Slipher was measuring the distance of 'nebulae' like Andromeda using a phenomena called Doppler redshift. If a cosmic object is moving away from Earth, then we observe a very slight lengthening of the object's light waves, ie a shift to the red. Likewise, if an object is moving toward Earth, its light is blueshifted as the light waves become slightly compacted.

Slipher's discovery was that the majority of nebulae he could find were moving away from the Earth at up to 1,100 km/s (683 miles/s). Hubble used Slipher's data and his own calculations to conclude that an object like the Andromeda nebula - so far away, yet so fast and bright - must not be a cloud of gas at all, but another galaxy. The universe, Hubble revealed, was much bigger than the Milky Way.

But Hubble wasn't done yet. He started measuring the redshift of every galaxy cluster he could detect. What he found was that the redshift of the smallest, faintest galaxy clusters was greater than the redshift of brighter, larger galaxy clusters. When he plotted this data on a graph, he found that the further a galaxy was from Earth, the faster it moved away. Hubble's Law, as it became known, pointed to some astonishing conclusions. The only way for distant objects to move away faster than closer objects is if the universe is expanding. And if it's expanding, then there must be a point where that expansion originated. That point would later be known as the Big Bang.

In the decades since Hubble, astronomers have drawn detailed maps of our position in relation to all nearby galaxies. What is clear from those calculations is that the Milky Way, as well as other large spiral galaxies in our Local Group, are all moving in the same direction. This

The future of telescopes

James Webb Space Telescope
NASA's James Webb Space Telescope (JWST), due to launch in 2018, is the largest and most ambitious space telescope to date. The infrared JWST packs a primary mirror almost three times as large as Hubble's mirror. The mirror is too big for launch, so it will unfold in 18 hexagonal sections once in orbit. JWST will scan the skies for the earliest galaxies, inching ever closer to the remnants of the Big Bang itself.

European Extremely Large Telescope
Fifteen times bigger than any existing telescope, the near-infrared European Extremely Large Telescope will boast a 39m (128ft) primary mirror. Located in northern Chile, it will offer sharper and deeper views into the cosmos. ESO researchers hope to seek out the very first stars formed in our universe and identify scores of exoplanet candidates in the inhabitable zone.

implies the existence of a celestial body of enough mass to influence the course of galaxies hundreds of millions of light years away.

In the Seventies, astronomers believed they found the source, a massive supercluster of galaxies called the Great Attractor, located roughly 250 million light years away. The problem was that the Great Attractor lay in the Zone of Avoidance, so named because it is obscured by the Milky Way's own dusty disc. By 2005, advances in X-ray and infrared telescopy shone a clearer light on the Great Attractor region, revealing that it contained only a tenth of the mass required to pull so strongly on our Local Group of galaxies.

Astronomers now believe that the majority of the gravitational influence on the Local Group is created by the Shapley Supercluster, a collection of thousands of galaxies roughly 250 million light years beyond the Great Attractor. Shapley's mass is four times greater than the Great Attractor, equal to the mass of 10,000 Milky Ways. Together, the gravitational pull of the Great Attractor and the Shapley Supercluster would explain collective drift of the Local Group.

> "The current best estimate for the age of the universe is 13.7 billion years old"

Every year, astronomers uncover another supermassive cluster of galaxies deeper and deeper into space. In 2003, the Sloan Digital Sky Survey uncovered a cosmic structure that dwarfs the Shapley Supercluster. Called the Sloan Great Wall, it is described as a 'galactic filament' - a long, connected string of galaxies - 1.4 billion light years across. The Great Wall, located a billion light years from here, is currently the largest structure in space, but there are other contenders. The Phoenix Cluster, 5.7 billion light years away, is not only one of the largest superclusters we've seen, but one of the oldest.

One of the most exciting fields of astronomy is the search for extra-solar planets, or exoplanets. Planets are so hard to detect in deep space because they produce no light of their own, only the faint reflection from a very bright nearby star. Since 1992, astronomers have found evidence of hundreds of exoplanets. Most have been detected by the telltale warble of light as a planet passes between its sun and the Earth. Details about these exoplanets have been sketchy, though, since the light from the local sun outshines planetary features.

Astronomers are putting great hope in the James Webb Space Telescope, scheduled for launch in 2018. The Webb's infrared telescope will closely study exoplanets as they transit their suns, analysing light as it passes through the planet's atmosphere for evidence of methane, carbon dioxide or water vapour. By studying protoplanets in the inhabitable zones of nearby solar systems, astronomers hope to track the sequence of evolutionary events by which Earths like ours are formed.

The current best estimate for the age of the universe is 13.7 billion years. The deeper we peer into space, the closer we come to viewing objects formed in the infancy of time and space. In 2009, NASA's Swift satellite detected a bright, short-lived burst of light near the constellation Canes Venatici. The gamma ray burst, as it's called, signalled the death of a massive star 30 times larger than our Sun. By analysing the faint wavelengths of light as the burst faded, astronomers calculated that the event originated 13.14 billion light years away. The object, known as Gamma Ray Burst (GRB) 090429B, became the furthest known object in the universe. It also became the oldest.

One of the mind-boggling contradictions of our universe is that it is infinite in volume, infinite in mass, yet nearly empty in reality. The average density of the universe is 9.9 x 10-30 grams per cubic centimetre. That's 9.9 preceded by 30 decimal points. But perhaps the universe only appears empty because we are blind to what fills it. Dark energy and dark matter - an undetectable force and an invisible substance - make up 96% of the mass energy of the universe. The mass we can see and detect is only 4% of the whole.

The future of deep space exploration, fuelled by increasingly powerful telescopes and computing technology, will continue to defy our conventional understanding of the universe. With luck, not only will we see further, but we'll see more of the infinite beauty and deep mysteries that surround us. ●

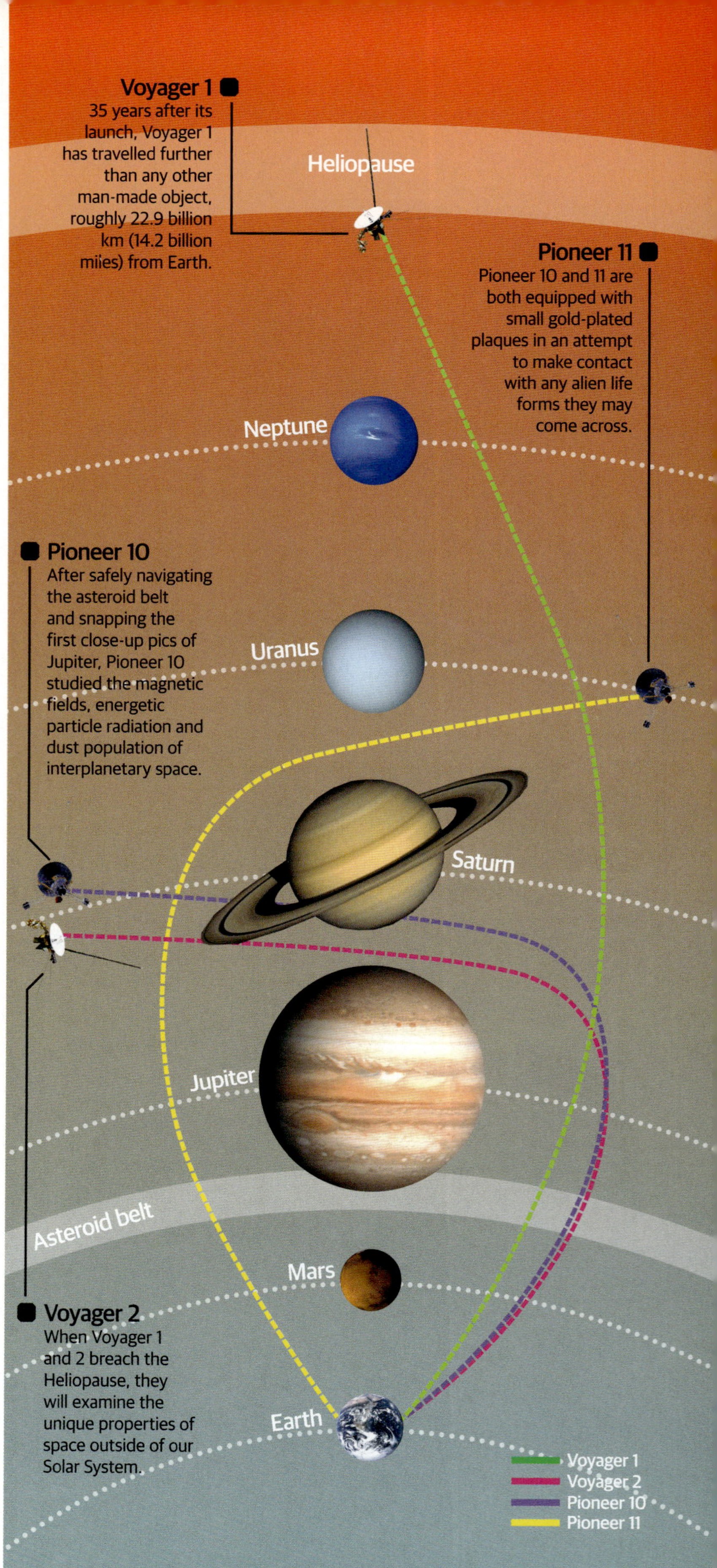

Furthest probes from Earth

The Voyager probes, and their predecessors, Pioneer 10 and 11, were launched in the Seventies as the first spacecraft to breach the thick asteroid belt between the orbits of Mars and Jupiter. The Pioneer probes sent back the first images of Jupiter and Saturn, and Voyager found new moons and new data on ancient frozen seas and active volcanoes. NASA received the last signal from Pioneer 10 in 2003, but the Voyager 'craft continue to transmit data as they prepare to breach the heliosphere, the outer shell of our Solar System.

The data used for the Hubble Ultra Deep Field image was accumulated between 24 September 2003 and 16 January 2004

"We can expect to learn more from Hubble about the most distant, infant galaxies"

Dr Jennifer Wiseman, senior project scientist on the Hubble Space Telescope, talks about deep space

What is Hubble Space Telescope looking for in deep space?
We use telescopes like Hubble to study the make-up and the development of the universe over its entire history. That includes everything from peering at the most distant galaxies to activity in our own Solar System.

Why does Hubble offer a dramatically clearer and deeper picture of space than an earthbound telescope?
Our atmosphere, with its water vapour and turbulence, smears light from objects in space. Space telescopes provide sharper images and a broad range of wavelengths to observe. Ground telescopes offer their own capabilities, including adaptive optics technology at some wavelengths that enable sharp viewing. Many astronomers use ground and space-based telescopes to gain a fuller understanding of celestial bodies.

How does the Hubble Space Telescope look 'back through time'?
All telescopes are 'time machines', because it takes time for the light from any celestial body to reach the lens. For the Sun, the light travel time is about eight minutes, meaning what we see is really the solar image and activity from eight minutes ago. The nearest grand spiral galaxy, Andromeda, is over two million light years away, so we are seeing it as it was two million years ago. With Hubble's new Wide Field Camera 3, we are now seeing the scraggly toddler galaxies shining to us from just a few hundred million years after the Big Bang.

What is the Hubble Ultra Deep Field image and what does it tell us about the origin of galaxies?
The Hubble Deep Fields are long exposures that provide awe-inspiring views of thousands of galaxies within a tiny cross-section of the sky. With this 'family album' of galaxies, we can compare the make-up of early galaxies to that of more evolved ones. Hubble scientists have determined that early galaxies contain very little of the heavier elements present in more mature galaxies with lots of stars.

How did Hubble help discover dark energy?
Hubble played a crucial role in the discovery that the expansion of the universe is accelerating; pushed apart by something we call 'dark energy'. The Nobel Prize-winning discovery hinged on the ability to accurately measure the distances between far-off galaxies. The trick was to identify a 'standard candle', a reference star whose brightness would never change. With the help of Hubble, a team of astronomers used Type 1A supernovae explosions as their standard candle, measuring the relative brightness of the starbursts as an indicator of their distance.

Has Hubble found extrasolar planets?
Most of the thousands of exoplanet candidates have been first discovered by ground-based telescopes or the Kepler space telescope. Once detected, Hubble helps to analyse the make-up of a planet's atmosphere.

Has Hubble witnessed the birth or death of stars?
With Hubble, we have seen stars at both ends of the 'life' spectrum. We see the telltale exhaust outflows from infant protostars in the process of coalescing. And the most massive stars end with a bang: a supernova explosion spreading stellar elements like carbon and oxygen into the interstellar medium.

What has Hubble taught us about black holes?
In 1994, Hubble first detected the presence of a black hole in the centre of galaxy M87 by measuring the velocities of the stars and gas around its nucleus. The Space Telescope Imaging Spectrometer, installed on Hubble in 1997, was hailed as a black hole hunter, because it could precisely measure the velocities of material on either side of the centre of a galaxy, determining the nature and existence of a black hole.

What is your favourite part of working with the Hubble Space Telescope?
I like being confronted with the extraordinary magnitude and majesty of the universe. Imagining that each of these galaxies contains billions of stars and potentially billions of planets provides a marvellous dose of curiosity and amazement.

What breakthrough discoveries can we expect Hubble to make in future?
Hubble is more scientifically powerful than ever before. We are conducting a wide variety of scientific investigations as proposed by scientists around the world. We can expect to learn more from Hubble about the most distant, infant galaxies, paving the way for the future work of the infrared James Webb Space Telescope, scheduled to launch in 2018. We can expect to find more incredible information about exoplanets and their atmospheres.

Celestial Witch's Broom

This stunning photo from the ESO highlights a magical feature in the Pencil Nebula

These two images, taken by the European Southern Observatory's La Silla Observatory in Chile, show a peculiar cloud of gas 800 light years away in the Vela constellation known as the Pencil Nebula (or NGC 2736).

The Pencil Nebula is a cloud of glowing gas left behind after a supernova explosion 11,000 years ago. It is only a portion of the entire supernova remnant, but it is the brightest region. The peculiar shape of this cosmic structure has earned it the moniker of the 'Witch's Broom' as the glowing filaments resemble the strands on a broom.

The whole remnant is known as the Vela supernova remnant, a giant expanding shell of gas from the initial explosion that moved at millions of kilometres per hour when it first formed. Having moved through the gas between stars, the expanding shell is now slowing down with certain regions of it glowing brighter than others, such as the Pencil Nebula imaged here.

The brightest regions of the Pencil Nebula are areas where the supernova's shock waves have hit dense regions of interstellar gas, at one point heating the gas to millions of degrees. The gas is now cooling down but it continues to give off a faint glow. The blue areas of the nebula are the hottest, full of ionised oxygen atoms, whereas the red regions are cooler and emit hydrogen.

The Pencil Nebula is 0.75 light years across and expanding at a 'leisurely' 650,000 kilometres per hour (400,000 miles per hour), about 0.06% the speed of light. Such is the rate of its expansion that within a human generation it will move to a different position in the night sky.

"HIP 56948 has physical properties and a chemical composition identical to that of the Sun"

The Sun's twin star

The most Sun-like star that we know of could kick-start the search for extraterrestrial life in the universe

Since the dawn of mankind our Sun has been regarded as unique. In ancient times it was thought to be the only star in existence, responsible for determining the day and night cycles on Earth. In the modern era we know it to be the heart and soul of the Solar System but it has long been regarded as one-of-a-kind in its composition and size. Now, however, it appears that our Sun could just be one of many similar stars in the Milky Way alone, providing a key piece of evidence to the belief that life could be lurking elsewhere in the universe.

The Sun is about 4.6 billion years old, born from a cloud of hot dust and gas at the start of the Solar System. In that time it has dictated the motion and characteristics of every body in its vicinity, including providing our own Earth with the ability to support life. As astronomers began to discover and study more and more stars elsewhere in the universe, they noticed several key differences between the Sun and every other star that seemed to make our own just that little bit special.

First, every star they came across was either much larger or significantly smaller. Second was that most other stars were considerably older or younger. Third, and perhaps most important, was the puzzling discovery that our Sun contained a very low amount of lithium compared to other stars. If all stars were essentially created in the same manner, why did this level of lithium vary so much?

A reason for this was theorised in 2009 in a paper published in Nature. "The explanation of this puzzle is for us rather simple," said lead author and astrophysicist Garik Israelian. "The Sun lacks lithium because it has planets." Rather than close the case, however, Garik's proposal carried with it a much more pertinent question. If we could find a solar twin with a similar lithium content, would that be indicative of that star also having a similar planetary system to our own?

Astronomers began to search in earnest for such a solar twin, but to little avail. That was until a paper published in 2012 proclaimed to have not only found a star similar in size and age to our Sun, but also nearly identical in its composition. HIP 56948 is about 210 light years away in the Draco constellation. It has a radius 1.14 times that of our Sun, a mass slightly smaller and is almost identical in age, meaning it is at the same point in its stellar evolution. In the paper, entitled 'HIP 56948: A Solar Twin with a Low Lithium Abundance', authors Jorge Meléndez and Iván Ramírez said: "HIP 56948 has stellar parameters identical to solar within the observational uncertainties, being thus the best solar twin known to date. Considering the age of this star and its location and orbit around the galaxy, if terrestrial planets exist around it, they may have had enough time to develop life."

Of most interest, however, was the revelation that HIP 56948 shared similar levels of lithium depletion as our own Sun, pointing to the presence of planets. However, there are no signs of large and hot Jupiter-like gas giant planets, suggesting that much smaller (and perhaps terrestrial) planets are in orbit. Finding such a star was a remarkable achievement, for our own Sun is regarded as one that has the optimal conditions around which such potentially habitable planets can form. Thus, in our continued search for life outside the Solar System, HIP 56948 represented a significant step forwards in the hunt for life-bearing exoplanets.

"HIP 56948 has physical properties and a chemical composition identical to that of the Sun, as well as a similar age," the paper continued. "Stellar ages are key in the search for complex life, especially if one considers that the formation timescale of complex life is similar to that for Earth. Furthermore, given its orbital properties, HIP 56948 is well within the galactic habitable zone. Considering these facts, HIP 56948 is an excellent candidate for life outside the Solar System."

In fact, the star is so Sun-like that Meléndez and Ramírez suggest it may completely change our understanding of how unique we are in the universe. "Besides the astrophysical significance of solar twins, there is another motivation to study them in detail: they help in answering the question of whether the Sun is unique or not, a question that has important philosophical consequences." Those consequences would be that there might be other places in the Milky Way, and the universe, where life such as ourselves could flourish. If the Sun were unique it would "suggest that our location in the universe is privileged for our existence as observers." The identification of HIP 56948, however, "can be used as an argument against [that theory]," and therefore allow us to theorise that there are many stars like our own Sun that have the necessary conditions around which life can form. Perhaps HIP 56948, our closest solar twin and a star not that far away in terms of astronomical distance, might just be one of those stars. ●

HIP 56948 is at the same point in its stellar evolution as our Sun

The universe's Sun-like stars Our Sun and its potential solar twins

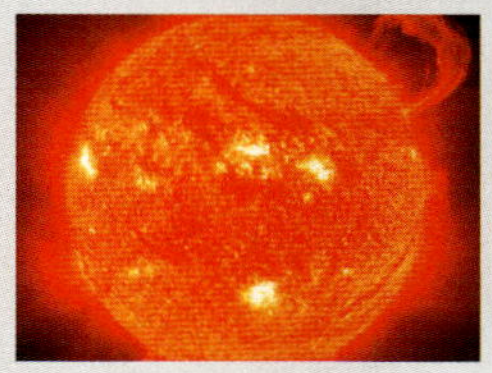

The Sun
Radius: 696,000km
Distance: 150 million km
Surface temp: 5,778 K
Age: 4.57 billion years

HIP 56948
Radius: 1.14 Suns
Distance: 210 light years
Surface temp: 5,748 K
Age: 3.6 billion years

18 Scorpii
Radius: 1.01 Suns
Distance: 45.3 light years
Surface temp: 5,433 K
Age: 4.7 billion years

HD 143436
Radius: Unknown
Distance: 142 light years
Surface temp: 5,768 K
Age: 3.8 billion years

HD 44594
Radius: 1.0 Suns
Distance: 82 light years
Surface temp: 5,840 K
Age: 4.1 billion years

HD 98618
Radius: 1.0 Suns
Distance: 126 light years
Surface temp: 5,843 K
Age: 4.21 billion years

This is the sharpest-ever image of the Whirlpool Galaxy, taken by NASA's Hubble Space Telescope

The Whirlpool Galaxy

This beautiful galaxy is one of the most famous galactic structures in the night sky

About 31 million light years away can be found one of the most observed galaxies in the night sky. Also known by its designations Messier 51a and NGC 5194, the Whirlpool Galaxy is a vast spiral galaxy that is of particular interest to both amateur and professional astronomers because of its large and intricate swirling arms.

This fantastic galaxy was first discovered on 13 October 1773 by French astronomer Charles Messier, and since then it has become one of the most studied objects in the universe by observers on Earth. Nicknamed the Whirlpool for its swirling structure, it is noticeable particularly for its two main curving arms, a hallmark of this particular type of grand-design spiral galaxy.

The highly pronounced nature of the Whirlpool Galaxy's two arms makes them huge star-forming factories, where compressed hydrogen gas creates new clusters of stars. The youngest stars are on the inner edge, moving to the bright pink star-forming regions and ending in the majestic blue star clusters on the outer edge.

On the right of this image you can see the small and yellow dwarf galaxy designated NGC 5195, also known as Messier 51b. It is thought that the interaction of the two galaxies may be responsible for the prominence of the arms. However, although NGC 5195 looks as if it is pulling on one of the arms of the Whirlpool, it is actually some distance behind the larger spiral galaxy and has been moving past for hundreds of millions of years.

Despite not being in direct contact, NGC 5195 still has a noticeable effect on the Whirlpool. As it glides past its gravitational pull sends ripples of waves passing through gas clouds in the disc of the Whirlpool. These waves move along the inner edge of each arm and compress the clouds of gas found there. In turn this stimulates the birth of stars, noted by the bright pink regions, and the larger stars in tandem with shockwaves from supernovas sweep away the remaining dust and gas. Left behind are bright blue star clusters that light up the Whirlpool's arms, giving rise to this most fantastic of astronomical phenomenon.

The Antennae Galaxies

How these colliding galaxies could reveal the fate of our Milky Way

The Antennae Galaxies, also known as NGC 4038 (left) and NGC 4039 (right), are a pair of interacting galaxies 45 million light years away that were first discovered by William Herschel in 1785. Located in the NGC 4038 group along with five other galaxies, they are currently in the process of colliding. This particular image was taken by the Hubble Space Telescope and shows how the collision is affecting the two galaxies.

They began colliding a few hundred million years ago, making them one of the youngest and nearest examples of a galactic collision. The hearts of each galaxy are the two orange blobs at the cores. These consist largely of older stars and also large amounts of dust, shown in brown.

As the two galaxies collide they spur the formation of new stars, shown in blue in the image, while glowing hydrogen gas is shown in pink. Over hundreds of millions of years ejected stars have streamed away from the collision, extending far into interstellar space as two long tails and giving rise to the name 'Antennae'.

In several hundred million years, after continually crashing into one another, the two nuclei will combine into one giant core and form an elliptical galaxy. Their interaction bears similarities to what will happen when our Milky Way collides with the Andromeda Galaxy in 4.5 billion years, providing an insight into the future of our own galaxy.

©NASA

Andr

omeda

The Andromeda Galaxy is similar to the Milky Way Galaxy in many ways. But what will happen if these two collide in the next 4.5 billion years?

When it comes to next-door neighbours, the Andromeda Galaxy, which rests within the constellation Andromeda, takes the cosmic biscuit. At a hefty 700 billion solar masses and an estimated 220,000 light years in diameter, this galactic giant does not follow its mythological namesake as a princess, but as a queen of the Local Group – a family of galaxies that, almost like Andromeda's minions, lie close by in the trillion star-strong galaxy's queendom. The group also includes the Triangulum Galaxy and our own whirlpool of stars, the Milky Way Galaxy, along with a collection of puny dwarf and irregular galaxies scattered around the more striking trio.

Around 2.5 million light years from the Andromeda Galaxy our own Milky Way, while smaller than the gargantuan queen, almost challenges its galactic ruler, threatening to steal her throne with a contending mass believed to be about 80 per cent of its superior. However, what the Milky Way very nearly matches in weight thanks to the hefty yet elusive dark matter, it loses in presence with a respectable if inferior diameter of 100,000 light years, making it about half the size of its brighter companion and therefore failing to steal the crown of 'size queen'. That said, there's no mistaking that the pair share a similar galactic type with both possessing winding arms that snake their way into space, protruding from luminous cores. Such breed of galaxy is known as the spiral.

While we have never seen our own galaxy from the outside, astronomers believe that its centrepiece is a glowing bulge of stars with a bar cutting through its middle, joining its arms. The origin of the bar is uncertain, perhaps having formed through some gravitational instability, but regardless it is funnelling stars and gas through the galactic centre and out the other end. Structurally Andromeda is not too dissimilar and so, when we look at this galaxy, it is almost as if we are looking at a larger version of how our own Milky Way Galaxy might look were we able to jump into a spaceship and travel hundreds of thousands of light years into intergalactic space to look at it from the outside. A brief glance at the majestic form of a spiral galaxy can easily fool you into thinking that its gigantic structure is just a pattern of swirling stars emanating from a great ball of light at its core. However, there is more to the likes of the Andromeda and Milky Way galaxies than meets the eye and such illusions start at the very heart; what is commonly known as the central bulge of a galaxy.

Through the eyes of visible light, the Andromeda Galaxy is just your typical spiral galaxy with a classic, bulbous central condensation of stars. However, when we look in infrared light, it's a different story as the galaxy's centre takes on a more boxy, angular appearance, leading astronomers to believe that the Andromeda Galaxy is even more similar to the Milky Way than previously thought; a galactic twin with matching barred centres. Perhaps their similarities are not so surprising as studies show that 70 per cent of spiral galaxies have bars.

There's something mysterious about the centre of our Milky Way's grand neighbour. The Hubble Space Telescope peered deep into its heart and found a pair of bright objects at the centre orbiting the dark monster that is a black hole up to 230 million times heftier than our Sun. Again, Andromeda shows our Milky Way to be inferior, with the black hole at the centre of our home only accounting for 4 million times the mass of our star. One of the glowing objects within the centre of Andromeda, which is also known as Messier 31 or M31 for short, is thought by astronomers to be a dense and compact star cluster. The other object is fainter and disc-shaped, spiralling hot gas swirling around the gravitational sinkhole of the black hole. The black hole and the cluster are snugly positioned just five light years from each other. The cluster is dicing with devastation so close to a giant black hole.

Out from the centre the bar links two spiral arms that wrap around Andromeda in a tight embrace. In the spiral arms is gas and dust and stars, with nebulae formed of the former two making the latter. Here too Andromeda triumphs over the Milky Way – deep images of the galaxy reveal a hidden outer layer that expands the spiral arms to around 220,000 light years, about twice the diameter of our galaxy.

Around the spiral arms and the centre is the stellar halo and while the spiral arms may be fresh-faced youngsters relatively speaking, the halo is positively ancient, home to the oldest of Andromeda's hundreds of billions of stars. The visible stellar halo also merges with the invisible dark matter halo that surrounds and encases the entire Andromeda Galaxy and holds it all together. Inside the halo there are also globular clusters, numbering around 460 in total and the biggest of them is called Mayall II, or alternatively G1, but this cluster of many guises is vastly greater in size and number of stars than any globular cluster around the Milky Way. It seems as though everything about Andromeda is bigger – a true giant.

Flanking Andromeda are around 14 dwarf galaxies which stick close to the structure. Perhaps the most famous of the group are the dwarf elliptical galaxies known as M32, also nicknamed Le Gentil, and M110. Messier 32 may have once been a larger galaxy – there is evidence that it is interacting with its bigger neighbour which is using its gravity to pluck the stars and gas from M32 and shrinking it. The evidence for this is that it has its own supermassive black hole about a million times greater in mass than our Sun, and only big galaxies get black holes so massive. Our Milky Way has its own satellite galaxies, including the Magellanic Clouds, but neither of them have black holes as big as M32. Andromeda wins again.

Watching Andromeda strut its stuff in visible light can only tell us so much about our nearest big neighbour but high above Earth are robotic eyes that have X-ray, ultraviolet and infrared vision. The Hubble Space Telescope isn't alone in space, with other space observatories covering the other parts of the electromagnetic spectrum of light. These include the Spitzer Space Telescope, which can see infrared light from cool things like clouds of gas that are turning into stars, or faint stars that only shine with a feeble glow. Meanwhile there is also the Galaxy Evolution Explorer that can see ultraviolet light from hot things such as bright, young stars – if a region of a galaxy is shining bright in ultraviolet light, then it is very young, forming lots of new stars. On the other hand, if it is dim in ultraviolet and bright at infrared wavelengths, it implies that the region of the galaxy is far older, with only the cooler, long-lived stars around. Together they have stared at Andromeda, showing the galaxy in a new light. At the wavelengths of ultraviolet and infrared, sunglasses aren't needed to cut down on the glare of the galaxy that we see in normal light. GALEX and Spitzer look right through, revealing the spiral disc to be harbouring several rings expanding away from the centre, possibly caused by M32 passing through the Andromeda Galaxy, causing ring-like ripples similar to waves in a pond where a stone has been dropped in. Some galaxies in the universe are ring shaped, with a starry circle of gas and dust lopping around and separated from a bright centre. Andromeda may be on the way to growing into a ring-shaped galaxy.

Across the vast reaches of the universe, galaxies are steadily rushing away from our own as the

> "The Hubble Space Telescope found a pair of objects at the centre orbiting the monster that is a black hole up to 230 million times heftier than our Sun"

The evolution of a spiral galaxy

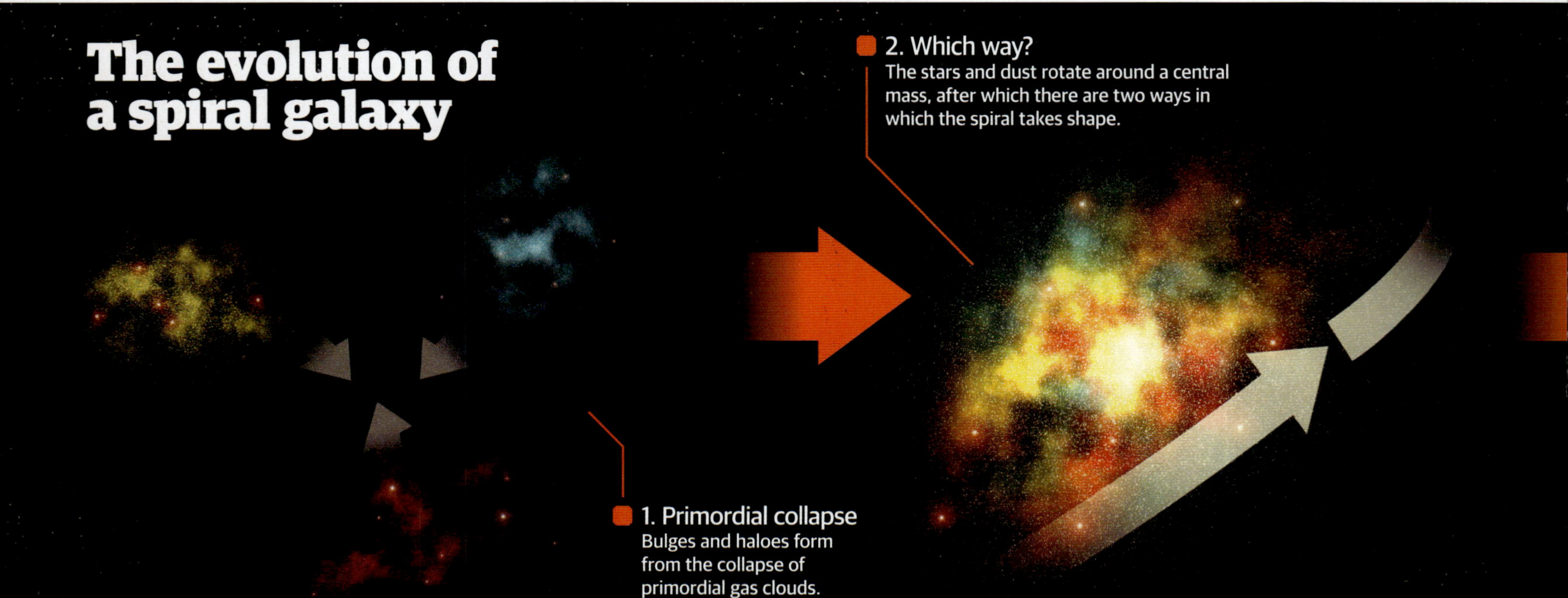

1. Primordial collapse
Bulges and haloes form from the collapse of primordial gas clouds.

2. Which way?
The stars and dust rotate around a central mass, after which there are two ways in which the spiral takes shape.

A galactic map

GALEX being mated to its Pegasus XL Rocket on 7 April 2003

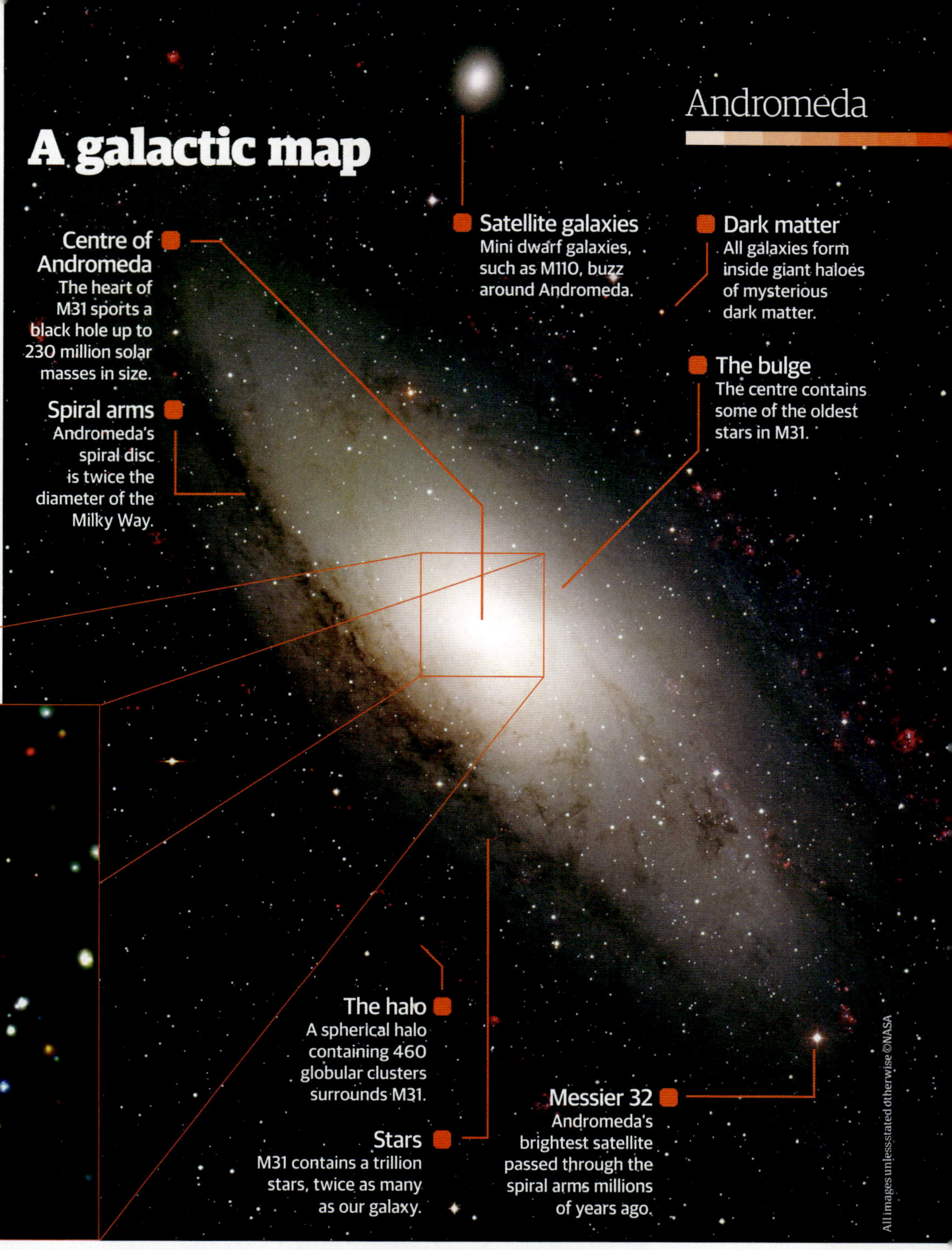

Andromeda is a large spiral galaxy that is very similar to the Milky Way

Anatomy of Andromeda

Tell-tale dust ring
Close examination of Andromeda in the infrared reveals a dusty inner ring believed to have been caused by satellite galaxy M32 ripping straight through its disc more than 200 million years ago.

S-shaped disc
Inclined at roughly 77 degrees relative to the Earth, Andromeda has a strange warped disc in the shape of an 'S', possibly caused by the gravitational interaction of satellite galaxies.

A 'misleading' bulge
In visible light, you wouldn't think that a bar streaks through Andromeda's centre. That is until you look at this section of the galaxy in the infrared.

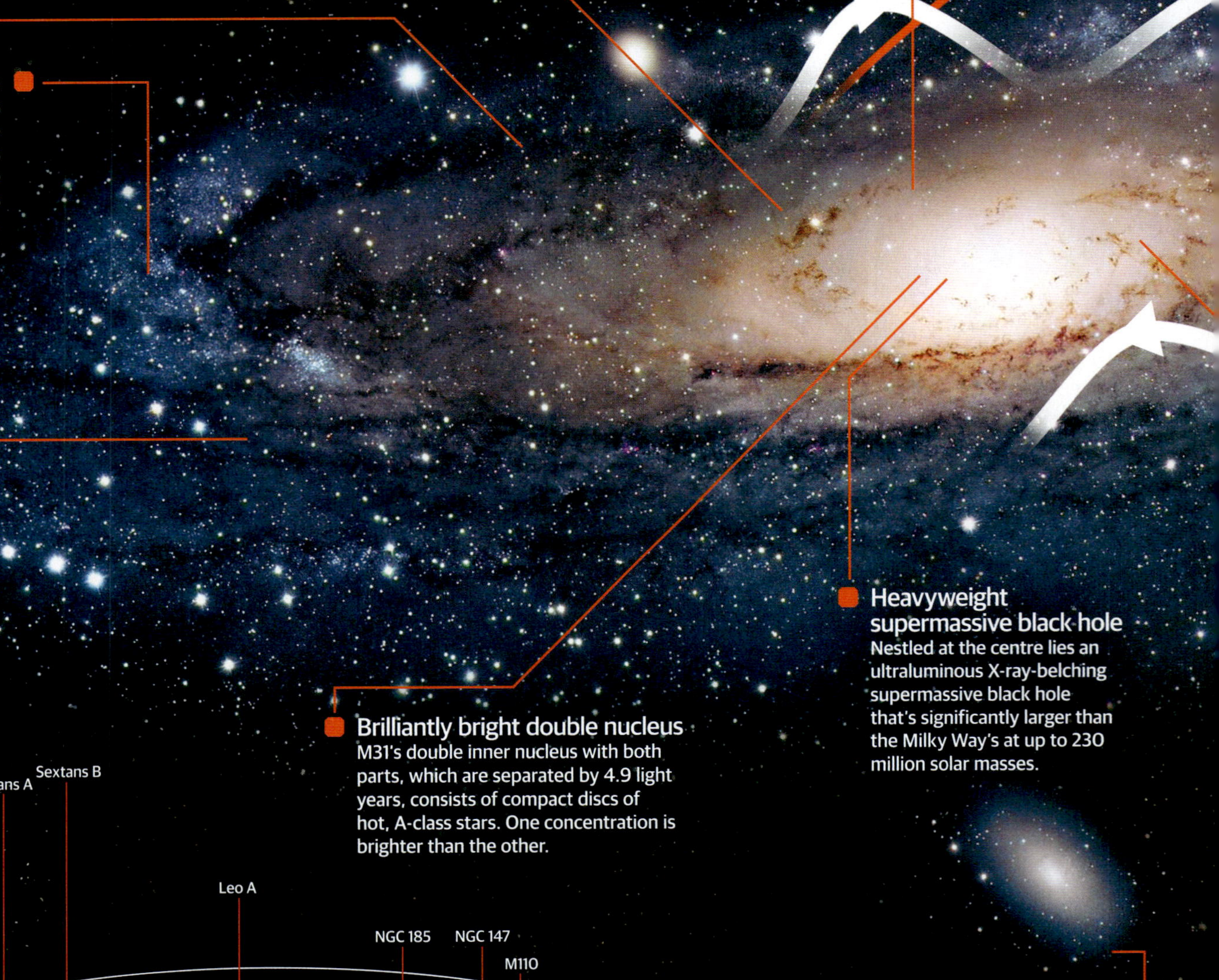

Winding arms
Wound up in a clockwise direction, M31's spiral arms are outlined by low-density clouds of partially ionised gas where the formation of young hot blue stars have recently formed.

Dust and gas
Cold dust and gas is arranged into overlapping rings according to an infrared to ultraviolet view, causing astronomers to believe that Andromeda may be transforming into a ring galaxy!

Brilliantly bright double nucleus
M31's double inner nucleus with both parts, which are separated by 4.9 light years, consists of compact discs of hot, A-class stars. One concentration is brighter than the other.

Heavyweight supermassive black hole
Nestled at the centre lies an ultraluminous X-ray-belching supermassive black hole that's significantly larger than the Milky Way's at up to 230 million solar masses.

Where is it?

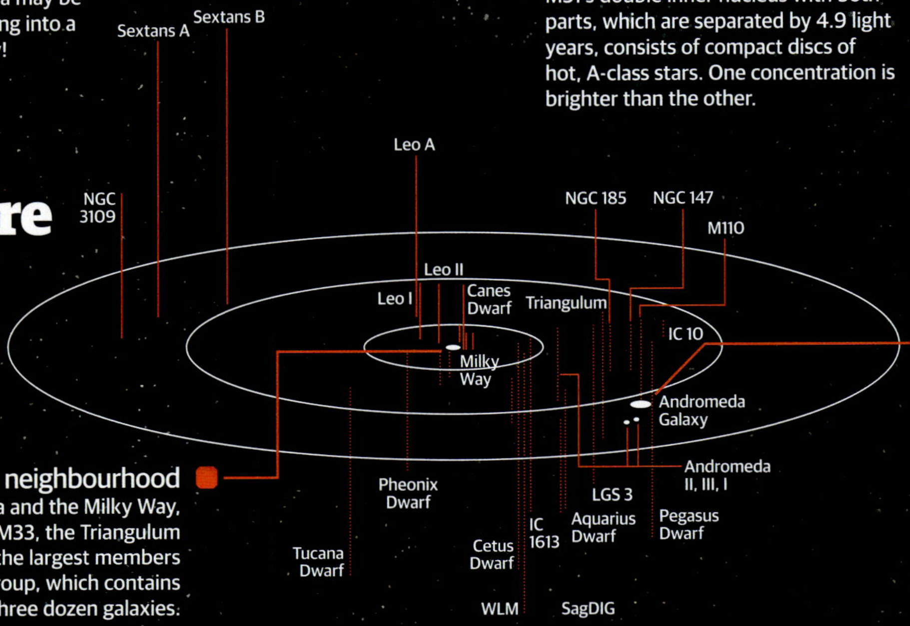

Our neighbourhood
Andromeda and the Milky Way, along with M33, the Triangulum Galaxy, are the largest members of the Local Group, which contains around three dozen galaxies.

Collision course
Andromeda and the Milky Way are speeding towards each other at 400,000km/h. There's also evidence that Andromeda and the Triangulum Galaxy interacted in the past.

Dwarf galaxies
Andromeda is accompanied by around 14 known dwarf galaxies, the most famous being M110 and M32, along with around 460 globular clusters. Faint galaxies around Andromeda could help astronomers learn more about dark matter.

Galactic star paths

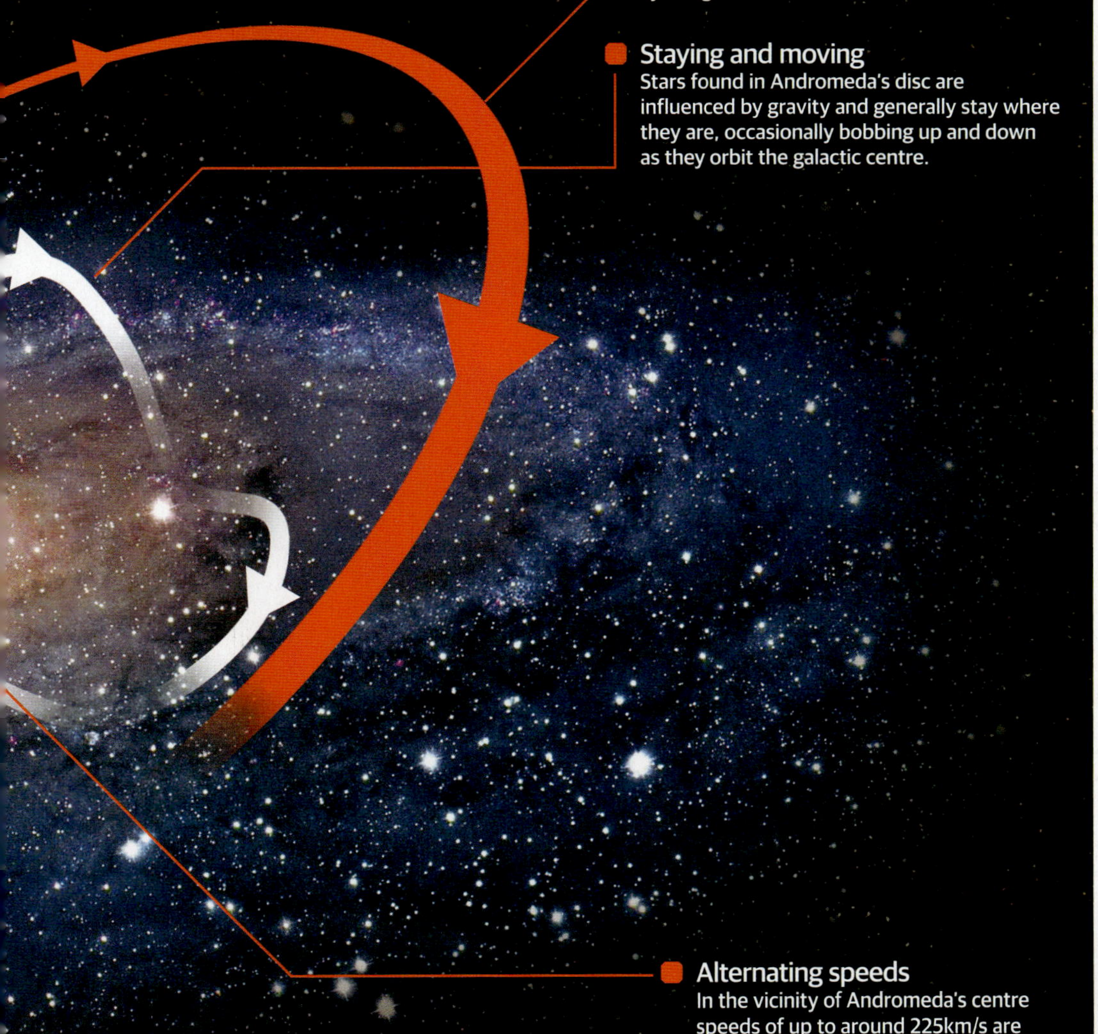

'Jumping' stars and clusters
Stars found in the galaxy's halo (and globular clusters) may 'jump' high above the disc before diving back in again popping out of the bottom of the galaxy before starting the cycle again.

Staying and moving
Stars found in Andromeda's disc are influenced by gravity and generally stay where they are, occasionally bobbing up and down as they orbit the galactic centre.

Alternating speeds
In the vicinity of Andromeda's centre speeds of up to around 225km/s are reached up to a radius of around 1,300 light years. Further out at 7,000 light years the speed of rotation drops as low as 50km/s before reaching speeds of around 250km/s even further from the centre. Finally, at around 80,000 light years, the speed becomes constant suggesting the presence of dark matter.

From the side

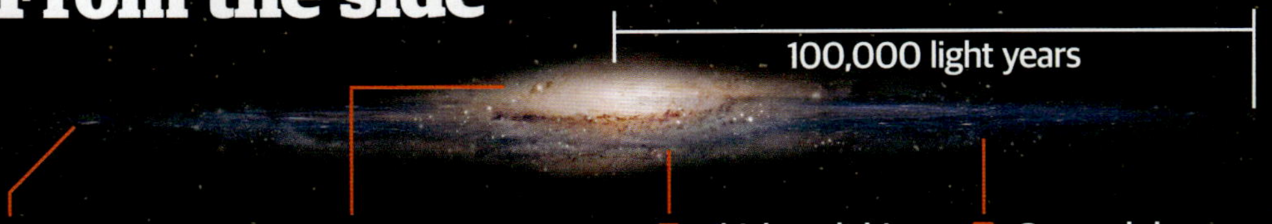

Globular clusters
The stellar halo is home to groups of stars called globular clusters. The largest around M31 is called Mayall II. It's twice as big as the Milky Way's largest.

Bulging out
The reason for the bulge's name is clear when the galaxy is viewed from the side. It hides a huge black hole, much heavier than the Milky Way's.

Thick and thin
The discs are divided into 'thick' and 'thin'. The thick disc contains stars over 8 billion years old, while a thinner disc houses younger stars.

Gas and dust
The spiral disc is filled with gas and dust. Dust is produced by dying stars and recycled into new stars born in nebulous regions of gas.

cosmos expands. It seems, however, that the Andromeda Galaxy has other ideas as it moves like a juggernaut in the opposite direction, charging at the Milky Way in what seems like slow motion - at a speed of around 400 light years every million years, Andromeda is set on a path of destruction that could see our galaxy getting walloped by it in the next four and a half billion years.

Crashes and cannibalism between galaxies isn't uncommon in the universe. Both the Milky Way and Andromeda Galaxy have form when it comes to gobbling up small galaxies and smashing into others. The former - our galaxy - is currently gaining more mass by snapping up several dwarf galaxies and cannibalising them - its next meal is likely to be our small elliptical companion the Sagittarius Dwarf Elliptical Galaxy (SagDEG), which has been drawn out into a loop around the Milky Way some 10,000 light years across by our galaxy's gravity. The loop is made up of spherical collections of stars also known as globular clusters, which are set to slowly merge with the larger Milky Way Galaxy. Meanwhile, evidence abounds in the form of tattered remnants of dwarf galaxies that shows the Andromeda Galaxy also has a track record of indulging in the odd galaxy or two.

While being in the path of a galaxy twice the size of our own would spell disaster in the minds of many, astronomers have been left wondering if the collision between our two giant stellar conurbations could happen at all. If the ultimate crash does come to pass, stars in both parties would largely miss each other as the space between stars is so enormous that the likelihood of any colliding is mind-bogglingly tiny. However, the gravitational fields of both galaxies will play havoc with the stars and gas clouds in both galaxies, throwing them around like toys. Just what will happen to our Solar System by the time 4.5

Spitzer after cryogenic telescope assembly integration

billion years rolls around almost seems irrelevant and will not affect us in the slightest for one main reason; our planet as we know it will by then have a swelteringly hot surface so high in temperature that water will boil away, ending all life upon it. The massive change from tranquility to hell on Earth will not be down to a sudden alteration on our planet's part, but will be down to the ageing of our Sun with it becoming brighter and therefore hotter a good 1.4 billion years from now, long before the end of its life.

The great event between the two galaxies might be a show that human beings are very unlikely to see, but that has not stopped astronomers from modelling just what will happen to our Solar System when the two do finally meet. They found that if Andromeda and the Milky Way do unite in the form of a merger, there is a possibility that our Solar System will be thrown out a good three times further away from its current position in the crook of the Orion arm, which rests around 28,000 light years from the centre of our galaxy. Another possibility, albeit a small one, is that our Solar System will be discarded and thrown out completely by the pair just as they collide to form a giant elliptical galaxy that astronomers have already nicknamed 'Milkomeda'.

That is not all. The mammoth collision between the gigantic duo could create a quasar at the centre of the newly formed Milkomeda. As the galaxies merge, so do the black holes, as the forces of the merger assist in pushing gas down the mouth of the giant black hole, and the gas heats up before it reaches the black hole, glowing brightly as it is sent to its doom. Such active black holes are called quasars, which are so bright they can be seen across the universe. Meanwhile the gas-laden cores of the galaxies will erupt with star formation - a final generation of new stars before all the gas is used up and the quasar runs out of gaseous food to chomp on. Then Milkomeda will become a quiet, ancient galaxy that will grow old respectably. ●

When galaxies collide

Although Andromeda is currently over two and a half million years from our own galaxy, in the next several billion years it will collide with the Milky Way. For any humans who are still around then, the sight is set to be remarkable. Our neighbouring galaxy will gradually grow larger and larger in the night sky before the two collide in a collage of exploding stars, twisting spirals and merging black holes.

2 billion years
The disc of the approaching Andromeda Galaxy will be noticeably larger.

3.75 billion years
Andromeda will fill the field of view and begin pulling the Milky Way.

4 billion years
Andromeda will be tidally stretched and the Milky Way will become warped.

5.1 billion years
The cores of the Milky Way and Andromeda will appear as a pair of bright lobes.

1. Clean room
White-suited workers at the Kennedy Space Center in Florida inspect the Spitzer spacecraft after its trip back to the clean room in May 2003.

2. Ready for launch
Spitzer is moved into position to have its launch faring installed atop its Delta rocket on 10 April 2003, ready for its launch later that year.

3. GALEX covered
Workers check the deployment of the cover of the telescope on the GALEX satellite.

4. CTA testing
The Spitzer cryogenic telescope assembly (CTA) being prepared for vibration testing.

5. GALEX launch
Being attached to a Lockheed L-1011 TriStar in preparation for launch.

Viewing our galactic neighbour

An old face
This Spitzer image shows Andromeda's older population of stars.

Ancient core
The halo and bulge of a spiral galaxy contain its oldest stars.

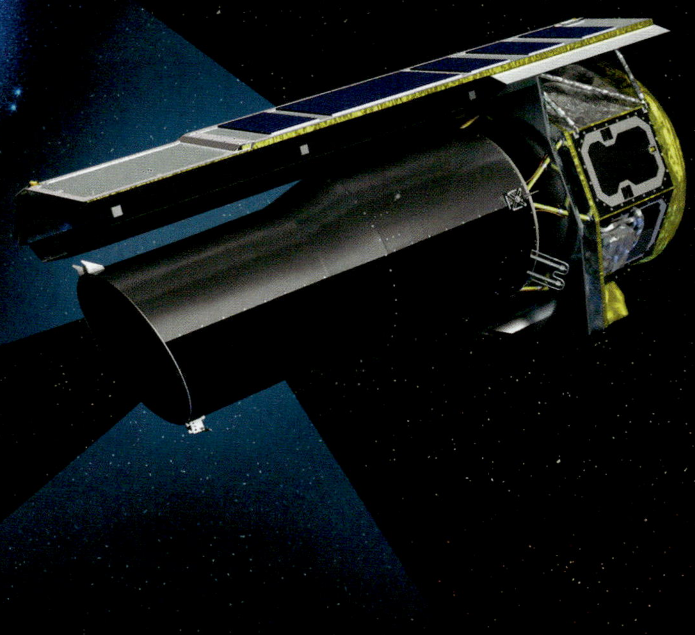

Mission Profile
Spitzer Space Telescope

Launch date: 2003
Launch vehicle: Delta II rocket
Mass: 950kg (2,100lb)
Telescope diameter: 0.85m (33in)
Mission: NASA's Spitzer Space Telescope observes the universe in infrared wavelengths, which can penetrate through interstellar dust.
Key discoveries: Spitzer probes the interiors of star and planet-forming regions, as well as the structures of galaxies, determining the interstellar chemistry of those regions. It has also probed the atmospheres of exoplanets.

Old and young
This false-colour composite of images reveals the ring structure of M31's disc, and the populations of old and young stars.

Hot and cold
The hottest stars (blue) are also the most massive and youngest, whereas older stars (green) are less massive and cooler.

Ring galaxy
M31 seen in ultraviolet light by GALEX. All the glare has gone, showing rings of hot young stars.

Dusty galaxy
Dark dust lanes line dense clouds of gas where star formation is actively taking place.

Mission Profile
Galaxy Evolution Explorer (GALEX)

Launch date: 2003
Launch vehicle: Pegasus rocket
Mass: 280kg (620lb)
Telescope diameter: 0.5m (19.7in)
Mission: This NASA ultraviolet space telescope is designed to study the structure and evolution of galaxies by observing its stars.
Key discoveries: GALEX has watched active black holes, captured images of galaxies plunging through other galaxies and spotted starbirth in the outer realms of galaxies.

Nebulae... Birth of a star

These beautiful and vast clouds of dust and gas show the remnants of dying stars, and are the birthplace of new generations of stars that bring life to the universe

The swirling, multicoloured clouds of nebulae are extraordinary visions of beauty that are truly awe-inspiring. They are like unique works of art, that use the ink-black bleakness of the surrounding heavens as a background to reinforce their stunning colours and intricate patterns of light and shade.

We can only glimpse them in the night sky as small, faint glowing clouds or as dark silhouettes against a lighter background. In Latin, a single celestial object of this type is known as a 'nebula', meaning a 'mist', 'vapour' or 'cloud', their plural is nebulae.

When astronomers first started training their new-fangled telescopes on them, we came to know far more about these fascinating stellar phenomena. One of the telescope pioneers was Charles Messier (1730-1817) who, when tracking the progress of a comet in 1758, observed a comet-like patch in the Taurus constellation.

It was not moving like a comet, and he determined that it was a nebula. To help him distinguish between comets and other celestial objects, he compiled a 'Catalogue of Nebulae and Star Clusters'. He designated the nebula seen in Taurus as Messier 1 (M1) - today it's more commonly known as the Crab nebula.

Sir William Herschel (1738-1822), conducted a more systematic survey of the Northern Hemisphere to find and catalogue 'deep sky' and nonstellar objects. Between 1782 and 1802, he recorded 2,500 separate nebulae. His son Sir John Herschel (1792-1871), who found and catalogued nebulae visible in the Southern Hemisphere, collected their combined work in 1864. This collection became the basis for an expanded New General Catalogue (NGC), which is still used today to number and designate nebulae.

Sir William Herschel categorised nebulae in terms of their size and brightness, and for those nebulae that had the oval-like appearance of planets, he named 'planetary nebulae'. Better resolution telescopes revealed some planetary nebulae to be star clusters. It was only when Sir William Huggins (1824-1910) first directed a spectroscope at the Cat's Eye (NGC 6543) planetary nebula in 1864 that it became clear that it was a cloud of gas rather than a group of stars.

Nebulae with a spiral appearance were first thought to be solar systems being formed. It was only in the Twenties, when Edwin Powell Hubble (1889-1953) measured the distance of Cepheid variable stars in spiral nebulae, that it was discovered that they are actually galaxies beyond our own, and not nebulae at all.

We now know that planetary nebulae are created by the dying throes of main-sequence stars. They live by converting hydrogen into helium, but after almost 10 billion

The Eagle nebula

Pictured far left, this 5.5-million-year-old emission nebula is still actively forming stars in the proximity of the 'Pillars of Creation' and 'Spire' regions

1. The Spire: This spire of cold hydrogen gas is 9.5 light years high. The ultraviolet radiation emitted from nearby stars heats the surrounding gas, which erodes the molecular cloud of hydrogen in a process called 'photoevaporation'. As the outside of the column is eroded, inside the extreme gas density can reach a point where gravity compresses the gas into clumps. Nuclear fusion is triggered, turning them into stars.

The dark areas inside the spire are where this star birth occurs, but as more stars are formed their intense radiation erodes the raw materials needed for new stars to grow. Starved of raw material, potential stars enter a 'frozen' state that categorises them as 'Evaporating Gaseous Globules'.

The gas at the top gets so hot that it sends a shock wave down the spire, which compresses the cold gas and triggers the creation of new stars.

2. The Pillars of Creation: These vast columns were first photographed by NASA's Hubble Space Telescope in 1995. The tallest column is four light years high, and is composed of cool hydrogen gas and microscopic particles of graphite and silicates.

The pillars are in the region of a cloud of dust that was heated by the explosion of a supernova. The shock wave from it could have toppled the them 6,000 years ago. Since they are 6,500 to 7,000 light years away, it will be 500 to 1,000 years before we know if they were destroyed.

years when most of the hydrogen supply runs out, the fusion process stops and the layers of the star collapse in upon its central core. As this compresses the stellar gas, it heats up causing the outer layers to expand and brighten by a factor of 10,000 per cent. The outer layers drop to a temperature of 3,000 to 4,000 Kelvin, and due to its appearance, it is described as a red giant star.

When the core temperature reaches 100 million K, helium burning begins; causing the star to lose its luminosity. For a time it becomes a red clump star, then when the helium burning stops it returns to being a red giant and enters the asymptotic giant branch (AGB) stage of its life.

A powerful wind will develop that takes away the outer layers of hydrogen, and they will contract and expand, in huge pulsations that can last up to a year. Seventy per cent of its stellar mass will be ejected by the wind. This material forms a tenuous envelope of gas around the star, and it is now a planetary nebula. The nebula is illuminated by the ultraviolet radiation emitted by the star, for a period of 10,000 to 50,000 years until the star ceases to give out any more radiation and becomes a white dwarf.

Besides planetary nebulae there are four other major types of nebulae. Supernova remnants (SNRs) are the most similar to planetary nebulae, though they are created by massive stars that explode with a force of 1,051 ergs (1,031 megatons) of energy to create a supernova.

Rather than it looking like the impressive end of its life, from the Earth this appears as if a new star has suddenly been born. The shock wave of the explosion ejects the atmosphere of the star creating the visible SNR, and its core can become a black hole or a neutron star.

There are three basic types of SNR. The first type is shell-like, as it sends out a hot ring of gas that heats up everything in its path. Crab-like remnants look more like blobs and send out radio waves, X-rays and visible light powered by a pulsar at the centre of the nebula.

Thirdly, there are composite remnants of which there are two-types. Thermal composite remnants look crab-like in the X-ray spectrum, but shell-like in the radio waveband. Plerionic composite remnants have a visible shell but will appear crab-like in the X-ray and radio wavelengths.

The remnants cast out by supernova are important to the formation of stars in galaxies, as they heat up the interstellar medium (ISM), accelerating the motion of cosmic rays. Most importantly for our own existence, they disperse heavy elements, such as iron, in the dense star-forming regions of the ISM, thereby creating a new generation of stars with rocky planets (like the Earth) orbiting them.

The remaining three major types of nebulae - emission, reflection and dark - are associated with areas that are actively forming stars, rather than with the demise of stars.

Emission nebulae can spread over several hundred light years and emit light in the visible wavelengths of the spectrum. They have a distinctive red colour due to the excitation of the hydrogen that dominates the nebula by the high-energy ultraviolet photons radiated by nearby O and B type stars.

Since they emit ionised hydrogen, they inhabit H II regions, where young hot stars are prevalent. In contrast, H I regions consist of nebulae that have neutral hydrogen that registers at the 21 centimetre (1,420.4 MHz) microwave

"For a time it becomes a red clump star, then when the helium burning stops it returns to being a red giant and enters the asymptotic giant branch (AGB) stage of its life"

What's the best way to see a nebula?

In the Northern Hemisphere, the most famous nebula is the Great Orion Nebula. You can see it with a pair of binoculars, but the view gets even more spectacular if you use larger telescopes.

The scale of the universe

Superclusters
Galaxies aren't randomly distributed throughout the universe, they gather in superclusters of several thousand galaxies instead.

Cluster
These contain local groups of about 50 galaxies. Our Milky Way galaxy is in a group of approximately 40 galaxies.

Galaxies
A galaxy can contain from 10 million to 100 trillion stars that rotate around its central mass.

Nebulae
Nebulae are interstellar clouds made of hydrogen, dust, helium and gases. New stars and planets form in nebulae.

Star systems
A planetary star system consists of a central star, with planets, satellites, asteroids, comets and dust orbiting around it.

Star
Most stars are of the main-sequence type, like our Sun. Stars release enormous amounts of energy, through the process of thermonuclear fusion of hydrogen.

Planets
Planets consist of bodies that are large enough to be rounded by their own gravity, and are terrestrial-type planets or gas giants.

How stars are formed

The part that nebulae play in stellar life cycles

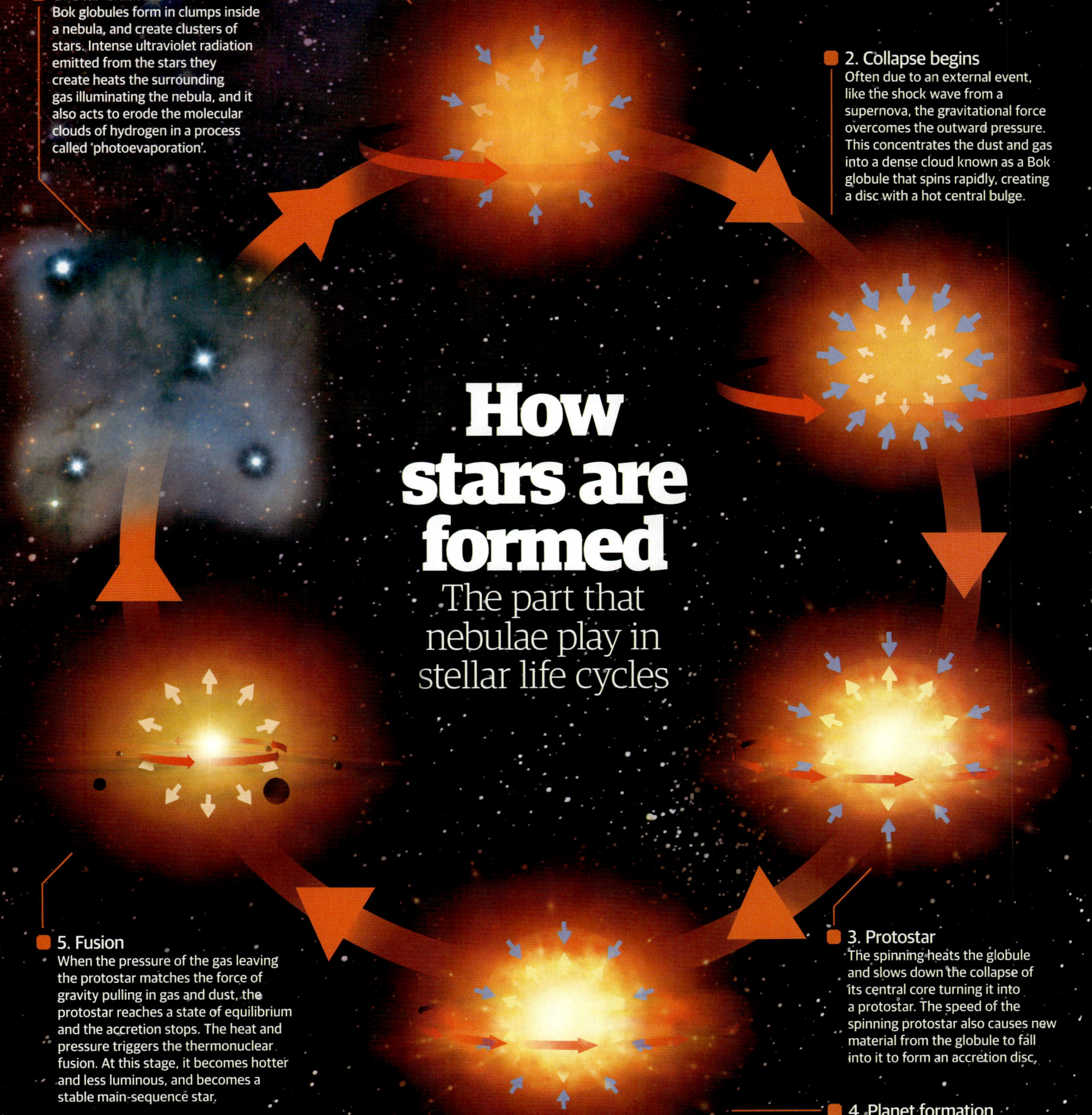

1. Collisions
Dust and gas drifts randomly inside a molecular cloud. Gravity pulls the cloud inwards to its centre, while collisions between dust particles create an outward pressure that keeps the cloud in a state of relatively stable equilibrium.

2. Collapse begins
Often due to an external event, like the shock wave from a supernova, the gravitational force overcomes the outward pressure. This concentrates the dust and gas into a dense cloud known as a Bok globule that spins rapidly, creating a disc with a hot central bulge.

3. Protostar
The spinning heats the globule and slows down the collapse of its central core turning it into a protostar. The speed of the spinning protostar also causes new material from the globule to fall into it to form an accretion disc.

4. Planet formation
As the protostar gathers material, it jettisons incoming gas. This bipolar outflow of gas can extend 3.26 light years and becomes visible if it collides with other gas in the nebula. As the gas is jettisoned, planets begin to form.

5. Fusion
When the pressure of the gas leaving the protostar matches the force of gravity pulling in gas and dust, the protostar reaches a state of equilibrium and the accretion stops. The heat and pressure triggers the thermonuclear fusion. At this stage, it becomes hotter and less luminous, and becomes a stable main-sequence star.

6. Star clusters
Bok globules form in clumps inside a nebula, and create clusters of stars. Intense ultraviolet radiation emitted from the stars they create heats the surrounding gas illuminating the nebula, and it also acts to erode the molecular clouds of hydrogen in a process called 'photoevaporation'.

radio frequency and do not emit visible light. Planetary nebulae can also be regarded as emission nebulae, although their emissions are caused by their dying central star rather than by nearby stars.

Rather than being dominated by hydrogen, dark nebulae consist of high concentrations of dust. This makes them difficult to spot in the visible spectrum unless they are illuminated. Their temperature can range from 10 to 100 Kelvin, and can vary in size from 652 light years across in the case of giant molecular clouds or three light years in the case of Bok globules.

Reflection nebulae are less dense than dark nebulae, and they reflect and scatter the light from a nearby star or stars. They do not contain enough hydrogen to become an emission nebula, and are mainly composed of microscopic particles of iron, nickel and carbon compounds. They tend to reveal a spectrum similar to the star that is illuminating them, though the dust particles scatter blue light better than red light, therefore giving them a blue appearance.

As in the past, when telescopes, spectroscopes and radio telescopes provided new information about the structure and formation of nebulae and their differences from other celestial objects, we are learning even more using space-based instruments.

One of the biggest advances was the launch of the Hubble Space Telescope in 1990; its 2.4-metre (7.9ft) aperture telescope has captured thousands of stunning images of nebulae. With this and other space telescopes we have discovered that nebulae are far more complex formations than we ever imagined. We are increasingly able to probe deeper inside them, and we are learning more about these fascinating stellar phenomena every day.

Yet, the swirling jets, rings, pillars, fingers and colossal columns of nebulae, with the dazzling clusters of new stars embedded inside them, are still as intriguing to us now, as they were to astronomers like Messier and Herschel all those years ago.

They still hold many mysteries about the complex interactions that force these clouds of dust and gas into fiery stars, which in the case of our Sun gives life to everything on Earth. And, we can barely conceive the enormous forces that power the spectacular death of stars, which in turn spew out new nebulae that propagate new clusters and stars, breathing new life into a constantly changing and evolving universe. ●

Types of Nebulae

Discover the different kinds of nebulae with an example of each

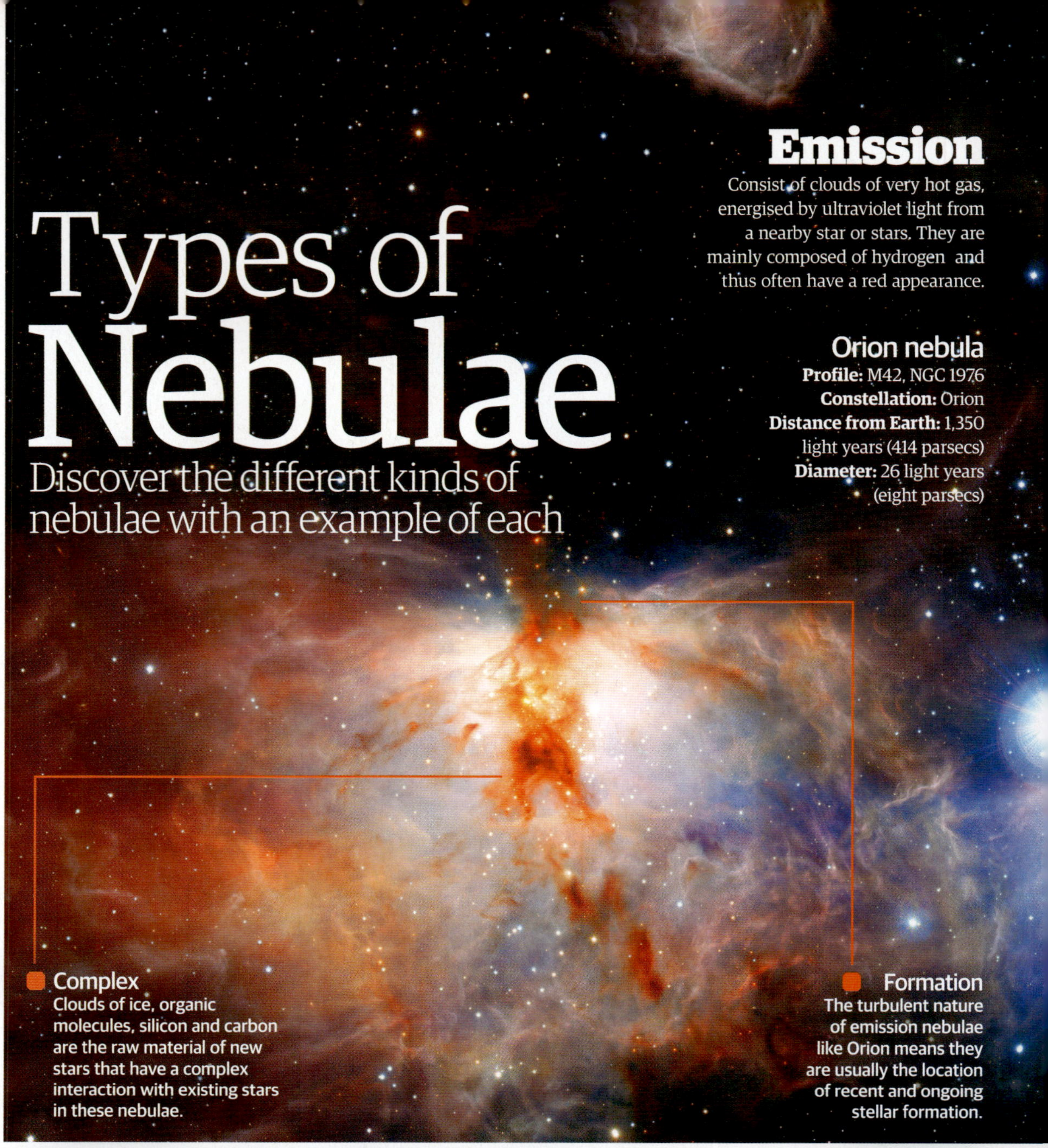

Emission

Consist of clouds of very hot gas, energised by ultraviolet light from a nearby star or stars. They are mainly composed of hydrogen and thus often have a red appearance.

Orion nebula

Profile: M42, NGC 1976
Constellation: Orion
Distance from Earth: 1,350 light years (414 parsecs)
Diameter: 26 light years (eight parsecs)

Complex
Clouds of ice, organic molecules, silicon and carbon are the raw material of new stars that have a complex interaction with existing stars in these nebulae.

Formation
The turbulent nature of emission nebulae like Orion means they are usually the location of recent and ongoing stellar formation.

Supernova remnant

Created by the violent explosion of a massive star at the end of its life span. For a few days, it casts off more energy than a whole galaxy and sends its atmosphere out to a distance of a few light years.

Crab nebula

Profile: M1, NGC 1952
Constellation: Taurus
Distance from Earth: 6,500 light years (1,992 parsecs)
Diameter: 11 light years (3.4 parsecs)

Expansion
These types of nebula can expand at over 1,500 kilometres (932 miles) a second due to the initil supernova explosion.

Neutron
At the centre of a supernova remnant nebula a dense ball of matter can often be found, known as a neutron star, left behind from the original star.

Amazing colours
The red or pinkish glow originates from hydrogen gas predominantly behind the Horsehead nebula.

Dark nebula

These are thick dust and gas clouds like reflection nebula. They completely block any light sources that are behind them.

Horsehead nebula

Profile: Barnard 33, IC 434
Constellation: Orion
Distance from Earth: 1,600 light years (490 parsecs)
Diameter: 13 light years (four parsecs)

Neck shadow
The darkness of the Horsehead is caused mostly by thick dust, although the lower part of the Horsehead's neck casts a shadow to the left.

Reflection

These do not produce visible light of their own. They mainly consist of dust that reflects light from nearby stars. They are linked with the creation of new star formations.

Witch Head nebula

Profile: IC 2118, NGC 1909
Constellation: Eridanus
Distance from Earth: 1,000 light years (300 parsecs)
Diameter: Unknown

Planetary

These have nothing to do with planets. They consist of gas cast off by a star at the end of its main sequence life.

Cat's Eye nebula

Profile: NGC 6543
Constellation: Draco
Distance from Earth: 3,300 light years (1,012 parsecs)
Diameter: Unknown

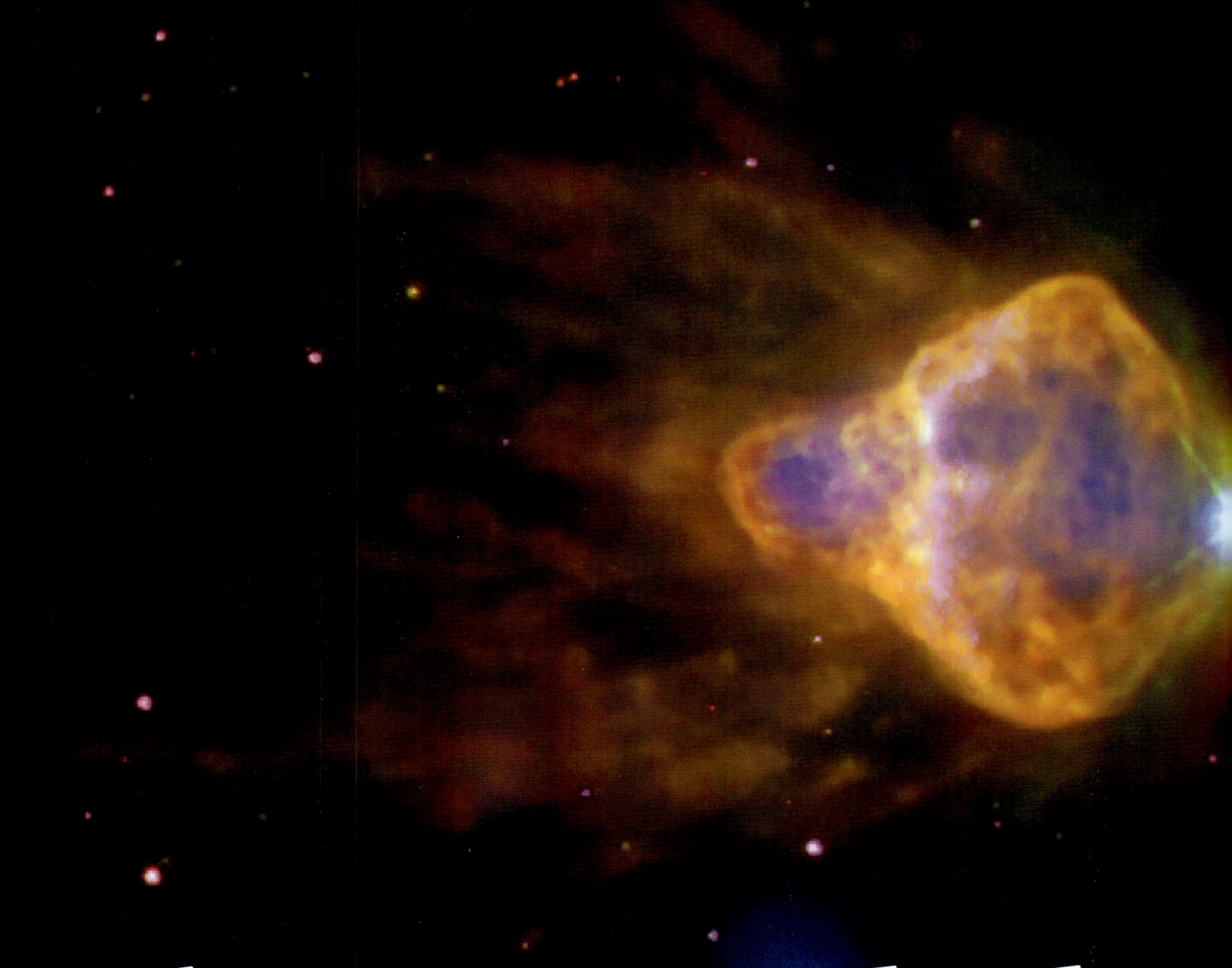

The Ant Nebula

This giant space ant could provide clues to the fate of our Sun

Planetary nebula Menzel 3 (Mz 3), known as the Ant Nebula due to its resemblance to the small insect, is up to 8,000 light years from Earth in the Norma constellation. It should be noted that 'planetary nebula' is a misnomer; Mz 3 is actually the result of a dying star, but the 'planetary' moniker stuck for these sorts of structures after they were incorrectly classified by astronomer William Herschel in the late 18th Century.

This bizarre nebula's similarities to an ant can be seen in the accompanying image. The 'head' is on the left, the 'thorax' is to the right and the 'legs' are the emissions streaming out from the nebula. From its 'head' to the end of the 'thorax' the Ant Nebula spans an entire light year across. At the centre of the nebula is a star in the last throes of its life that is ejecting material into the surrounding space.

In such an instance, it would be expected that the material would be flung in a spherical manner, but the cause of the odd symmetrical shape of the Ant Nebula is puzzling. The predominant theory is that the dying star is in a binary system with a companion at a distance comparable to that of the Earth and Sun, with the other star sweeping the material into the 'ant' shape. Another theory suggests that the strong magnetic fields of the dying star are directing electrically charged gas moving at 1,000 kilometres (600 miles) per second along the magnetic field lines to produce the 'ant'.

The Ant Nebula's central star is thought to be very similar to our own Sun and, because of this, astronomers are hopeful that by understanding what exactly is going on at the heart of Menzel 3 they may be able to predict what will become of the Sun, and indeed the Earth, in the distant future several billion years from now.

Rogue planets

Planet expert Thijs Kouwenhoven tells us why these nomad worlds are so important

"If the Earth were ejected temperatures would drop beyond the freezing point of the atmosphere"

Thijs Kouwenhoven, planet expert

Just eight planets make up our Solar System, ranging from the rocky terrestrial inner worlds to the huge outer gas giant planets, and based on our understanding of exoplanets so far it appears that there are many other planetary systems both like and unlike our own around other stars. But could there be planet-sized objects drifting through the universe unattached to a host star or planetary system?

"Rogue planets, also known as free-floating planets [FFPs], are planets that are freely floating through space. They are not orbiting a star or any other massive object, such as a white dwarf or black hole," says Thijs Kouwenhoven, the co-author of a paper entitled 'On the origin of planets at very wide orbits from the re-capture of free floating planets' with colleague Hagai Perets. The two have been pivotal in the study of rogue planets, and believe that the universe is teeming with these nomad worlds that may have once been part of a planetary system like our own.

"Theory suggests that all rogue planets are formed through the ejection of planets from planetary systems," says Kouwenhoven. "If we look at our Solar System, we see that comets and asteroids can be ejected with high velocities when they come too close to Jupiter or Saturn. In the same way, a planet can be ejected from a planetary system after a strong gravitational interaction with another planet. In fact, computer simulations suggest that Mercury is most likely to be the first planet to be ejected from our Solar System in the distant future [in billions of years]."

It's not only the interaction between planets that can deprive a world of its host system, however. Two stars passing close to each other in a crowded part of a galaxy could result in planets being flung from their system. One example of such a region is something known as a globular cluster, a compact collection of stars "where the density of stars is so high that most of the planets are likely to have left their parental star. Star clusters are therefore good places to look for free-floating planets."

While we can simulate their existence, the detection of rogue planets is rather more difficult, not least because our most successful current method of finding exoplanets, namely by observing their transit across their host star, is nigh-on impossible without such a star to transit. Therefore, scientists have been using the microlensing technique (see 'How do we find them?' boxout) to find rogue planets in densely packed regions such as globular clusters.

So, if we can't see rogue planets, how do we know they're there? "Traditionally, the existence of rogue planets came from theory, and later from computer simulations," says Kouwenhoven. "Everyone playing with a simple planetary system simulator on an iPhone, or with the most sophisticated astrophysical software, will notice that many planetary systems are unstable, which often results in the ejection of one or more planets into deep space. Observationally it is very difficult to find free-floating planets. They do not emit light and are almost impossible to see with telescopes. In addition, their mass is much smaller than that of stars. Unlike for the detection of black holes, the gravitational pull of planets on their surroundings cannot be used to infer their existence."

If the theory and simulations hold true, then from our knowledge of planetary systems, and our simulations of the gravitational interaction of planets, the expected number of such nomad worlds according to Kouwenhoven should be huge. "Based on observations, one can infer that there are roughly twice as many free-floating planets as there are stars in the neighbourhood of the Sun," he says. "In crowded environments, such as in the centre of the Milky Way and in globular clusters there may be many more due to the destruction of planetary systems by close stellar encounters. A rough estimate gives 100 to 150 billion rogue planets in our Milky Way galaxy, and there are hundreds of billions of galaxies in the observable universe. That's a lot of planets."

But what of the conditions on such worlds? As they are drifting freely through space, it would be expected that almost all of them would be uninhabitable. With no star to heat their surface, every rogue planet is expected to be freezing cold and therefore it might seem impossible that the surface of any such world is habitable. Hope is not lost, however, says Kouwenhoven: "We know that our planet Earth is very warm on the inside. Sometimes we see molten lava coming out of volcanoes, so the heat source is clearly not the result of the Sun heating up the Earth [but rather a molten core].

"Some rogue planets may also have an internal heat source, just like the Earth. Although the surface of the planet might be frozen, underground oceans could exist due to the presence of the internal heat source. In fact, even in our own Solar System, several cold moons have subsurface water oceans. The most famous example is Jupiter's moon Europa, which has an icy cold surface, but a warm water ocean below. Rogue planets could be habitable to small creatures that like to live in subsurface oceans in total darkness. But it is not a very nice place for humans to go. If the Earth were ejected, the oceans would probably freeze quickly, and temperatures would drop rapidly beyond the freezing point of the oxygen and nitrogen in the atmosphere."

So, do these giant floating rocks pose any threat to Earth? Could they drift into the Solar System and impact our planet? "Yes, this is possible. However, the chances are extremely small, and it is unlikely that this has ever happened or will ever happen. On the other hand, it can happen that the Sun or another star captures a rogue planet into a wide orbit, far beyond the orbit of Pluto. This formerly rogue planet would then have found a parent star again, perhaps after billions of years of loneliness in deep space." ●

There could be up to 150 billion rogue planets in the Milky Way

How do we find them?

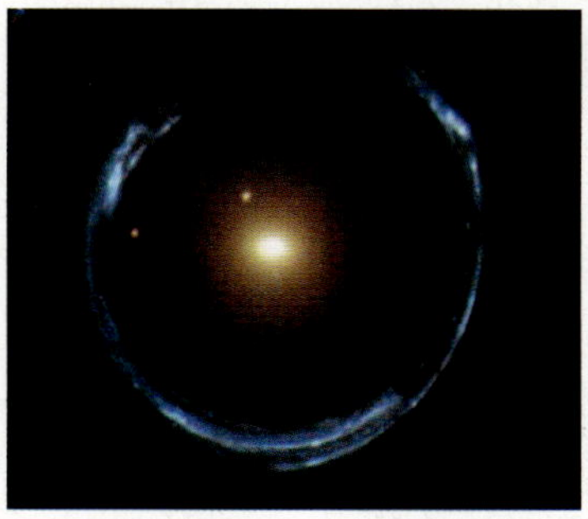

Kouwenhoven explains how we hunt for these lonely worlds: "Einstein's theory of relativity comes to help when finding free-floating planets. The gravity of each object in the universe deflects light. Under certain circumstances, this light deflection can act as a lens, and the light of a background star can be briefly enhanced. When a free-floating planet passes right in front of a background star, the background star suddenly becomes brighter for a brief time, and then faint again. The brightness changes due to microlensing have characteristics that allow the observer to derive the mass of the lensing object. In this way, several objects of planetary mass have been discovered, freely floating through space."

Pleiades

What makes this famous cluster of stars in the night sky so interesting?

The Pleiades has been observed for millennia, with its proximity to Earth and large stars making it observable to the naked eye and also an important tool for astronomers. Over 1,000 stars are contained within the cluster, and its characteristics have made it a stepping stone to understanding other clusters and stars in the universe.

Some of the earliest known depictions of Pleiades date back to 1600 BC, but it was not until 1771 AD that Charles Messier measured the position of the cluster and classified it as M45. Its nine brightest stars are named after the Seven Sisters of Greek mythology along with their parents. In order of brightness they are Alcyone, Atlas, Electra, Maia, Merope, Taygeta, Pleione, Celaeno and Sterope.

The Pleiades is between 390 and 460 light years away, making it one of the most easily viewable star clusters from Earth. This has seen it become an important calibration tool for calculating the distance to other stars in the universe.

The core cluster of stars within Pleiades have a radius of about eight light years. The cluster is dominated by bright hot blue stars, 14 of which are visible to the naked eye. These stars are typically between 15 and 90 times the mass of our own Sun with a luminosity at least 30,000 times greater and as much as 1,000,000 times more. However, owing to their large mass, they burn through their hydrogen fuel very quickly. Whereas our Sun is thought to have a lifetime of ten billion years, a hot blue star will live for just tens of millions of years.

A quarter of the Pleiades cluster is made up of brown stars, stars with less than eight per cent of the Sun's mass that are not heavy enough to ignite nuclear fusion in their cores. The relative proximity of Pleiades to the Earth has made it an excellent location to study these dim and diffuse stars, as in older clusters further away they are much more difficult to observe.

The cluster itself seems to bear some signs of being a reflection nebula. Dust in Pleiades reflects the light of the hotter blue stars, which may be a remnant of when the cluster first formed. However, its age would suggest that most of the dust from its formation should now have dispersed, suggesting that the nebula elements may merely be the result of the Pleiades passing through an especially dusty region of interstellar space.

The Pleiades is estimated to have an age of between 75 and 150 million years. It is an open star cluster, which means it will not stay gravitationally bound forever, and indeed calculations suggest it will disperse within 250 million years after interaction either with spiral arms in the Milky Way or the Orion constellation.

Fourteen stars in Pleiades are visible to the naked eye from Earth

Space Science

From the big bang to travelling faster than the speed of light

162
Life in space

164
Light-speed travel

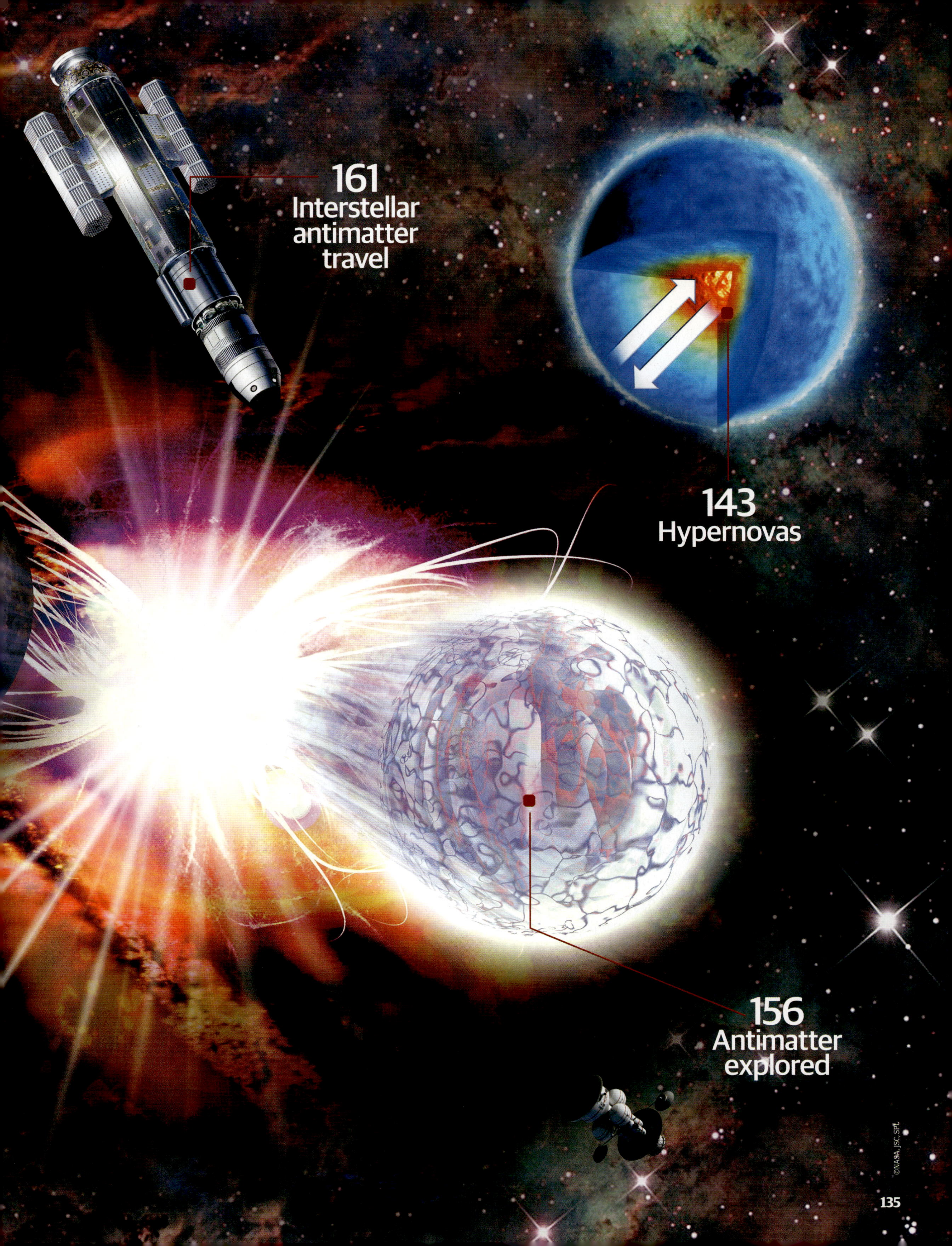
161
Interstellar antimatter travel
143
Hypernovas
156
Antimatter explored
©NASA, JSC, SPL

THE MOST POWERFUL FORCES IN THE UNIVERSE

Join us as we explore the objects in the cosmos that pack the biggest punches of all

The universe is an incredibly violent place, populated by explosions and torrents of radiation, pulled this way and that by powerful fundamental forces, and lit up by active centres of galaxies and massive stars. All these forces are in interplay - supernovas create black holes, while gravity battles dark energy to decide the fate of the universe. Energies far greater than the Sun can produce in 10 billion years are wielded in a matter of seconds, and our knowledge of physics is put to the test by the most extreme and most powerful events in the universe.

THE EXPLOSION THAT CREATED THE UNIVERSE

The Big Bang

Our universe sprang into existence around 13.77 billion years ago; a great event that created everything we know of - from stars and galaxies to planets and Solar Systems. Nothing existed before the Big Bang. While it's easy to imagine that a great explosion created our universe, this is far from the truth. Currently we understand that, at first, there was nothing and, during and after that moment, time and space came into existence - beginning as an infinitesimally small, infinitely hot and dense object. Just where it came from, is however, something experts are still not sure of.

What we do know is that this point began to expand and is continuing to do so according to the rate at which galaxies are moving away from us. The story of how the cosmos came to be as it is today is a tale of high energies, thick 'fog' and sizzling temperatures which gradually calmed, cleared and cooled, creating the first particles and the beginnings of the fundamental forces that surround us. These are the electromagnetic, weak, gravitational and strong forces, the latter being the one that holds nuclei together.

As the universe cooled further it shifted from being radiation dominated to being matter dominated, introducing the hydrogen atoms along with the cosmic microwave background radiation - the thermal radiation that fills every part of the universe - which crackles its presence when radio dishes are turned upon it.

The final transformation saw the emergence of large-scale structures as the earliest stars, quasars, galaxies, clusters of galaxies and superclusters were added to the cosmic mix.

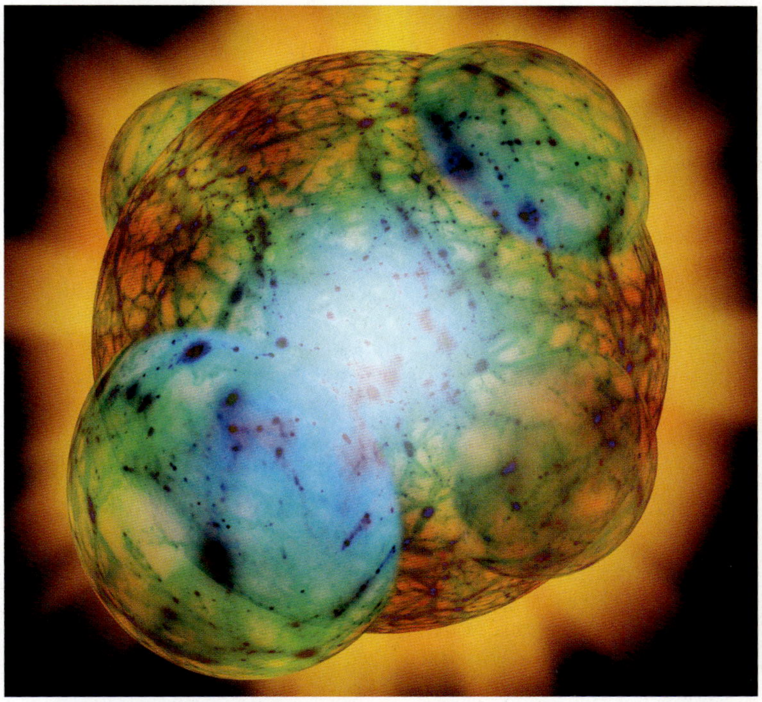

An artist's impression of the inflation theory which suggests that during the Big Bang, a false vacuum created a force which drove a very rapid expansion of the universe

Birth of the universe

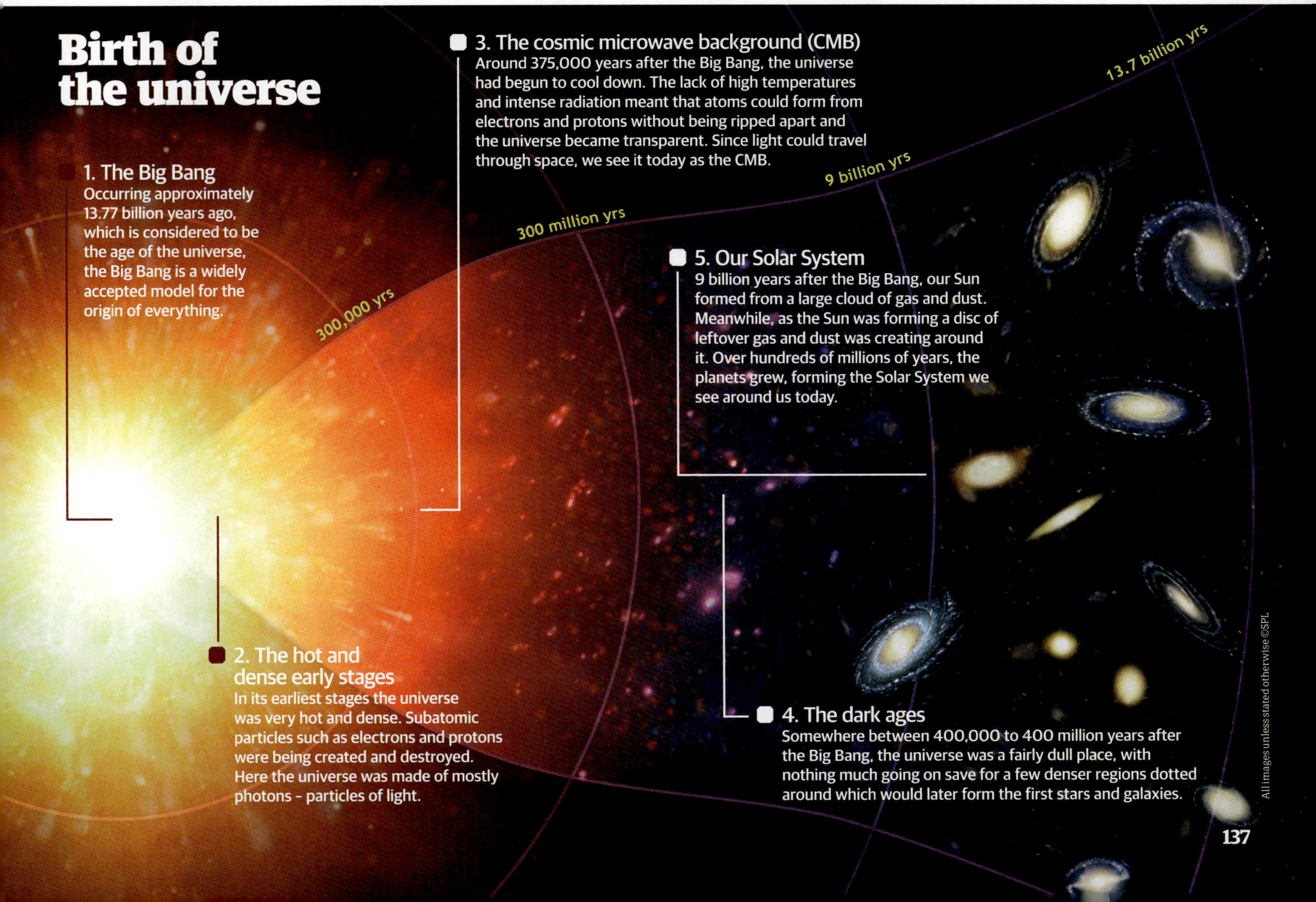

1. The Big Bang
Occurring approximately 13.77 billion years ago, which is considered to be the age of the universe, the Big Bang is a widely accepted model for the origin of everything.

2. The hot and dense early stages
In its earliest stages the universe was very hot and dense. Subatomic particles such as electrons and protons were being created and destroyed. Here the universe was made of mostly photons - particles of light.

3. The cosmic microwave background (CMB)
Around 375,000 years after the Big Bang, the universe had begun to cool down. The lack of high temperatures and intense radiation meant that atoms could form from electrons and protons without being ripped apart and the universe became transparent. Since light could travel through space, we see it today as the CMB.

4. The dark ages
Somewhere between 400,000 to 400 million years after the Big Bang, the universe was a fairly dull place, with nothing much going on save for a few denser regions dotted around which would later form the first stars and galaxies.

5. Our Solar System
9 billion years after the Big Bang, our Sun formed from a large cloud of gas and dust. Meanwhile, as the Sun was forming a disc of leftover gas and dust was creating around it. Over hundreds of millions of years, the planets grew, forming the Solar System we see around us today.

POWERING THE EXPANSION OF THE UNIVERSE

Dark energy

We can't see it, but we know it's there. The mysterious dark energy, which accounts for roughly 70 per cent of the universe, is the driving force behind why galaxies are moving away from us in an almost eternal expansion, which, according to experts, isn't showing any signs of slowing down.

Permeating through every corner of space, scientists didn't even realise it existed until 1997. Two groups of astronomers had been competing against each other to measure the expansion rate of the universe by using the light of supernovas. As the universe expands, the light is stretched and reddened. Because certain types of supernovas - the explosions of merging white dwarf stars - detonate with practically identical energy and luminosity, they believed it would be possible to measure their 'redshift' and consequently the expansion of the universe. They expected it to be slowing down - instead it was found that it was actually speeding up!

Nobody knows what dark energy is or even precisely how strong it is. It acts a bit like anti-gravity, pushing the universe apart. On the biggest scales it overcomes all of the other forces in the universe, including gravity, and that could prove to be bad news for the universe. If dark energy was to become too powerful, it could tear the universe apart in a 'big rip', starting with galaxy clusters, then galaxies themselves, then stars, planets, us and even our constituent atoms until the fabric of space and time itself is destroyed completely.

At best dark energy will accelerate the expansion of the universe so that every other galaxy is moved so far away from us that we will no longer be able to see them, but astronomers need not panic yet - this is not expected to happen for approximately another 2 trillion years.

A ring of dark matter can be seen in this image of galaxy cluster CI 0024+17

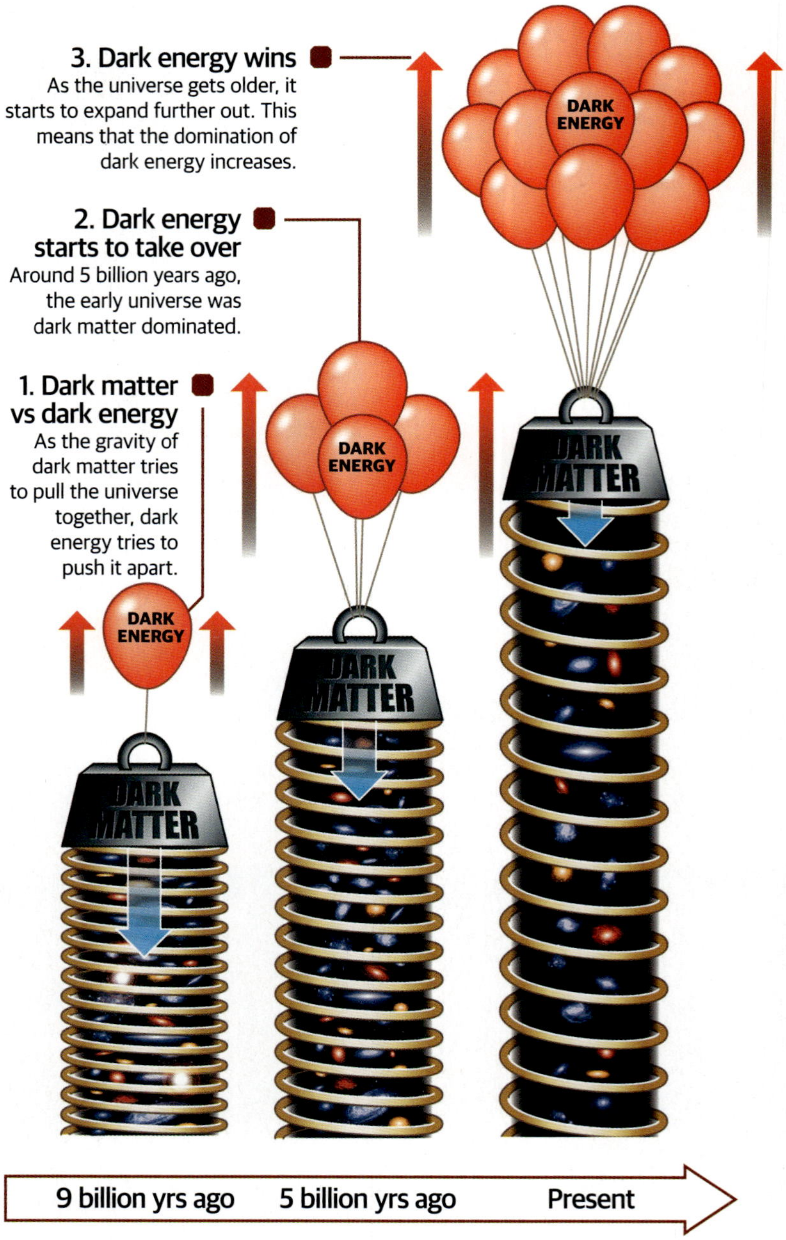

Gravity

THE FORCE THAT BINDS THE UNIVERSE TOGETHER

In *Star Wars*, there was The Force - the mystical field that binds together all life. In the universe, however, there is another 'force' that binds together all matter, and that's the somewhat mysterious force of gravity. That famous (and probably false) story of an apple falling on Isaac Newton's head was only the beginning of gravity's remarkable story.

What makes the planets round? Gravity. What keeps us from floating away? Gravity. What causes temperatures and pressures to grow so high in the core of the Sun that it can ignite nuclear fusion? Gravity. What keeps the planets orbiting the Sun? Gravity. And so on.

So, gravity is a big deal. Newton's laws of motion and his law of universal gravitation describe how gravity operates in everyday life. However, things can get a little strange when we start to talk about really massive objects, or things that are moving at close to the speed of light. This is where Einstein's general theory of relativity comes in, describing such concepts as gravitational time dilation, black holes and neutron stars with immense gravity, gravity wells in space-time, and gravitational lenses where massive objects like galaxy clusters are able to bend and magnify the light of more distant objects. And when neutron stars merge, or black holes crash into each other, they unleash a torrent of 'gravitational waves' that ripple through space-time. Nobody has ever detected a gravitational wave (see our space mysteries feature on page 54) , but scientists are always on the lookout and hope to meet with some success in this area in the coming years. Oddly, for a force that is so important, gravity is quite weak on small scales. A bar magnet, for example, can overpower gravity, picking bits of metal up for fun. But on much larger scales gravity dominates, holding entire galaxy clusters together. It's only when it comes face to face with the ever-growing force of dark energy that gravity starts to become unstuck. Ultimately, the fate of the universe will be decided by the battle between gravity and dark energy: will dark energy rip the cosmos apart, or will gravity be strong enough in the long run to pull the universe back in a 'big crunch'? The end of the universe may be decided by one of these theories.

SO BRIGHT THEY CAN BE SEEN FROM THE EDGE OF SPACE

Quasars

They might be distant, but packing a punch of high energy and indescribable luminosity are quasars - objects believed to be glowing strongly since their creation in the universe's early days.

Usually found in the very centres of active galaxies, quasars are among the most powerful objects in the universe; with most throwing out a luminosity equivalent to around 2 trillion Suns, while others emit strongly as sources of radio emission and gamma rays. So what gives them so much power?

In the nuclei of the galaxies they occupy, a supermassive black hole munches on the material from the disc of gas around it. This gas is then fed into the centre of the galaxy with the dazzling quasar light all coming from this million-degree hot disc and the jets of energy it unleashes. The jets form because the disc is a tangle of magnetic fields that become tightly wound as the disc rotates, trapping charged particles within them until they're fired out at almost the speed of light. It's only when we look almost head-on at these jets that we see a quasar. Indeed, they are so bright and powerful they can be seen right across the known universe.

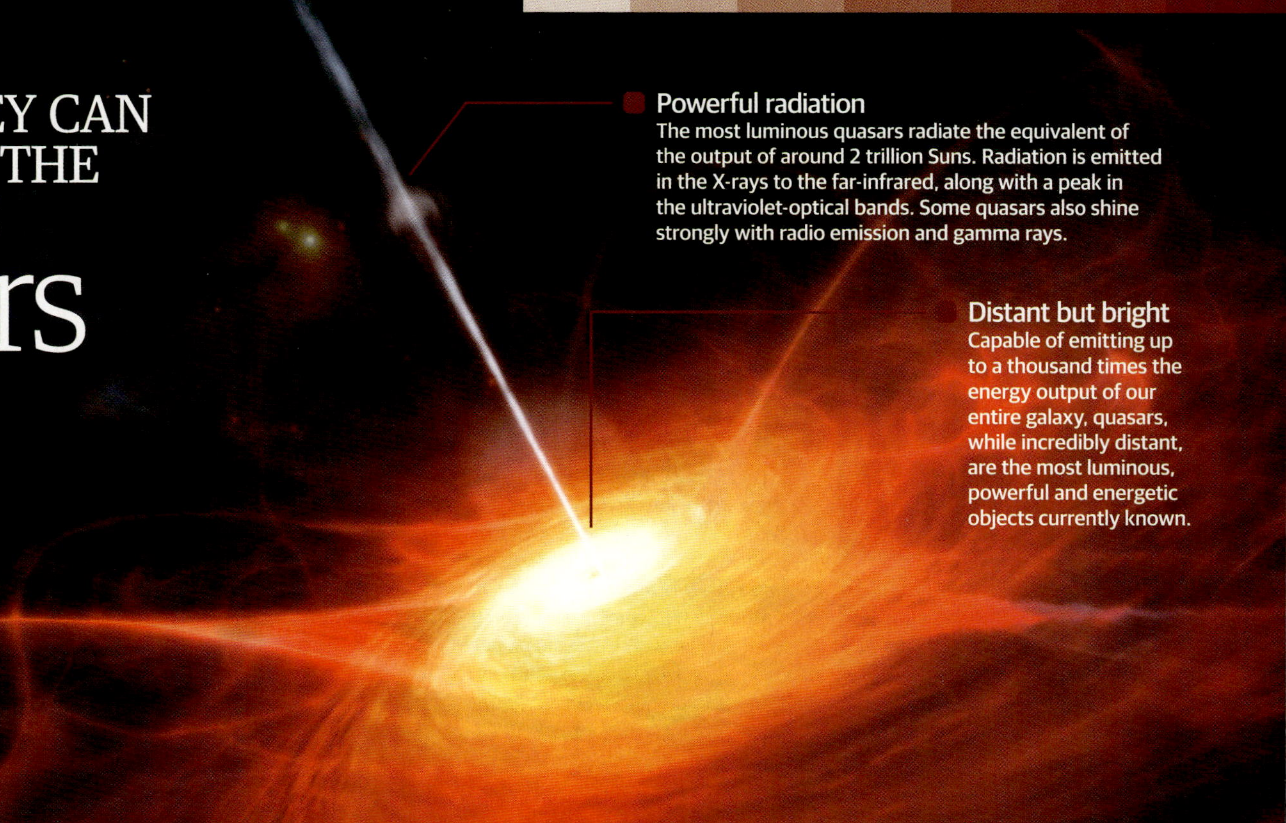

Powerful radiation

The most luminous quasars radiate the equivalent of the output of around 2 trillion Suns. Radiation is emitted in the X-rays to the far-infrared, along with a peak in the ultraviolet-optical bands. Some quasars also shine strongly with radio emission and gamma rays.

Distant but bright

Capable of emitting up to a thousand times the energy output of our entire galaxy, quasars, while incredibly distant, are the most luminous, powerful and energetic objects currently known.

Accretion disc power

Quasars are believed to be powered by the accretion of material into centralised supermassive black holes, some of these high-gravity objects have masses of over 1 million solar masses.

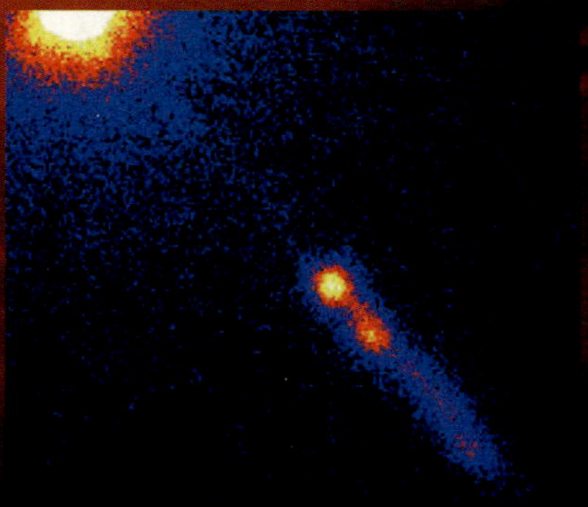

An X-ray image of quasar 3C 273 and its jet. This quasar is the closest to Earth at a distance of almost 3 billion light years

Gravity wells

The Sun

Since our Sun is so heavy, its gravity well is by far the deepest.

Inner planet gravity

Out of the terrestrial planets, Earth has the deepest gravity well. The deeper the well, the harder it is to escape the gravity of the planet.

Jupiter's gravity well

Because this gas giant is much more massive than each of the planets in our Solar System, it has the deepest gravitational well. In comparison, its moons have shallower dips which are quite easy to escape.

Outer planet gravity

Out of Saturn, Uranus and Neptune the deepest gravity well is made by Saturn.

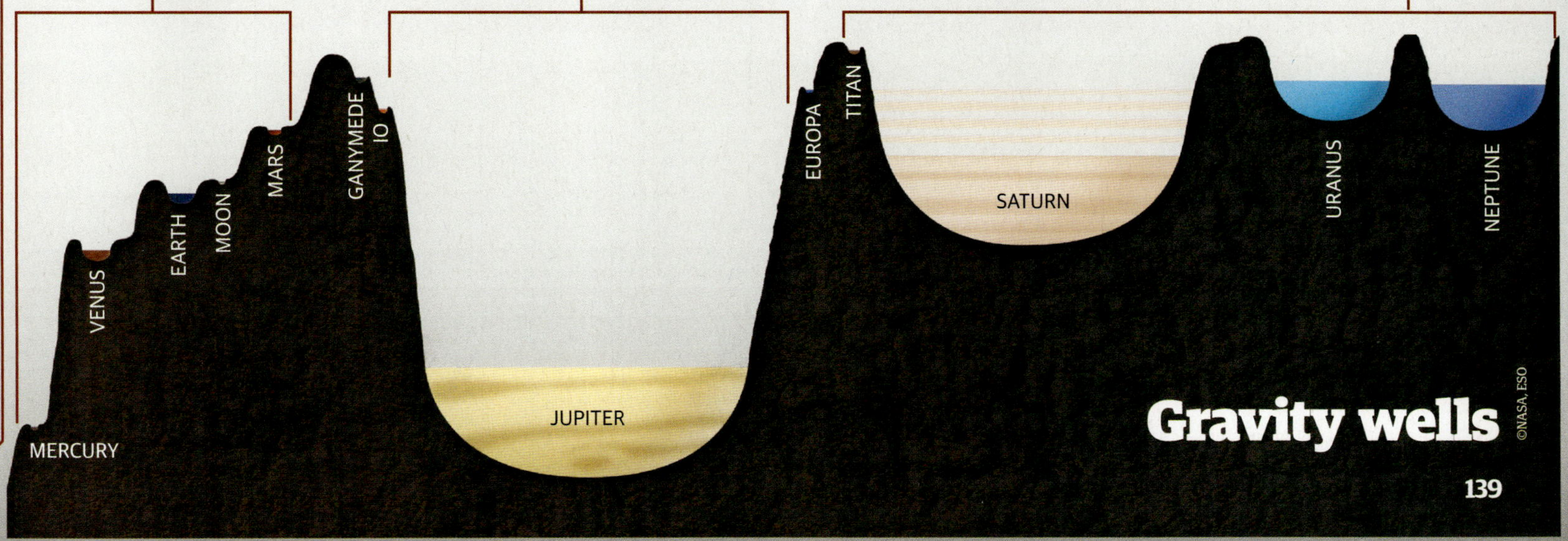

This coloured image snapped by the Chandra X-ray telescope shows the heart of our Milky Way Galaxy

This distant galaxy houses a quasar, a supermassive black hole encircled by a torus of gas and dust

THE POWER TO HARNESS A GALAXY

Supermassive black holes

The ultimate consequence of gravity is a black hole. Imagine a region of space where gravity has caused a star to collapse at the end of its life to a point so small and dense that its gravity is practically infinite and completely overwhelms everything else. It's so strong that not even light can escape its grasp - the point of no return is known as the event horizon - explaining where the name black hole came from. And black holes don't come any more massive than a hefty supermassive black hole. With a mass ranging anywhere from hundreds of thousands to billions of times the mass of the Sun, these exotic high-gravity objects are, more often than not, the centrepiece of the many galaxies that litter our universe. Our own Milky Way even has one, called Sagittarius A*, which is a monster of around 4.3 million times the mass of our Sun, located deep in the middle of our galaxy amid myriad stars and vast clouds of gas and dust. So powerful are these galaxies that they have the strength to switch star formation in a galaxy on and off at will.

Think back to quasars - these are the most extreme form of active supermassive black hole. But less energetic black holes can still produce lower power jets, yet even though they're lower power, they still dominate the galaxy that they are in. Stars need gas to form, and the gas in galaxies often falls on to them from wandering clouds of intergalactic gas. Yet as clouds fall on to galaxies, and as the galaxies merge with other galaxies, gas gets funnelled towards the black hole, ending up in a disc surrounding it, some of which is then beamed back out into the galaxy by jets, or 'winds', of stellar radiation.

These jets and radiation heat the gas that is creating stars, causing it to become too hot for star formation and sometimes even blowing right out of the galaxy itself. This is called feedback, and when it happens it brings star formation in a galaxy to a stuttering halt.

"Sagittarius A* is a monster of around 4.3 million times the mass of our Sun"

Supermassive formation

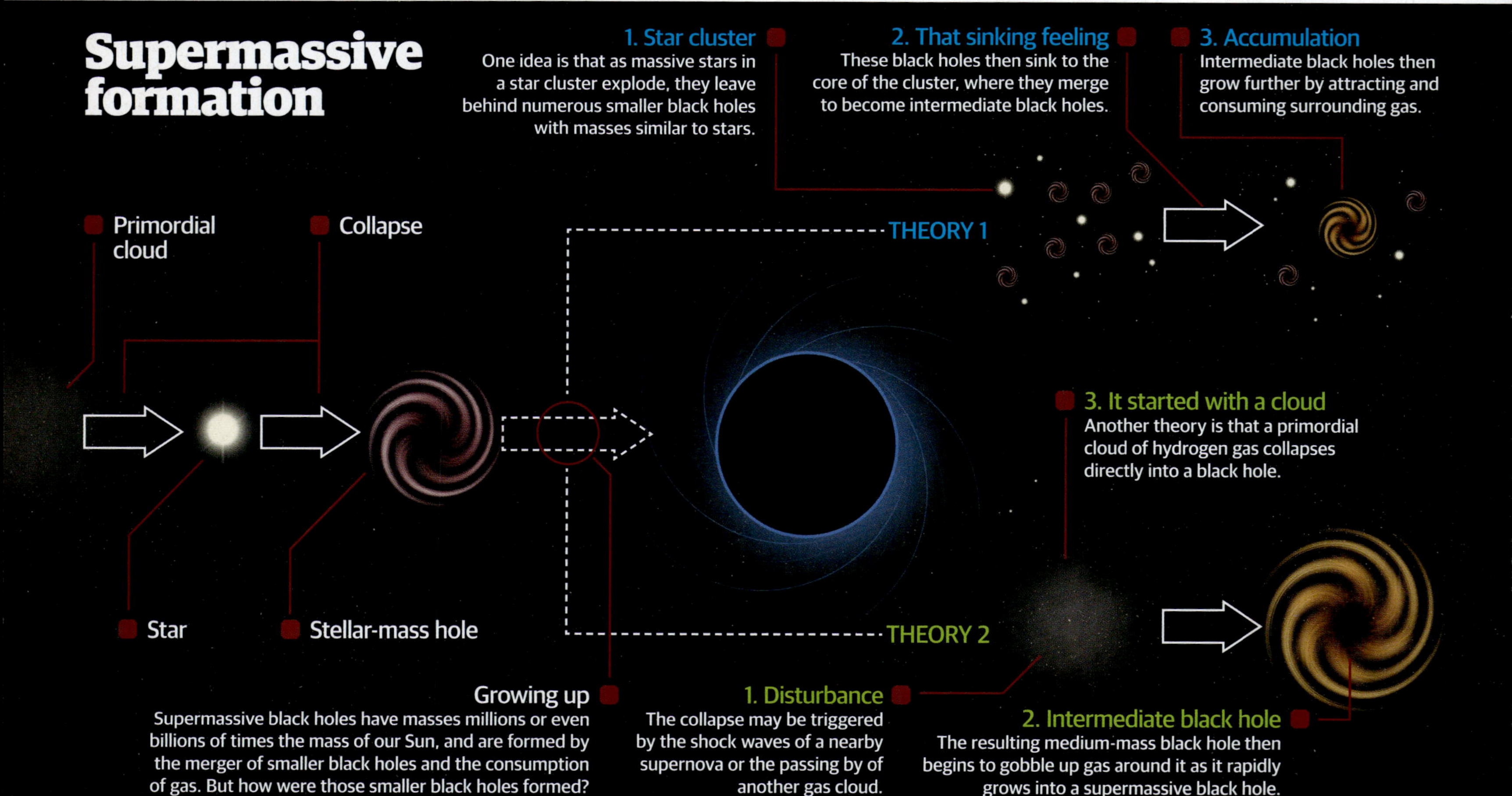

A rapidly growing supermassive black hole rests at the centre of one of the nearest and brightest galaxies to Earth – NGC 1068

The supermassive black hole at the heart of the Milky Way

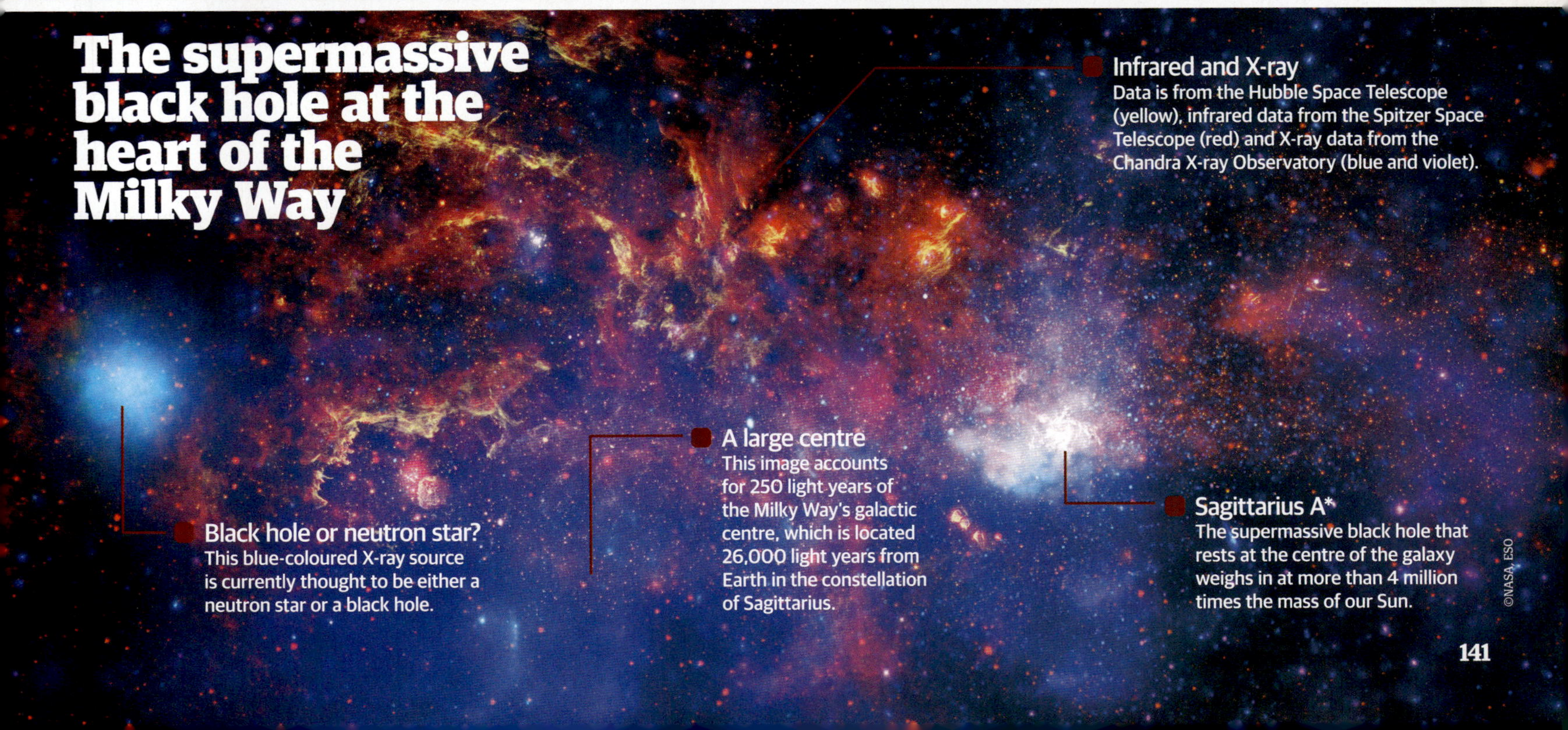

THE ENERGY OF A THOUSAND SUNS

Gamma ray bursts

Gamma-ray bursts (GRBs) signal the biggest explosions in the universe. They were discovered in 1973, after analysis of data from the Vela satellites, which the USA launched to try to detect Soviet nuclear tests in space. Instead, they found ferocious bursts of gamma rays from outer space. It took almost 25 years to figure out what they were. Scientists call them 'collapsars'. When the most massive stars of all reach the end of their lives, they can no longer hold back gravity and their core collapses into a black hole. Gas from some of the layers surrounding the core rain down on to it and, just like how the black holes in quasars produce jets, so do the black holes inside the collapsing star. All of this happens in merely a fraction of a second, and the jets blast out through the star's outer layers at close to the speed of light, as the star explodes.

But this isn't what creates the gamma rays. The jets are formed from highly entwined magnetic fields, and when charged particles like electrons and protons spiral around magnetic fields like this, they produce gamma rays, and it's these gamma rays that we see as a burst. As for their power, there's nothing else like them in the known universe, releasing the equivalent amount of energy that a thousand Sun-like stars will release over their entire lifetimes! If a GRB's energy could be harnessed on Earth, it would meet the world's energy demands for billions of years. ●

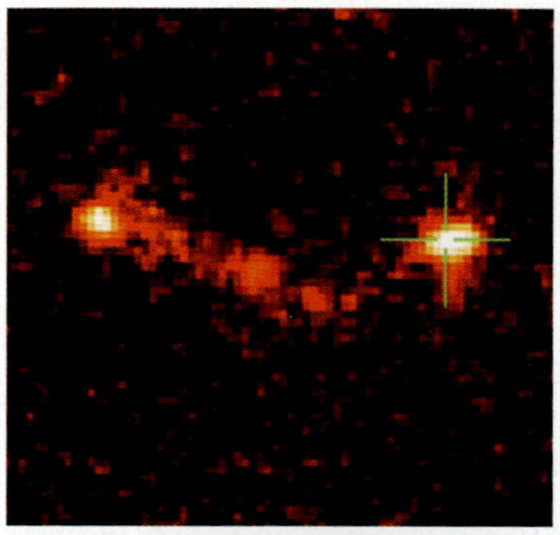

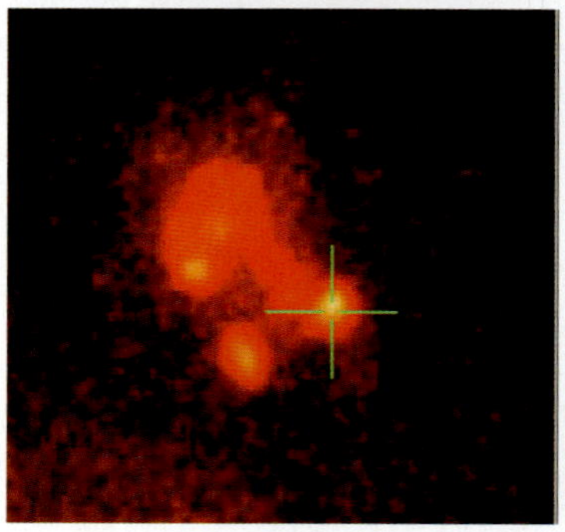

A selection of images of galaxies that host long-duration gamma-ray bursts as taken by the Hubble Space Telescope

Beautiful bursts

1. Fusion
Stars generate energy through nuclear fusion. In massive stars it is via the CNO – carbon, nitrogen, oxygen – cycle, which acts as catalysts for fusion involving hydrogen atoms.

2. Onion layers
Nuclear fusion of hydrogen creates helium. Temperatures grow so high that the helium begins to fuse to create oxygen, then nitrogen, carbon, silicon and so on.

3. Living fast
Massive stars struggle to stay aloft against the pull of gravity, so they have to generate a lot of energy, which uses up their vast stores of gas in just a few million years.

4. Iron star
Massive stars end up with cores of iron, which cannot undergo further nuclear fusion without putting in more energy than it produces. Fusion ceases in the star's core.

5. Collapse
As the massive star reaches the end of its life and is unable to generate any more energy, the core of the star begins to collapse in on itself to form a black hole.

6. Jets
Gas inside the star swirls around the black hole and forms powerful jets that destroy it in a hypernova. Charged particles spiralling around the magnetic jets produce gamma rays.

THE POWER OF AN EXPLODING HYPERGIANT

Hypernovas

As you might imagine, the supernovas that create gamma-ray bursts are no ordinary type of exploding star; instead we call them hypernovas, and they make normal supernovas look like a mere pop in comparison.

Hypernovas can be 20 times more luminous and up to 50 times more energetic than a normal supernova. It's not entirely clear why hypernovas are different to normal supernovas, but mass undoubtedly has something to do with it: some stars like Eta Carinae have masses around 100 times that of our Sun, while other stars that explode as supernovas may have only a dozen solar masses. In addition, massive stars that have been deprived of heavy elements – elements heavier than hydrogen or helium – have a tendency to explode as hypernovas.

However, not all hypernovas create gamma-ray bursts. It seems the most extreme examples are completely annihilated without even leaving a black hole behind. These are known as 'pair instability' supernovas and happen when electrons and their anti-particles – or positrons – are formed en masse by collisions between energetic gamma rays and atoms inside the dying star.

Not only does this lead to reduced pressure inside the supermassive star, which then prevents the core of the star from fully collapsing to create a black hole, but when matter and antimatter come into contact with each other in this way they create what's known as a runaway thermonuclear explosion that utterly destroys the star, without leaving a black hole remnant behind.

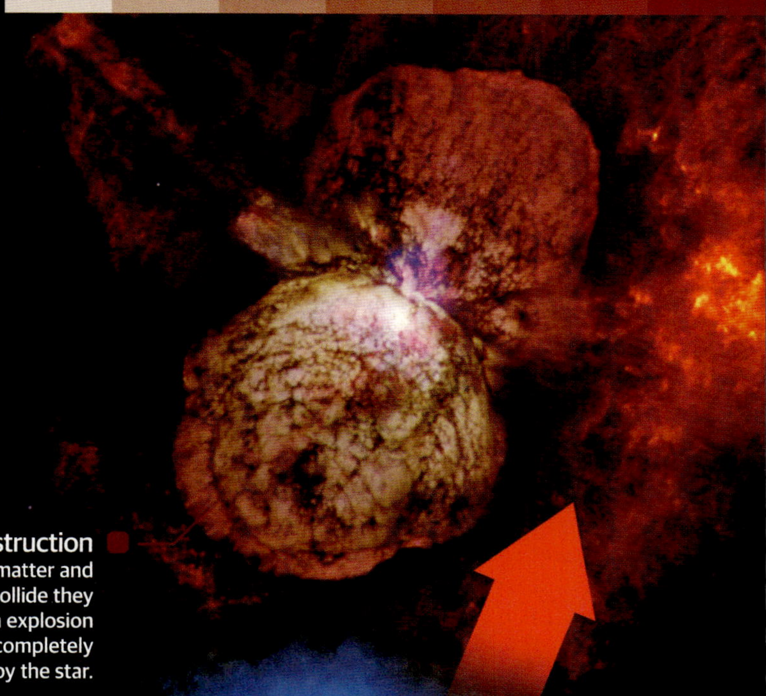

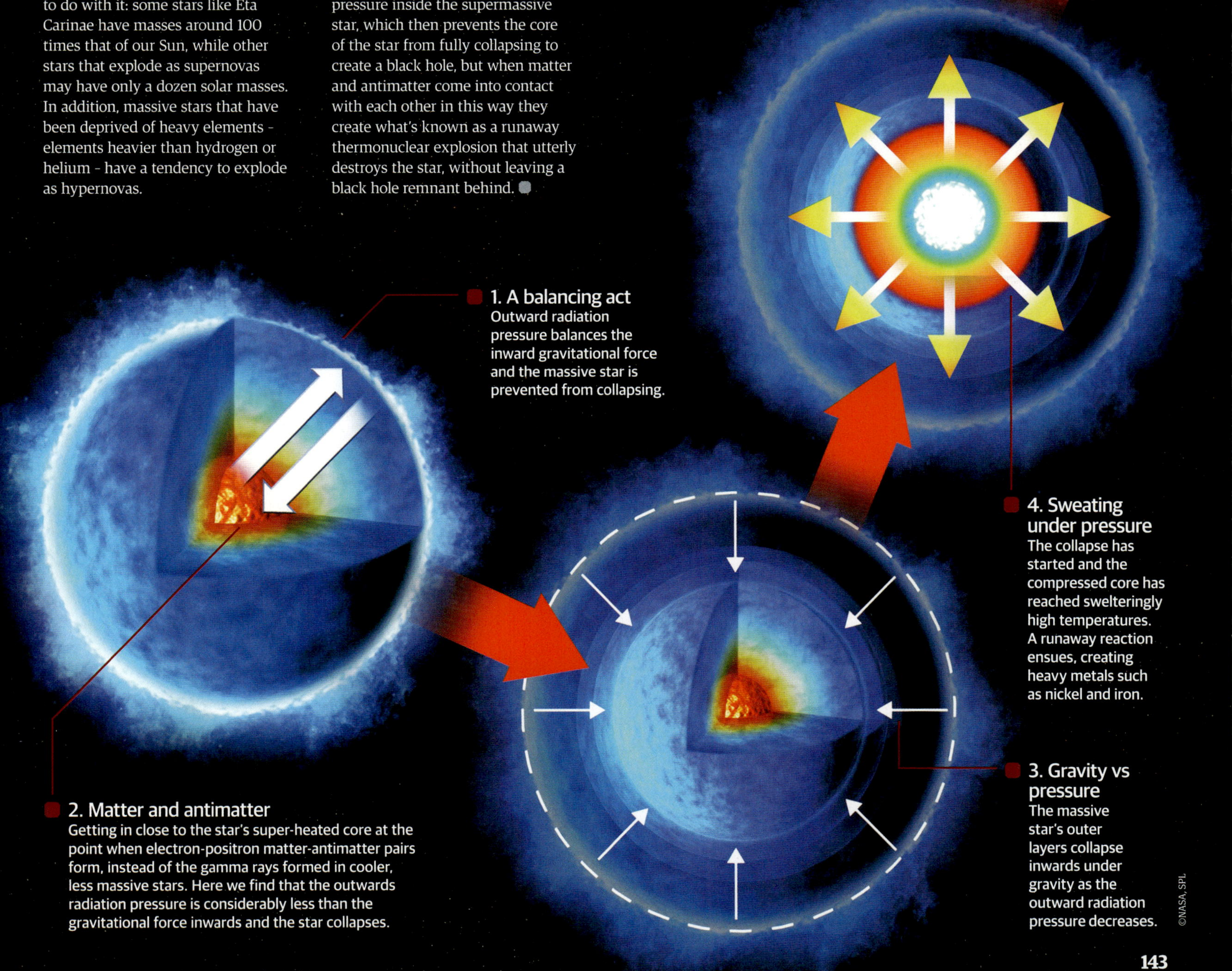

Seeing double: Gravitational lensing

A phenomenon that allows us to see an object simultaneously at two different points in time

In 1916, Albert Einstein published his groundbreaking paper on general relativity, which, among other things, showed that space and time were intertwined as space-time, and that every object with mass exerted a gravitational influence on its surrounding space.

This brought with it an interesting conclusion, namely that an object with enough mass would not only exert a gravitational influence on other celestial objects, but also on light itself. This theory was confirmed during a solar eclipse in 1919 when British astrophysicist Arthur Eddington observed that stars passing close to the Sun appeared out of position because their light was being bent.

It was postulated that if a distant object, an intervening one and the Earth were all aligned, then the image of that distant object would appear distorted or even multiplied as its light bent around the intervening object on its way to Earth. However, scientists including Einstein, only considered the gravitational lensing effects of a single star, which they deemed would be almost impossible to observe. It was not until 1937 that Swiss astronomer Fritz Zwicky suggested that larger objects like galaxies could produce the same effect, although sadly he would not live to see his theory proved.

In 1979, five years after Zwicky's death, the first gravitational lens was discovered, albeit by accident. A team using the Kitt Peak National Observatory in Arizona, USA was responsible, but their discovery was the cause of contention for some time. What they saw was the Twin Quasar, an occurrence of apparently two quasars located over 8 billion light years from Earth in the Ursa Major constellation. They were remarkably similar, with an almost identical redshift and visible light spectrum, suggesting that they were actually the same object appearing in two different images due to an intervening galaxy cluster located over 4 billion light years closer to Earth.

However, later in 1979 further studies revealed a relativist jet emerging from quasar A, but the same could not be seen at quasar B. This put the suggestion that the Twin Quasar was the first gravitationally lensed object to be observed in doubt, until similar jets were discovered at quasar B in 1983.

It was also found, through three decades of observations, that the intervening galaxy cluster was off-centred. So, although the two quasars were the same object, the light from quasar A reaches Earth 14 months before quasar B. This is one amazing aspect of gravitational lensing; it allows us to see an object simultaneously at different points in time.

But the Twin Quasar was not finished with its surprises just yet. One other type of gravitational lensing, called microlensing, occurs when a smaller object like a planet in the lensing object further distorts the light of the distant object. In 1996, such a distortion was observed in the lightcurve of the Twin Quasar, which was controversially attributed to an extragalactic planet (one found outside the Milky Way) three times the mass of Earth. At a distance of 4 billion light years this would make it the most distant planet known to date, but the chance alignment will never occur again and therefore we will never know for sure.

However, microlensing such as this has proven very useful in the search for planets. A Polish astronomical project called the Optical Gravitational Lensing Experiment (OGLE), which began in 1992, has successfully discovered several extrasolar planets by observing the distortion in the lensing effect of distant objects (see the 'Finding planets through microlensing' boxout). This led to the discovery of OGLE-2005-BLG-0390Lb, a super-Earth 21,500 light years away that is one of the most distant confirmed planets we know of to date.

We now know of many gravitationally lensed objects in the universe, and by using this technique we are able not only to discern the properties of massive distant objects like quasars, but also to map the amount of expected dark matter in the universe. Gravitational lensing is a remarkable effect but it has taken us nearly a century to truly appreciate and understand its uses. Continued observations will no doubt uncover more of these fantastic phenomena and help us to comprehend the effect of massive objects on space-time even further. ●

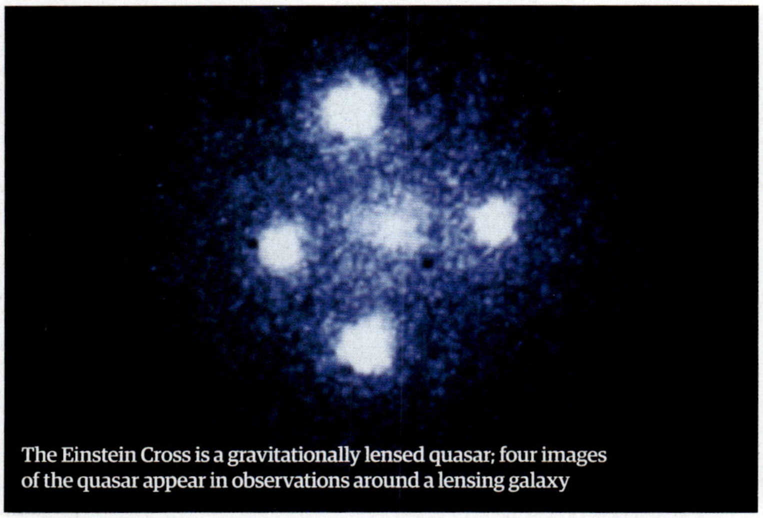

The Einstein Cross is a gravitationally lensed quasar; four images of the quasar appear in observations around a lensing galaxy

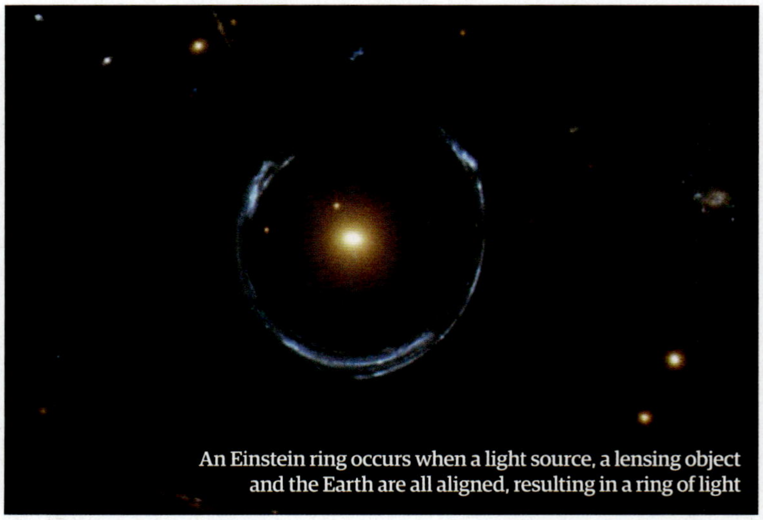

An Einstein ring occurs when a light source, a lensing object and the Earth are all aligned, resulting in a ring of light

Looking through the lens

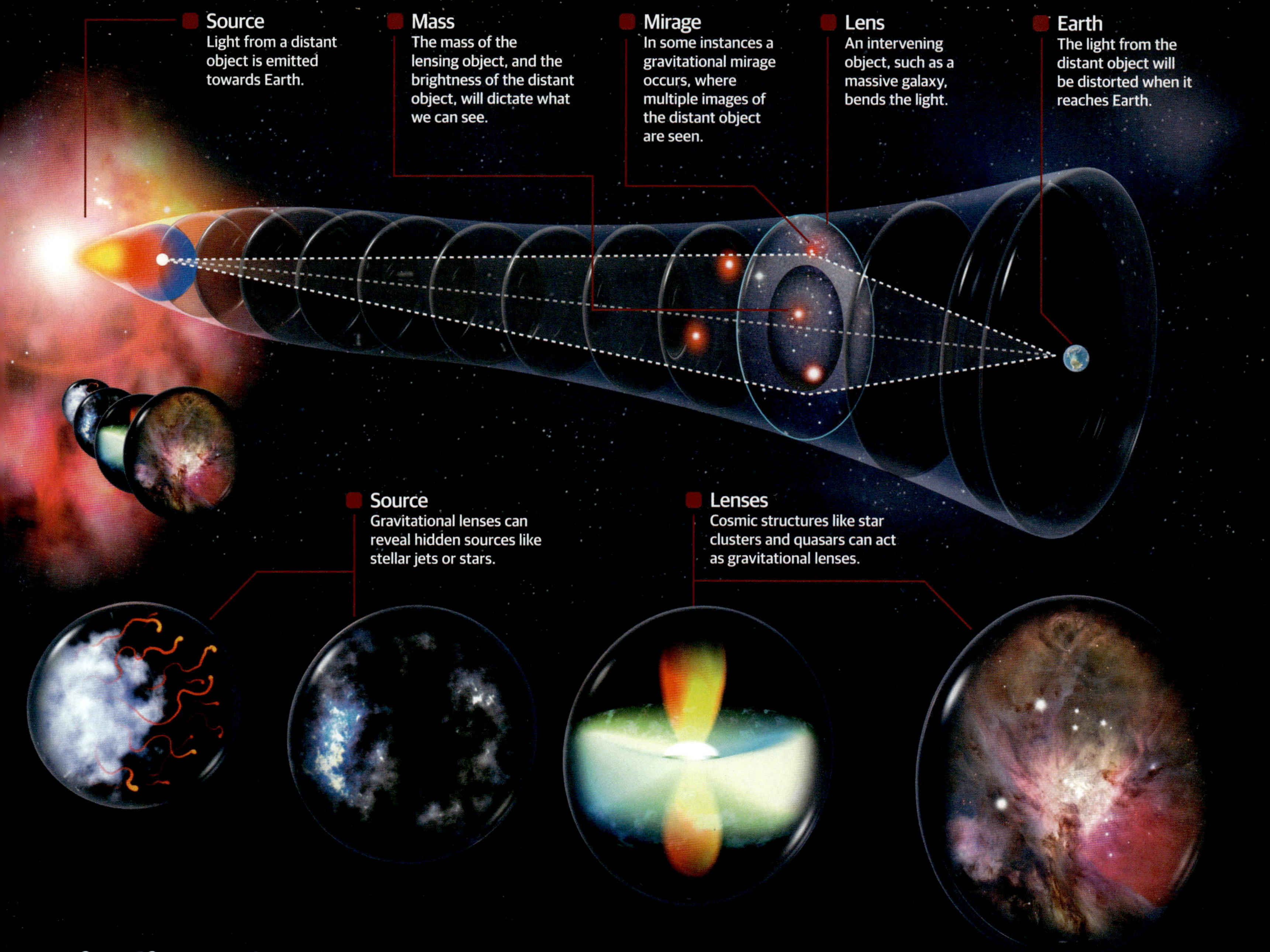

Finding planets through microlensing

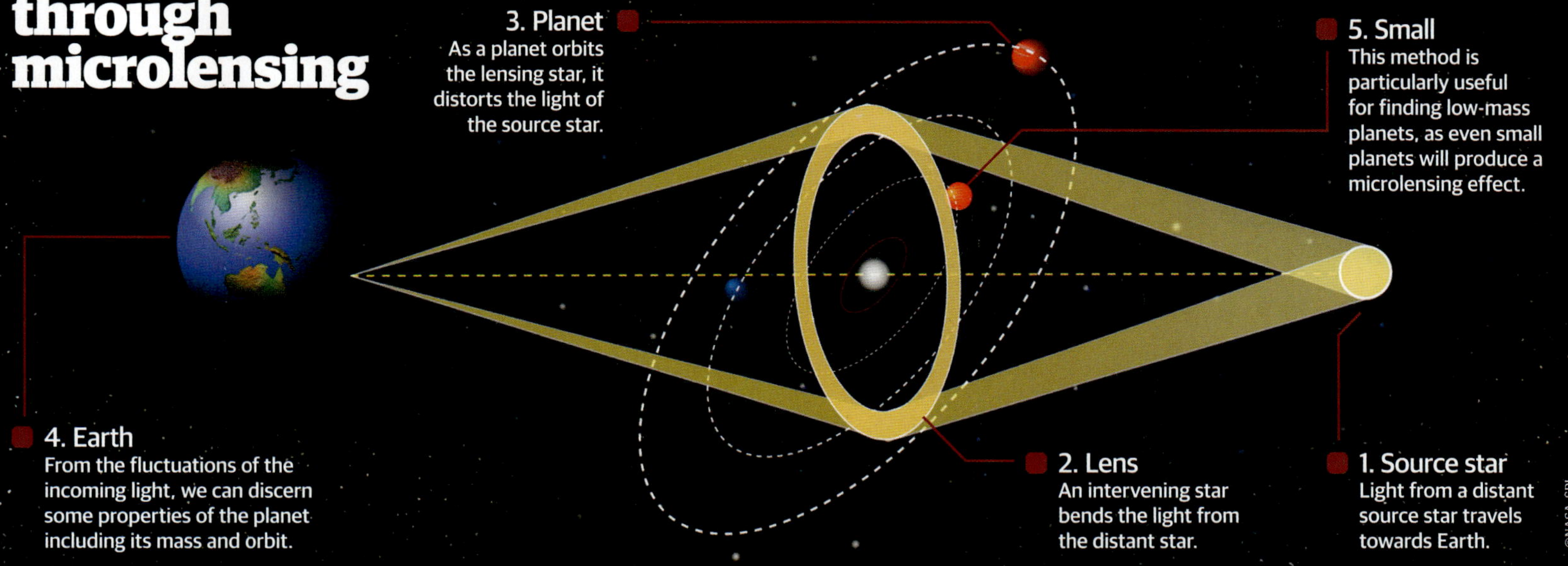

Tails

These two galaxies were nicknamed the Mice Galaxies due to their huge and pronounced galactic tails, which dramatically extend outwards and away from each other. The long tails were generated by tidal action, with the difference in gravitational attraction pulling on the near and far side of each.

Colours

The colours of both galaxies, but notably the upper NGC 4676A, are interesting, with the tails especially differentiating from other examples. Starting out blue and terminating in a yellow colour, the tails reverse the standard colour pattern for spiral galaxies – most likely caused by galactic tidal forces.

Coalesce

While not all orbiting pairs of galaxies converge, in the case of the Mice Galaxies this is predicted, with the pair predicted to continue to collide until they coalesce and form into one larger galaxy.

Spiral

The Mice Galaxies (NGC 4676) are two spiral galaxies in the constellation Coma Berencies, which is approximately 290 million light years from Earth. Both galaxies, which are members of the Coma cluster, are presently colliding and may have done so in the past.

> "Galactic tides affect the shape and composition of stellar objects"

The power of Galactic tides

Galactic tides are capable of shearing entire galaxies in two and ejecting stars and debris into interstellar space

A galactic tide is a cosmic process in which an object of small mass is distorted gravitationally by one of larger mass, such as a satellite galaxy being influenced by a larger galaxy. This process occurs as gravitational attraction between two objects increases with a decrease in distance, with objects in close proximity to each other experiencing stronger attraction and greater probability of generating a galactic tide.

A good theoretical example of a galactic tide is two galaxies located close to each other, one with a large mass and the other with a smaller mass. Here, the stronger gravitational attraction of the large galaxy causes the outer layers of the smaller one to be siphoned and drawn off from its core, warping and elongating it from a rough disc shape to an uneven one. This shearing tidal force is experienced by the larger galaxy too, however, due to the smaller one's lesser mass and gravitational attraction - as described in Isaac Newton's law of universal gravitation - it does not experience the effect as strongly.

Interestingly, galactic tides do not necessarily result in galactic collisions, as tidal forces are dependent on the gradient of gravitational field as well as strength. For example, in the aforementioned example of two galaxies, the result of close proximity will not necessarily lead to a collision as the tidal forces involved will distort each galaxy along an axis both pointing towards and away from its opposite number. As the two galaxies orbit each other, which can be temporarily, these distorted stretched-out regions are sheared off the corresponding cores due to their differential rotation (different layers are rotating at different angular velocities) and ejected into intergalactic space. This ejection generates galactic tails, strongly curved expanses of stars and gas that extend out from the galaxy cores (a good example of this can be seen in the image of the Mice Galaxies on the opposite page).

Galactic tides not only affect the shape and composition of stellar objects but also other factors, too. In small-scale objects such as dwarf galaxies, tidal forces can alter their interior structure and motions, luminosity factor and - in galaxies - star formation rate. A good example of these effects can be seen in the case of dwarf galaxy M32, a satellite of the mighty Andromeda Galaxy. Here, not only has M32 had its spiral arms accreted by Andromeda in a tidal stripping process but also it has an anomalous mass-to-luminosity ratio as well as an abnormally high star formation rate in its core - the latter theorised to be generated by tidally induced motions in its remaining molecular clouds.

While galactic tides occur outside of a galaxy, tidal forces in general occur both outside and inside them, with the gravitationally weak boundaries of systems most prone (the region where the Sun's gravitational influence is overpowered; referred to as the tidal truncation radius). A good example of this can be visualised with our own Solar System, with the hypothetical Oort cloud that surrounds it being gravitationally distorted by the Milky Way's tidal forces. This distortion is postulated to be one of the primary generators of comets within our Solar System, with the galactic tide bending and distorting the orbits of bodies (such as comets) and drawing them towards the galactic centre. ■

Tides in space

Galactic tides are generated by galaxies due to their huge gravitational attraction and tidal forces. As such, satellites of major galaxies are the most common places to find evidence of the galactic tidal processes.

One of the best currently known interactions of this type can be found in the relationship between the dwarf elliptical galaxy M32 and Andromeda. Here, not only has the significantly smaller M32 had almost all of its outer layers (spiral arms) sheared away by the tidal forces of Andromeda but it is also having its core manipulated by them. This manipulation consists of tidally induced motions within its central molecular clouds, with the tidal forces kneading and compressing them on a large scale. This is inducing the creation of large quantities of new stars within the heart of the system and rapidly accelerating their full formation.

The Antennae galaxies are currently undergoing a galactic collision

Roche limits

The Roche limit - also referred to as the Roche radius - is described as the distance within which a celestial body held together by its own gravity will disintegrate under the influence of tidal forces. See how this works with our step-by-step process.

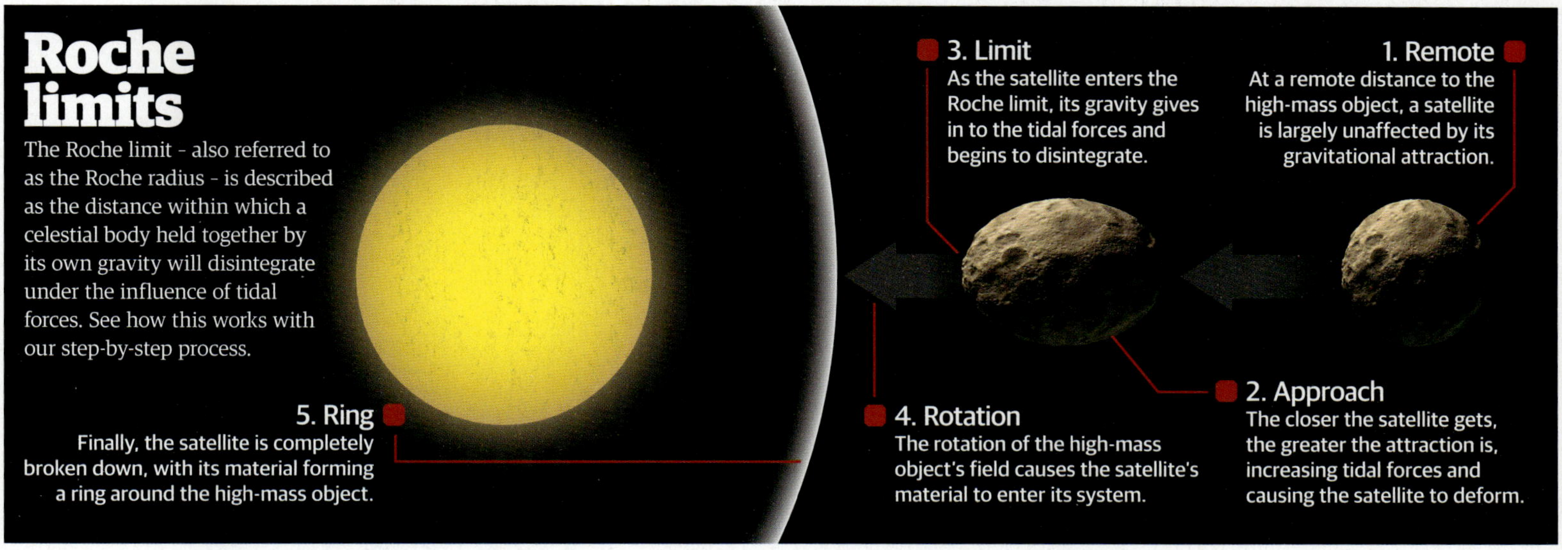

Hubble's tuning-fork classification system

Sc Open Spiral
This contains more young population I stars and interstellar gas. They have loosely wound untidy arms and a small central bulge. These consist of 10% gas and dust compared with 2% in Sa spirals.

Sb Intermediate Spiral
Found between the Sa and Sc galaxy formations, intermediate is the most common form of spiral galaxy. All spirals are rich in gas and dust and contain young population I stars along with older population II stars.

SBc Open Barred Spiral
This type of galaxy has the least defined central bar and a looser structure.

Sa Spiral
The spiral arms are tightly wound, with a bright central bulge and small amounts of interstellar gas. The S prefix refers to this being a spiral galaxy and the lower case letter refers to how tightly wound the galaxy arms are.

SBb Intermediate Barred Spiral
Our Milky Way galaxy is thought to be of this type.

E5 and E7 Elongated Elliptical
The most flattened galaxies are given this designation. Elliptical galaxies tend to contain old stars and are loosely structured indicating they were formed before spiral galaxies.

SBa Barred Spiral
The B designates that the galaxy has a bar of stars at its centre that the spiral arms wind away from. Just like the normal spiral galaxy classification system, the lower case letter refers to how tightly wound the spiral arms are.

SO Lenticular
This is lenticular shaped with a prominent central bulge, but has no spiral arms. It is an intermediate type between E7 and Sa galaxies. They are like elliptical galaxies because they tend to contain old stars and have less gas and dust than spirals.

E3 Elliptical
Elliptical galaxies are given higher numerical designations according to how flat they look. The E prefix refers to this being an elliptical galaxy and the number refers to how flat the galaxy is.

EO Spherical
The roundest-looking galaxies are given this rating. This corresponds to the physical structure of the galaxy, the rest of the E-type galaxies refer to how they look from Earth rather than their actual structure.

Galaxy classification

Edwin Hubble's monumental discoveries revealed that the universe consists of a variety of vast galaxies that exist far beyond our Milky Way galaxy

Edwin Hubble can be ranked as one of the great astronomers, whose discoveries are as important as those of Nicolaus Copernicus and Galileo Galilei.

In 1919, he began working at the Mount Wilson Observatory in California. A few years later, he used the newly built 2.5-metre (100-inch) Hooker Telescope to study Cepheid variable stars located in spiral nebulas. From these observations, he found that they must exist far beyond the Milky Way. In 1925, he presented his finding that these nebulas are galaxies in their own right, proving that the Milky Way is just a small part of the universe as opposed to the existing view that nothing existed beyond it.

Another major discovery was that the spectra of the light emitted by galaxies shifted towards the blue end of the spectrum if they were moving towards the Earth and that those moving away from the Earth showed a shift to the red end of the spectrum. From studying 18 galaxies, Hubble determined that the further away the galaxy is the faster it is moving away from us, which became known as Hubble's Law. From his measurements he reasoned that 2 billion years ago the universe began in a single burst of energy and has been moving away from this point of origin ever since. Today, it is thought the universe began 13.77 billion years ago but this was an important foundation for the influential Big Bang theory.

In 1926, Hubble created his morphological classification of the different types of visible galaxies. He divided galaxies into three major groups that he arranged in his famous Hubble tuning fork diagram. Elliptical galaxies represent over half the visible galaxies and are given the prefix E, while a number from 0 to 7 denotes how round or oval they are. Giant ellipticals exist at the centre of galactic clusters that can contain billions of stars, though there are also dwarf elliptical galaxies that contain a few hundred thousand stars.

Spiral galaxies

Spiral galaxies are equally divided between spirals with a central bulge (S types) and spirals with a central bar (SB types). Stars form in the spiral arms and centres of these galaxies. A further designation running from a to c was given to indicate how tightly or loosely wound the arms are. A 'd' type represents galaxies that have luminous, fragmentary and loosely wound arms, and an 'm' type is for galaxies with no bulge and irregular appearance.

Lenticular galaxies

Lenticular (S0 type) galaxies do not have spiral arms but do have a bright central bulge of stars like the spiral galaxies. Unlike the spirals they do not have significant amounts of stars forming inside them.

Irregular galaxies

Hubble identified a further group of irregular galaxies. He designated two types, the asymmetric Irr I that lacks a spiral or bulge structure that contains young stars, and Irr II, asymmetric galaxies that have no clearly visible stars or clusters.

Classifying galaxies

Although lenticular and elliptical galaxies are often called 'early type' galaxies, and spirals look more perfectly formed, Hubble was at pains to point out that his scheme did not show the evolutionary path of galactic formation. Instead, the diagram should be used as a guide to the visual appearances of the galaxies as seen from Earth.

Hubble's system is not perfect because it depends on a subjective assessment of which category a galaxy fits into. Another problem is that it only deals with the galaxies as two-dimensional objects and does not fully represent their true three-dimensional structures. French astronomer Gérard de Vaucouleurs found several shortcomings with the scheme. In 1959, he extended it to include ring-like galactic structures and he gave numerical values to the different classes of galaxy. Certainly, advances in astronomy have provided more information about the structure of galaxies and more complex classification systems exist, but Hubble's system remains a useful guide to understanding their appearance and basic structures.

Hubble studied law at Oxford University before deciding on a career in astronomy

Galactic identity parade

Abell S0740

The giant ESO 325-G004 E/S0 elliptical galaxy dominates the centre of the Abell S0740 galaxy cluster. The cluster is located in the Centaurus constellation at around 463 million light years from Earth.

M101 – The Pinwheel Galaxy

M101 is only 21 million light years away in the Ursa Major constellation. It is the most prominent grand design Scd spiral galaxy in the sky and is 170,000 light years across.

NGC 1300

This is an SBbc spiral barred galaxy with a diameter of around 110,000 million light years. It is at a distance of 61 million light years away and located in the southern constellation of Eridanus.

NGC 5866 – The Spindle Galaxy

This S0 lenticular galaxy is found in the Draco constellation. Only its 60,000 light year long edge is visible, from above it might reveal itself to be a spiral galaxy.

The Large Magellanic Cloud

Under Hubble's classification system, this irregular galaxy is on average 200,000 light years away. It is a satellite of our Milky Way galaxy and is full of glowing nebulas.

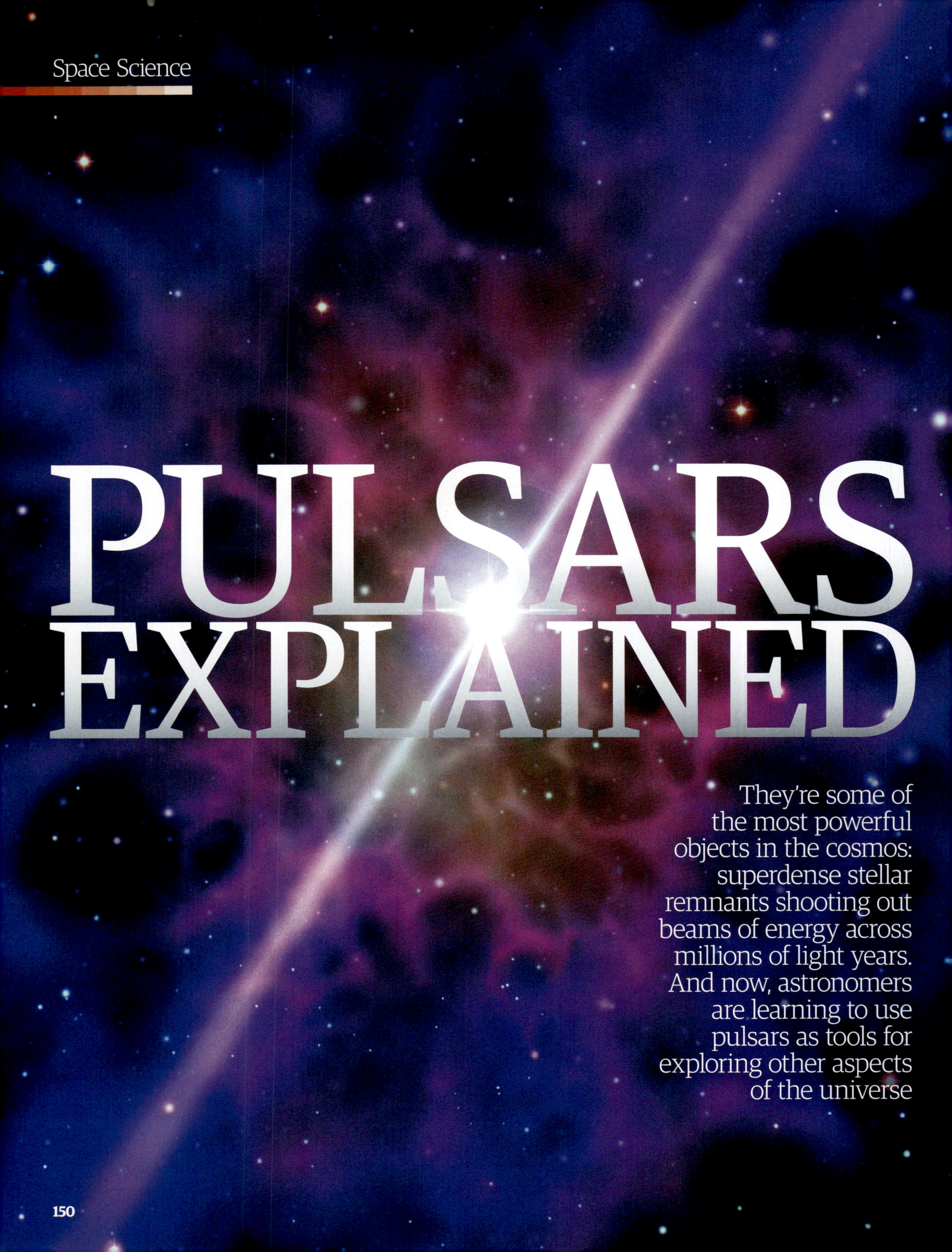

PULSARS EXPLAINED

They're some of the most powerful objects in the cosmos: superdense stellar remnants shooting out beams of energy across millions of light years. And now, astronomers are learning to use pulsars as tools for exploring other aspects of the universe

One afternoon just before Christmas 1967, a strange meeting took place at Cambridge University's famous Cavendish Physics Laboratory. A group of astronomers huddled in the office of Professor Antony Hewish arguing over how to announce a mysterious new discovery: a pulsating radio signal from an apparently empty part of the sky that might - just might - be a signal from an extra-terrestrial civilisation.

The signal had been discovered by Jocelyn Bell Burnell, one of Hewish's PhD students, using a revolutionary new radio telescope in the fields near Cambridge. A 16-millisecond burst of radiation, it repeated with a period of just 1 1/3 seconds - characteristics that suggested it could be no larger than a planet. At the time, most of the known radio sources in the sky were either enormous glowing gas clouds or fluctuating quasars associated with the central regions of remote galaxies. In stark contrast to these, Bell Burnell's precisely timed signal appeared to be remarkably compact and distinctly artificial - and it presented something of a problem for its discoverers, who jokingly nicknamed it LGM-1 (short for "Little Green Man" - see box).

This mysterious signal turned out not to be a message from an alien world, but a first glimpse of the extraordinary natural phenomena known as pulsars. These superdense burnt-out stellar remnants announce their presence through a spectacular burst of radiation that can be seen across many thousands of light years.

At their simplest, pulsars are often called celestial lighthouses, but they could equally be described as cosmic particle accelerators. Their brilliant emissions are created by subatomic particles moving at high speeds through powerful magnetic fields around rapidly spinning neutron stars.

When the heaviest stars (with at least eight times the Sun's mass) near the end of their lives and begin to exhaust the supplies of fuel in their cores, they first swell to an enormous size, becoming huge supergiants whose outer layers are only supported by the torrents of radiation that flood out from the star's core. But when the star exhausts the last of its nuclear fuel, that radiation is abruptly cut off. The star collapses under its own tremendous weight, with such speed and force that atomic nuclei in the core are torn apart into their constituent particles - positively charged protons, and electrically neutral neutrons floating in a 'sea' of negatively charged electrons. This subatomic soup can compress itself into a much smaller volume, and continues to shrink until internal pressure finally asserts itself. As the collapsed core finally stabilises, a powerful shockwave ricochets back through the star's upper layers, generating such immense pressures and temperatures that the remaining stellar material ignites in a firestorm of nuclear fusion that can outshine an entire galaxy - a supernova.

As this stellar cataclysm gradually fades away, a city-sized neutron star emerges from the wreckage. Despite its name, free neutrons are thought to dominate only in the heart of this compact remnant. Its upper layers contain a variety of neutron-rich atomic nuclei, and its crust is composed of nuclei alone. Neutron stars typically have a mass of between 1.4 and five Suns - so dense that a single pinhead of its material would weigh as much as a fully laden supertanker. Their surface temperatures, meanwhile, may reach more than 1 million °C (1.8 million °F).

Given their tiny size, you might expect neutron stars to be all but invisible. After all, white dwarf stars (the planet-sized burnt-out cores of stars like the Sun) are extremely faint despite being so hot. So how can they produce such intense radiation? The answer, as astronomers Gold and Pacini figured out, lies in the dramatic nature of the dying star's collapse.

All stars have an innate property called angular momentum, created by their rotating mass. Most also have a substantial magnetic field, generated by the churning "plasma" or electrically charged gas within them. When a star's inner regions collapse, both of these properties are not just preserved, but intensified. Just as a spinning ice dancer can speed up by drawing their arms in towards their body, so the concentration of mass closer to the centre of the star's rotation causes it to spin far more rapidly, rotating up to several dozen times per second. At the same time,

With their beams of energy, pulsars are awesome phenomena

Alien messages

Jocelyn Bell Burnell famously described the first pulsar signal as a "bit of scruff" on her charts, repeating like clockwork with a period of 1 1/3 seconds, and moving across the sky in sync with the stars. Cambridge colleagues confirmed the object's existence using a second radio telescope. The team now faced a dilemma: announce their problem signal to the wider scientific community and risk the onslaught of publicity, or keep quiet and see if they could come up with a natural solution.

Bell Burnell worked late that night and discovered traces of a similar "scruff". A late-night trip out to the radio telescope confirmed it - a second signal, this one pulsing with a period of 1.2 seconds. Observations over Christmas and early in 1968 confirmed the second signal and revealed two more.

The final piece of the puzzle came from Hewish's analysis, looking for tell-tale shifts in radio frequency that would be generated by the Doppler effect if the source was on a planet whose orbit carried it towards and then away from us. The absence of such changes confirmed that the source was stellar rather than planetary, and ended speculation about "Little Green Men".

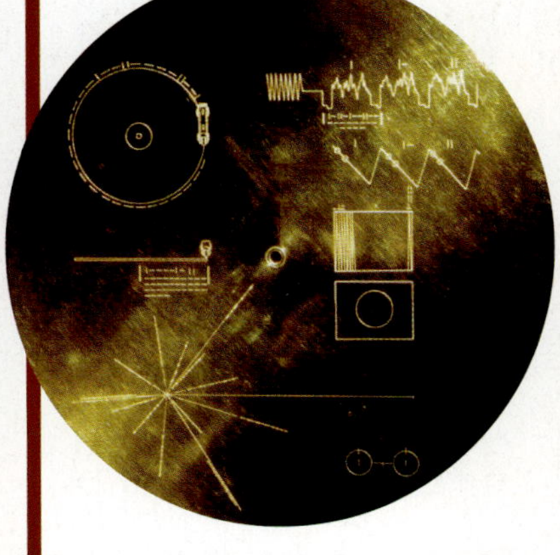

Although pulsar signals are natural phenomena, space scientists have chosen to use them in messages to aliens. The "starburst" engraved on the Voyager probes' 'Golden Record' shows our Solar System's location relative to 14 prominent pulsars.

Pulsar stars: Bell Burnell and Hewish

Antony Hewish and Jocelyn Bell Burnell built the Interplanetary Scintillation Array on 4.5 acres of land outside Cambridge. Bell Burnell's pulsar discovery came as a surprise to everyone, and Hewish took some convincing.

However, by the time he announced the discovery in early 1968, Hewish had a hunch that they were linked to compact stellar remnants. Within months, he was proved right - American astronomer Thomas Gold and his Italian colleague Franco Pacini produced a plausible mechanism by which neutron stars could generate such strong signals. And before the end of the year, US radio astronomers announced their discovery of a pulsar at the heart of the Crab Nebula.

Hewish and his colleague Martin Ryle were awarded the 1974 Nobel Prize for Physics. Bell Burnell's omission from the Nobel citation proved controversial but she went on to enjoy a distinguished career of her own.

Bell Burnell and Hewish: putting pulsars on the cosmic map

Bell Burnell and Hewish pose amidst the Interplanetary Scintillation Array. This groundbreaking radio observatory had more than 1,000 antennae

the magnetic field is magnified to become perhaps a trillion times more powerful than Earth's. This intense magnetism exerts such great forces that it can overcome the star's intense gravity, stripping away the electrically charged particles that persist in the neutron star's upper layers and trapping them in spiralling paths that accelerate them to tremendous speeds before spitting them out along the magnetic poles, generating beams of radiation in the process.

The pulsar's distinctive signals arise because the magnetic field rarely lines up perfectly with the neutron star's poles of rotation (just like on Earth, where the magnetic poles emerge in northeastern Canada and some way off the Antarctic coast). With each spin of the pulsar, the twin jets of radiation and escaping particles sweep a circle around the sky like a lighthouse beam. And if one of them happens to briefly point towards Earth, we see a short, intense pulse of radiation.

This is the basic mechanism behind all pulsars, but there are a number of important variations. Since those first discoveries, pulsars have only got stranger and more extreme. Radio waves proved to be just the most easily spotted element in a spectrum of radiation that pulsars emit, ranging through visible light up to high-energy X-rays and gamma rays. Some pulsars emit sudden bursts of radiation, while others show 'glitches', in which they suddenly speed up for a short period of time before returning to more or less the same rotation period as before. Experts speculate that these events may be caused by changes in the pulsar's internal structure.

Based on four decades of research, astronomers now distinguish between three different classes of pulsar. Typical pulsars are powered by the rotation of the star and its magnetic field, and release most of their energy as radio waves and visible light. X-ray and gamma-ray emitting "magnetars", meanwhile, have magnetic fields that are exceptionally powerful even for a pulsar, and seem to be generated during the neutron star's initial collapse. It is the rapid decay of this field that powers most of their emission. A final class of X-ray-emitting "accretion pulsars" exist in binary star systems, where they pull gas away from the outer layers of their companion stars. As this material spirals in towards the neutron star, intense tidal forces heat it up and generate the X-ray emission.

Of course there's no such thing as a free lunch in the universe, and despite their immense power, pulsars are not perpetual motion machines. As the magnetic field strips particles away from the star's crust to power its radiation, the neutron star very gradually slows down. Eventually, it seems, the rotation slows so much that the pulsar mechanism can no longer sustain itself and cuts out. As a result, the slowest known pulsar has a period of roughly 9.4 seconds.

For this reason, you'd naturally expect newly formed pulsars to spin the fastest, and indeed the pulsar at the heart of the Crab Nebula, at less than 1,000 years old, does rotate at an impressive 30 times per second. But amazingly, some pulsars spin even faster, flashing hundreds of times every second. These so-called "millisecond pulsars" spin far too quickly for their momentum to have come entirely from their initial

How a pulsar works

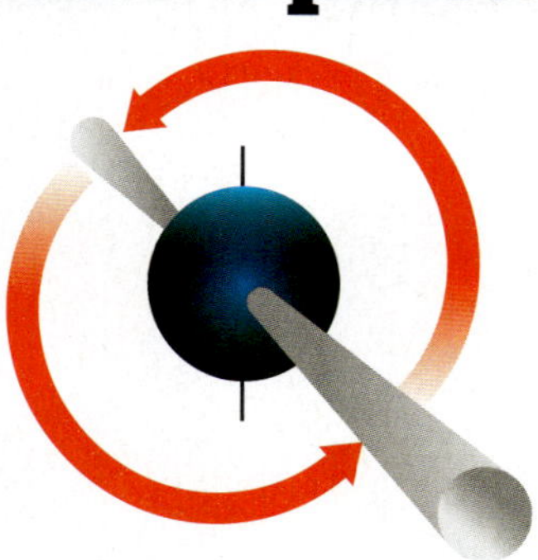

1. Pulsar off
Most of the time, a pulsar's radiation beams are directed away from Earth.

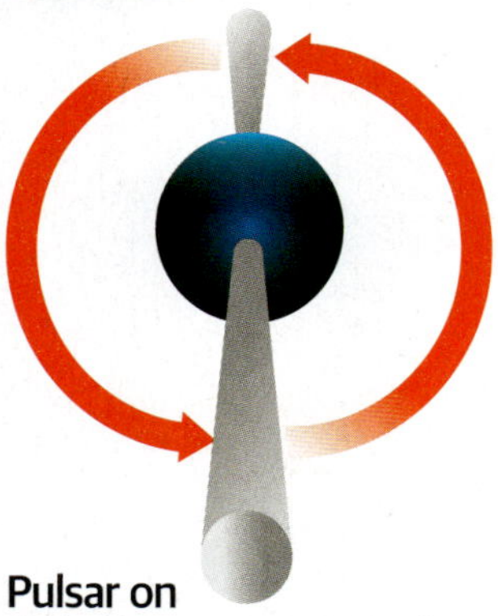

2. Pulsar on
As the beam sweeps across Earth, it creates a briefly intense radiation pulse.

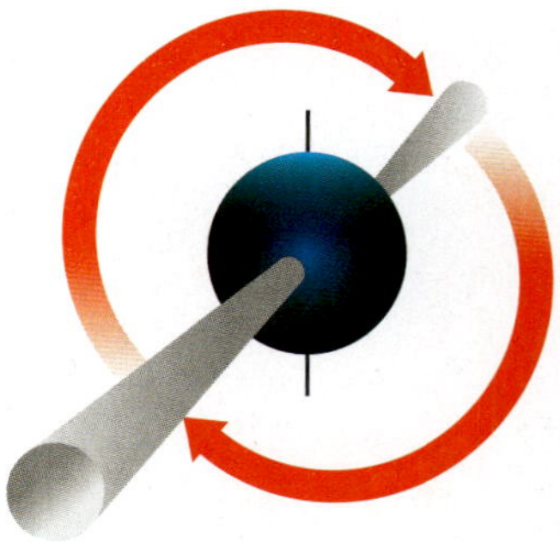

3. Pulsar off
As the beam moves, the burst fades away, to repeat on the next rotation.

Anatomy of a pulsar

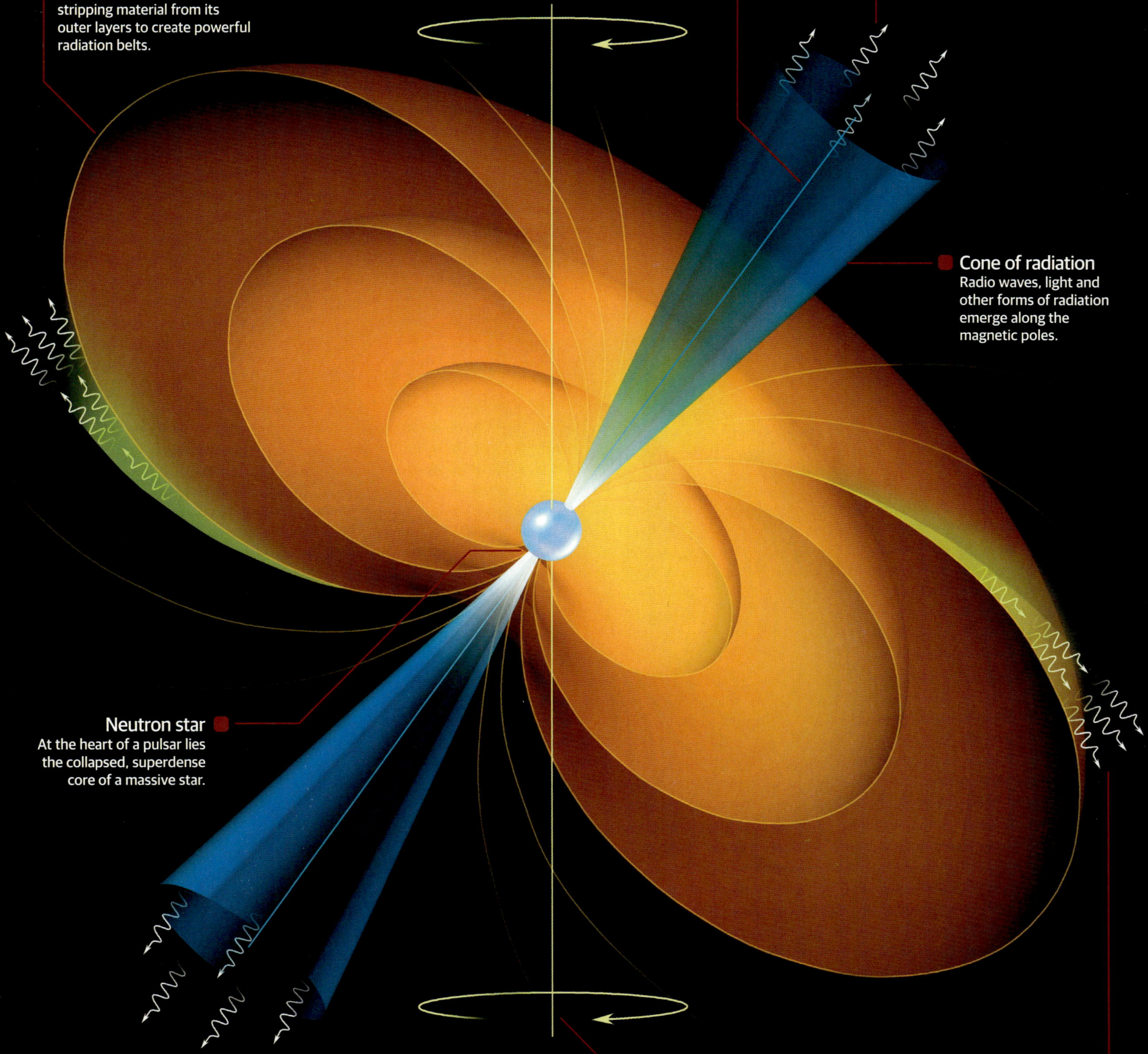

"Astronomers now distinguish between three different classes of pulsar"

formation. In fact, astronomers think that they're actually accretion pulsars that have "spun up" to their current speed by accumulating mass from their companion stars. This process somehow buries or suppresses the magnetic field, weakening the pulsar's output but also shielding it from the forces that would normally slow it down. Thanks to this fountain of youth, some millisecond pulsars have persisted for billions of years without appreciable slowdown.

Aside from being fascinating objects in their own right, pulsars are also powerful weapons in the astrophysicist's arsenal - they have already proved the key to some important discoveries, with the promise of more in the future. Their usefulness is due in large part to the precise nature of their signals, particularly those of millisecond pulsars. By providing such accurate clocks, they allow astronomers to measure and analyse tiny variations caused by a variety of phenomena.

For instance, the first detection of a solar system beyond our own came not from a Sun-like star, but from a pulsar known as PSR B1257+12. In 1992, Dale Frail and Alexander Wolszczan identified slight variations in its 6.2-millisecond pulse and traced them to the influence of not one but four planets in orbit around it.

Perhaps the most intriguing prospect for pulsar research, however, lies in the field of gravitational waves. These hypothetical distortions in the fabric of the universe itself arise naturally from Einstein's Theory of General Relativity, and should be radiated by objects in orbit around each other. The denser the objects and the more extreme their gravity fields, the more powerful the waves should be. This should mean that in theory binary pulsar systems, with two neutron stars in orbit around each other, should be the strongest gravitational wave sources of all.

And not only are pulsars thought to generate gravitational waves, they may also be the key to measuring them for the first time. As their distortions ripple out across the universe, they stretch and compress space in distinctive ways that affect the time light and other radiations takes to reach Earth. The precisely timed heartbeats of pulsars offer the best way of measuring such changes. If astronomers can track their early or late arrival, it may be the first sign that another of Einstein's predictions has proved true. ■

Pulsars in our skies

The Crab Pulsar

Constellation: Taurus
Distance from Earth: 6,500 light years

1. Neutron star
The Crab Pulsar is the central neutron star at the heart of the famous Crab Nebula.

2. Shockwaves
A high-speed stellar wind of particles blowing away from the pulsar's surface forms shockwaves as it collides with the surrounding nebula.

3. Visible light
In this image, observations from the Hubble Space Telescope are colour-coded in red.

4. X-ray view
Radiation detected by the Chandra X-ray Observatory is colour-coded in blue.

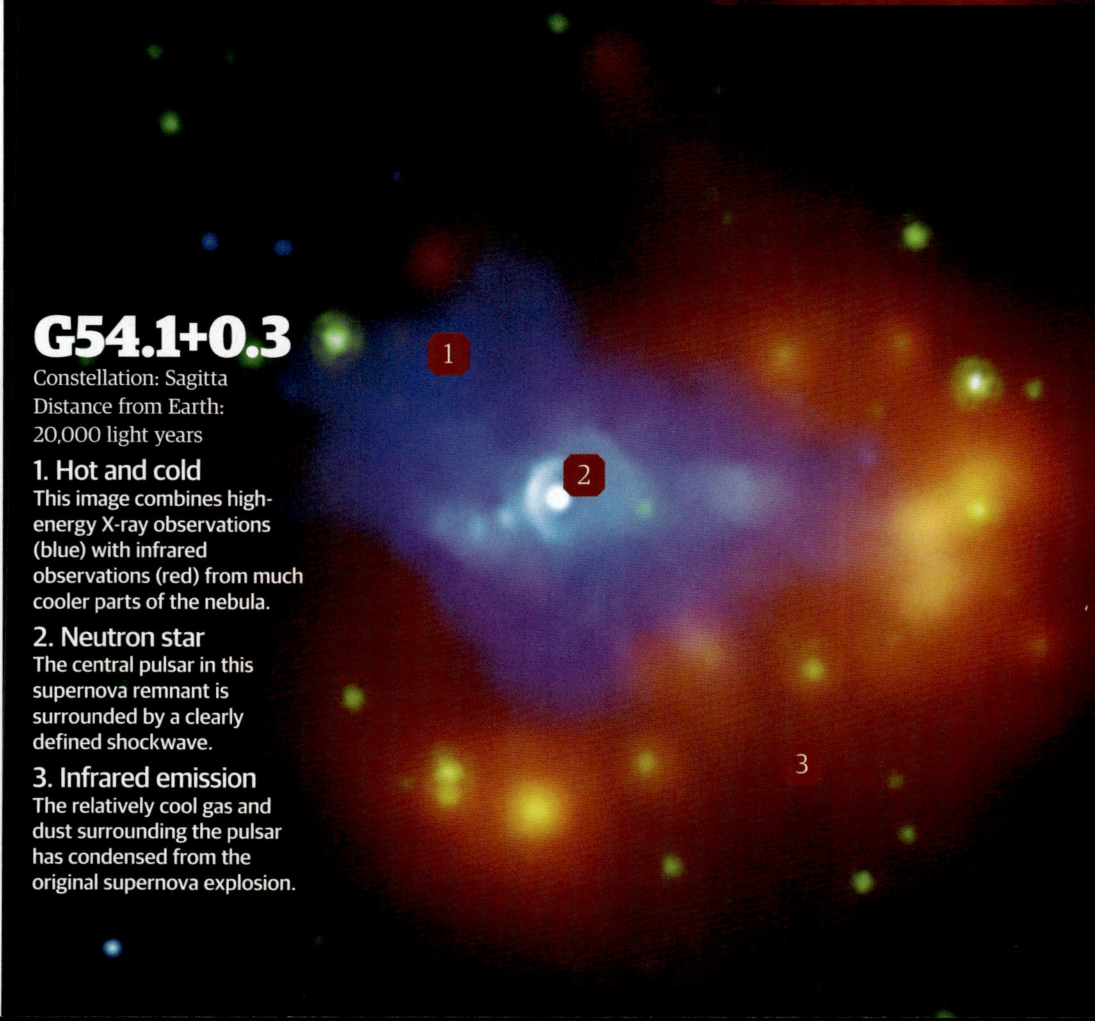

G54.1+0.3

Constellation: Sagitta
Distance from Earth: 20,000 light years

1. Hot and cold
This image combines high-energy X-ray observations (blue) with infrared observations (red) from much cooler parts of the nebula.

2. Neutron star
The central pulsar in this supernova remnant is surrounded by a clearly defined shockwave.

3. Infrared emission
The relatively cool gas and dust surrounding the pulsar has condensed from the original supernova explosion.

A young pulsar

Constellation: Circinus
Distance from Earth: 17,000 light years

1. Central star
Pulsar B1509 is around 1,700 years old, and rotates seven times per second.

2. X-radiation
In this Chandra image, low, medium and high-energy X-rays are colour coded red, green and blue.

3. Illuminated cloud
High-energy particles from the pulsar collide with the nearby gas cloud RCW 89, causing it to emit X-rays itself.

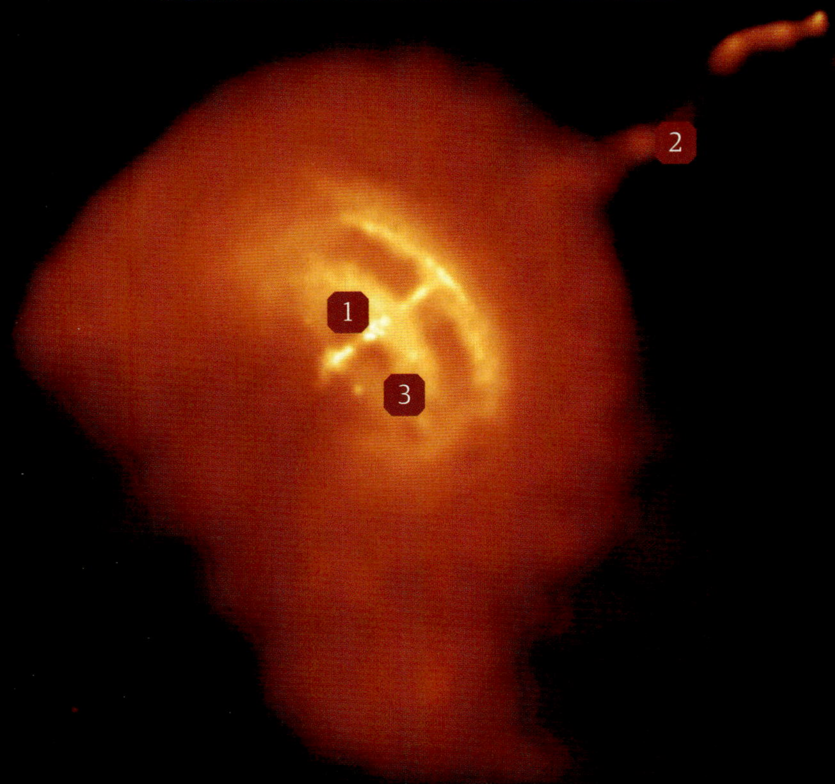

DEM L 190

Constellation: Dorado, Distance from Earth: 180,000 light years

1. Supernova remnant
Pulsar DEM L 190 is still surrounded by a shredded supernova remnant about 30 light years across.

2. Extragalactic pulsar
Located in the Large Magellanic Cloud, this pulsar is one of the most distant so far detected.

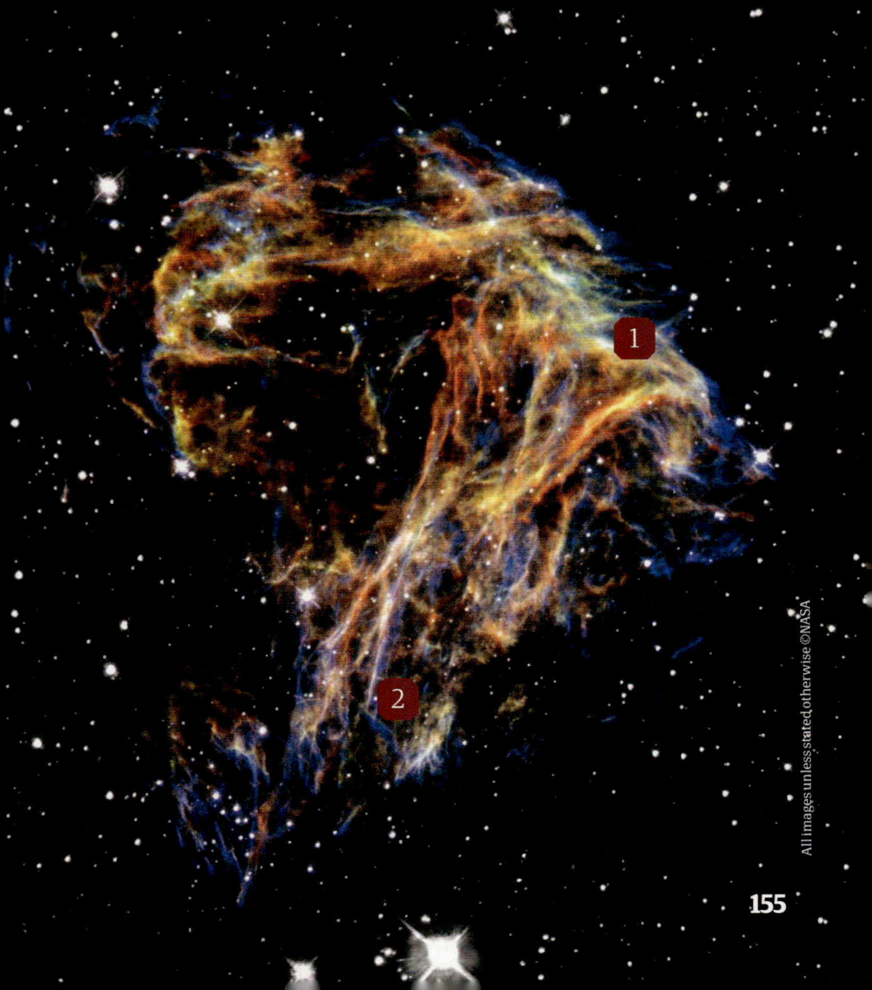

The Vela Pulsar Jet

Constellation: Vela, Distance from Earth: 1,000 light years

1. Central star
The Vela Pulsar is the brightest persistent object in the gamma-ray sky, and the third brightest pulsar at visible wavelengths.

2. Firehose jet
Following the lines of the neutron star's magnetic field, the pulsar's jets wiggle all around like an out-of-control firehose.

3. Hot gas
The hottest regions of the surrounding nebula appear yellow and orange in this Chandra X-ray image.

THE POWER OF ANTIMATTER

Is antimatter the key to understanding more about our universe and propelling future spacecraft between the stars? We investigate how close we are to finding out more about this exotic matter

Imagine a mirror held up to the universe, one that reflects matter on the scale of particles. Just like a normal mirror, the image would be reversed. Particles like protons with positive charge would suddenly look to be negatively charged, while electrons that spin in quantum fashion one way would appear to spin the other way. While the universe doesn't really have a mirror, particles of matter do have mirror images of themselves, known as antimatter.

"[Matter and antimatter] are equal and opposite, that's the theory so far," says antimatter researcher and spokesperson for CERN's Antihydrogen Laser Physics Apparatus (ALPHA), Jeffrey Hangst. "The antiparticle equivalent - antiprotons, antineutrons and positrons - are just like their matter counterparts but they have an opposite charge in the case of the charged particles and when they meet they annihilate."

So when the two clash, they do so explosively. Just as Einstein's famous equation $E=mc^2$ describes the equivalence of mass and energy, when a particle and an antiparticle come into contact with each other, they utterly annihilate in a flash - there one moment, gone the next - converting all their mass directly into energy. It's for this reason that, if antimatter could be harnessed, we would have an impressive energy source on our hands. The trouble is, there's just not that much antimatter about.

That's the major problem with antimatter, especially when its far more common counterpart - common matter - is found lurking everywhere. Antimatter can be created then destroyed in such a short space of time that experts do not have much time to hold antimatter down long enough for us to question what about its existence makes it special. As a result, there are not only gaps in our knowledge when it comes to this shy matter itself, but also in our theories of how the cosmos came into existence. "The names matter and antimatter are a bit arbitrary," adds Hangst. "We believe that if you built a universe out of antimatter it would behave in the same way, so we don't know why nature chose one over the other."

Without a doubt, the Big Bang is a widely supported theory and it tells us that matter and antimatter should have been created equally at the beginning of time around 13.8 billion years ago. They should have annihilated each other leaving nothing behind, but we exist today in a universe with plentiful matter and scarcely a drop of antimatter. Thanks to our natural curiosity for exploring things and taking things apart to reveal the fundamental building blocks of matter, one thing remains unclear; what happened to the antimatter that once existed?

"[The study of antimatter] is motivated by the fact that we believe that matter and antimatter should have been produced in equal quantities at the [time of the] Big Bang and as far as we can observe so far the universe just contains matter, so we don't really know what happened," explains Hangst. "None of the theories that we have, or the so-called standard model [of particle physics] tell us what happened to the antimatter. That's one of the biggest

©SPL

unsolved questions in physics - why is there a universe at all?"

While the Big Bang is an extraordinarily successful theory, as it currently stands, we shouldn't exist since the matter from which we are built from should have been annihilated away. The University of California's Professor Joel Fajans, who has recently enlisted the help of the ALPHA experiment to investigate if antimatter and matter are affected differently by gravity, echoes Hangst's and other scientists' thoughts that maybe there has been an error in our understanding of how much matter and antimatter was produced when the universe began. "I wish I knew why the amounts produced are not equal," he tells **All About Space**. "Understanding antimatter is important to our very existence."

And so, that's what experts have been trying to do ever since antimatter was first proposed by physicist Paul Dirac in 1931; study the ying to matter's yang in the hope of locking down something substantial, providing the answers to the mysteries of space that have eluded us for so long. A year after Dirac's proposition the first antiparticle - the positron - was discovered, followed by the antiproton and antineutron two decades later.

But in our attempts to delve into ways of pinning down antimatter, scientists have hit a few snags. Creating it artificially is one thing, but making enough of it and keeping it within our grasp for long enough is quite another. "First you have to produce [antimatter], it can't exist naturally [in significant quantities] in a matter universe so there are lots of very difficult technologies that you have to master to produce it and then to hold on to it," explains Hangst. "It needs to be held in a vacuum, a very, very good vacuum."

While the likes of Hangst and other scientists all over the world have been trying to get this down to a tee, Hangst insists that we still have much to figure out. "We are still learning how to efficiently produce it and handle it in a matter universe and even if you master these techniques, you are typically dealing with small quantities. It is not like you can buy a bottle of antihydrogen and make it [many] atoms at a time, so even after all that technology you are still left with very little of the substance."

CERN has been able to produce thousands of atoms of the simplest antiatom, antihydrogen, at a time, yet capturing it has proven to be problematic. "We've only managed to trap one atom at a time," explains Hangst. "We are really talking about a very, very rare substance." Nevertheless, ALPHA has been able to trap some antiatoms for as long as 1,000 seconds - holding them still long enough for scientists to study them before they annihilate.

As a result of the painstaking methods used to make antiatoms, antimatter is deemed to be the most expensive material to produce with NASA suggesting that it would cost around $62.5 trillion (£41 trillion) to produce just one gram of antihydrogen. To date, only a few tens of nanograms have been created at particle accelerators like the Large Hadron Collider at CERN.

That's why as things stand antimatter is never going to be a power source of the future; there's just not enough of it to do anything with. "It takes more energy to make it than

> "We are still learning how to efficiently produce it and handle it in a matter universe"
> **Jeffrey Hangst, CERN**

Hunting antimatter

Mounted on the International Space Station, the Alpha Magnetic Spectrometer (AMS), or AMS-02, studies cosmic rays - beams of high-energy particles that permeate space - before they have a chance to interact with the Earth's atmosphere. Cosmic rays, which are believed to originate from beyond the confines of the Solar System, carry an excess of antimatter that has been detected by this sensitive particle physics experiment. This unusual excess in antimatter, or positrons, could help us to find evidence for the elusive dark matter - one of space's biggest mysteries - that is believed to account for a huge chunk of the universe's mass.

Here the AMS-02 is inside the Maxwell electromagnetic radiation chamber at the European Space Research and Technology Centre (ESTEC) for electromagnetic capability and interference testing prior to launch

Reaching a sensitivity that allows the instrument to test a greater volume of the universe than its predecessor for primordial antimatter, the AMS will study the composition of cosmic rays with a high accuracy for a decade from the ISS

A history of hunting for antimatter

1931

Existence of antimatter predicted

Theoretical physicist Paul Dirac pointed out that the Schrödinger wave equation for electrons, when considered in its relativistic form, suggested the existence of antielectrons.

1932

Scientists discover positron

During his investigation of cosmic rays, Carl Anderson from the California Institute of Technology came across unexpected particle tracks in his cloud chamber that seemed to have the same mass as the electron but an opposite, positive charge; the positron.

1955

The discovery of the antiproton

Confirmed at the University of California, Berkeley, Emilio Segrè and Owen Chamberlain were awarded the 1959 Nobel Prize in Physics for their discovery of the antiproton.

1956

Scientists discover the antineutron

Discovered at the Lawrence Berkeley National Laboratory, the antineutron was uncovered by physicist Bruce Cork in a proton-proton collision experiment.

Inside the AMS

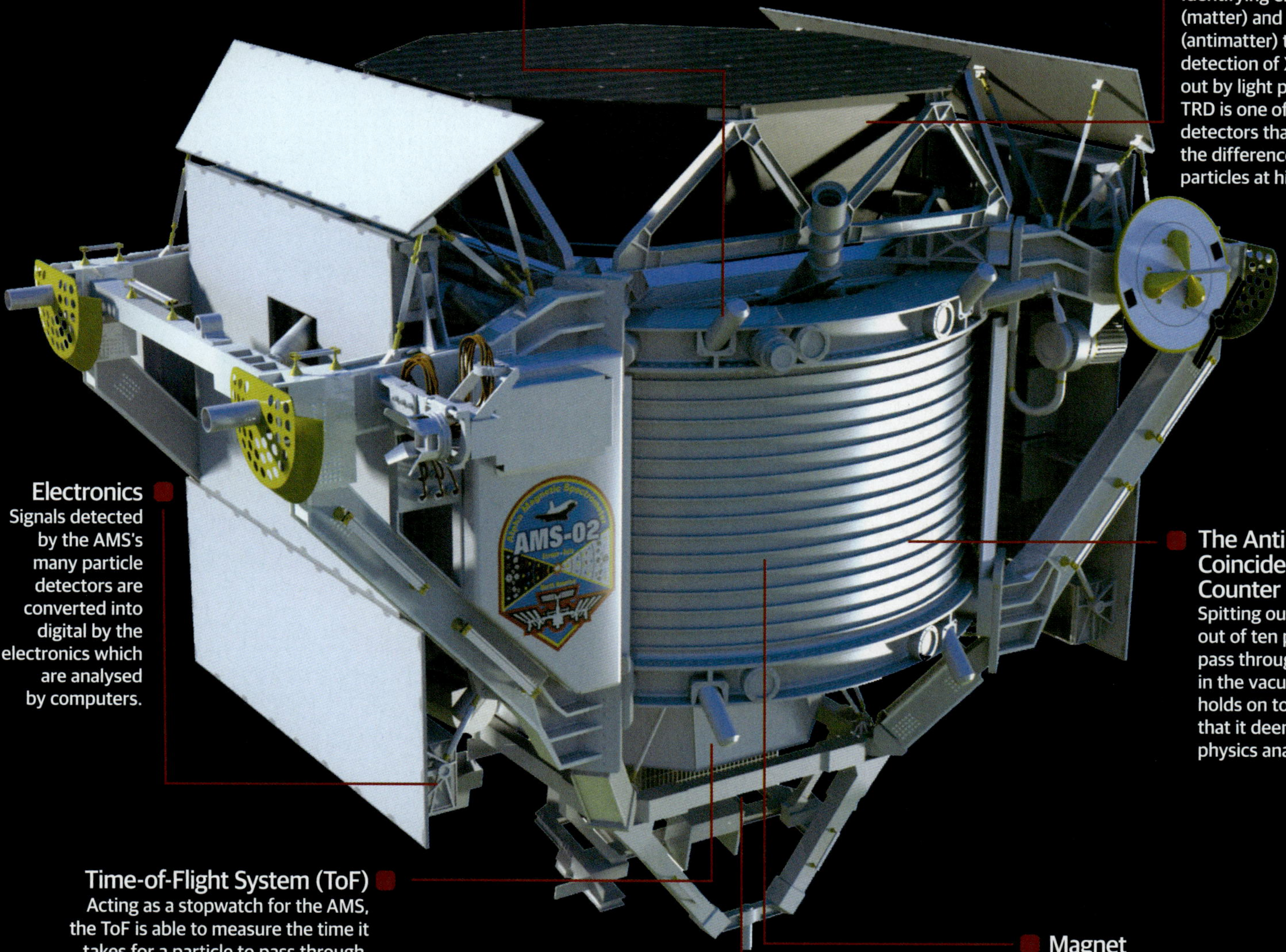

Silicon Tracker
Hunting for matter and antimatter, this tracker is able to separate the two by determining the charge of the particle entering the AMS by measuring the deflection of the matter and antimatter.

Transition Radiation Detector (TRD)
Identifying electrons (matter) and positrons (antimatter) through the detection of X-rays thrown out by light particles, the TRD is one of the few detectors that can tell the difference between particles at high energies.

Electronics
Signals detected by the AMS's many particle detectors are converted into digital by the electronics which are analysed by computers.

The Anti-Coincidence Counter (ACC)
Spitting out a good eight out of ten particles that pass through it, the ACC, in the vacuum case, only holds on to particles that it deems useful for physics analysis.

Time-of-Flight System (ToF)
Acting as a stopwatch for the AMS, the ToF is able to measure the time it takes for a particle to pass through. The velocity of the particle can be measured up to an accuracy of 98% the speed of light. It also warns the sub-detectors of incoming cosmic rays.

Ring-Imaging CHerenkov Detector (RICH)
The velocity of a charged particle is determined from the Cherenkov effect - radiation which can travel faster than the speed of light in a particular material that produces a blue cone of light which is detected by RICH.

Magnet
At the heart of the AMS experiment rests the magnet which is able to separate matter from antimatter. It does this by bending the matter particles in an opposite direction to the antimatter particles thanks to their opposite charges.

1965
Antideuteron created in laboratory
The antiparticle of a nucleus of deuterium, antideuteron, was originally created at the Proton Synchrotron at CERN as well as at the Alternating Gradient Synchrotron at Brookhaven National Laboratory.

1995

CERN scientists observe antihydrogen
Antihydrogen was made artificially in accelerator experiments. However, the subsequent annihilation with matter meant that it could not be examined in detail.

2010
Atoms of antihydrogen trapped at CERN
The Antihydrogen Laser Physics Apparatus (ALPHA) team at CERN produced and managed to confine cold antihydrogen for about a sixth of a second, marking the technique that would see antihydrogen maintained for over 15 minutes.

2013
Scientists study antigravity for first time
Scientists uncovered the first direct evidence of how antimatter interacts with gravity. However, while it is undecided if antigravity truly exists, measuring antimatter gravity is proven to be possible.

Why is antimatter important?

1 To understand our existence
"The Big Bang should have produced as much antimatter as matter and then it should have all mutually annihilated, leaving nothing," says Professor Joel Fajans. "Yet we are here, and we've observed almost no antimatter. It's the biggest outstanding problem in our understanding of the early universe."

2 It could be used as fuel
Spacecraft might one day be powered by the annihilation of matter with antimatter. NASA believes that the amount of antimatter required to supply power for an engine for a one-year trip to Mars could be a millionth of a gram, providing huge thrust while being a very efficient form of propulsion.

3 For medical purposes
"Practical applications of antimatter are mostly in Positron Emission Tomography, which is revolutionising many medical fields," says Fajans. With physicians using beams of electrons, protons, neutrons or photons as well as chemotherapy, could a beam of antimatter eliminate cancer cells?

4 Possible interstellar travel
Using antimatter to voyage between the stars is currently not possible. "Making macroscopic quantities of antimatter would require all of the Earth's energy production for thousands of years," says Fajans. However, if we could create enough antimatter, we could propel starships through the cosmos.

5 Using antimatter to probe dark matter
Cosmic rays emanating from the outer reaches of the universe carry an excess of antimatter thought to be directly related to the extremely elusive dark matter. It is believed that the high amount of positrons is a result of when two particles of dark matter collide and annihilate.

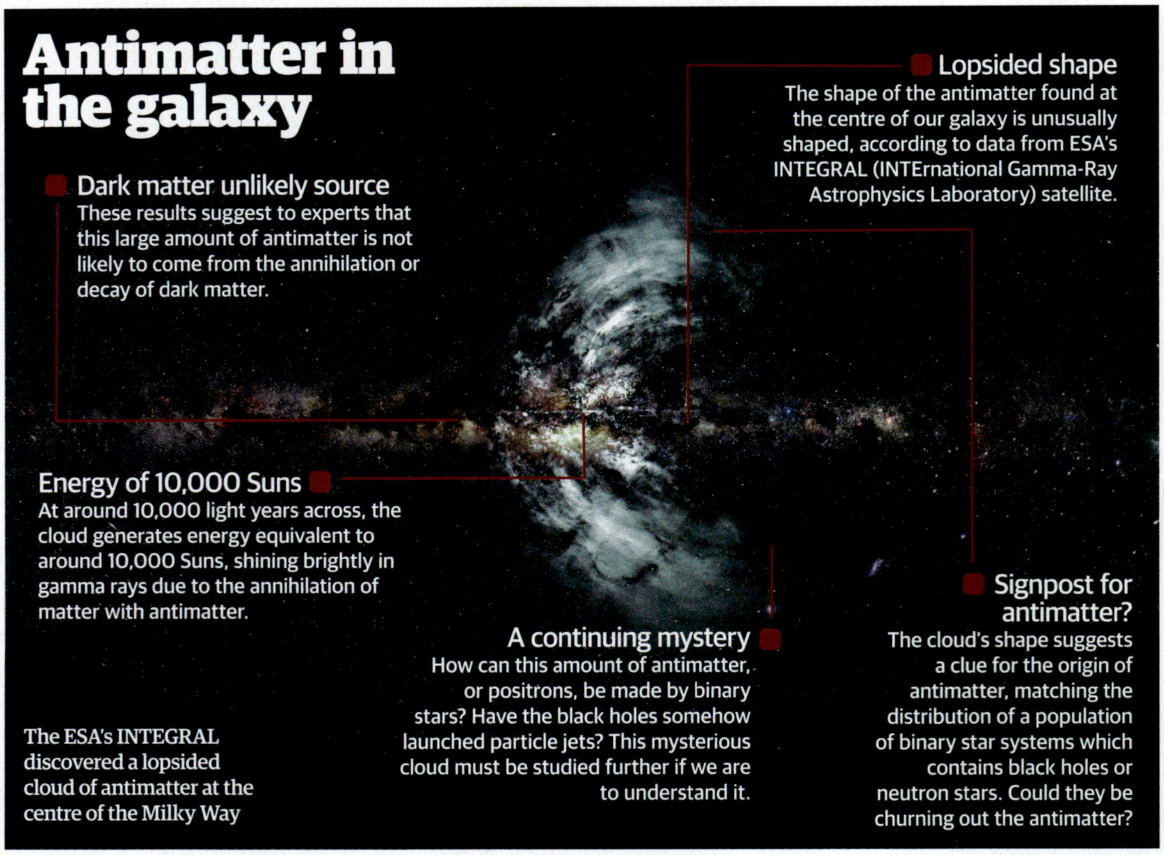

The ESA's INTEGRAL discovered a lopsided cloud of antimatter at the centre of the Milky Way

you would get back, so that's a loser – that's not what you want from an energy source," states Hangst. "If some antimatter flew by and you could get a hold of it, that would be an energy source, but as far as producing it on Earth, that's just not even close."

Sadly, that means we may have to forget about antimatter-powered starships, for the moment at least. However, particle accelerators are not the only places where we can find antimatter. In 2011, 160 nanograms of antiprotons were discovered trapped in the Van Allen radiation belts above Earth, with similar amounts expected to exist in the magnetically organised radiation belts of other planets, including up to 260 nanograms around Saturn. Yet this is still a very tiny amount – add it all up and it still doesn't even come to a gram.

In the same year, astronomers announced that the Fermi Space Telescope, which observes the universe in gamma rays, had detected antimatter not coming from space, but streaming into space from above thunderstorms in Earth's atmosphere. Fermi detected high-energy gamma rays at just the right energy to indicate they were created when an antimatter particle annihilated a matter particle.

"Thunderstorm electric fields accelerate electrons to high energies," explains Professor Joseph Dwyer of the Florida Institute of Technology. "These electrons make gamma rays, which then pair-produce electrons and positrons, which are the antimatter version of the electron. The positrons may play an important role in the electrical properties of thunderstorms – it has been quite surprising how common positron production is in our atmosphere and how the positrons can actually be important for understanding thunderstorms and lightning."

> "Understanding antimatter is important to our very existence" **Joel Fajans, University of California**

Fermi was actually expecting to see gamma rays from matter-antimatter annihilation near the centre of the galaxy, as was its European counterpart, the INTErnational Gamma-Ray Astrophysics Laboratory (INTEGRAL), which discovered a lopsided cloud of positrons in the galactic centre where annihilation is taking place and producing gamma rays with energies of around 511,000 electronvolts. Meanwhile the state-of-the-art Alpha Magnetic Spectrometer (AMS) on board the International Space Station is searching for antimatter in cosmic rays.

So it seems we are really starting to make headway in our quest to solve the mysteries of matter and antimatter and ultimately the grand mystery of why the matter-dominated universe as we know it exists at all.

"There's lots going on," says Hangst. "It's a very interesting time to be working in this field because we are getting more and more capabilities. At CERN we are studying antimatter to see if it behaves in the same way as matter; that's a long-term project. We're also looking for matter/antimatter asymmetry – does antimatter somehow behave different to what the laws of physics describe for matter? We'd like to study the spectrum of antihydrogen and compare that with what we have measured in hydrogen, or look at how antimatter behaves in a gravitational field. So those are the two big things: is antihydrogen quantum mechanically the same as hydrogen and does it fall up or down in gravity?"

The answers might unlock the secrets of the expanding universe and we could be extremely close to doing just that. ■

Interstellar antimatter travel

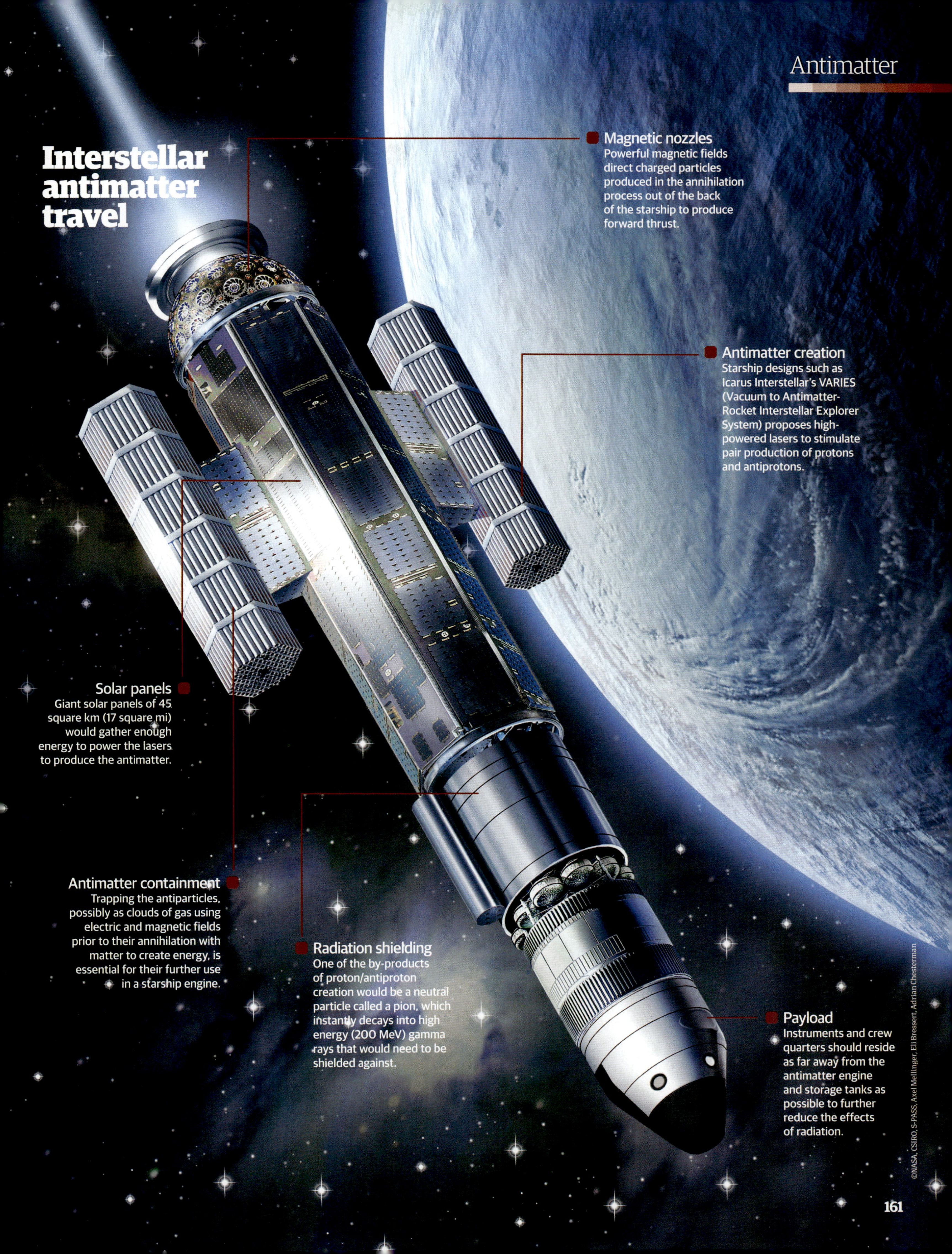

Magnetic nozzles
Powerful magnetic fields direct charged particles produced in the annihilation process out of the back of the starship to produce forward thrust.

Antimatter creation
Starship designs such as Icarus Interstellar's VARIES (Vacuum to Antimatter-Rocket Interstellar Explorer System) proposes high-powered lasers to stimulate pair production of protons and antiprotons.

Solar panels
Giant solar panels of 45 square km (17 square mi) would gather enough energy to power the lasers to produce the antimatter.

Antimatter containment
Trapping the antiparticles, possibly as clouds of gas using electric and magnetic fields prior to their annihilation with matter to create energy, is essential for their further use in a starship engine.

Radiation shielding
One of the by-products of proton/antiproton creation would be a neutral particle called a pion, which instantly decays into high energy (200 MeV) gamma rays that would need to be shielded against.

Payload
Instruments and crew quarters should reside as far away from the antimatter engine and storage tanks as possible to further reduce the effects of radiation.

10 amazing facts about Living in space

The heart takes a breather

Due to the low gravity, the heart has a far easier time of pumping blood around the body in space than it does on Earth. This can be dangerous, as it gradually pumps less and less and becomes weaker, so astronauts must exercise for several hours a day to keep it working hard.

You can stay in space for more than a year

The longest amount of time ever spent in space was 437 days by Russian cosmonaut Valeri Polyakov aboard the Mir Space Station in 1994 and 1995, proving that a prolonged stay in the weightlessness of space is indeed possible.

You see a sunrise every 90 minutes

The International Space Station orbits the Earth at about 17,000mph (27,000km/h). This means astronauts aboard the ISS see the sun rise and set every 90 minutes. However, their clocks run to UTC and they work 9-5, just like on Earth, to keep their days ordered.

Food needs water to be eaten

Food on the ISS has come a long way from the freeze-dried examples in early space missions, but it still needs preparation. It is stored in dry form so that it doesn't rot, and water must be added to it to make it edible.

Space sickness is common

On Earth we rely on gravity, signals from our ear and pressure receptors on our limbs, but in space vision is the only useful sensor. This has meant astronauts often suffer from space sickness, where they spend several days adjusting to the environment.

Preparation for a spacewalk takes hours

Astronauts don their space suits hours before going on a spacewalk, during which time they breathe pure oxygen in preparation for the activity.

Shaving is extremely difficult

The surface tension of water, and the absence of gravity, causes it to clump together in globules in space. This poses problems when shaving, as any water applied to the face won't spread evenly, so astronauts must be very careful with the sharp razor.

You'll drop things back on Earth

Several astronauts have reported that when they come back to Earth they inadvertently drop objects like cups. This is because they're so used to the weightless environment in space.

Velcro is a must

In a weightless environment everything has a tendency to float around. To counteract this astronauts hold things down with Velcro.

You must sleep next to a fan

Good ventilation is vital for sleeping astronauts, as warm air does not dissipate in space. Instead, it forms a bubble of carbon dioxide around them and, eventually, they'd run out of breathable oxygen.

Interstellar antimatter travel

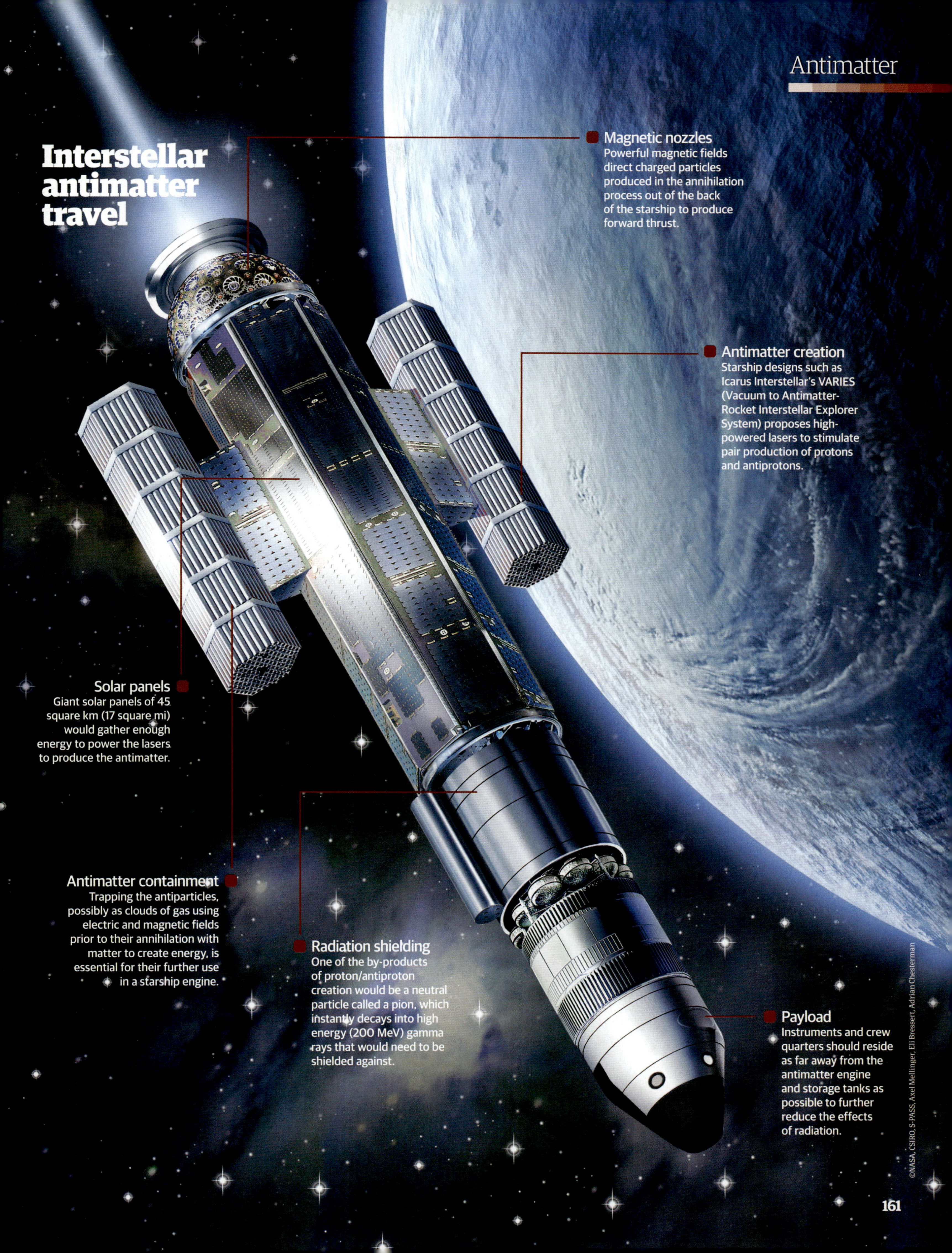

10 amazing facts about Living in space

The heart takes a breather

Due to the low gravity, the heart has a far easier time of pumping blood around the body in space than it does on Earth. This can be dangerous, as it gradually pumps less and less and becomes weaker, so astronauts must exercise for several hours a day to keep it working hard.

You can stay in space for more than a year

The longest amount of time ever spent in space was 437 days by Russian cosmonaut Valeri Polyakov aboard the Mir Space Station in 1994 and 1995, proving that a prolonged stay in the weightlessness of space is indeed possible.

You see a sunrise every 90 minutes

The International Space Station orbits the Earth at about 17,000mph (27,000km/h). This means astronauts aboard the ISS see the sun rise and set every 90 minutes. However, their clocks run to UTC and they work 9-5, just like on Earth, to keep their days ordered.

Food needs water to be eaten

Food on the ISS has come a long way from the freeze-dried examples in early space missions, but it still needs preparation. It is stored in dry form so that it doesn't rot, and water must be added to it to make it edible.

Space sickness is common

On Earth we rely on gravity, signals from our ear and pressure receptors on our limbs, but in space vision is the only useful sensor. This has meant astronauts often suffer from space sickness, where they spend several days adjusting to the environment.

Preparation for a spacewalk takes hours

Astronauts don their space suits hours before going on a spacewalk, during which time they breathe pure oxygen in preparation for the activity.

Shaving is extremely difficult

The surface tension of water, and the absence of gravity, causes it to clump together in globules in space. This poses problems when shaving, as any water applied to the face won't spread evenly, so astronauts must be very careful with the sharp razor.

You'll drop things back on Earth

Several astronauts have reported that when they come back to Earth they inadvertently drop objects like cups. This is because they're so used to the weightless environment in space.

Velcro is a must

In a weightless environment everything has a tendency to float around. To counteract this astronauts hold things down with Velcro.

You must sleep next to a fan

Good ventilation is vital for sleeping astronauts, as warm air does not dissipate in space. Instead, it forms a bubble of carbon dioxide around them and, eventually, they'd run out of breathable oxygen.

Interstellar antimatter travel

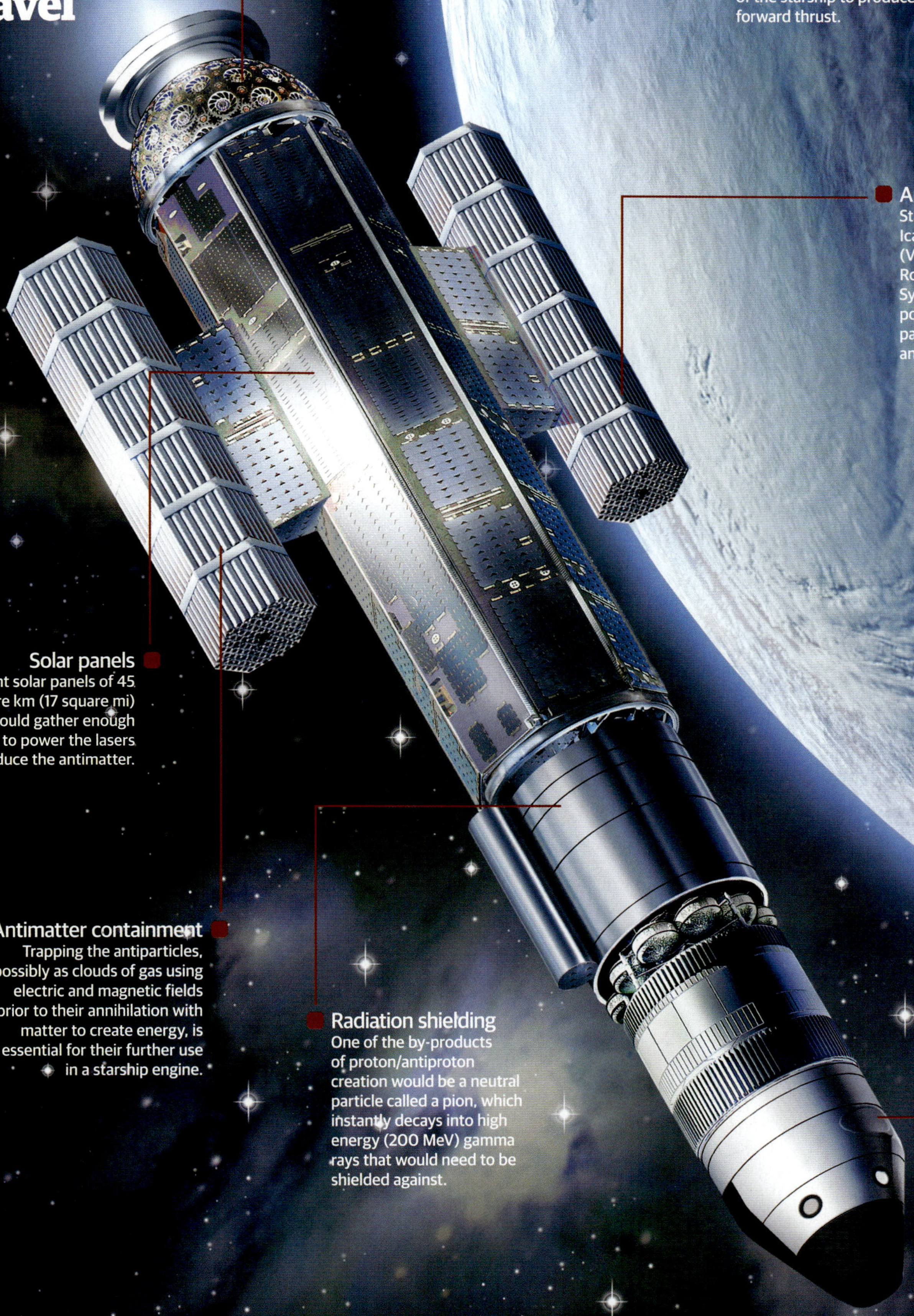

Magnetic nozzles
Powerful magnetic fields direct charged particles produced in the annihilation process out of the back of the starship to produce forward thrust.

Antimatter creation
Starship designs such as Icarus Interstellar's VARIES (Vacuum to Antimatter-Rocket Interstellar Explorer System) proposes high-powered lasers to stimulate pair production of protons and antiprotons.

Solar panels
Giant solar panels of 45 square km (17 square mi) would gather enough energy to power the lasers to produce the antimatter.

Antimatter containment
Trapping the antiparticles, possibly as clouds of gas using electric and magnetic fields prior to their annihilation with matter to create energy, is essential for their further use in a starship engine.

Radiation shielding
One of the by-products of proton/antiproton creation would be a neutral particle called a pion, which instantly decays into high energy (200 MeV) gamma rays that would need to be shielded against.

Payload
Instruments and crew quarters should reside as far away from the antimatter engine and storage tanks as possible to further reduce the effects of radiation.

10 amazing facts about

Living in space

The heart takes a breather

Due to the low gravity, the heart has a far easier time of pumping blood around the body in space than it does on Earth. This can be dangerous, as it gradually pumps less and less and becomes weaker, so astronauts must exercise for several hours a day to keep it working hard.

You can stay in space for more than a year

The longest amount of time ever spent in space was 437 days by Russian cosmonaut Valeri Polyakov aboard the Mir Space Station in 1994 and 1995, proving that a prolonged stay in the weightlessness of space is indeed possible.

You see a sunrise every 90 minutes

The International Space Station orbits the Earth at about 17,000mph (27,000km/h). This means astronauts aboard the ISS see the sun rise and set every 90 minutes. However, their clocks run to UTC and they work 9-5, just like on Earth, to keep their days ordered.

Food needs water to be eaten

Food on the ISS has come a long way from the freeze-dried examples in early space missions, but it still needs preparation. It is stored in dry form so that it doesn't rot, and water must be added to it to make it edible.

Space sickness is common

On Earth we rely on gravity, signals from our ear and pressure receptors on our limbs, but in space vision is the only useful sensor. This has meant astronauts often suffer from space sickness, where they spend several days adjusting to the environment.

Preparation for a spacewalk takes hours

Astronauts don their space suits hours before going on a spacewalk, during which time they breathe pure oxygen in preparation for the activity.

Shaving is extremely difficult

The surface tension of water, and the absence of gravity, causes it to clump together in globules in space. This poses problems when shaving, as any water applied to the face won't spread evenly, so astronauts must be very careful with the sharp razor.

You'll drop things back on Earth

Several astronauts have reported that when they come back to Earth they inadvertently drop objects like cups. This is because they're so used to the weightless environment in space.

Velcro is a must

In a weightless environment everything has a tendency to float around. To counteract this astronauts hold things down with Velcro.

You must sleep next to a fan

Good ventilation is vital for sleeping astronauts, as warm air does not dissipate in space. Instead, it forms a bubble of carbon dioxide around them and, eventually, they'd run out of breathable oxygen.

Astronauts carry out work on the ISS with New Zealand in the background

Faster than light

If humanity is to truly explore the universe it must first conquer the vast distances of space. We investigate the fact and theory behind travelling at the speed of light

Scientists have recognised the speed of light as the ultimate speed limit of the universe for more than a century now - ever since Albert Einstein put forward his revolutionary special theory of relativity in 1905. Einstein developed his theory in order to account for a series of problems that beset the physics of the time - most importantly the fact that light seemed to travel through a vacuum at the same speed, regardless of the relative motions of source and observer. In other words, light arrives at Earth from a distant star at the same speed regardless of whether the star is moving towards or away from us - think for a moment about how that compares with the behaviour of a tennis ball thrown by someone on a moving train and you'll see why that's so weird. The speed of light in vacuum, 299,792.5 kilometres per second (186,282 miles per second), is a universal constant, often written as 'c'.

In order to explain this strange behaviour, Einstein realised he would have to rewrite the laws of physics from the bottom up. The resulting theory of special relativity mimics the well-established rules of 'classical' physics in everyday situations, and only diverges when objects are travelling at speeds comparable to c (so-called 'relativistic' speeds). Here, though, things start to get very strange - from the point of view of a distant observer, relativistic objects appear to get shorter in the direction of their travel; to increase in mass (making it harder to accelerate further); and strangest of all, to experience time more slowly.

These weird effects, Einstein explained, were inevitable consequences of the principle of relativity - the long-established idea that the laws of physics behave the same way in all 'inertial' (non-accelerating) frames of reference. In other words, if a moving train is travelling at a constant speed, then it's actually impossible for someone on board to conduct an experiment that proves they're the one in motion, rather than someone doing the same experiment on the platform rushing past the window. (If that sounds weird, then remember how many thousands of years it took people to figure out that Earth is rotating daily on its axis and orbiting the Sun, rather than sitting still among countless spinning celestial spheres.) From the point of view of a person on a relativistic spaceship, everything would seem to be perfectly normal - in fact the strange effects would seem to be happening to the rest of the universe!

Einstein realised that these effects got increasingly extreme towards c, until they spiralled out of control at the speed of light itself: an object travelling at the speed of light would have zero length, infinite mass, and no experience of time. Such a situation was clearly impossible, so travel at light speed was impossible and c set an ultimate speed limit for the universe (photons of light and other radiations can only travel at c because they are completely massless). Special relativity has now been proven by any number of experiments - for example, atomic clocks flown aboard satellites or high-speed jets, have been shown to slow down compared to those in ground-based laboratories, thanks to the effects of time dilation.

The speed limit of c seems to frustrate our dreams of exploring the universe. The scale of interstellar space is daunting - even the closest stars are light years away from Earth, our galaxy is more than 100,000 light years across, and most other galaxies are many millions of light years away, so even if a spacecraft could somehow propel itself to 99.999 per cent of the speed of light, it would still require these kind of timescales to explore the universe. As a result, even the most enthusiastic advocates of interstellar exploration have assumed it would require crews in deep-frozen suspended animation for many years, or enormous 'generational' starships that would eventually deliver the descendants of the original crew to a home in a new solar system.

But even though astronomers and physicists accept special relativity as a fact of life, they've still discovered a variety of situations - some natural, some highly artificial, in which faster-than-light motion, or at least the illusion of it, can take place.

For instance, one intriguing effect, which at first seems to break Einstein's rules, is known as a 'superluminal jet'. These strange phenomena are usually associated with the violent conditions around black holes, and involve streams of genuinely

"One could stimulate space-time to behave in such a way that it mimics the classical warp drive"

Dr Richard Obousy, president of Icarus Interstellar

Lightspeed pioneer: Miguel Alcubierre

Born in Mexico in 1964, Alcubierre studied physics at the Mexican National University before studying for his doctorate at the University of Wales. Specialising in the investigations of general relativity and black holes, he later moved to Germany's Max Planck Institute before returning to Mexico in 2002. Although his work is largely concerned with the long-standing problem of reconciling quantum physics and general relativity, he is best known for his 1994 proposal for a 'warp drive' - a means of carrying a bubble of space across large distances at faster-than-light speeds without violating the rules of Einsteinian physics. Because space-time within such a 'warp bubble' would remain essentially flat, a spacecraft within it can move through its local environment at relatively low speeds, avoiding many problems associated with relativistic motion, such as time dilation.

relativistic particles shooting out in a jet pointing almost (but not quite) directly towards the Earth. In these special circumstances, light emitted by a particular region of the jet at a later time can 'catch up' with that emitted at an earlier stage, giving the impression that the jet itself is moving faster than light (see the 'Superluminal jet illusion' boxout on page 33).

So far, all the natural phenomena observed in the universe have turned out to be consistent with relativity and the ultimate speed limit of c. But in March 2011, a team of astronomers at Italy's Gran Sasso National Laboratory reported measurements that seemed to show that beams of neutrinos fired from the Large Hadron Collider at CERN on the Swiss-French border, some 731 kilometres (454 miles) away, were arriving at their own OPERA detector slightly sooner than expected - so fast, in fact, that they appeared to be travelling slightly faster than the speed of light.

The Gran Sasso team did not really believe that they had found neutrinos breaking the rules of relativity. Instead, their announcement was an appeal to the wider scientific community for help in analysing their experiment and pinpointing possible errors. And indeed, within a year several equipment issues had been identified and the revised measurements brought back into line with expectations.

But what if particles could travel faster than light? In 1967, Columbia University physicist Gerald Feinberg put forward the suggestion that an entire universe of new hypothetical particles with speeds greater than that of light might exist. These 'tachyons' (from the Greek word for swift) would avoid the problem of travel at c itself by never travelling that slowly. However, other theoretical physicists soon showed that the tachyon properties Feinberg proposed would have different consequences from those he predicted. What's more, the widely accepted models of particle physics seem to work pretty well without faster-than-light particles, so tachyons remain little more than a fascinating thought experiment.

Another particle phenomenon, however, really does seem to break Einstein's golden rule. This is quantum entanglement - an effect in which two atomic or subatomic particles interact with one another in such a way that certain properties or 'quantum states' become intrinsically linked together. According to quantum theory, on the smallest scales particles have an uncertain, wave-like nature, with properties that only become fixed when they are measured. In theory, it should be possible to prepare a pair of entangled particles, then separate them by a great distance (perhaps taking one away in a spaceship while keeping the other one on Earth). When the state of the one particle is finally measured, the other particle's complementary state also 'collapses' instantaneously, wherever it is in the universe, and can then be measured. Einstein himself memorably referred to entanglement as "spooky action at a distance", but since his time it has moved beyond the realms of theory into reality. In September 2012, scientists at laboratories on the islands of La Palma and Tenerife demonstrated the phenomenon of simultaneous collapse across a record distance of 143 kilometres (89 miles).

In the future, quantum entanglement could form the basis

Tachyons: the faster-than-light particles

This diagram visualises the appearance of a hypothetical faster-than-light particle or tachyon passing an observer

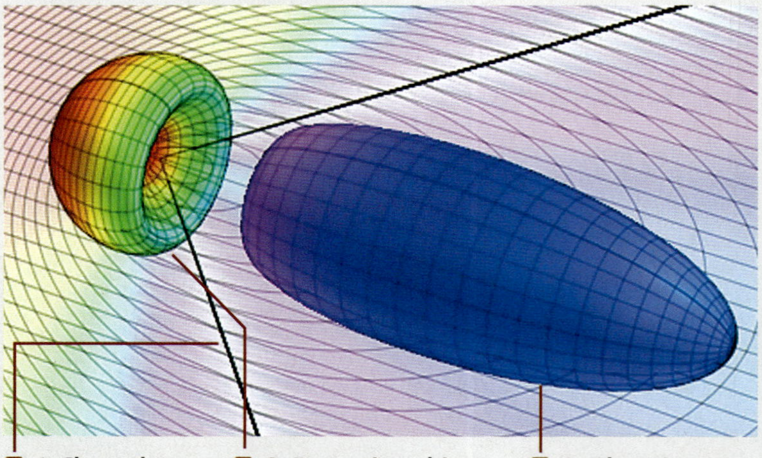

1. Cherenkov radiation The particle emits an expanding wave of radiation equivalent to a sonic boom.

2. Departing object Because it is travelling faster than light, the particle is invisible until it passes the observer. We can only see it once it is already retreating.

3. Ghost image Once the particle has passed by, light waves emitted during its approach finally reach the observer, creating a ghostly image.

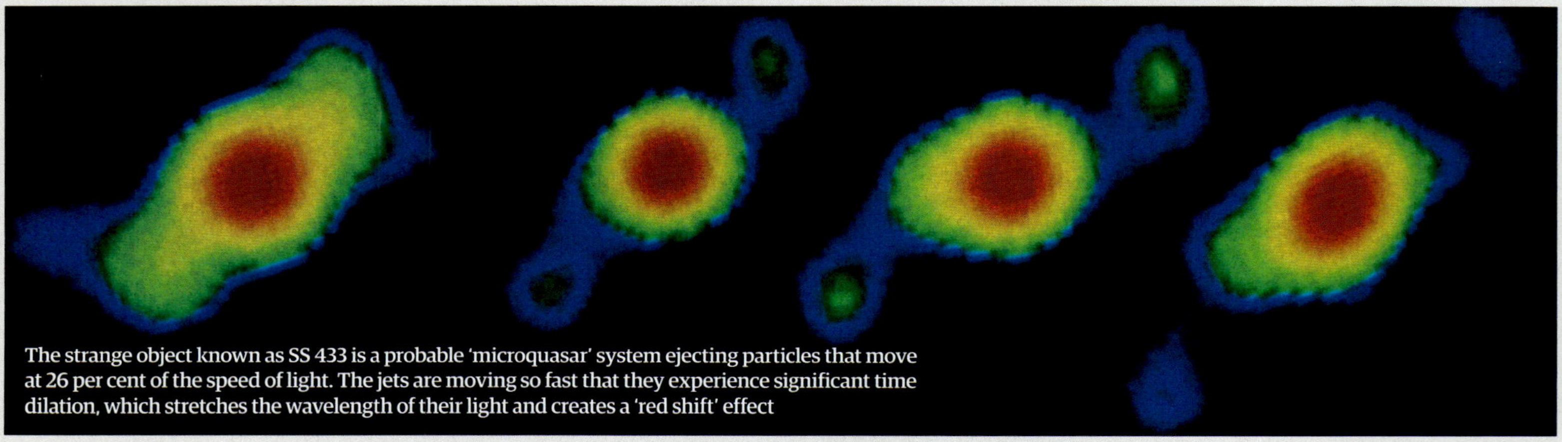

The strange object known as SS 433 is a probable 'microquasar' system ejecting particles that move at 26 per cent of the speed of light. The jets are moving so fast that they experience significant time dilation, which stretches the wavelength of their light and creates a 'red shift' effect

of a new generation of superfast computers, but does the phenomenon really break the speed of light? Not strictly, say the experts, explaining that the phenomenon only enables observers at two locations to instantaneously discover the same information - nothing is communicated directly from one observer to the other.

This, then, is the fundamental rule of relativity - that it's impossible to transmit information faster than the speed of light. If it was then causality itself, the universal law of cause and effect, could be undermined - for instance, you could send a message that would arrive before you had even sent it, and the recipient might then send one back in the same way, arriving in time to stop you sending them the original message and creating a paradox.

However hard we might try, it seems that the cosmic speed limit is unbreakable - so are we doomed to stay trapped forever in our small corner of the universe, with dreams of star travel limited to science fiction or the most ambitious, one-way-ticket projects? Not necessarily - we can't break the speed of light, but Einstein's own work gives rise to ways in which we could bend it.

Ten years after the special theory, Einstein published his theory of general relativity, which remodelled space and time as a four-dimensional 'manifold' that can be warped by the effects of gravity. He suggested that the bending of space and time around massive objects such as stars could create similar effects to those seen at relativistic speeds in special relativity. For instance, the three dimensions of space might become compressed or curved, while the time dimension could become extended. It's another idea that sounds crazy, but was developed from the simplest principles and was soon proved to be correct thanks to the discovery of 'gravitational lensing' - the way in which the straight paths of light rays travelling through space are deflected as they pass through the warped space close to massive objects.

> "Wormholes offer a potential shortcut that gets around the cosmic speed limit"

One common way of thinking about general relativity is to think of space-time as a rubber sheet in which heavy objects create dents or 'gravitational wells'. The heavier or more concentrated the object, the deeper the well and the greater the effect on its surroundings. In 1935, Einstein and his colleague Nathan Rosen published a paper in which they outlined the theoretical possibility that two such wells in different regions of the universe might connect together, creating a shortcut known as an Einstein-Rosen bridge. Today, most

Exploring new frontiers - the Alcubierre drive

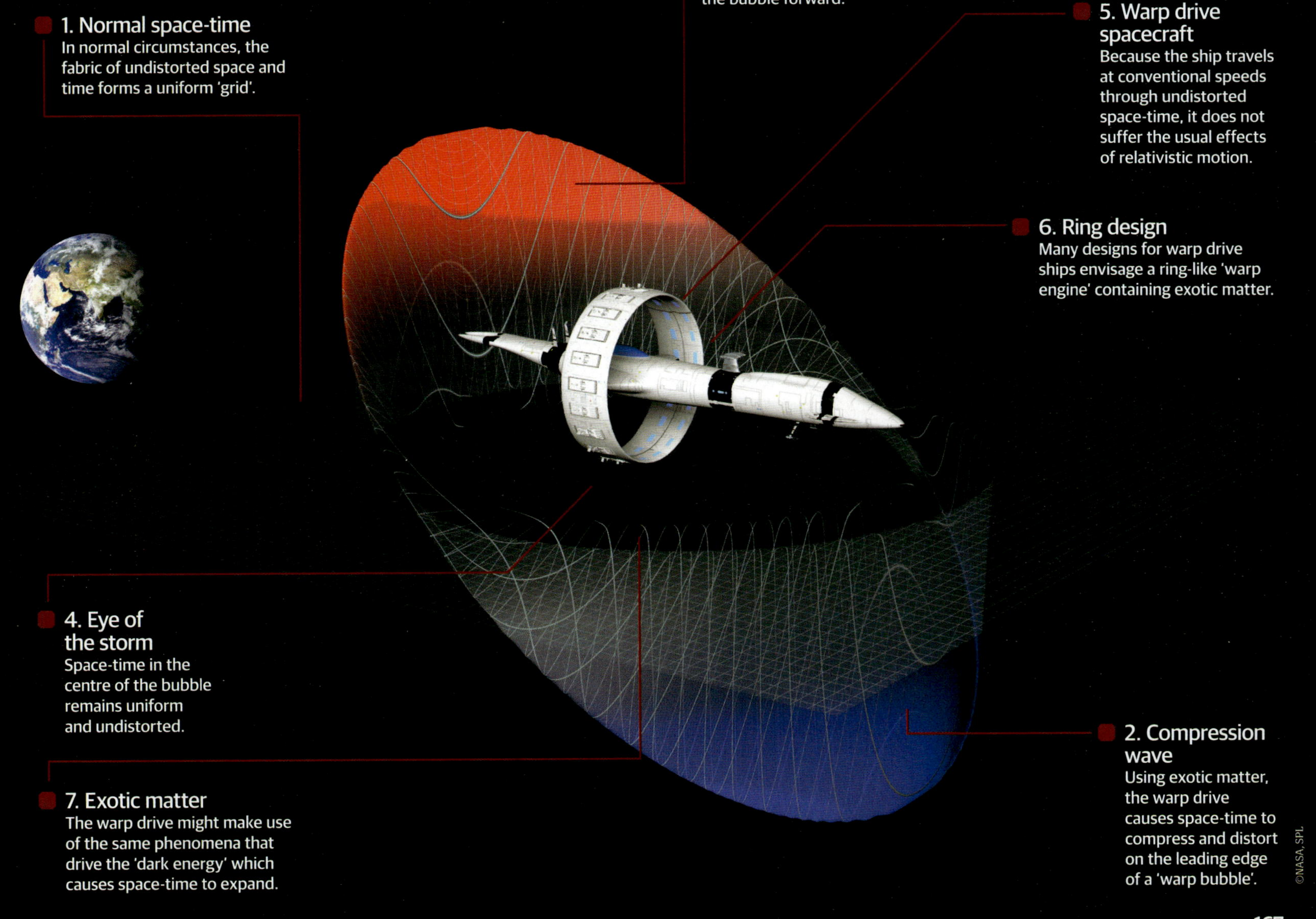

Wormhole theory

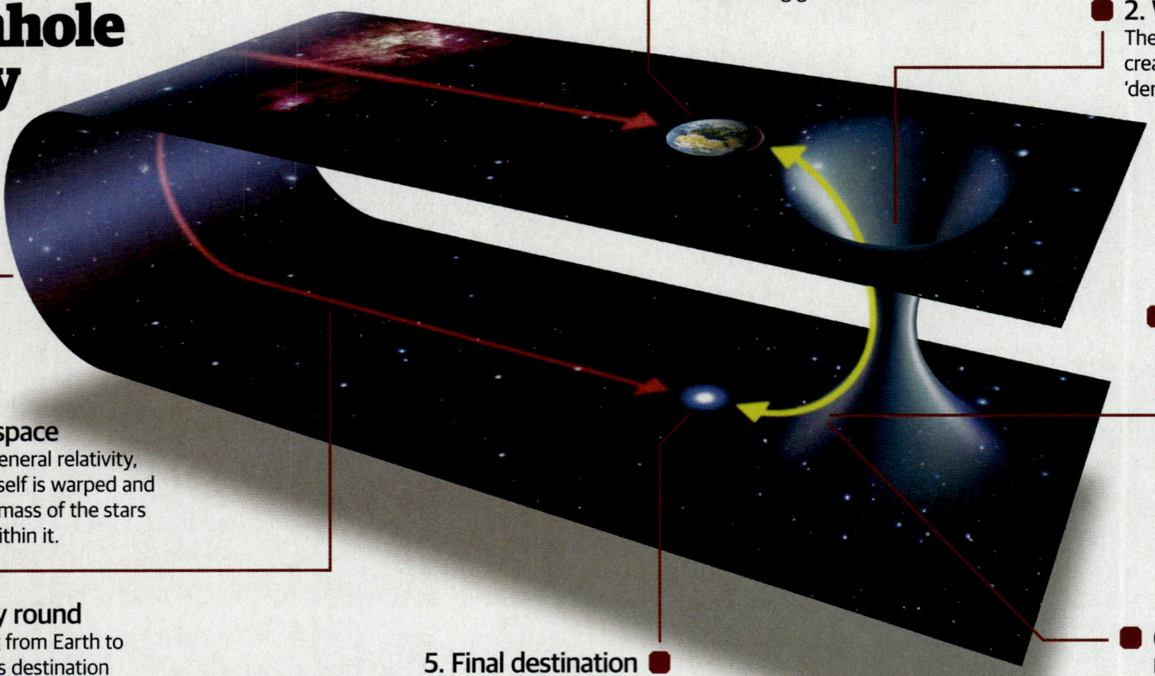

science fiction fans know the concept better by the popular nickname coined by physicist John Wheeler in 1957.

Wormholes offer a potential shortcut that gets around the cosmic speed limit – in theory the distance connecting two points through a wormhole might be much shorter than the distance across normal space – so you could fly down a wormhole at conventional or 'subluminal' speed and still reach your destination more quickly than a beam of light taking the long route between the same two points.

Wormholes are a fascinating area of study for theoretical physicists, but they still present huge problems. Although nothing in general relativity forbids their existence, their existence could undermine causality and even (as American cosmologist Kip Thorne proved) be used to build a time machine. For this reason, some experts have speculated that a real-life wormhole would have to connect with a parallel universe rather than another part of our own.

What's more, in 1962 John Wheeler showed that the forces around any naturally forming wormhole would cause it to close up within an instant of its creation – sustaining an artificial wormhole would require the use of 'exotic matter' with negative energy density (something which sounds entirely fantastical but may not be as far-fetched as it sounds – see our interview with Dr Richard Obousy, the president of Icarus Interstellar, on the following page).

But even if wormholes do turn out to be impossible, things aren't quite as bad as they seem. If a starship could achieve sufficient speed for the effects of special relativity to kick in, it could take advantage of the time dilation effect. While everything would seem normal for the crew, their experience of time would be slowed down considerably compared to the surrounding universe, so that a journey of several dozen light years at near-light speed might only take a few months for those on board the starship. Such a mission would be a one-way ticket into the future, leading to some rather strange phenomena – for example, an explorer might witness their twin sibling left behind on Earth age much more rapidly. Sceptics about Einstein's theories have tried to suggest there is a paradox here – surely both twins should see the same phenomenon? But this is ignoring the fact that special relativity only applies to 'inertial' (non-accelerating) situations – and the explorer twin will likely spend a great deal of their voyage either accelerating or decelerating.

In theory, if a spacecraft could reach sufficient speed, time dilation would allow humans to make not just interstellar, but even intergalactic trips in manageable time spans. But there are huge practical challenges in generating the power needed to reach such speeds – suggested mechanisms include controlled nuclear explosions, and the transfer of energy from powerful laser beams.

Perhaps the most intriguing possibility of all, though, is the 'warp drive' whose principles were outlined by Mexican physicist Miguel Alcubierre in 1994. Alcubierre's research described how a bubble of space-time, driven forward by the expansion of space-time behind it and contraction in front of it, could theoretically propagate across the universe at hyperfast speeds, without requiring the spacecraft within this bubble to break the light-speed barrier in its own frame of reference. Alcubierre's idea was purely theoretical, but it has so far stood up to scientific criticism, and scientists such as Dr Richard Obousy of Icarus Interstellar have now proposed ways in which such a drive might be created in practice. ●

> "In theory time dilation would allow intergalactic trips in a manageable time frame"

Lightspeed pioneer: Kip Thorne

US physicist Kip Thorne is one of the world's leading voices on wormholes. He has spent much of his career investigating the plausibility of these tunnels in space-time, showing how they could be used for faster-than-light travel. He first investigated the possibility of wormhole-based time travel when Carl Sagan asked him for advice on the time machine featured in his novel *Contact*, and has since made contributions to the investigation of time travel, suggesting that 'backwards time travel' (to a period before such a time machine was created) should be impossible, and that the laws of physics may prevent many of the paradoxes beloved of science fiction authors.

"Loopholes in the restrictions of special relativity have been appearing in physics for some time"

Researching warp drives and wormholes

Dr Richard Obousy, president of Icarus Interstellar, tells us how science is beginning to encroach on the stuff of science fiction

What first got you interested in the subject of interstellar travel?
My interest in space and space exploration was galvanised by my interest in astronomy. I remember in my early teens happening upon a book on astronomy which opened my eyes to the vastness of the universe and helped me realise that there's so much more than our small planet. I also developed an interest in science fiction around the same time and read everything I could by sci-fi greats like Clarke and Asimov, which compelled me to explore the technical aspects of interstellar flight.

Conventional proposals for travel to the stars still present huge technical challenges, even if they don't require groundbreaking physics...
Yes, because the stars are so far away one typically has two options. Either you travel very fast, or you take a very long time to get there. For the first option chemical rocket fuel is inadequate to make trip times on the scale of human lifetimes, so one has to look into more exotic means. One proposal made initially by the British Interplanetary Society in the Seventies called Daedalus involved detonating thermonuclear pulse units inside a reaction chamber at a rate of 250 detonations per second over a period of several years. This would have allowed the spacecraft to reach a top speed of 12% the speed of light.

But if you get close to the speed of light, strange things start to happen...
Yes, Einstein showed us that, as an object's velocity increases, relativistic effects manifest themselves. One example is time dilation, famously explained through the 'twin paradox'. In this example twin A stays on Earth, and twin B crews a starship travelling close to the speed of light. When twin B returns to Earth she's aged but a few months, while twin A is now in old age.

But even with time dilation, you're still looking at very long journey times – are there any other options?
You'd be looking at long trip times from the context of an Earth-based observer. Loopholes in the restrictions of special relativity have been appearing in physics for some time. The two most famous examples are the wormhole and the 'warp drive'. Wormholes are essentially tunnels through space-time that connect two distant points and allow for near-instantaneous travel between them. A warp drive is a specific distortion of space-time that contracts the space-time in front of a 'craft, allowing one to travel by manipulating space instead of moving through it. Space-time itself isn't restricted by special relativity, which is why these constructs are so fascinating.

However, all faster-than-light (FTL) schemes are speculative at this stage and require exotic matter to create and prodigious amounts of energy. None are practical with today's technology.

You've recently been looking at how a warp drive might operate in practice?
That's not strictly correct. I was looking at a model of dark energy, which is an energy field that has the effect of causing space-time to inflate. I examined the energy requirements necessary to artificially amplify the magnitude of dark energy in the vicinity of a spacecraft to create the type of space-time modification one would need.

But the nature of dark energy is a big mystery in itself...
It's called theoretical physics for a reason. Under the models I looked at, dark energy can be explained through an enigmatic form of energy known as Casimir energy, which has a non-zero value in the higher dimensions of space that have become popular in recent 'superstring' theories of the universe's fundamental structure. Dark energy itself is an artefact of higher-dimensional Casimir energy, showing up in the four dimensions that we can perceive.

My analysis showed that the energy requirements to create a warp bubble could be reduced dramatically – instead of requiring the mass energy in a typical galaxy to create the warping effect, 'all' you'd need is the mass energy contained within the planet Jupiter.

And by manipulating space in this way, you could actually reach or exceed the speed of light?
Yes, one could stimulate space-time to behave in such a way that it mimics the classical warp drive.

Is there any hope of testing it?
Some work I did in 2009 indicated that it could be tested with energy levels accessible by the Large Hadron Collider. I'd like to encourage theoreticians not to shy away from using theoretical physics to explore novel propulsion paradigms. It was barely 70 years from the discovery of the subatomic constituents of the atom to the first working nuclear thermal rocket. First comes the physics, next comes the technology.

Future Tech

Take a look at the technology of tomorrow

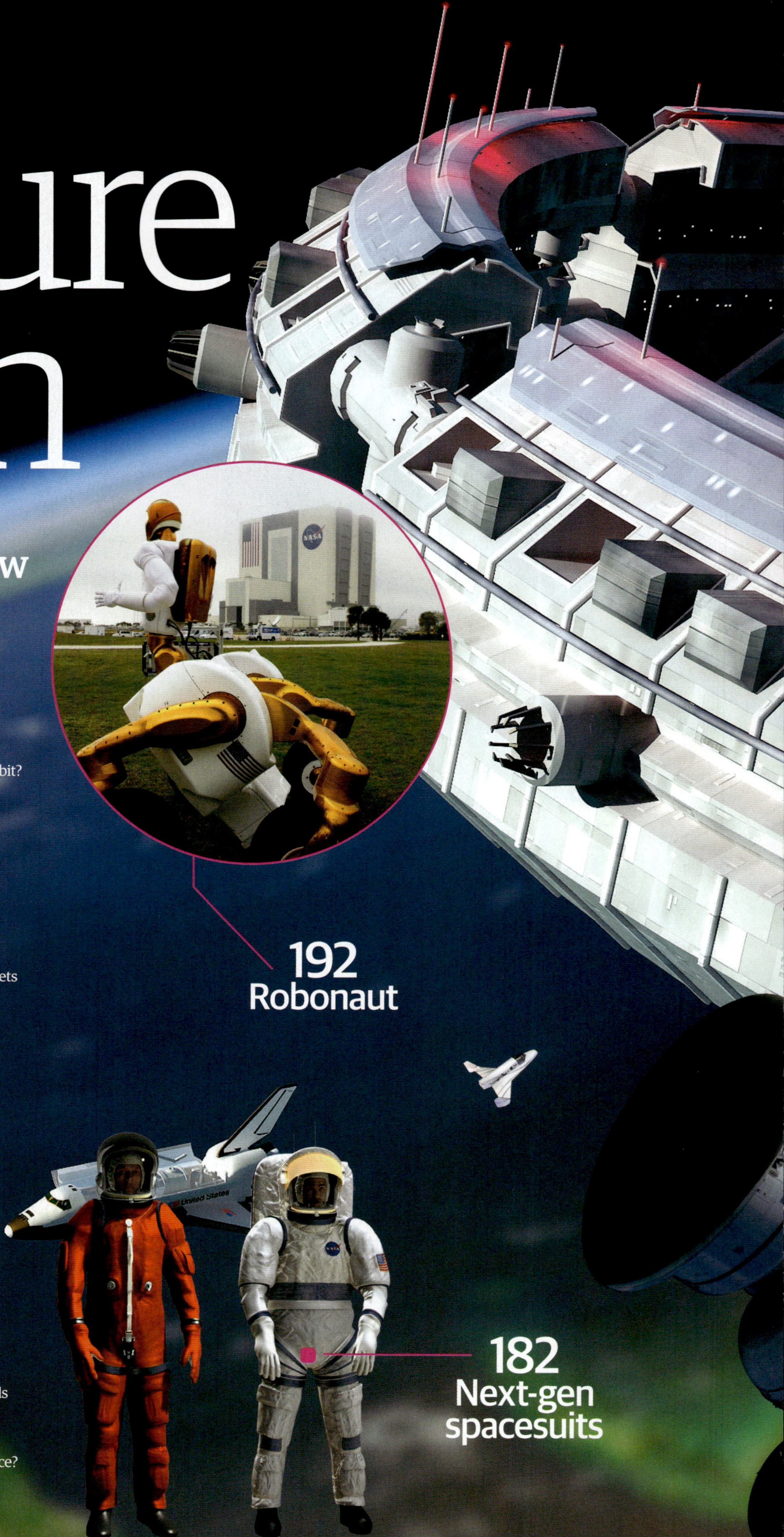

192
Robonaut

182
Next-gen spacesuits

200
Space colonies
198
Project Icarus

Space planes of tomorrow

Already in development, the next generation of reusable spacecraft will turn science fiction into science fact

"The impact of Skylon on the space business is going to far exceed any revolution in the aircraft industry"

1. Aerodynamic
Control of Skylon is provided by various aerodynamic components. Its tail fin can move to change the yaw of the vehicle, while the two small fins at the front alter the pitch. The wings, as well as providing lift, also offer roll control. The overall sleek design allows Skylon to attain orbital speed without being hindered by atmospheric drag.

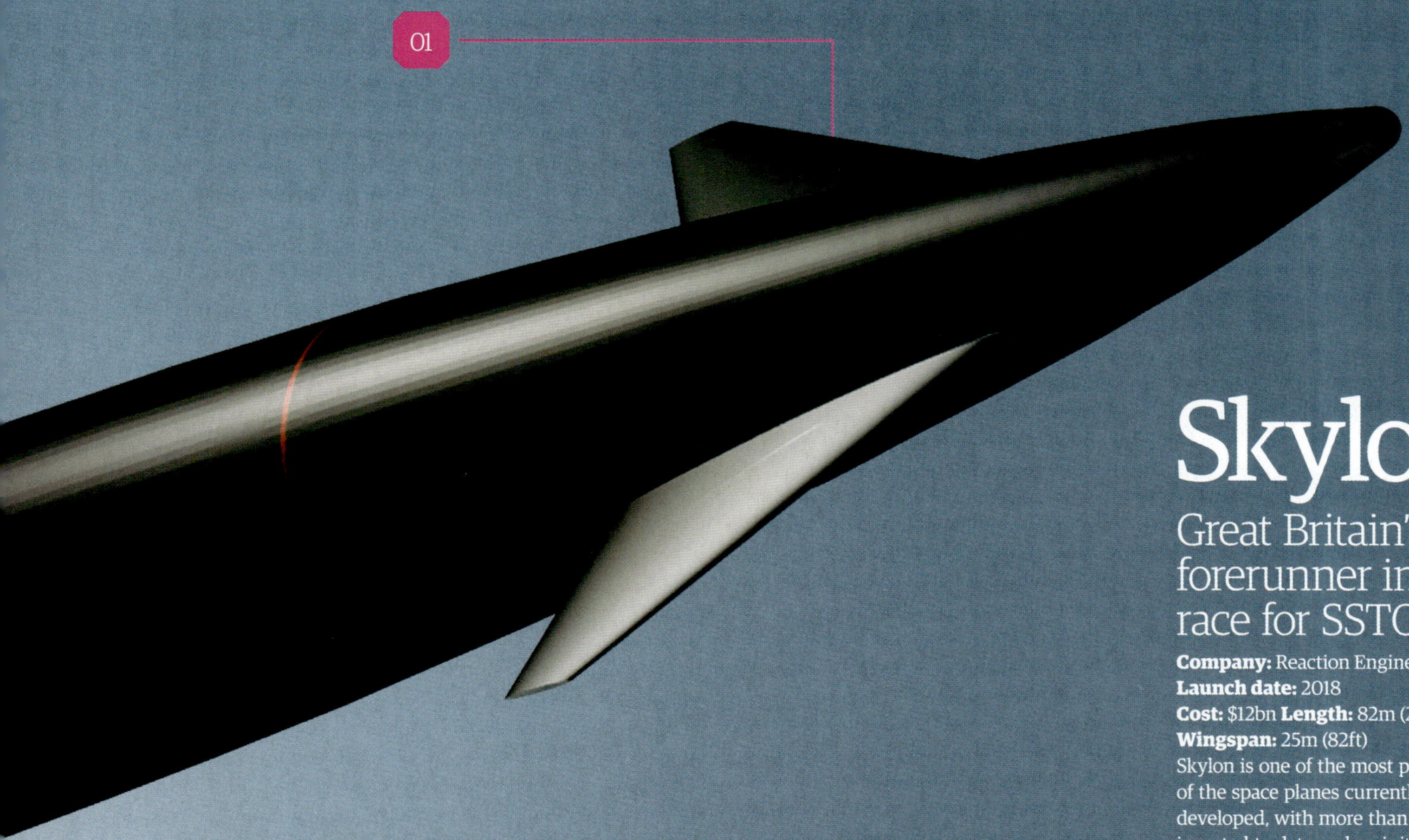

Skylon

Great Britain's forerunner in the race for SSTO

Company: Reaction Engines Ltd
Launch date: 2018
Cost: $12bn **Length:** 82m (269ft)
Wingspan: 25m (82ft)

Skylon is one of the most promising of the space planes currently being developed, with more than $544m invested to date and an initial test flight planned for 2018. It's a single-stage-to-orbit (SSTO) craft designed to take off without boosters and accelerate into a stable orbit before deploying its payload and returning.

The problem with SSTO is that the vehicles ideally need to use air-breathing engines like a jet within the Earth's atmosphere, but once they are in the vacuum of space they must rely on a new method of propulsion. Richard Varvill, the technical director and chief designer at Reaction Engines Ltd, told us that Skylon aims to tackle this problem head-on: "The unique feature of Skylon is SABRE. The same engine can burn the hydrogen fuel with either air when it is within the atmosphere or with liquid oxygen when it is in space. This allows Skylon to fly to 25km [15.5 miles] altitude and a speed of over five times the speed of sound while consuming relatively small amounts of liquid hydrogen. When it switches to rocket mode Skylon has only 80 per cent of the work to do compared to a rocket taking off from the ground and this makes a big difference in the feasibility of the vehicle."

So, when will Skylon take to the skies? "With adequate funding we could plan a development programme with the first orbital test flight in 2018 followed by a further 403 test flights," said Varvill. "Skylon would then go into operational service in 2020."

2. SABRE

Skylon's revolutionary Synergistic Air-Breathing Rocket Engine (SABRE) uses both a jet-like air-breathing cycle and a pre-cooler heat exchanger to travel to and from the edge of space. Once airborne Skylon switches to rocket mode at a height of 25km (15.5 miles), accelerating to over 28,150kph (17,500mph) to reach Low Earth Orbit.

3. Cargo

It is currently planned that each Skylon vehicle will be unmanned and autonomous for the first few years of operation, but the ultimate goal is that for later flights it will be able to take humans into orbit. To do this, Skylon would carry a Personnel/ Logistics Module, which could carry 24 passengers and a pilot.

4. Angle

Skylon will fly at a slight angle in order to generate lift. For this reason the engine intake of the nacelles is curved seven degrees downwards to ensure sufficient air is taken in. At the back of the nacelle the thrust chambers are again pointed down by seven degrees to ensure that they point through the centre of mass of the vehicle.

Dream Chaser

Vertical-take-off space plane ready to launch in 2014

Company: Sierra Nevada Corporation
Launch date: 2014
Cost: $1bn **Length:** 9m (30ft)
Wingspan: 7m (23ft)

The Dream Chaser is a crewed space plane based on the HL-20 space taxi concept developed by NASA in the Eighties and Nineties, and is designed to carry humans into both sub-orbit and Low Earth Orbit.

As a space plane the Dream Chaser differs in design to Skylon and Lynx, which are both single-stage-to-orbit (SSTO) vehicles capable of taking off horizontally from a runway and landing in the same manner. Instead, Dream Chaser is a vertical-take-off, horizontal-landing (VTHL) space plane, designed to launch atop the nose of a conventional rocket, before gliding back to Earth in much the same way NASA's Space Shuttle did. Unlike the Space Shuttle, though, Dream Chaser carries no hazardous fuel and does not need to be decontaminated, therefore greatly reducing the time between flights. Aside from the rocket it launches on it will have its own propulsion in the form of SNC's hybrid rocket motor technology which will power it once it reaches orbit.

Dream Chaser is primarily being designed to travel to the ISS to collect cargo. However, it will also be able to carry humans.

Earlier this year it was to perform unmanned atmospheric drop-tests, where it will be carried into the sky by Virgin Galactic's WhiteKnightTwo mothership and dropped from a high altitude to test its gliding capabilities. If it manages to stay on schedule, Dream Chaser will launch into orbit on an Atlas V rocket in 2014.

Dream Chaser will launch on an Atlas V rocket

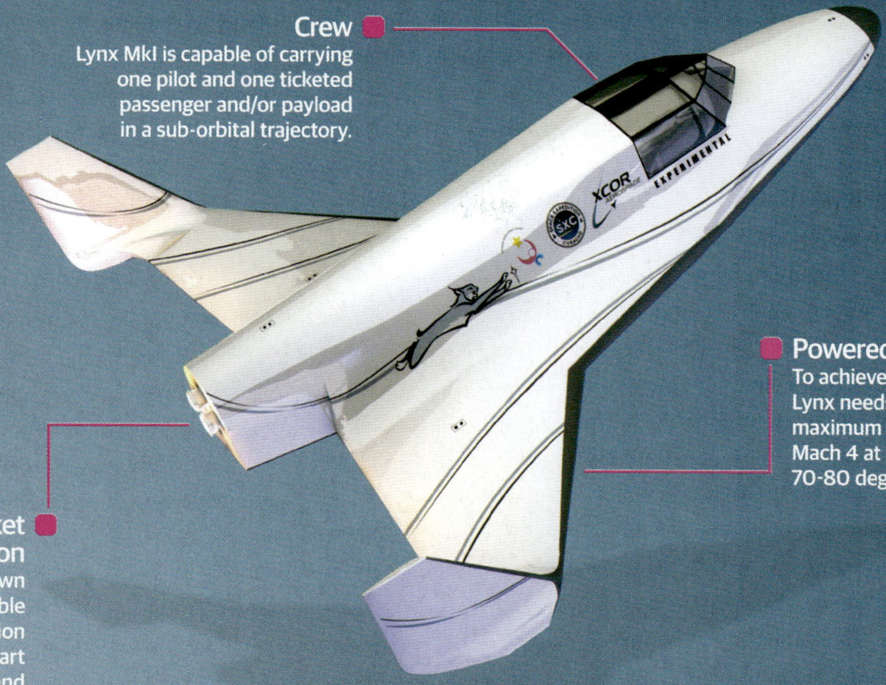

Crew
Lynx MkI is capable of carrying one pilot and one ticketed passenger and/or payload in a sub-orbital trajectory.

Powered ascent
To achieve sub-orbit the Lynx needs to reach a maximum airspeed of Mach 4 at a climb of 70-80 degrees.

Rocket propulsion
Lynx uses its own fully reusable rocket propulsion system to depart from a runway and return safely.

Lynx

Single-stage vehicle developed in California, USA

Company: XCOR (US)
Launch date: Q4 2012
Cost: $10m **Length:** 9m (30ft)
Wingspan: 7.5m (24ft)

Lynx is a single-stage vehicle that will travel to space and back without using any single-use rocket boosters. One key difference between the two is that the first class of Lynx space planes will only be able to reach sub-orbit, not full orbit like Skylon. However, the smaller design of Lynx allows it to both take off and land on a conventional runway, rather than just the latter for Skylon.

To achieve sub-orbit Lynx must take a steep climb of 70-80 degrees, the optimal angle at which to get into space. Once in space it will be able to perform a variety of tasks. It has a payload bay on its top to deploy satellites into orbit. It could also be used as an observation platform, with a telescope in its payload bay used to observe stars, the Sun, Earth or another celestial body.

Upon its return from sub-orbit, XCOR – the company behind Lynx – expects the space plane to have a turnaround time of just 35 minutes before it can fly again, compared to several weeks for NASA's Space Shuttle. Up to eight flights a day are possible with this configuration.

The fuels used by Lynx are non-toxic, which also helps keep the turnaround time to a minimum. This is because when Lynx lands it doesn't need to go through extensive restoration and decontamination, again a disadvantage of NASA's Space Shuttle and one that often took weeks or even months to sort out.

Lynx is made a test flight before at the start of 2013 and is expected begin operational flights before the end of the decade. XCOR also has plans to create an orbital class of Lynx vehicles as opposed to just sub-orbit. This new class will be a two-stage-to-orbit vehicle. An orbital spacecraft using Lynx technology would fly on top of a larger first stage vehicle and, once a reasonable altitude had been reached, it would detach and fire its own engines to reach Low Earth Orbit while the first stage would return safely to Earth.

"To achieve sub-orbit Lynx must take a steep climb, roughly 70-80 degrees, the optimal angle at which to get into space"

The Lynx MkI has a Primary Internal Payload of up to 120kg

Solar sails

Will humanity ever breeze through the cosmos?

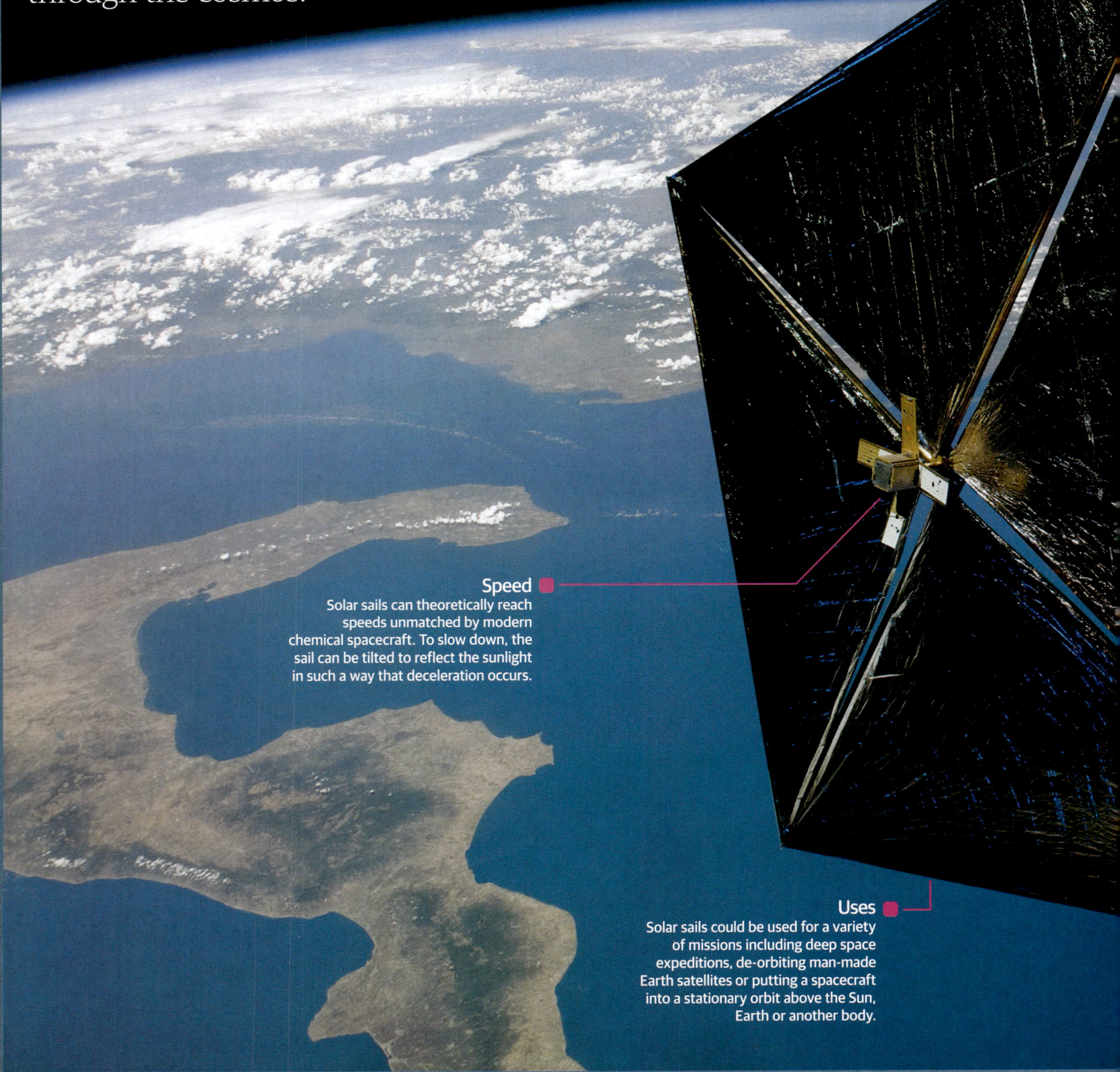

Speed
Solar sails can theoretically reach speeds unmatched by modern chemical spacecraft. To slow down, the sail can be tilted to reflect the sunlight in such a way that deceleration occurs.

Uses
Solar sails could be used for a variety of missions including deep space expeditions, de-orbiting man-made Earth satellites or putting a spacecraft into a stationary orbit above the Sun, Earth or another body.

Solar sails could be used to propel spacecraft indefinitely in Earth orbit

For decades we've sought to find better and more powerful types of fuel to allow us to explore the cosmos. From primitive kerosene-based rocket fuels to modern day liquid hydrogen and oxygen engines, and from chemical engines to long-lasting ion drives, our methods of producing more powerful rockets have come on leaps and bounds. But could it really be that the answer to future space exploration is the same method used by our ancestors to venture into strange new lands on Earth: the sail?

Solar sails work by using the influence of the Sun. Our Solar System's star emits photons that produce a tiny force when they come into contact with another object. This small force is incredibly minute but, over time and given that space is a frictionless vacuum, it can slowly push a small object like a spacecraft faster and faster.

In theory, a giant solar sail would take about 100 days to reach 16,000kph (10,000mph). It could accelerate to 58,000kph (36,000mph) in one year, and in three years it could travel over 160,000kph (100,000mph). While the latter is still only 0.015 the speed of light, at this speed you could reach Pluto from Earth in under five years, compared to the nine-year journey time for humanity's current fastest chemical propulsion spacecraft, New Horizons.

Several solar sail concepts have already flown, including Japan's successful 2010 spacecraft IKAROS and now NASA is planning a 1,200 square-metre solar sail for late 2014 under the direction of L'Garde in Tustin, California. The aim of this solar sail will be to demonstrate an early warning system for solar flares. Between the Earth and the Sun is an area known as Lagrange point 1 where the gravity of the Sun and Earth are equal, allowing spacecraft to remain at a stationary position relative to the Sun and the Earth. This solar sail spacecraft will create an artificial Lagrange point about twice as close to the Sun. By using the photons emitted from the Sun as radiation the solar sail-powered spacecraft will be able to sit much closer to the Sun as it will have a constant force pushing it away from the Sun which, combined with the gravity of Earth, would balance out the gravity of the Sun. This could be very useful for providing an early warning system for a dangerous solar storm, and is just one of the many uses of solar sails that are currently being researched.

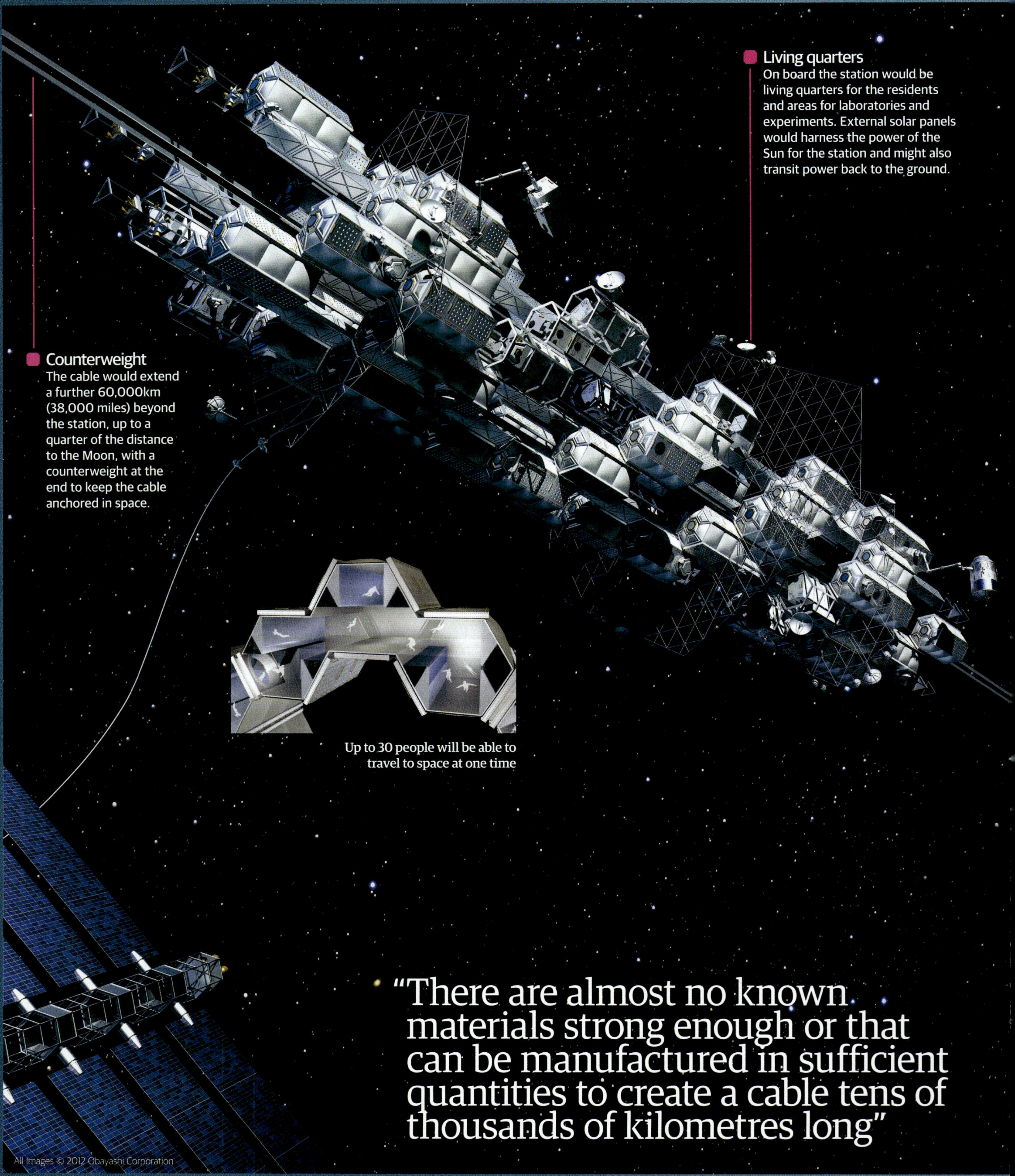

Up to 30 people will be able to travel to space at one time

"There are almost no known materials strong enough or that can be manufactured in sufficient quantities to create a cable tens of thousands of kilometres long"

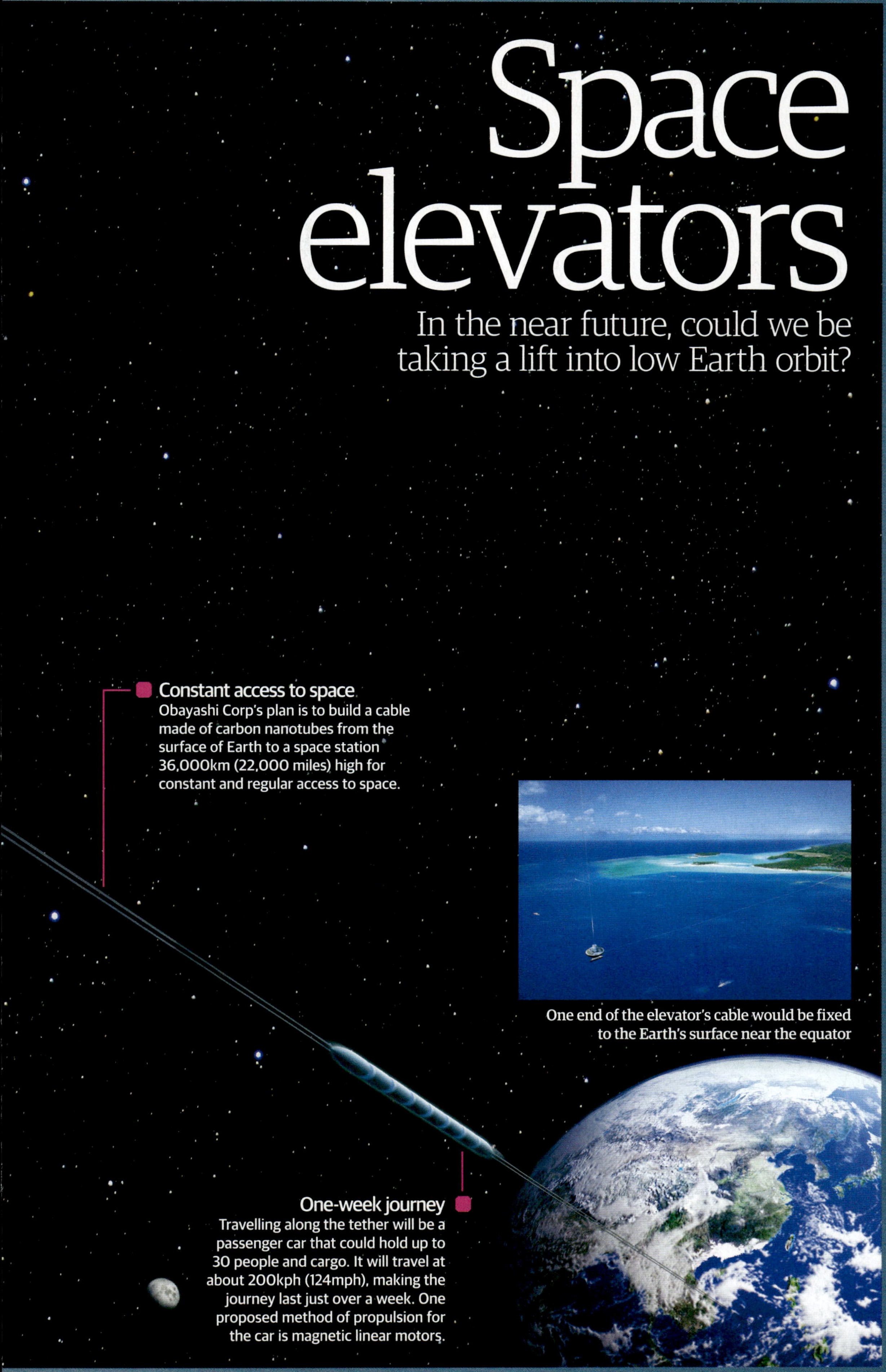

Space elevators

In the near future, could we be taking a lift into low Earth orbit?

Constant access to space
Obayashi Corp's plan is to build a cable made of carbon nanotubes from the surface of Earth to a space station 36,000km (22,000 miles) high for constant and regular access to space.

One end of the elevator's cable would be fixed to the Earth's surface near the equator

One-week journey
Travelling along the tether will be a passenger car that could hold up to 30 people and cargo. It will travel at about 200kph (124mph), making the journey last just over a week. One proposed method of propulsion for the car is magnetic linear motors.

Getting into space is no easy feat. At the moment we use huge tanks of propellant powered by giant explosions at their base, which are better known as rockets, but these are both dangerous and very expensive.

That's why various agencies have spent years looking for other ways to reach space. Last issue we looked at space planes, but this time we're focusing on a more ambitious way to have a constant connection to space.

The idea of a space elevator was first inspired by Russian scientist Konstantin Tsiolkovsky in 1895. In principle it sounds simple - have a tether extend from the surface of Earth to space and just travel up and down it. In practice, however, it's incredibly difficult to construct such a device. For starters, there are almost no known materials strong enough or that can be manufactured in sufficient quantities to create a cable tens of thousands of kilometres long. Second, the tether would need to be anchored both at a geostationary station and further out with a counterweight point to ensure it didn't break. Finally, you'll need some sort of elevator that can attach itself to the cable and travel into space.

Thankfully, there are solutions. One of the primary candidates for the cable's material is carbon nanotubes, which could possess the tensile strength needed for such a structure. Meanwhile, a counterweight beyond the orbit of the space station could be an asteroid or an additional space station. This would ensure the cable had a centre of gravity beyond the space station it was attached to, allowing it to remain anchored in space. Finally, by making the cable much wider at its centre point, cars could climb up it without destroying it. The counterweight would move to ensure the cars did not cause the cable to rotate too much and be destroyed. There are also several proposed methods to power the cars including solar power and wireless energy transfer.

In 2012, Tokyo-based company Obayashi Corporation announced plans to build an operational space elevator by 2050. Although the project is merely in a concept phase, Obayashi Corp's proposal (pictured) isn't too out of this world. We won't be seeing one any time soon but, if all goes to plan, by 2050 we could all be taking regular trips to the stars.

Space elevator, space plane or a rocket - which would you choose? @spaceanswers #SpaceElevators

Plasma drives

Ad Astra, the corporation behind the 'Mars-in-a-month' engine, tells us why this next-generation technology will change space travel forever

The Variable Specific Impulse Magnetoplasma Rocket (VASIMR) is a type of electromagnetic thruster that could be used to power spacecraft at great distances and speeds. It uses a revolutionary form of propulsion, namely using radio waves to ionise and heat a propellant, with magnetic fields then accelerating the plasma and generating a thrust. Its most exciting use would be to create high-speed spacecraft unlike anything that had ever been seen before.

VASIMR is currently being developed by the Ad Astra Rocket Company in Texas, USA. In the image a concept spacecraft using VASIMR is shown. We spoke to Dr Franklin Chang-Díaz, a former NASA astronaut and inventor of VASIMR, to find out how this cosmic powerhouse could revolutionise space exploration.

"Right now, the prototype VASIMR is the most powerful plasma engine in the world, at 200kW," said Dr Chang-Díaz. "Most other electric thrusters are maybe only as high as 10kW.

"The applications of high power propulsion are many. We're interested in missions to Mars, of course, but for now we are interested in moving satellites or the International Space Station. We can bring huge savings to these kinds of services, and we feel that the ISS is not the only station that will be operating in the world that will need VASIMR."

The VASIMR rocket has been extensively tested, but there are some vital steps that must be completed before this type of propulsion can become mainstream. According to Dr Chang-Díaz, the next stage of development would involve "testing multi-megawatt VASIMR engines on the surface of the Moon, where we intend to set up a testing facility."

However, if we're serious about exploring Mars and beyond, Dr Chang-Díaz believes the use of nuclear power will become a necessity. "Nuclear power is an essential ingredient for energy and robust human exploration of the Solar System. I don't think humans are going to get very far if we don't get to grips with nuclear power."

Currently it takes over six months for a spacecraft to get to Mars, but Dr Chang-Díaz is confident that VASIMR could do it in just over a month. "We've been mentioning trip times of 39 days, which would require advanced nuclear reactors to provide electricity. We would use four VASIMR engines at 50MW each, so 200MW in total, equivalent to the power of a Boeing 747 jet on take-off. The top speed at the mid-point of a trajectory to Mars would be 198,000 kilometres per hour (120,000 miles per hour)."

In comparison, the world's current fastest spacecraft, the New Horizons probe on its way to Pluto, can reach 'just' 55,000 kilometres per hour (34,500 miles per hour). "If you go to places like Jupiter or Saturn, or places further out, the top speed would be higher," added Dr Chang-Díaz.

So, when will we see these amazing thrusters powering the next era of spacecraft? "By 2020 we should be able to do some testing on the Moon. Assuming a nuclear reactor component has been developed, we'd then be able to make very fast trips to other places later in the 2020s."

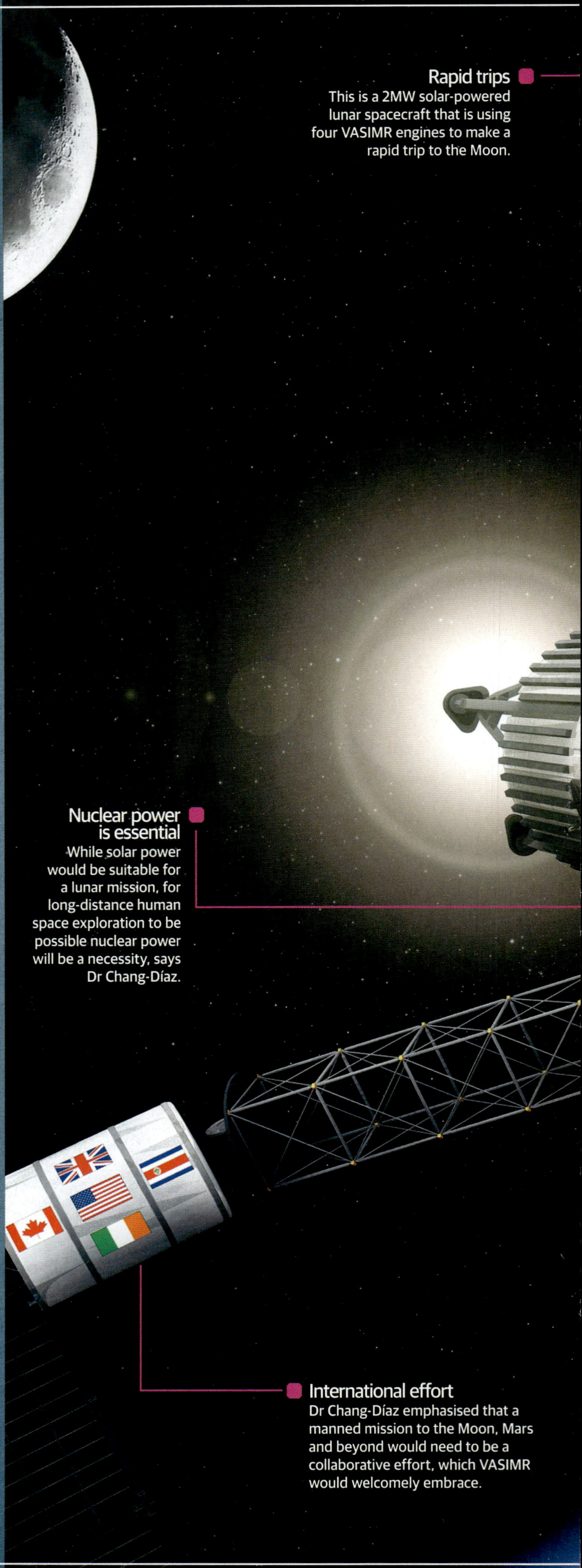

“A trip to Mars would be reduced to just 39 days”

Dr Chang-Díaz, VASIMR inventor

Ultra-fast propulsion

Gases such as argon will be stored on the spacecraft in tanks to be used by the VASIMR engine for ultra-fast propulsion.

To Mars in just over a month

Using current methods of propulsion a mission to Mars could take more than six months, depending on the position of Mars relative to Earth at the time. VASIMR could cut that down to just under 40 days.

Next-gen spacesuits

What is the next generation of spacesuit technology that will help humans explore the cosmos?

Spacesuits are one of the most important parts of any human space exploration mission. The large spacesuits used for spacewalks have most of the capabilities an astronaut would need to survive in space, at least for a short time.

However, spacesuits are, and always have been, reasonably bulky. They limit movement and, as was found in the early space exploration missions of the Sixties, they can be very tiring to use. So, since the dawn of the space age, NASA and other agencies have been looking for spacesuits with added manoeuvrability that still retain the same safety factor found in previous suits. In addition, for operations on other bodies such as the Moon or Mars, astronauts would need new technologies to ensure they make the most of their mission.

NASA has three ways in which it tests a spacesuit. First, it has its 12-metre (40-foot) deep swimming pool, the Neutral Buoyancy Lab. An underwater environment is the closest we can get to replicating the vacuum of space on Earth. NASA also uses ARGOS, the Active Response Gravity Offload System. Astronauts are suspended in midair, with ARGOS able to replicate the gravity they'd feel on the Moon, Mars or in space. NASA's final testing 'facility' is an aeroplane that flies in steep parabolas to create moments of simulated zero gravity. Dubbed the 'Vomit Comet', would-be astronauts can practise space manoeuvres or try out new spacesuit technologies, as was done recently with the Advanced Crew Escape Suit.

Read on to find out some of the new technologies that could be used on future spacesuits.

Advanced Crew Escape Suit

Developer: David Clark Company
Planned use: Orion spacecraft
Estimated date: 2016

First worn by Space Shuttle astronauts, the original Advanced Crew Escape Suit (ACES), which was affectionately known as the 'pumpkin suit' due to its orange appearance, was used to keep astronauts safe during launch and re-entry.

The upgraded ACES will be used by NASA on its Orion spacecraft to keep the astronauts safe and also allow them to perform light activities while in space. It carries a few design changes from the original Space Shuttle design to ensure it's the best spacesuit an astronaut could use with present technology. Its main difference is the use of a 'closed loop' system rather than an 'open loop'. This means ACES is able to get rid of the carbon dioxide an astronaut breathes out.

Integration
The new ACES suit will be fully integrated with the life support systems on board the Orion spacecraft.

Mobility
This suit will have more hard elements in the joint areas, which will give the astronauts more mobility for surface exploration.

Launch and re-entry
Although predominantly used to keep astronauts safe during launch and re-entry, ACES will also be used for minor spacewalks.

Lunar operations
The white suit will be used mainly for extended spacewalks, such as operations on the lunar surface.

"ACES is able to get rid of the carbon dioxide an astronaut breathes out"

Suiting up on Mars

There are a number of problems that need to be overcome before astronauts will be able to suit up on Mars. First, using current technology a spacesuit would have to weigh about 43kg (95lb) on Mars. While the Martian gravity is only about a third that on Earth, this would still exhaust astronauts wearing it for a prolonged period of exploration. Therefore, lighter spacesuits will be needed for astronauts to operate efficiently on Mars, but they will need some smart technological advances to ensure that, although they will have less equipment, they will still be able to keep the astronauts safe.

Suitports

Developer: NASA
Planned use: Spacewalks
Estimated date: 2020

Getting into your spacesuit while in space can be a tricky business, especially in the confines of a spacecraft. While in the pressurised environment of a spacecraft astronauts are able to wear regular clothes, as they do on the International Space Station (ISS), so NASA has been trying to devise a way for astronauts to quickly and easily get into their spacesuits when they need to perform extra-vehicular activities (EVAs), or spacewalks. One concept currently being tested is a suitport. This would basically be a suit attached to the side of a lander or space station into which an astronaut could climb.

Entry
A hatch in the back of the spacesuit, which can be sealed once inside, allows astronauts to enter and exit the spacesuit quickly.

Pressure
The astronauts are pressurised and depressurised while inside the suit, eliminating the need for a depressurisation chamber.

Activity
Once sealed the astronauts detach from the suitport and perform their activities outside the spacecraft before returning and re-attaching themselves.

Debris
Essentially leaving the spacesuit outside the spacecraft ensures that no debris, like dust or microparticles, makes its way back into the spacecraft.

Bio-Suit

Developer: Massachusetts Institute of Technology
Planned use: Moon, Mars
Estimated date: 2025

Under development at the Massachusetts Institute of Technology, the Bio-Suit is a radical attempt to produce a space activity suit (SAS) that provides astronauts with unprecedented manoeuvrability. An SAS is a spacesuit that uses skin-tight garments to adhere to the body of an astronaut, rather than inflating like many modern spacesuits.

Pressure
Life-support is provided by pressure being applied to the body, while a helmet is used to protect the head.

Second skin
The Bio-Suit aims to provide enhanced movability for astronauts performing spacewalks by giving them a 'second skin'.

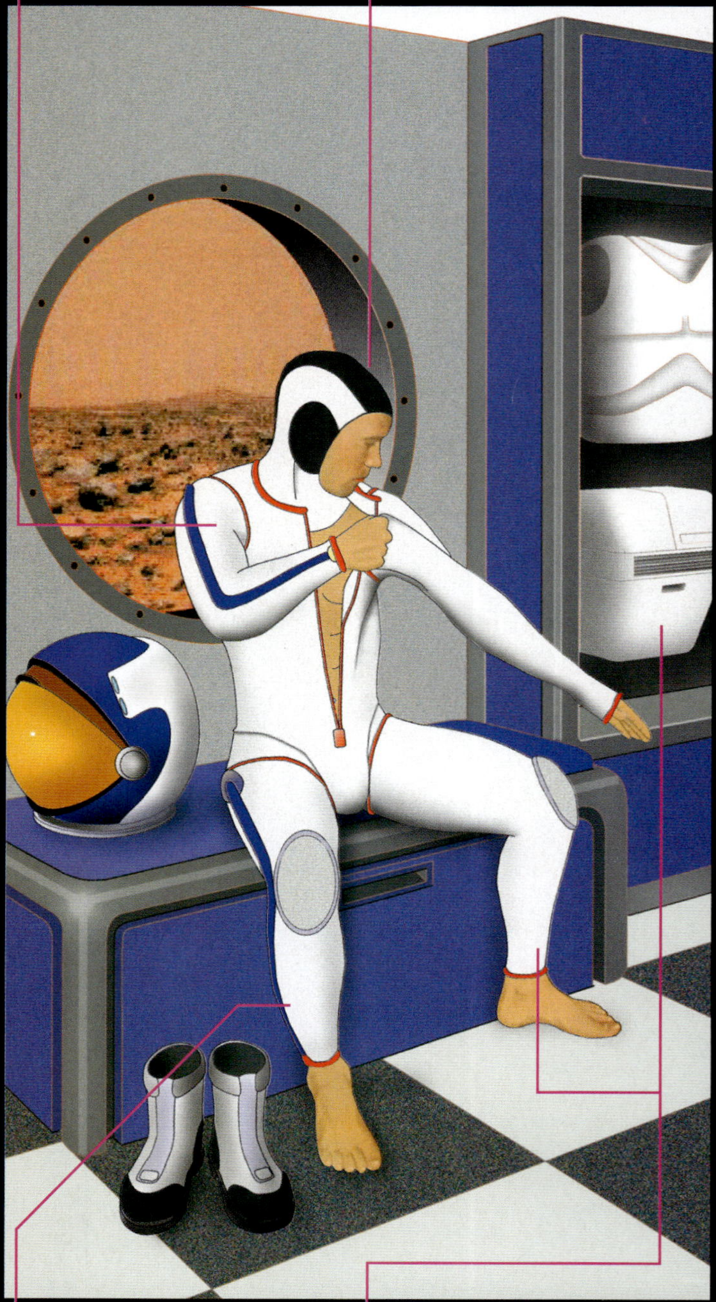

Layers
The Bio-Suit is made of different layers to protect the astronauts from harmful radiation and the surrounding environment.

Shell
An astronaut on Mars would wear the elastic inner Bio-Suit layer before putting on the hardened torso shell for added protection.

The Bio-Suit's skin-tight design offers astronauts unprecedented movement

©MIT

"Instead of being built underground, the launch tube is levitated and kept aloft by two sets of superconducting cables"

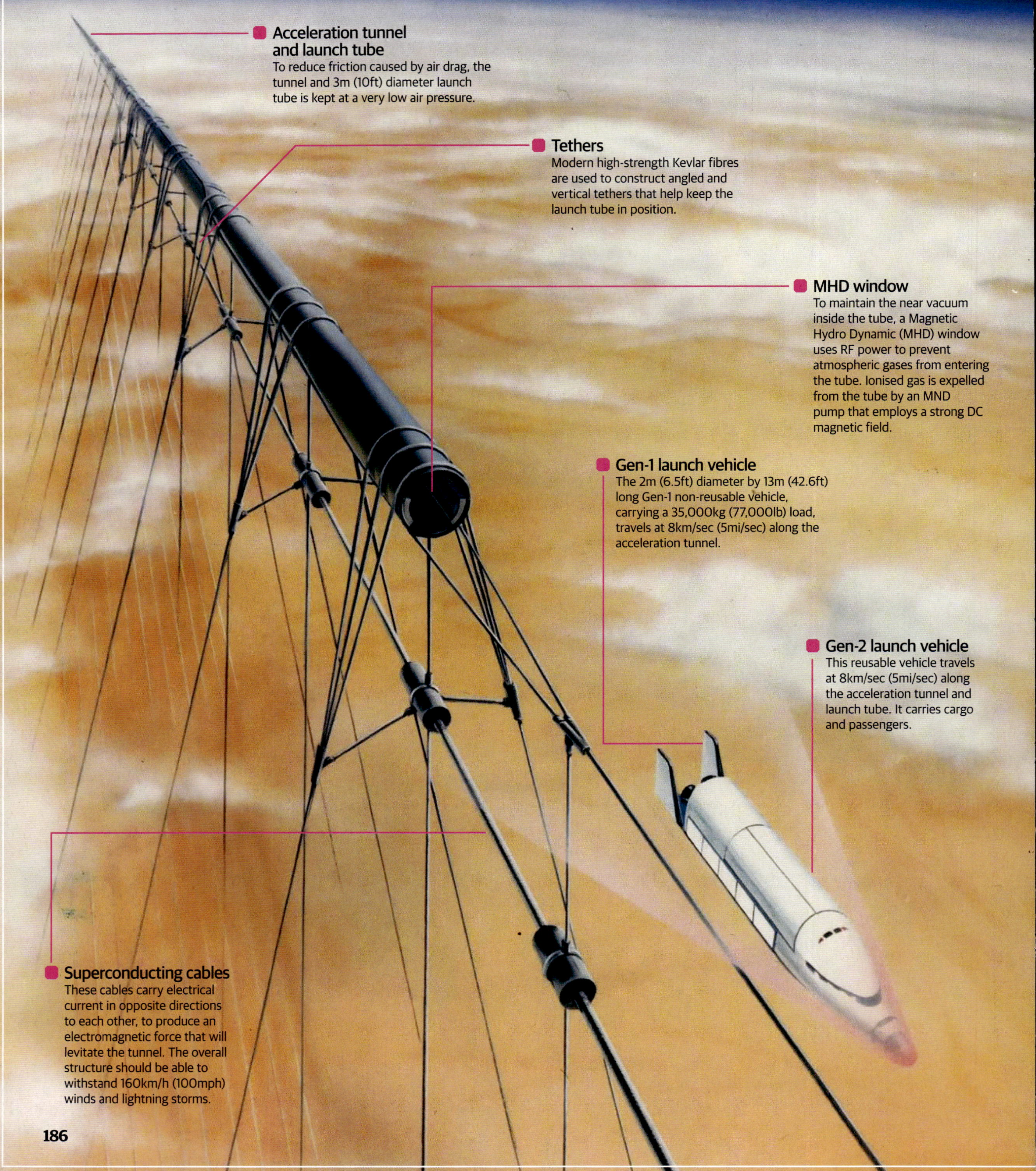

The StarTram Space Launcher

Forget about expensive rockets or even reusable space planes, the StarTram system launches space vehicles along an elevated tube using magnetic levitation

The concept of the StarTram is within the bounds of today's technology, and in the long-term will bring the price of sending one kilogram of payload into space down from around £6,500 ($10,000 USD) to £26 ($40). In the short-term, it will cost £13 billion ($20 billion) and at least ten years of development to construct the cargo-carrying Gen-1 version.

The Gen-1 system consists of a 100-kilometre (62-mile) long acceleration tunnel that is built into a mountain to reach an exit height at the mountain's surface of 6,000 metres (20,000 feet).

The launch vehicle will operate using the same principles as the magnetic levitation (maglev) trains currently operating in Japan. Their speed is limited to less than 600 kilometres per hour (370 miles per hour) due to air drag, but this factor will be drastically reduced, as the acceleration tunnel will have a near-vacuum environment.

Powerful superconducting magnets on the vehicle interact with aluminium loops in the tunnel to levitate it by 100 millimetres (four inches), and propulsion is provided by a linear synchronous motor (LSM) that will take its energy from a second set of energy storage loops positioned along the tunnel. After leaving the tunnel, it fires a small rocket motor to put it into orbit. Annually, it could take around 135 million kilograms (300 million pounds) of payload into low Earth orbit.

The Gen-1 system would only carry cargo as the acceleration forces are in the range of 10-30g making it unsuitable for passengers. The Gen-2 system, however, will carry cargo and passengers but is a far more ambitious project. This needs a 1,000-kilometre (620-mile) long acceleration tunnel, elevated to a height of 21,000 metres (70,000 feet), to bring the acceleration forces down to 2-3g.

Instead of being built underground, the launch tube is levitated and kept aloft by two sets of superconducting cables. The ground level cables carry up to 100 million amps, while the cables below the tunnel carry over 40 million amps to produce a magnetic interaction that can create a force of four tons per metre along the tube.

It would take about 20 years to develop and construct at a cost of at least £38.5 billion ($60 billion). To fund this it could carry 1 million passengers a year into space at a cost of £3,200 ($5,000) per ticket.

StarTram is a massive, bold project that would make living and working in space as easy as boarding a jet plane today.

Can the StarTram really succeed? @spaceanswers #StarTram

Antarctica, Greenland, Siberia, Northern Canada and Alaska are regarded as suitable launching sites for the StarTram

The future of space travel

Dr James Powell reveals why StarTram could replace conventional space launch systems

1. Reduced costs
"The reason it costs so much to launch payloads into space, almost $5,000 [£3,200] per pound to low Earth orbit (LEO), and much more to geostationary Earth orbit (GEO), the Moon, Mars, and beyond, is that the very expensive rocket hardware is usually thrown away. It's like delivering a refrigerator by helicopter that crashes after every delivery."

2. Reusable
"In contrast, StarTram keeps all the expensive hardware on the ground, and uses it over many thousands of launches, making the amortised cost per pound very low. The cost of electric energy for launch is trivial. For launch to low Earth orbit at eight kilometres per second [five miles per second], it costs only $0.30 [£0.19] per pound of payload. For GEO and beyond, it would be a bit higher, about $1 [£0.64] per pound."

3. Technology already exists
"The basic technology for Gen-1 cargo launch system – ie maglev levitation and propulsion, superconducting energy storage, magneto-hydraulic control of air flow – already exists. The excavation volume for the Gen-1 acceleration tunnel is only 1/10th of that for the English Channel Tunnel. The magnetically levitated tube technology for the Gen-2 passenger and cargo system can be developed within the next 20 years."

Tractor beam technology

Tractor beams have been the stuff of science fiction for many years. Here we look at how the technology could soon become reality

Many scientists are now working on how tractor beam technology can be created, exploited and used in real life.

In 2011, NASA awarded funding to scientists at the Goddard Space Flight Center to investigate the possible methods of using laser light to manipulate objects. Their work explores three major methods of manipulating and collecting particles, molecules and viruses using laser light, which could be used on board space exploration vehicles.

One method involves using optical trapping or optical tweezers. When laser light is passed through a microscope lens, it produces an hour-glass-shaped beam, which can trap a small particle in the 'waist' of the beam. The particle can then be moved around by changing the position of the beam's waist.

Optical tweezers can be operated by using two rings of light. By strengthening and weakening one of the light rings, the heat around a trapped particle can be varied to make it move up or down the central core of the light rings. At the Australian National University they have been able to move a small bead of glass a distance of 1.5 metres (five feet) using this method.

The second technique, unlike the optical tweezer method, can be used in the vacuum of space. It uses optical solenoid beams that spiral around the axis of propagation, which can be used to trap and expel a particle away from it.

The third concept involves the use of Bessel beams. Rather than firing a focused beam of light like a normal laser that spreads out the further it travels, Bessel beams produce a central beam surrounded by concentric rings. Even over a long distance, the central beam will remain focused and if it is partially blocked by an object, the beam can reconstruct itself on the other side of the obstacle. Unlike the other techniques, Bessel beams are capable of pulling objects back down the light beam.

Professor Andrei V Rode, of the Australian National University, notes that all these methods work "on the precise manipulation and pin-point delivery of micron-size particles with optical vortex beams. We aim to develop new controllable ways of trapping and transport of micron-size particles, biological macromolecules, and viruses by analysing various catching techniques through the laser beam properties, such as polarisation, intensity distribution, and laser-vortex formation methods, and their influence on the transport speed, and delivery accuracy."

He warns that, "In principle, assuming unlimited laser power, it may be possible to form a tornado in the atmosphere, which may raise objects from the Earth's surface. However, I believe it would be a very destructive exercise."

John E Sinko at Nagoya University, Japan is investigating another promising use of laser beams. This involves spacecraft being fitted with laser thruster motors, which can be activated by a laser beam up to 100 kilometres (62 miles) away. It is easy to repel or steer the spacecraft, but a complex system of mirrors would be needed to send the spacecraft towards the laser beam. Using this system, satellites could be put into a higher orbit, or activated to re-enter the Earth's atmosphere.

These various forms of tractor beam technology show that real spacecraft could actually be using such devices very soon, moving it out of the realms of science fiction and into reality.

"It may be possible to form a tornado in the atmosphere, which may raise objects from the Earth's surface"

The underwater space cannon

Jules Verne imagined using a cannon to send humans to the Moon, now one could be built to send cargo into Earth orbit

The Quicklaunch project plans to put into reality Verne's 19th Century dream of using a cannon to launch space vehicles, though in this case it will be used to send cargo into low Earth orbit (LEO) rather than humans to the Moon.

The cannon, known as the Quicklauncher, will be submerged 183 metres (600 feet) under water. The initial scheme is to build a 400-metre (1,300-foot) long QL-100 launcher to carry payloads of 45 kilograms (100 pounds) into LEO. To benefit from the slingshot effect of the Earth's rotation, it would be located near the equator. It would cost $50 million USD (£32 million) to build and be capable of launching ten vehicles a day.

The cannon is fired by heating hydrogen gas in a confined space so that it generates enough pressure to blast the space vehicle out of the end. When fired, the cannon produces a staggering 5,000 gs, which would easily crush a person, so it is mainly practical for carrying satellites or cargo, such as rocket fuel.

Within a minute, the vehicle will reach an altitude of 100 kilometres (62 miles), and after six minutes at an altitude of 450 kilometres (280 miles), it will fire its rocket motor to rendezvous with an orbiting fuel depot. Once docked, the propellant can be accessed from the central hub of the depot. Such depots could bring the price of fuelling a mission to Mars down from $50 billion (£32 billion) to $5 billion (£3.2 billion).

A bigger QL-1000 launcher costing $500 million (£320 million) to build, would have a 1,100-metre (3,600-foot) long barrel to carry 450-kilogram (1,000-pound) payloads into LEO. This could deliver 1.8 million kilograms (4 million pounds) of payload into LEO yearly and would be seven times more efficient than a standard multi-stage rocket. This would reduce the cost of sending 0.45 kilograms (one pound) of payload into space from $5,000 (£3,200) to $500 (£320).

Dr John Hunter, Dr Harry Cartland and Dr Richard Twogood, who, in the Nineties, worked on the Super High Altitude Research Project (SHARP) that used a land-based hydrogen gun to fire high-speed projectiles, created the Quicklaunch Inc company. At the moment it is still looking for funding, and Dr Cartland admits: "Quicklaunch is never going to replace rockets for fragile payloads (like people), but something like Quicklaunch is going to happen; it's just a question of who is going to do it and when.

"In fact, Quicklaunch can stage most of the mission mass for something like Mars exploration, and the financial case for replacing expendable launch vehicles that are used once and dumped in the ocean with a reusable ground facility, whose cost is amortised over many launches, is simply too compelling to avoid."

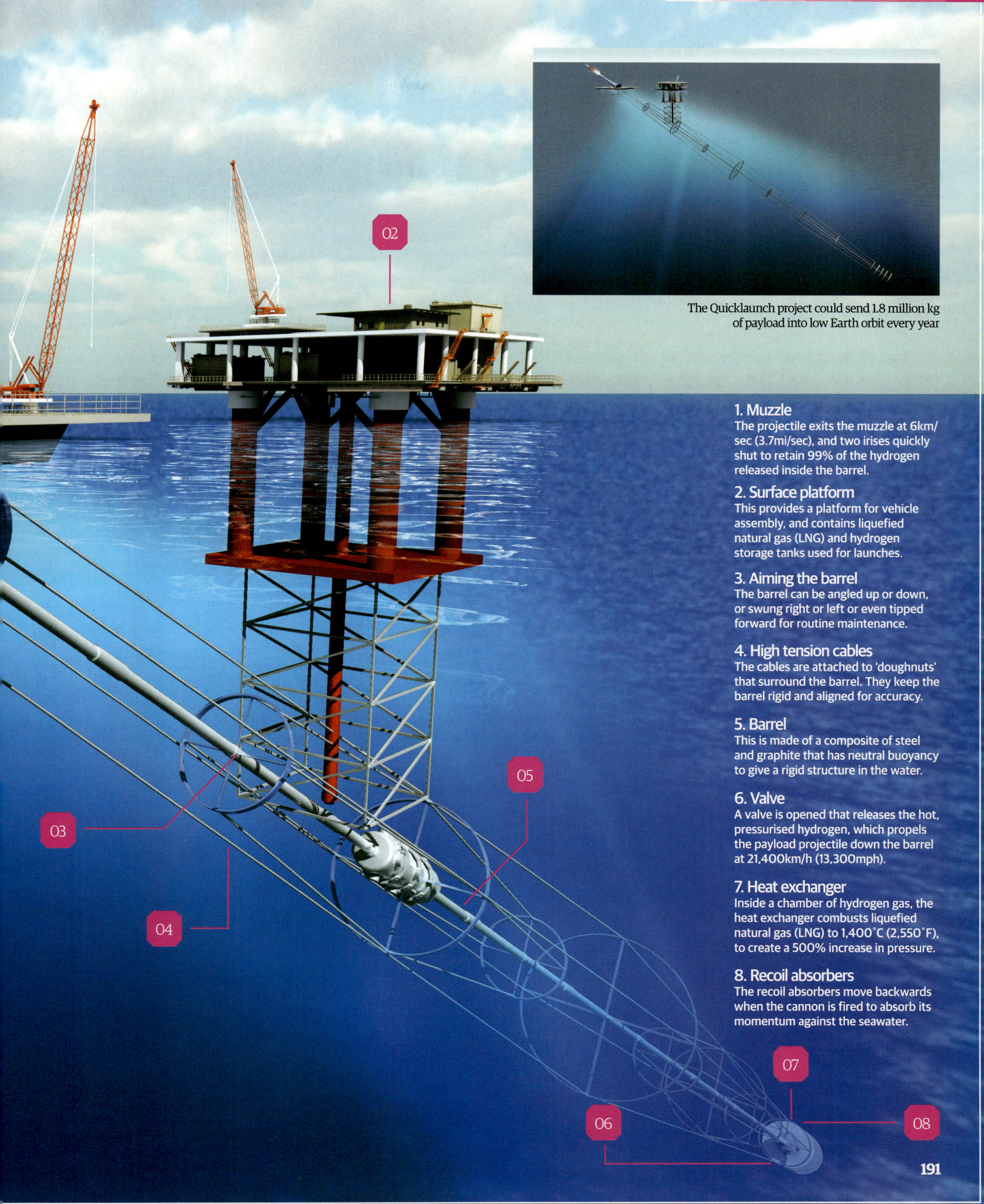

The Quicklaunch project could send 1.8 million kg of payload into low Earth orbit every year

1. Muzzle
The projectile exits the muzzle at 6km/sec (3.7mi/sec), and two irises quickly shut to retain 99% of the hydrogen released inside the barrel.

2. Surface platform
This provides a platform for vehicle assembly, and contains liquefied natural gas (LNG) and hydrogen storage tanks used for launches.

3. Aiming the barrel
The barrel can be angled up or down, or swung right or left or even tipped forward for routine maintenance.

4. High tension cables
The cables are attached to 'doughnuts' that surround the barrel. They keep the barrel rigid and aligned for accuracy.

5. Barrel
This is made of a composite of steel and graphite that has neutral buoyancy to give a rigid structure in the water.

6. Valve
A valve is opened that releases the hot, pressurised hydrogen, which propels the payload projectile down the barrel at 21,400km/h (13,300mph).

7. Heat exchanger
Inside a chamber of hydrogen gas, the heat exchanger combusts liquefied natural gas (LNG) to 1,400°C (2,550°F), to create a 500% increase in pressure.

8. Recoil absorbers
The recoil absorbers move backwards when the cannon is fired to absorb its momentum against the seawater.

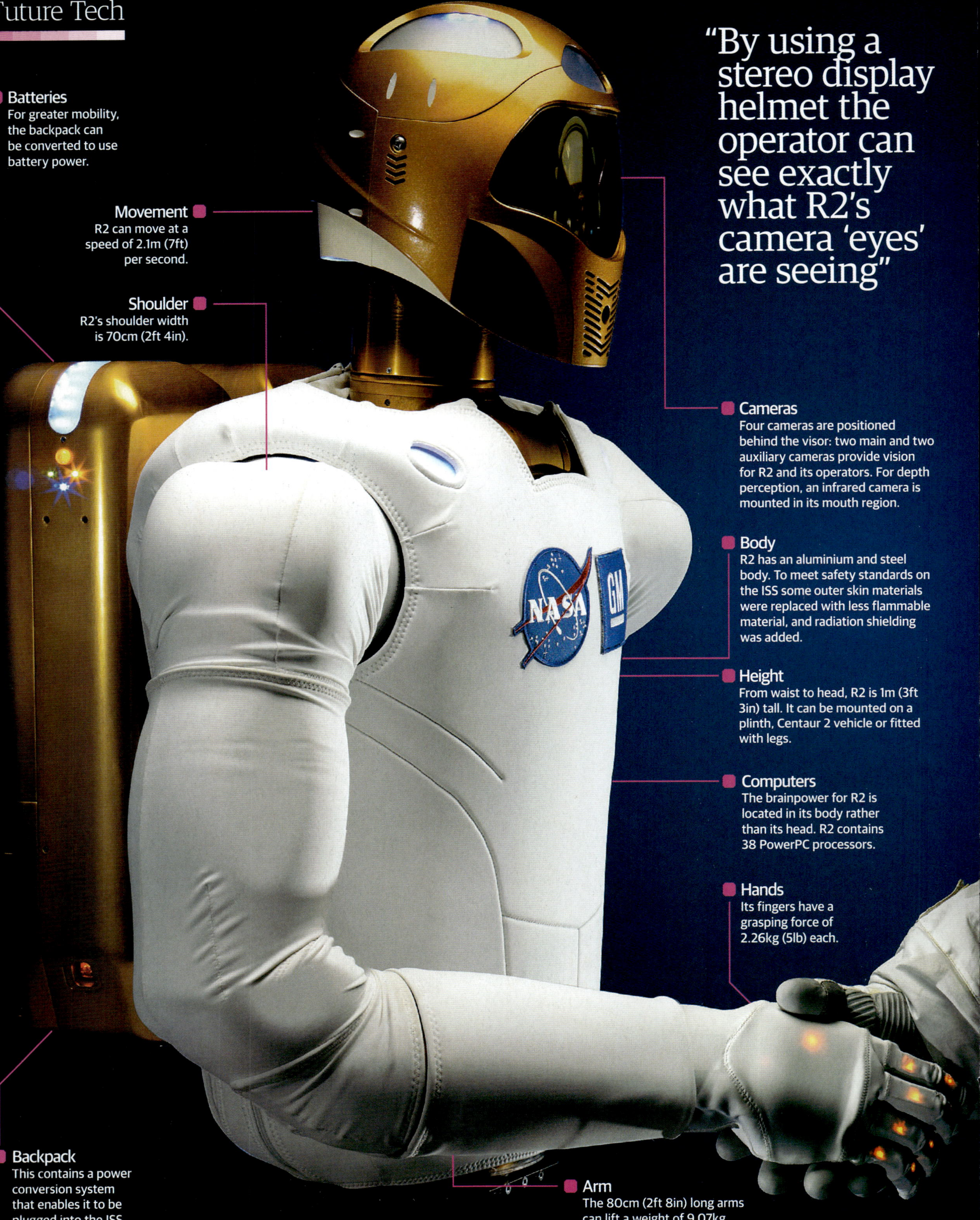

"By using a stereo display helmet the operator can see exactly what R2's camera 'eyes' are seeing"

Batteries
For greater mobility, the backpack can be converted to use battery power.

Movement
R2 can move at a speed of 2.1m (7ft) per second.

Shoulder
R2's shoulder width is 70cm (2ft 4in).

Cameras
Four cameras are positioned behind the visor: two main and two auxiliary cameras provide vision for R2 and its operators. For depth perception, an infrared camera is mounted in its mouth region.

Body
R2 has an aluminium and steel body. To meet safety standards on the ISS some outer skin materials were replaced with less flammable material, and radiation shielding was added.

Height
From waist to head, R2 is 1m (3ft 3in) tall. It can be mounted on a plinth, Centaur 2 vehicle or fitted with legs.

Computers
The brainpower for R2 is located in its body rather than its head. R2 contains 38 PowerPC processors.

Hands
Its fingers have a grasping force of 2.26kg (5lb) each.

Backpack
This contains a power conversion system that enables it to be plugged into the ISS electrical supply.

Arm
The 80cm (2ft 8in) long arms can lift a weight of 9.07kg (20lb) on Earth.

Meet the Robonaut

Robonaut is a NASA-led project to create a human-like robot to carry out dangerous tasks in outer space

NASA has many types of robot vehicles and robotic equipment, but the task given to its Robot Systems Technology Branch in 1997 was to create a robot that could work alongside human astronauts.

With the construction of the International Space Station (ISS), there was a need for regular extra-vehicular activity (EVA or spacewalks) to maintain and service the station, which could only be fulfilled by a mobile human astronaut. Most of these tasks are essential and dangerous, yet dull and do not require a lot of brainpower. For example, every 90 days one of the ISS crew has to hold a gauge in front of five airflow vents scattered throughout the station to check whether they're working correctly or not. A robot is perfect for this task because it does not breathe, whereas human breathing can contaminate the results, and it can hold the gauge more steadily in the microgravity environment.

In 2000, the outcome of this project was Robonaut 1. It had a head, torso and two arms with dextrous hands. Ten years of development in conjunction with General Motors produced Robonaut 2 (R2). Each R2 costs $2.5 million (£1.5 million) and weighs 150 kilograms (330 pounds). It is essentially the same as R1 but has better dexterity, speed of movement and sensing abilities.

R2's hands consist of two sections that allow it to manipulate and grasp objects. 14 motors and 12 circuit boards inside its 20cm (8-inch) long, 10cm (4-inch) diameter forearms control the hands. The head contains five cameras: four provide stereo vision and one infrared camera offers depth of perception.

Robonaut can be given simple jobs to do and its computers can work out how to do them, or it can be operated from Earth. By using a stereo display helmet the operator can see exactly what R2's camera 'eyes' are seeing and sensors on the operator's hands and body can be duplicated by R2 to move and manipulate objects.

On Earth, Robonaut can be mounted on a four-wheel Centaur 2 rough terrain vehicle platform that is also suitable for use on the surface of other planets. When R2 was sent to the ISS in 2011, it was unpacked and mounted on a plinth, though there are plans for legs to be fitted to it to help it move around the station.

In future, Robonauts with better body protection and mobility could work outside the International Space Station and even service other satellites and take part in missions to the Moon or Mars.

Robonaut 2 can be mounted on a number of different bases

Robonaut 2's hands have 12 degrees of freedom

Robots in space

Space probes
Even the earliest space probes had robotic pre-programmed systems to keep them operational. Today, probes like the Cassini spacecraft need robotic systems as they are so far from mission control on Earth.

Remotely operated vehicles
The Curiosity rover is the latest example of a robot vehicle sent to explore the surface of another planet. It used pre-programmed computer software for the descent and landing.

Remote Manipulator System
This robotic arm system was fitted to the Space Shuttle and ISS. Astronauts can use it to deploy or gather payloads. For more delicate jobs a grappling hand can be used.

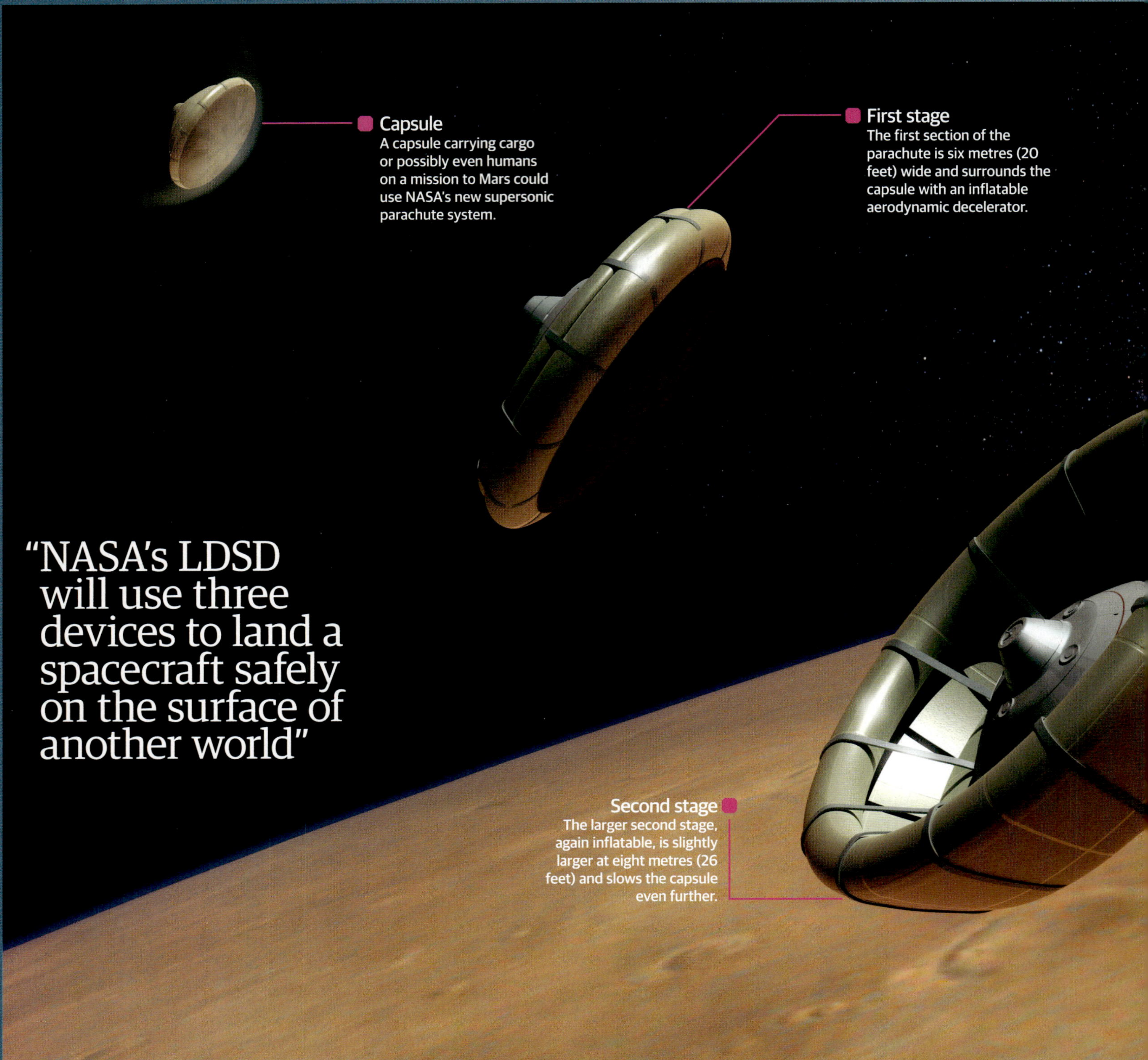

> "NASA's LDSD will use three devices to land a spacecraft safely on the surface of another world"

An inflatable decelerator being tested on rocket sled by NASA in mid-2012

Supersonic parachutes

The next generation of parachute technology will land bigger and better payloads on other worlds

When the Curiosity rover landed on Mars's surface on 6 August 2012 it employed the largest supersonic parachute to ever operate outside the confines of Earth, measuring a whopping 16 metres (52.5 feet) in diameter and being able to withstand a force of 29,500 kilograms (65,000 pounds). However, even this mammoth parachute wasn't enough to lower the rover all the way to the planet's surface, and it needed additional rocket boosters to touch it down safely. If we want to use a parachute to make it all the way to the surface of another world we're going to have to greatly enhance their capabilities, and NASA is in the process of doing just that.

Affectionately called the Low-Density Supersonic Decelerator (LDSD), NASA's next generation of supersonic parachutes will be unlike anything ever seen before. When landing on a world with an atmosphere, such as Mars, the atmospheric drag is a great way to slow down a spacecraft. For a single sheet parachute like that used on Curiosity, however, there's a limit to how much force it can handle, so NASA has been looking at a multiple component parachute to get large payloads safely and comparatively cheaply to the surface.

The LDSD will use three devices to land a spacecraft safely on the surface of another world. The first two sections are inflatable aerodynamic decelerators that will expand as the capsule passes through the atmosphere. These large, balloon-like pressure vessels, one measuring six metres (20 feet) in diameter and the other eight metres (26 feet), would surround the capsule and slow it from Mach 3.5 or higher to Mach 2. The last device will be a huge parachute 33.5 metres (110 feet) wide, which would slow the capsule to subsonic speeds (lower than the speed of sound).

It is estimated that this new type of supersonic parachute could double the payload capability of a capsule going to the surface of Mars, and improve landing accuracy from a margin of ten kilometres (6.2 miles) to just three kilometres (1.9 miles). In mid-2012, NASA conducted the first test of such a parachute system, using a rocket-powered sled to test its aerodynamic resilience. In the coming years NASA will test the parachute system in the atmosphere of Earth, in preparation for its use on Mars or potentially elsewhere in the Solar System with an atmosphere.

Comet harpoon

Could we fire a capsule into a comet to return samples to Earth?

On page 188 we looked at how tractor beams might be used to transport particles from a celestial body to a spacecraft. Elsewhere, scientists at NASA's Goddard Space Flight Center have been looking at something just as innovative to return a sample from a comet - a harpoon-wielding spacecraft.

If you're imagining a boat's harpoon gun in space, then you're not far off. This remarkable concept would place a spacecraft in the vicinity of a comet before firing a sample capsule, attached to the spacecraft with a tether, into the comet. It would retrieve a sample before winching it back to the spacecraft and flying back to Earth.

The testing so far has seen scientists develop a large crossbow 1.8 metres (six feet) tall to fire a projectile into a mock comet with a force of around 450 kilograms (1,000 pounds) at 30 metres (100 feet) per second. A similar device could be attached to a spacecraft and sent to space where it would use explosive powder to fire a capsule into a comet and winch a sample back.

The desire to research the comet harpoon method came about after scientists discussed how best to return a sample from icy and mineral-rich comets, which are of great interest as they may have carried the building blocks of life in the early Solar System. Landing on a comet has been mooted for some time, although no nation has yet accomplished it.

Some comets tear through the Solar System at up to 240,000 kilometres per hour (150,000 miles per hour), making retrieving a sample incredibly difficult. NASA's new comet harpoon mission offers several benefits over a landing mission. "The harpoon mission does not need to land, so it can sample from virtually any terrain," said lead scientist on the project Dr Joseph Nuth. "A harpoon obtains a sample very quickly, in less than a minute, rather than over days or weeks for a drill on a lander."

A harpoon could bring back samples up to a metre (3.3 feet) beneath a comet's surface, which would "be a collection of dust and volatiles that should contain a representative sample of the materials making up the comet," said Dr Nuth. This in turn could provide useful data on the formation of the solar nebula.

So, when can we expect to see such a mission? "The next New Frontiers opportunity will not be until at least 2016," said Dr Nuth. "The time to build and launch a mission of this complexity is four to five years and the cruise time is also on the order of five to seven years. Sample return could take another three to five years. This means that the sample would return sometime in the 2030s."

"Comets tear through the Solar System at around 240,000km/h, making retrieving a sample incredibly difficult"

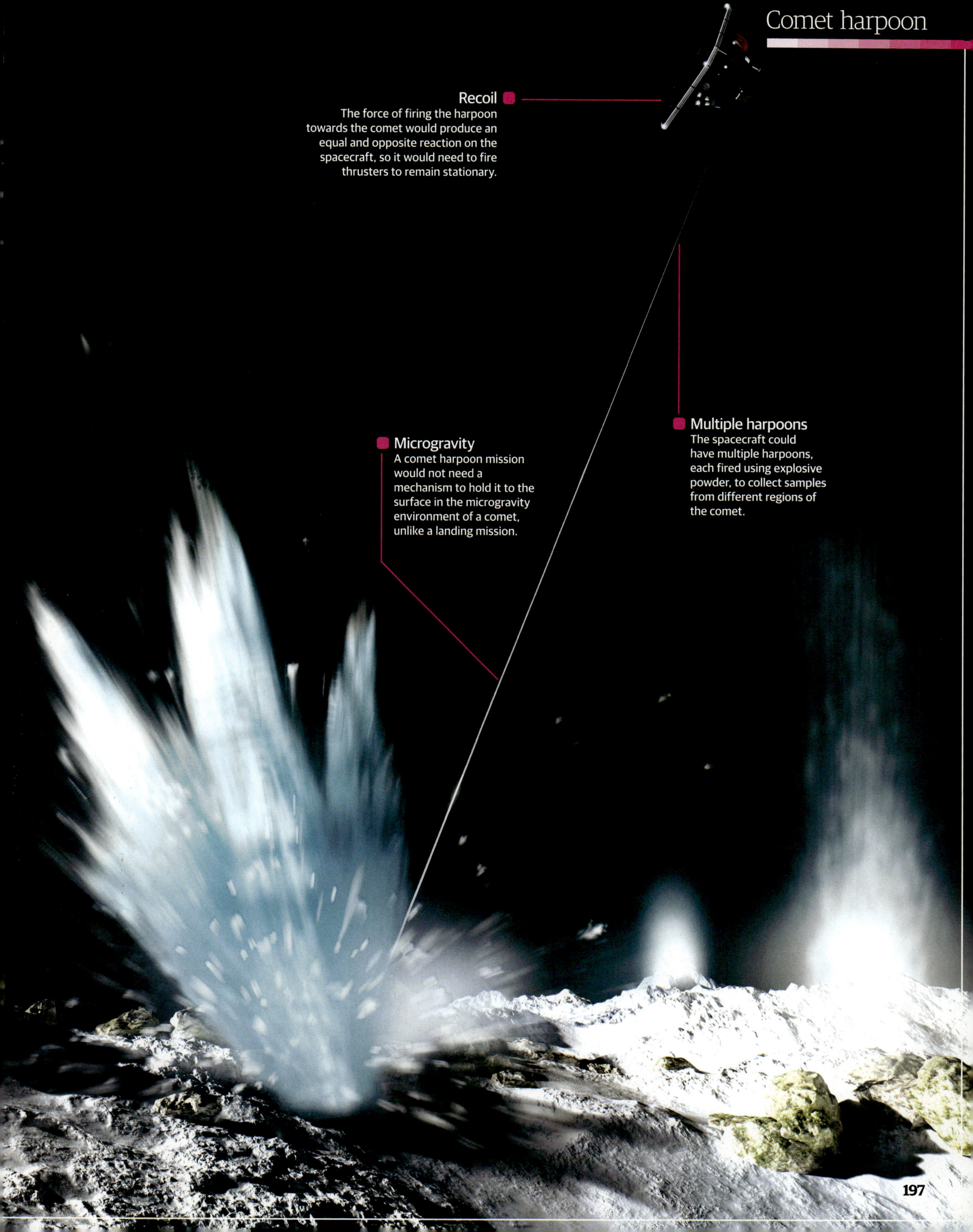
Recoil
The force of firing the harpoon towards the comet would produce an equal and opposite reaction on the spacecraft, so it would need to fire thrusters to remain stationary.
Multiple harpoons
The spacecraft could have multiple harpoons, each fired using explosive powder, to collect samples from different regions of the comet.
Microgravity
A comet harpoon mission would not need a mechanism to hold it to the surface in the microgravity environment of a comet, unlike a landing mission.

Project Icarus Starfinder MkI

Erosion shield
A lightweight beryllium shield protects the 63,500kg (140,000lb) 'craft from the impact of dust particles.

Dustbug Spacecraft
As it approaches its target, small 'Dustbug' spacecraft could seed clouds of particles 200km (124 miles) ahead of the 'craft to intercept any large debris.

Payload
Contains the super-computer that runs and controls all the spacecraft's systems throughout the journey. The decks in this area contain unmanned probes that will be sent out to explore regions of deep space as it approaches and reaches its target.

A Gasdynamic Mirror, seen above, is an example of a magnetic mirror based fusion propulsion system

Project Icarus

Launched in 2009, Project Icarus is a five-year mission to make real the dream of interstellar exploration

By any standards, Project Icarus is a very ambitious attempt at assessing the requirements for an unmanned interstellar probe, using current and developing technology. In the process of producing technical reports on the physics, functionality, engineering and performance requirements of the 'craft, needed for different types of mission profiles, it is hoped to provide inspiration for a new generation of scientists and to boost the possibility of bringing such a scheme into reality.

The project is an update of the British Interplanetary Society's Project Daedalus that ran from 1973 to 1978. Daedalus envisaged a huge two-stage 54 million kilogram (119 million pound) nuclear fusion-powered spacecraft fuelled by deuterium helium-3.

The intentions of Project Icarus are to design a similar unmanned fusion-powered space probe that can be targeted at a variety of nearby star systems, and can reach and scientifically study them within a span of 100 years. The goal is to initiate the launch of such a vehicle by 2100 at the least.

The vast scale of this project is underlined by the fact that the helium-3 fuel to power the Daedalus 'craft can only be gathered in the atmosphere of Jupiter. This would take 20 years for robot factories, held afloat by huge balloons, to mine and process the fuel into coin-sized pellets.

The 'craft would be constructed in Earth orbit or near Jupiter, and propelled by a fusion pulse propulsion engine. 250 fuel pellets per second would be injected into the engine's reaction chamber and detonated by electron beams. To provide the forward thrust, magnetic field coils channel the plasma produced out of a nozzle.

A variety of smaller 'craft based on the Daedalus proposal are being considered by Project Icarus, including the Starfinder MkI that could travel the 10,000 AU distance to the Oort cloud in 50 years and could be launched in 2050. Twenty years later, the Starfinder MkII could visit a star system 50,000 AU away in a period of 100 years. It would take until 2200 to launch anything as ambitious as the original Daedalus spacecraft.

With the increasing amount of extrasolar planets being discovered, it is an exciting possibility that Icarus-inspired 'craft could explore worlds much like our own by the end of the century.

Space stations of the future

For decades astronauts have lived on temporary outposts in low Earth orbit, but could we begin to further our horizons and permanently colonise the cosmos?

Hundreds of kilometres above the Earth a handful of astronauts are living aboard an orbital outpost. They are encircling the Earth at over 27,000km/h (17,000mph) in a self-sustaining environment that was constructed in space, and every few months spacecraft dock to this space station to deliver cargo or new crewmembers. In simple terms it sounds like something out of a science-fiction novel, but living in space is now very much a reality. Our next steps in space settlement, however, could venture towards the realms of what was once pure fantasy.

When Russia decided to shift their focus from lunar missions to manned space stations in the Seventies they ushered in the era of space occupation. Barring a few brief periods, humanity has almost continuously occupied the cosmos with a variety of independent and international endeavours since the first space station, Salyut 1, in 1971. We've gradually learned more about how to live and adapt in space, and furthered our technologies to enhance the experience that much more.

It is thanks to these accomplishments that we can allow ourselves to look further into the future. The ISS has been a mainstay in space for the last 14 years, providing astronauts with an orbital outpost to observe Earth and conduct microgravity experiments. However, it will not last forever, with current estimates expecting it to be de-orbited some time after 2020. For that reason, space agencies and private companies around the world are deciding what the next step in permanent space habitation will be, and the answer could be something rather fantastic.

Our work so far has provided us with a variety of answers to questions we need to solve. Early endeavours taught us how to dock with a space station, and also how the human body would cope with a prolonged period in space. We then had to work out how to re-supply and sustain an extended presence in space. We've achieved this by recycling many of the resources used in space, including air and water. It was also important to recognise the biological effects on the human body of living in a microgravity environment. We now know the limits of a human's activities in weightlessness, and we know that they must exercise frequently to keep their bodies conditioned.

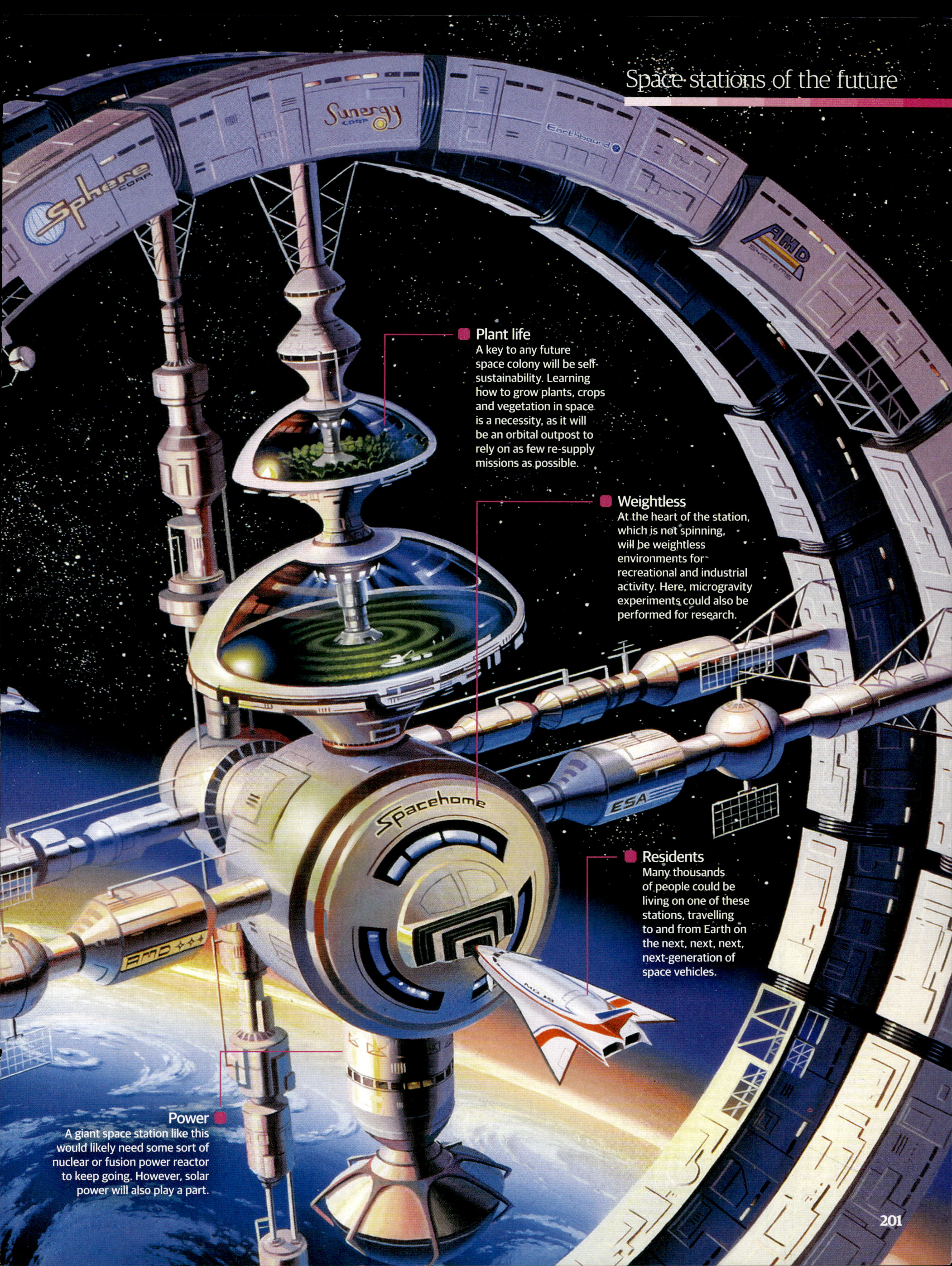

Plant life
A key to any future space colony will be self-sustainability. Learning how to grow plants, crops and vegetation in space is a necessity, as it will be an orbital outpost to rely on as few re-supply missions as possible.

Weightless
At the heart of the station, which is not spinning, will be weightless environments for recreational and industrial activity. Here, microgravity experiments could also be performed for research.

Residents
Many thousands of people could be living on one of these stations, travelling to and from Earth on the next, next, next, next-generation of space vehicles.

Power
A giant space station like this would likely need some sort of nuclear or fusion power reactor to keep going. However, solar power will also play a part.

But what if weightlessness was not a problem? Back in 1951 Werner von Braun, designer of the V-2 and Saturn V rockets, envisaged a space station shaped like a donut, known as a toroid, with a circular exterior and a hollow interior. He suggested that if such a space station could be rotated around a central point then the centrifugal force would push the inhabitants outwards, allowing them to live in artificial gravity. This has been the cornerstone of many works of science fiction that have portrayed humanity living in space, but would it really work?

To answer this question, NASA conducted the first artificial gravity experiment on its Gemini 11 mission in 1966. It attempted to induce a g-force by rotating a Gemini capsule around an Agena Target Vehicle in Earth orbit and used the centrifugal force to create artificial gravity. The two vehicles were tethered together and astronauts Pete Conrad and Richard Gordon experienced a force of 0.00015g, a tiny push but significant enough to prove that it was possible to create artificial gravity in space. By using this same concept, it could be possible to one day build a futuristic space settlement with levels of artificial gravity closer to the 1g experienced on Earth. That day will almost certainly be some point far into the future, but it's fascinating to know that when we do decide to undertake such an endeavour there is no obvious reason why it wouldn't work.

Of course, the issue of weightlessness is not the only obstacle that must be overcome in order to seriously consider colonising the cosmos. One of the other issues is that of self-sustainability. If we're truly going to live in the stars, we can't rely on constant re-supply missions. Eventually we'll need to devise ways for space-farers to fend for themselves, through the development of new machines that can recycle almost all the waste created.

Another key component of a future space settlement will be the source of power. Every cosmic base so far has relied largely on solar power for operations. However, as space stations get bigger, and possibly further from Earth and therefore the Sun, it is likely that new sources of power will be needed. Most space exploration agencies view the future of power for cosmic vehicles as nuclear, and this would certainly be the case for a large space settlement. A nuclear power

"The first artificial gravity experiment occurred on the Gemini 11 mission in 1966"

Near-future

Russia's revolutionary OPSEK space station will act as a base for mankind to reach Mars and beyond

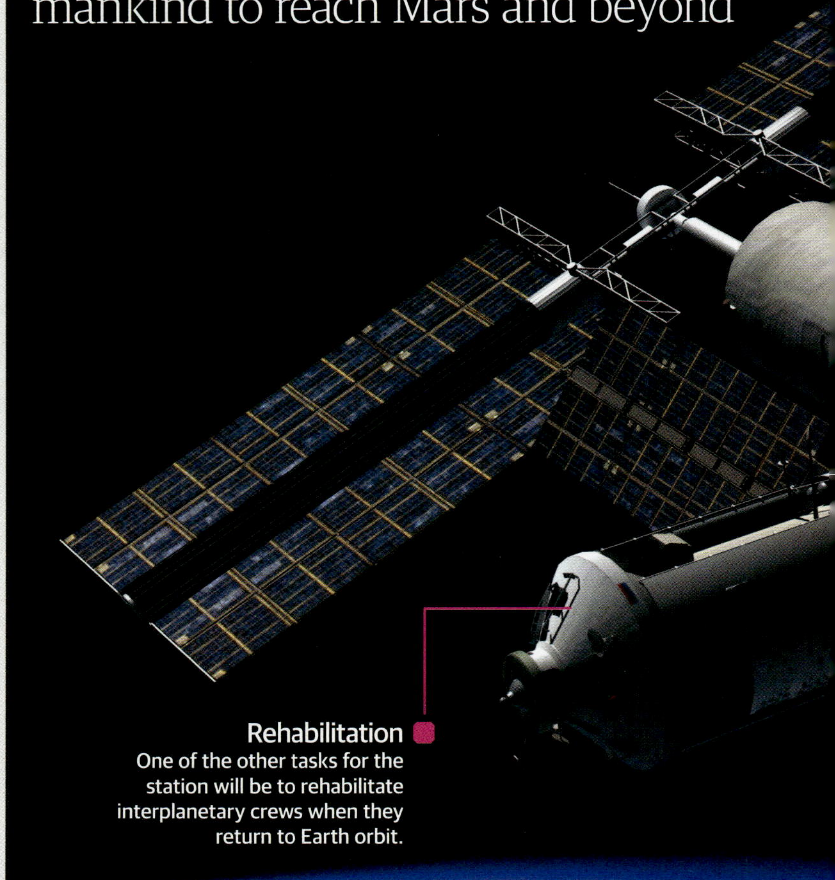

Rehabilitation
One of the other tasks for the station will be to rehabilitate interplanetary crews when they return to Earth orbit.

Space hotels

Bigelow Aerospace is the first company of what is thought to be several that will build and operate tourist destinations in space. It will use inflatable modules to build these orbital hotels. Two experimental modules, Genesis I and II, have already been tested in space, and the first true space hotel - BA 330 - is expected to launch by 2014 at the earliest. However, a trip to one of these modules will cost millions of dollars. Perhaps several decades down the line, when we have new launch capabilities to reach space, the cost will come down, making space exploration more accessible.

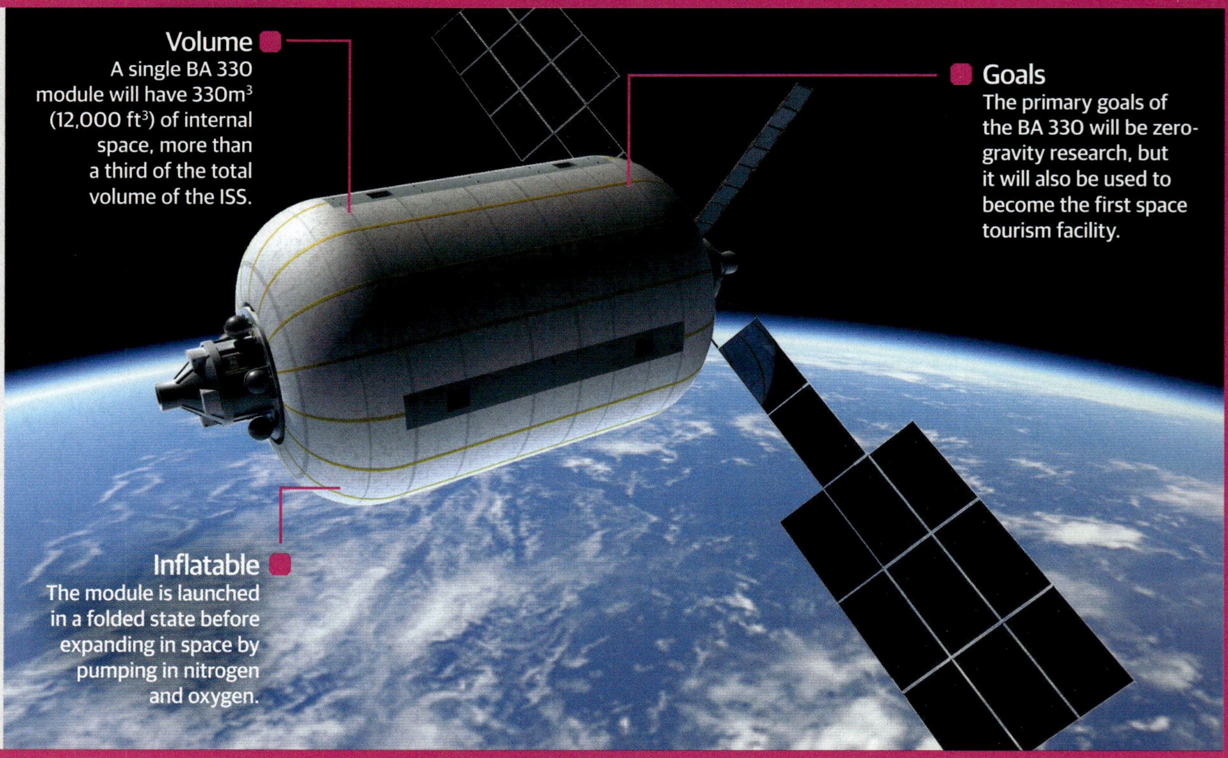

Volume
A single BA 330 module will have 330m^3 (12,000 ft^3) of internal space, more than a third of the total volume of the ISS.

Goals
The primary goals of the BA 330 will be zero-gravity research, but it will also be used to become the first space tourism facility.

Inflatable
The module is launched in a folded state before expanding in space by pumping in nitrogen and oxygen.

Orbital construction yards

In 2009 Russia outlined a proposal to build the Orbital Piloted Assembly and Experiment Complex, or OPSEK. Currently, the Russian modules are all capable of being detached and moved as they have their own propulsion and self-sustaining systems. When the ISS is decommissioned some time after 2020, Russia plans to use its existing modules to build the new OPSEK space station. This revolutionary platform will be used to assemble manned spacecraft or simply act as a docking port, and therefore from OPSEK spacecraft will be able to travel to the Moon, Mars and possibly beyond.

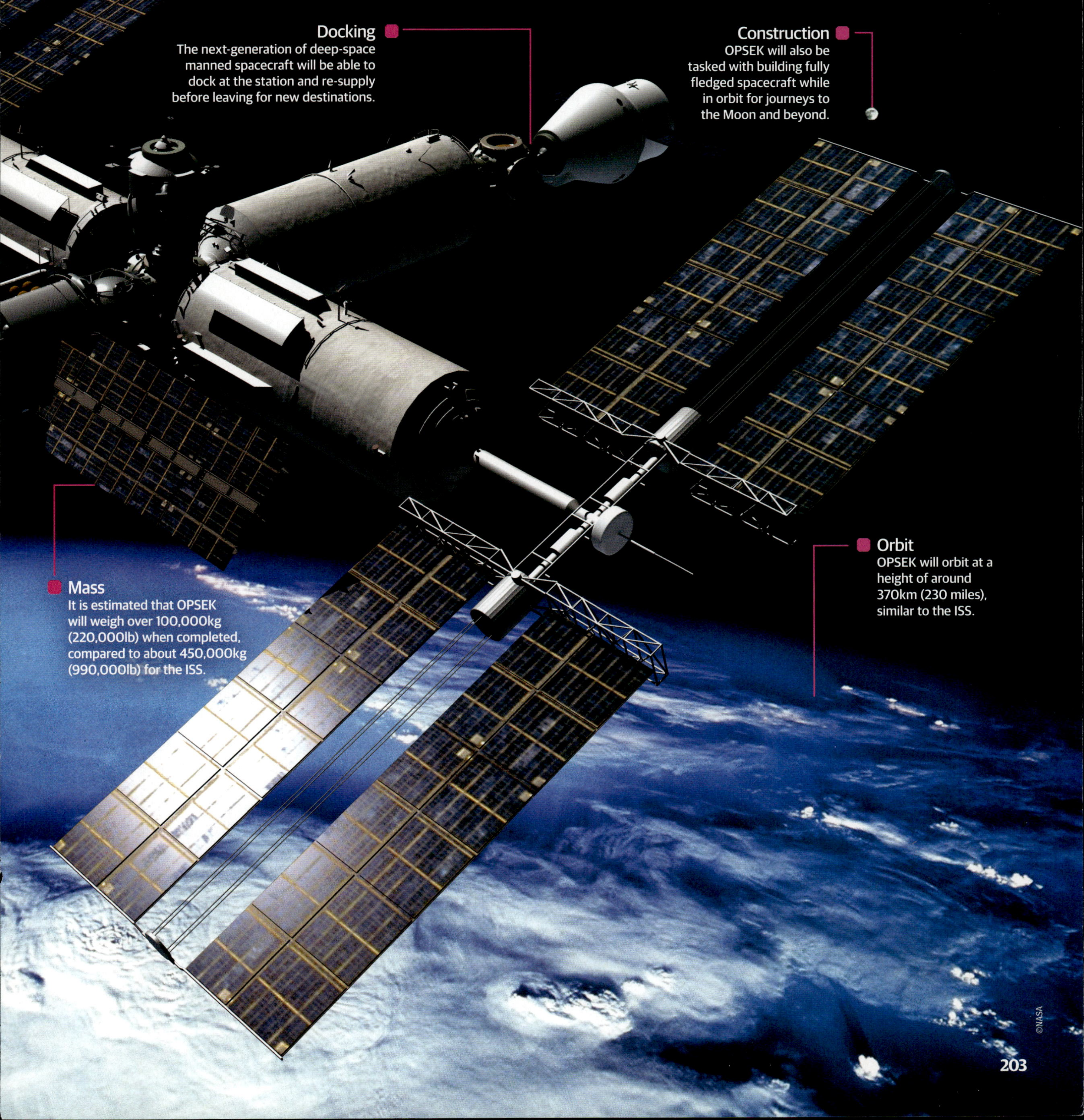

plant at the heart of the station could supply enough power for many years for a colony of thousands of people to survive. Other proposals include building a giant power satellite with huge solar panels, harnessing the Sun's energy and beaming it to a space station for use as power.

These are all practical problems that can be solved with continued research and technological developments, but there are other logistical issues that will have to be considered. For example, what are the implications of actually sending a colony of humans to live in space? What sort of ethical questions does it pose? Since the dawn of mankind we've colonised large swathes of Earth, but moving to the stars poses an entirely new challenge. We know that humans can safely operate in space for more than a year, but we know nothing about permanent occupation of space for a decade or more. From a technical standpoint we are making great strides towards one day settling in space, but the prospect of an ordered civilisation is something that is only in the realms of science fiction and not science fact.

Don't let that dampen your imagination. Giant space settlements might, for now, be limited to humans many decades into the future, but there are more than enough developments in the coming years, including space hotels and orbital construction yards, that will move us closer to one day creating colonies outside Earth's atmosphere and truly colonising the cosmos.

Far-future

Far into the future, beyond 2100 at the earliest, space settlements such as that pictured here could become a reality

Giant space colonies

For the moment it's merely the stuff of science fiction, but giant orbiting space stations could be used to house thousands or perhaps millions of people. Their construction would take decades to complete, with either resources taken from asteroids or the Moon used to build the giant structures. Alternatively, a new method of getting material into Earth orbit, such as a space elevator, could be used to provide these huge space cities with the resources they would need to be built.

How do current space stations compare in size?

From Salyut to Tiangong-1, find out how different stations and spacecraft stack up

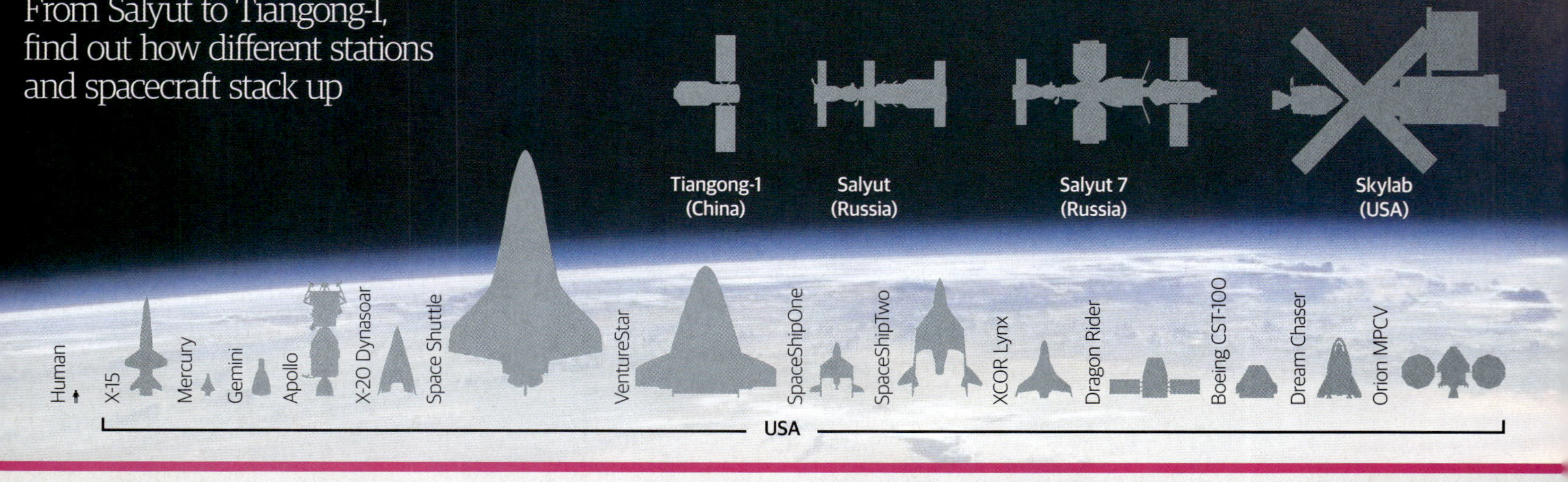

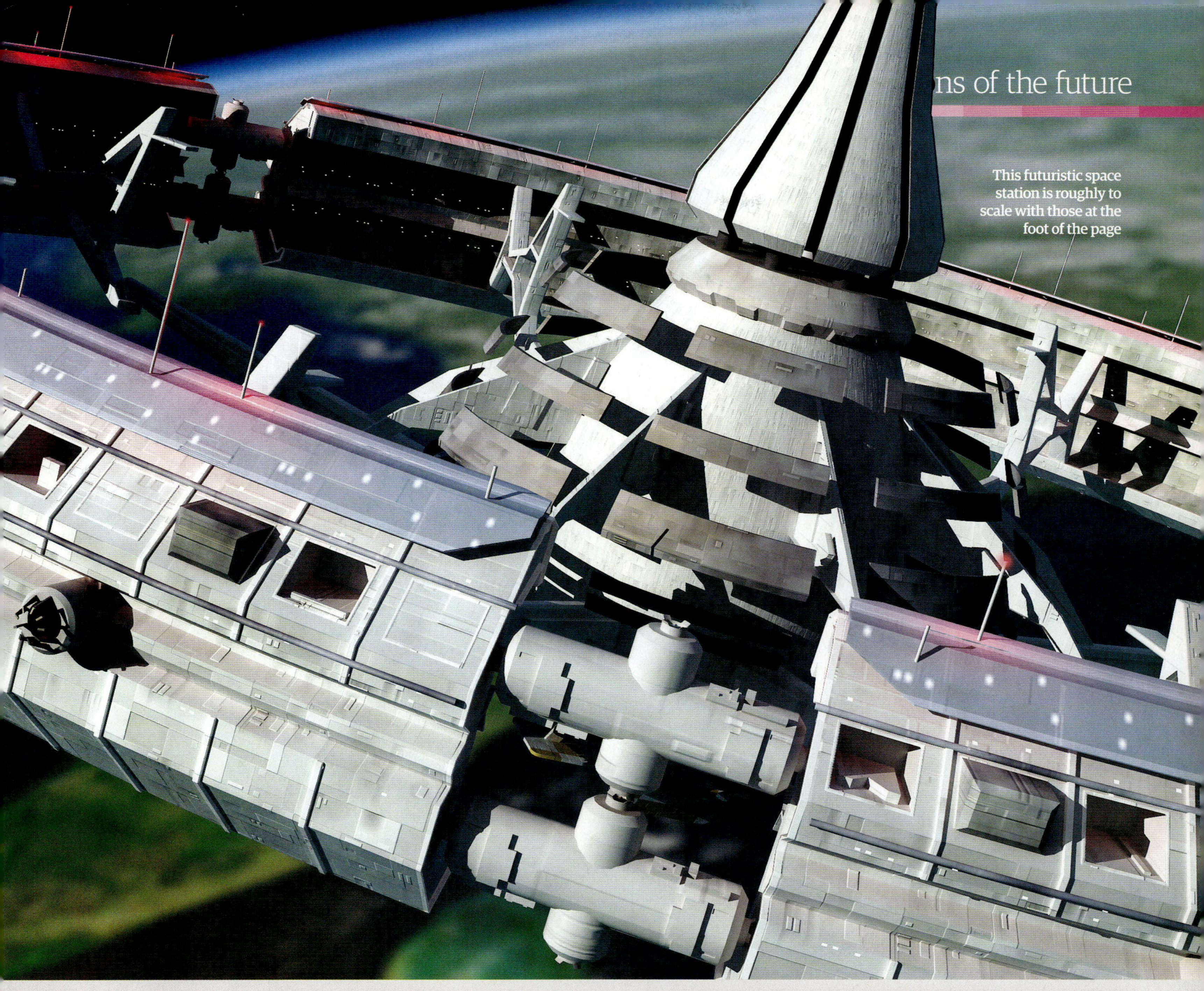

This futuristic space station is roughly to scale with those at the foot of the page

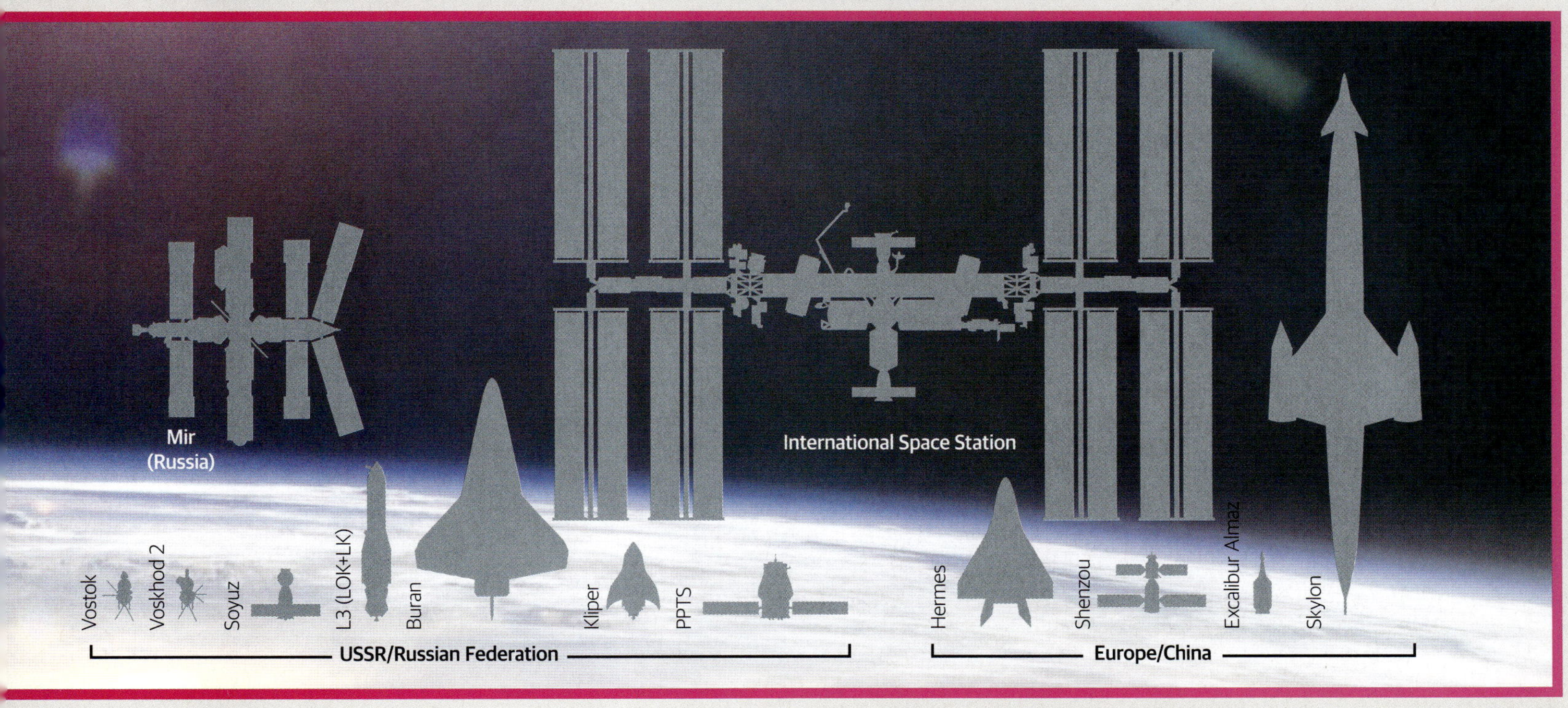

"You can have hundreds of thousands or even millions of people in orbit"

Space station expert Albert Globus tells us why the colonisation of space is so important

INTERVIEWBIO

Albert Globus

After earning a BA in Information Science at the University of California in 1979, space settlement expert Albert Globus worked on the Hubble Space Telescope and the International Space Station at NASA Ames Research Center. In the Nineties he initiated the annual National Space Society Student Space Settlement Design Contest, which continues today. He is now chairman of the NSS's Space Settlement Advocacy Committee, and is also a Senior Engineering Associate for Human Factors Research and Technology at San Jose State University at NASA Ames Research Centre. He has written many papers on space settlement, and his numerous awards include the NASA Software of the Year prize.

How did you get so involved in space settlements?

Well I used to be a musician, but I decided to go back to school and get a technical degree. I was at the University of California and while I was there my housemate had a job cleaning out somebody's garage. There was a stack of [magazines] and in that stack was an issue on space colonies. I was just totally blown away, so I decided this was what I was going to do. If you really look at it, it turns out that building settlements in free space is actually significantly easier than on the Moon and Mars, and it has a number of very important advantages in terms of living there. So I had an opportunity to work at NASA Ames Research Center. I've been pursuing space elements in one form or another ever since.

Are we making good progress with space stations?

Well, the fundamental problem is that the current model is way too expensive. The ISS cost, depending on who you ask, $100bn to build, and it houses six people, costing a couple of billion dollars a year to operate. Unless the world was to do something really radical, like decide that settling in space was more interesting than [war], which doesn't seem likely, then it's just way too much money, and we have to find a much cheaper way. And the thing that's actually most encouraging to me is the new space developments and, from the point of view of space stations, Bigelow Aerospace's proposal. They've got a couple of small stations [Genesis I and II] up there for tests and they're basically just waiting for a way to get customers [there]. It's a much lower cost, and it could be made pretty widely available.

Are inflatable stations better than the rigid modules of the ISS?
Well, it's definitely got some advantages. I don't know how well it will scale, though. I don't know if you can scale one of those up to a kilometre in size, which is the size that's most of interest to me. If you're building a hotel then the whole module approach is a good way to go because you can build up over time. If you're trying to build a settlement somewhere where people can raise kids, then you need something big because you want to rotate it and get 1g. You could do it with a bunch of little modules but you're probably better off building one large one or a few very large pressurised vessels.

What are the key technologies we are yet to master in order to colonise space?
The number one is launch. As long as it costs five or ten thousand dollars a kilogram to get from here to low Earth orbit, forget it. And reliability is not the greatest either. The second big one, which I actually think will be fairly easy, is the life support system. You need something that recycles air, water and food indefinitely. We don't know how do to that, and it's essential. The third one, in terms of actually building the settlements, is you'd really like to build your settlements out of material that is already there, either lunar or asteroid materials. There's actually some interesting progress in that area, with the stated goal of Planetary Resources to do asteroid mining, and then there's also the Shackleton Energy Company who have plans in the near future to mine the Moon for materials. The last thing, which would make a huge difference in the materials requirements, is if cancer was not a problem. There's a lot of radiation in space, particularly above the Van Allen belts where there are lots of galactic cosmic rays, and there are various problems that radiation causes, but the number one showstopper is cancer. If cancer didn't matter very much, if it was really easy to cure, then you wouldn't need so much radiation shielding, and that could drop the mass requirements for a space settlement by a factor of ten or more.

Globus is chairman of the NSS's Space Settlement Advocacy Committee as well as having worked on major NASA projects like the ISS and Hubble

"Sooner or later, this planet is going to become uninhabitable for civilisation or even for life itself"

What are the primary benefits of building a space settlement?
The long-term benefit [of building a space settlement] is survival of the human species, and survival of life for that matter. Sooner or later, this planet is going to become uninhabitable for civilisation or even possibly for life itself eventually. We don't know when and it's probably going to be a long time, but it's going to happen. So if we want to keep going then we need to get into space. That's the sort of big biological imperative long-term vision. In the short term, short meaning a few decades, the main advantage is to let people who want to go into space do it, and to establish new societies and new resources and have the freedom that involves. It's also possible to access space resources, most of which you can do without a settlement. Settlement would certainly be extremely helpful in getting access to those materials, but a much more viable method would be the other way around. We'll be going to get those materials, and we'll have work camps and space power satellites and hotels for tourists, and some people will want to stay. And so rather than say we'll settle in space and then get access to materials it'll be the other way around. We'll go out to get access to energy and materials in order to build tourist destinations and that will evolve into settlements.

We've seen various space stations over the last few decades, but what's the next step?
I think the most important development will be hotels. The reason for this is volume. Exactly how many people are we going to support in space with tax-payer dollars? The answer right now is six, but if you can get a viable tourism industry going, and you can get the price low enough, then you can have hundreds of thousands or even millions of people in orbit. The experience base you are going to get from a few thousand people in orbit in hotels is vastly in excess of what you're going to get from keeping a few guys alive doing science. Now, the exception to this is that if the International Space Station or something similar discovered something that makes space really valuable that you can't make on Earth, then you can imagine an industry developing in low Earth orbit to produce whatever it is and bring it back to the ground.

If money was no object, what sort of space stations should be built next?
Well, if you're doing something along the lines of the ISS, it would be really interesting to have a couple devoted to nothing but materials science. You could also have separate power satellites that beam energy from huge solar arrays. And then I'd have some to do biology at variable gs, with a particular interest in plant growth. You could also have one that's completely devoted to life support in space, and they'd basically be their own experiment. The whole thing would be recycled – including water, food and air – and you could see how close you can get to [self-sustainability]. Finally, I would want one that looked to gather asteroids and lunar materials and figure out how to process them into making things we want.

Further into the future, are these big donut-shaped (toroids) space stations the way to go?
Well, it depends on what you want to do. For one thing, I'm a cylinder guy. Cylinders are better than toroids because they give you a lot more volume, and the mass to volume ratio is optimised by cylinders not toroids. What you get is your shielding on the outside, so all of your shielding is right next to where people [live on the station] as opposed to a toroid where each section has shielding all the way around. The other thing is you can use interior cylinders to give you additional area for growing crops and doing industrial work, so you can preserve the outer 1g area for living. And finally, one of the biggest attractions of going into space is weightlessness, and in a toroid you don't get it. With a cylinder you just go to the centre of the space station and bingo, you have got weightlessness.

What should we be looking out for, development-wise, in the coming years?
Well, the tourist industry started about ten years ago when Dennis Tito flew [to the ISS], although the industry is at a very low level. And there are two companies [Virgin Galactic and XCOR] that believe they are going to be flying people into sub-orbit maybe by next year. And we have a NASA programme to develop orbital vehicles, the Commercial Crew Development Program, and those same private vehicles can be used to go to a Bigelow Aerospace station or a hotel built by anyone else, so that's very promising. In terms of mining materials we have two companies [Planetary Resources and Shackleton Energy Company] that have said what they're going to do, and they're headed in the right direction. The other piece that I see in terms of what you need to develop towards space settlements is solar power, and the Japanese have a pretty good programme to do that.

But it's space hotels that we should be most excited about, right?
Bigelow Aerospace is trying to go after the national space programmes of smaller powers, but that market isn't that large. There are maybe only ten or 20 nations that will want to get involved. There's nothing wrong with going for that market, but you are not going to build a thousand modules for that market. But for the tourism industry, it could easily be a thousand hotels if you can get the price down.